A Second Look at the Second Coming

Sorting Through the Speculations

By T. L. Frazier

Conciliar Press
Ben Lomond, California

Published by   Conciliar Press
                    P.O. Box 76
                    Ben Lomond, California 95005-0076

Printed in the United States of America

ISBN 1-888212-14-4

Table of Contents

To my daughters Arianna and Tatiana:
May the Lord uphold their steps in His paths,
that their footsteps may not slip (Psalm 17:5),
whatever the future may bring.

Foreword

I T WAS A GREAT PLEASURE to read T. L. Frazier's book, *A Second
Look at the Second Coming*. I found it a breath of fresh air in an atmosphere polluted with pop theology and trendy end-times speculations.
Without a doubt, Mr. Frazier offers the best-documented, the most serious,
and the most historically accurate critique of modern millenarianism to date.
His critique is based firmly upon the beliefs of the people most ignored in the
prophetic debates of our times: the people of the Christian East.

The "Christian East" comprises those Christians of the ancient Orthodox Churches of Antioch, Alexandria, Constantinople, and, not least of all,
Jerusalem itself. These are the Christians found everywhere from the frozen
regions of Siberia to the jungles of Africa and as far east as the shores of
Japan. These are the Christians who belong to that original Church born in
the East, as described in the Acts of the Apostles. Western Christians of every
denomination should seriously heed the forgotten witness of this Apostolic
Church of the East.

The reader might legitimately ask, Why? What does the Christian East
have to teach me? With the reader's patience, I would like to answer that
question with a few paragraphs of personal background.

Fulfilled prophecy, especially with regard to the Holy Land, has always
held a prominent place in my life. As a sixteen-year-old Jewish boy living in
New York City, I read the Old Testament prophecies concerning the Messiah
and came to the inevitable conclusion that they were fulfilled in Jesus of
Nazareth. I thus came to believe that Jesus was the Messiah, and entrusted
myself to Him. This decision profoundly shocked my family, especially my
father, who had been born in the Old City of Jerusalem and had been raised
to be an Orthodox Jewish rabbi.

I gravitated into evangelical Protestantism, since it was the only form of
Christianity with which I was familiar. From there, I slowly drifted into fundamentalism, accepting uncritically its prevailing dispensationalist theology
with its premillennial, apocalyptic views. I became like many "born-again"
fundamentalists in that anticipating future prophetic fulfillment eventually

came to define my world-view. While I was spending a year in Jerusalem during 1967, the Six-Day War erupted and Israel took possession of the Old City. I, like millions of other fundamentalists, interpreted this event as a confirmation of my belief that prophecy was being fulfilled in my lifetime. It seemed self-evident that the "time of the Gentiles" was ending and that God would soon resume His original plan for the Jewish people and the state of Israel.

In 1971, I moved from New York to San Francisco with Moshe Rosen to assist in founding a brand new ministry to Jews called "Jews for Jesus." The success of this ministry, we believed, would provide further evidence that we were living in the generation that would witness the Second Coming of Christ. During the 1970s, I met the leaders of this new wave of prophetic speculation, Hal Lindsey and Dave Hunt (both of whom are discussed at length in this book). Lindsey and Hunt were greatly inspired by the phenomenal success of our Jews for Jesus Ministry, which was experiencing growth beyond everyone's most optimistic expectations.

As a fundamentalist, I believed the life in Christ meant studying the Bible and uncovering its hidden, esoteric secrets. However, my understanding of Christianity was beginning to change, and I eventually became disillusioned with the shallowness and rootlessness of parachurch ministries like Jews for Jesus. Now that I look back on it, such an amazing change of heart must have been the work of the Holy Spirit. I experienced a leading to search for the ancient Church of the Apostles, and soon discovered the Orthodox Christian Church.

The road to historic Orthodoxy was not an easy one. (But then, Christ never promised the Way would be easy.) I needed to learn that Jews are not the center of God's creation, nor is the state of Israel—nor, for that matter, am I. God Himself is the center of His creation; and, insofar as it is "in" Christ, the Church as the New Israel also shares center stage with her divine Bridegroom (see Matt. 25:1–13; Eph. 5:30–32). Orthodoxy taught me that the Christian Church is not merely a Bible study or a prayer group (as good as these things are), but is actually the Bride of Christ, who raises to maturity her spiritual children by her Bridegroom, the Lord Jesus Christ.

On Christmas Eve, 1981, I was received into the Orthodox Church. It is a profound paradox that in sacrificing my former Jewishness in Christian Orthodoxy, I became truly Jewish in becoming one with Christ, the true center of creation. I now declare that I am by ancestry an Israelite, by faith a Christian, by vocation an Orthodox priest, and by grace a "fulfilled Jew," in that my Judaism has found its fulfillment in the Gospel. Thus with the Apostle Paul I can proclaim unequivocally, "I am indeed a Jew" (Acts 22:3).

As a Jew, I find great significance in the fact that the indigenous Christian Church of Jerusalem, the Church that exists in the land where the Prophets and the Apostles lived and taught, is the Orthodox Church. To this day, the Orthodox Church in the Holy Land is a Semitic Church, composed of the descendants of the Lord's first disciples. Before coming to Orthodoxy, I had learned prophecy from charismatic (and often immoral) televangelists. As an Orthodox Christian, however, I was reintroduced to biblical prophecy as it has been interpreted throughout two millennia by faithful Orthodox saints, martyrs, and Spirit-filled Church Fathers. As T. L. Frazier repeatedly emphasizes in his well-documented book, the historic Christian teaching on such issues as the rapture, the millennium, the state of Israel, and the role of the Church in the last days is something quite different from what is commonly taught in the pop religion of today's televangelists.

We discover declarations throughout the New Testament that the Church is indwelt by the Holy Spirit, who leads it "into all truth" (John 16:13). Not by human means, but by the indwelling of the Holy Spirit has the Church preserved for two millennia "the faith which was once for all delivered to the saints" (Jude 3). The epitome of pride is to ignore that truth which the Holy Spirit has taught the Church for two thousand years in order to "reform" (or "reinvent") Christianity to one's own liking. Such pride leads people to believe they know better than the historic Church how to interpret the "prophetic word," an attitude condemned in Scripture itself (2 Pet. 1:19–21; Heb. 13:7). This sort of pride is at the heart of today's apocalyptic movements and is the source of its many destructive heresies.

I found one portion of T. L. Frazier's book particularly important. For many "born-again" fundamentalists, belief in Christ is intimately linked with belief in the state of Israel. An ardent support of Israel, regardless of Israeli state policy, is often used as a litmus test for a true Christian. Criticism of Israel is interpreted by the "born-again" fundamentalist as evidence of an allegiance to Satan's camp, of a complicity in the New World Order and the coming system of Antichrist, and of a lust for the great whore of Babylon.

Frazier argues that the heart of modern apocalyptic fundamentalism is its view of the state of Israel, a nation conspicuous for its persecution of Arab Orthodox Christians. The Church's presence in the Holy Land today is becoming a pale shadow of its former self as Christians flee to other countries. (Frazier reports that three Christians flee the Holy Land every day.) Yet fundamentalists are among the Jewish state's most fanatical allies, little caring that they are accomplices in the destruction of Christianity in the land of its birth. The eradication of the Jerusalem Church is simply rationalized away by fundamentalists for the sake of their interpretation of prophecy.

In his book, Frazier reveals that so-called prophecy "experts" have transformed Christianity into an extreme form of Jewish nationalism. This observation explains their indifference to the Church of the Holy Land as they seek to "stand with Israel" in the latter days. In this respect, "millennial mania" is not only heretical, but even anti-Christian. Could we be witnessing the beginning of that "strong delusion" mentioned in 2 Thessalonians 2:11? Is aiding in the destruction of the indigenous Church of the Holy Land, believing it is "God's will" as revealed in prophecy, anything less than a strong delusion?

In this destruction of the Jerusalem Church one recalls the Lord's words to His disciples when He was last in the Holy City: "The time is coming that whoever kills you will think that he offers God service" (John 16:2). It is a great irony that while these prophecy "experts" anticipate the coming persecution by the Antichrist, the Christians of the Holy Land are already experiencing that persecution at the hands of the Israeli state, a state that these "experts" virtually worship and adore.

The strength of T. L. Frazier's book is that it fully embraces the historic Christian teaching on the end times, a teaching handed down for two thousand years through the Spirit-indwelt Church. Frazier never dismisses or ignores this teaching simply to concoct his own theories on the end times.

Nor does Frazier invent bogus "facts" to convince us some prophecy has been fulfilled, as do so many ministries specializing in end-of-the-world scenarios. His treatment of the subject is sober and unapologetically within the mainstream of the Church's Tradition. The author's presentation is not only in continuity with the Christian Tradition, but builds upon it to respond to fundamentalism's challenge. Frazier's work is patristic, balanced, comprehensive, sensitive, compassionate, articulate, and, at times, amusing.

This book has greatly blessed me. I pray it will do the same for you.

Fr. A. James Bernstein
St. Paul Antiochian Orthodox Church
Lynnwood, Washington
The Feast of the Dormition, 1998

Introduction

Apocalypse is in fact all but an industry. It may not be very absurd because our world, as we are at least everywhere now told, is very absurd.
—Historian Christopher Nugent, *Masks of Satan* (1983)

THE SECOND COMING OF CHRIST will probably happen within a decade, by the year 2009.

Also, the Antichrist is more than likely alive at this very moment and readying himself for world domination. Who is he? Nobody yet knows for sure; however, he will undoubtedly be a Jew. Biblical prophecy is unfolding exactly as foretold. Prepare yourself—the apocalypse is nigh.

Perhap . . . or perhaps not.

Who knows?

The Reverend Jerry Falwell seems to know. He made the foregoing claims at an evangelism conference of 1,500 people in Kingsport, Tennessee, on January 14, 1999. Falwell's statements were duly reported two days later in the *New York Times*, though not without a hint of scorn.

Personally, I hope Falwell is right. What Christian wouldn't get excited over the prospect of the Lord returning in the immediate future? As an Eastern Orthodox Christian who resolutely clings to the Nicene Creed, I have little doubt Christ will someday come again in glory to judge the living and the dead. Better sooner than later.

But soon isn't soon enough for some, as evidenced by the shelves at local Christian bookstores crammed with books and tapes bearing titles like, *The End: Why Jesus Could Return by A.D. 2000* and, *How Close Are We?* In fact, anticipation of the Second Coming over the last few decades has spawned an incredible industry manned by prophecy pundits ready to decipher every minor detail of every arcane revelation in every obscure niche of the Bible (except, of course, Jesus' words in Matthew 24:6, "For all these things must come to pass, *but the end is not yet*"). And with each major news story (and some not so major) the prophecy industry steps up its efforts to crank out yet more doomsday forecasts, both in print and over the broadcast airwaves.

This frenzy over prophecy has its good side. The Second Coming of

Christ, the resurrection, the judgment: all these teachings are a prominent part of Scripture, Christian Tradition, and the Church's liturgical prayers. Such an expectation of Christ's coming constitutes the ultimate hope of the gospel; in fact, it is at the heart of the Lord's Prayer: "Thy kingdom come . . ." As such, this renewed interest can only be welcome.

However, there is also a negative side to the current prophecy craze. What is being popularly taught in most instances bears little resemblance to what has been believed by the Church for the last two thousand years. For instance, today's popular belief that Christ will establish a thousand-year "millennial" kingdom on earth at His return is hopelessly irreconcilable with the Nicene Creed's plain assertion that Christ's Kingdom will have "no end."

Nor is this all. Today's prophecy industry is also notorious for such things as date setting, Antichrist naming, and wild end-times speculation. The prophecy peddlers frequently stoop to sensationalism to keep their audience, exploiting people's fears and curiosity about the future. These "experts" on biblical prophecy create a climate obsessed with a single facet of the Christian message, a climate I call "millennial mania."

Trusting what they've been told by an elite class of prophecy "experts," sincere believers have on various occasions quit their jobs, put their pets to sleep, and sold their property believing the end was near. The result has inevitably been crushing disillusionment when the Lord fails to arrive on schedule. Many of the disillusioned have even come to distrust all of Christ's promises, and so have abandoned the gospel altogether. In short, real people have been hurt by what is being passed off as "Bible prophecy."

Hence the need for this book. In the pages that follow, I take a long and hard look at today's millennial mania, comparing it to what has traditionally been believed by Christians through the centuries. My goal is to clear up the prevailing misunderstandings of what Scripture and historic Christianity actually teach concerning the end of the age and the return of Christ.

And are there ever lots of misunderstandings! A proper response to these necessitates the wide-ranging scope of this book. In large part, it is a handbook designed to give answers to many common questions about the end times: Is modern Israel the key to end-times prophecy? Is AIDS one of the plagues heralding the end? Will the Church be raptured off the planet before the appearance of the Antichrist? What is the "mark of the beast"? My answers may surprise you—perhaps even astonish you.

Before I begin astonishing anyone, however, I should make one thing clear: I am not an unbiased author disinterested in his subject. The awesome Second Coming of the Lord in glory is too grand a topic to leave one either unbiased or disinterested. I am compelled to approach this topic as I see it, which is from an Eastern Orthodox point of view.

When I say I write "from an Eastern Orthodox point of view," I don't mean to imply that it is a *peculiarly* Eastern Orthodox point of view. The truth is, the teachings that I set forth in this book are by and large also shared by Roman Catholics, Oriental Orthodox, and most mainline Protestants. Though there may be some charitable disagreement over points of detail or emphasis, there has traditionally existed a happy concurrence of belief among most Christians on the end of the age and the full manifestation of Christ's Kingdom.

An "Orthodox point of view" on any subject is basically little more than the point of view of the Church Fathers, those early leaders and teachers whose lives and writings exemplify authentic Christianity. I consequently refer extensively to the Fathers throughout this book. The non-Orthodox reader who wants to learn more about a particular Church Father (or all of them!) might try consulting either the *Dictionary of Saints* published by Penguin Books or *The New International Dictionary of the Christian Church*, part of the Regency Reference Library published by Zondervan. Either of these two inexpensive references will provide basic biographical information on most of the Fathers cited. Two Orthodox resources are *Orthodox Saints* by George Poulos, a relatively inexpensive four-volume set from Holy Cross Orthodox Press in Brookline, Massachusetts; and the four-volume *Prologue from Ochrid* published by Lazarica Press in Birmingham, England. Though rather expensive, the *Prologue* is a classic that deserves to be in every Christian home.

Those desiring to look up my references to the Fathers are referred to the following: The Ante-Nicene Fathers as well as The Nicene and Post-Nicene Fathers (First and Second Series), published by Hendrickson; The Loeb Classical Library, published by Harvard University Press; Classics of Western Spirituality, published by Paulist Press; the Popular Patristics Series, published by St. Vladimir's Seminary Press; The Fathers of the Church, published by The Catholic University of America Press; *The Faith of the Early Fathers* (a three-volume set of patristic citations), published by Liturgical Press; and *The Philokalia*, published by Faber and Faber.

To treat our subject thoroughly, we need to begin from the end. Therefore, we are first going to look at the end of the world with one of today's most popular prophecy "experts." Then, in Chapters 3, 4, and 5, we will indulge in a historical survey on the end of history. We will then proceed in the rest of the book to dissect today's millennial mania, analyzing it in light of the Bible and the Tradition of the Church.

Ready? Let's turn the page and find out what our apostles of Armageddon have in store for the late, great planet Earth.

To those who eagerly wait for Him He will appear a second time, apart from sin, for salvation.

The Epistle to the Hebrews 9:28

Hail! Thou king of all the living;
Hail! Thou judge of all the dead,
At the right hand of thy Father,
Thou art throned in highest power,
And from thence just judge of sinners,
Thou shalt one day come again.

Aurelius Prudentius Clemens, A.D. 348–410

Chapter One

Prologue to Armageddon

And [they] said to the mountains and rocks, "Fall on us and hide us from the face of Him who sits on the throne and from the face of the Lamb! For the great day of His wrath has come, and who is able to stand?"
　　　　　—The Apocalypse of St. John 6:16, 17

Surely some revelation is at hand;
Surely the Second Coming is at hand.
The Second Coming! . . .
And what rough beast, its hour come round at last,
Slouches towards Bethlehem to be born?
　　　　　—William Butler Yeats, *The Second Coming* (1919–1921)

AMERICANS were having difficulty coming to terms with their world in 1970.

The Cold War was in full swing, and the planet had already come to the brink of nuclear annihilation with the Cuban missile crisis in 1962. In June of 1967, the Six-Day War came close to involving the superpowers— the U.S. and the Soviet Union—in an Armageddon in the Middle East. As the late Eldridge Cleaver had poignantly noted in his 1968 book, *Soul on Ice*, it seemed that "all the gods are dead except the god of war." Or, as Bob Dylan put it, the world seemed to be on "the eve of destruction."

By 1970, the United States was trying to grope its way out of a prolonged "police action" in Vietnam that was polarizing the American public. Student protests against the war were becoming common, and some were veering into outright terrorism. These protests resulted in 1970 in students being shot at both Kent State and Jackson State Universities. Such incidents contributed to a general suspicion of established institutions—collectively

15

dubbed "the Establishment"—which would give way to a full-blown cynicism after the Watergate scandal broke in 1973.

By 1970, the country had witnessed the assassinations of President John F. Kennedy and two other noted leaders, Robert Kennedy and Martin Luther King, Jr. The very glue that held society together seemed to dissolve as racial strife tore cities apart. Race riots occurred in Harlem in 1964, in Watts in 1965, and in Chicago in 1966. In 1967, America experienced 164 racial disturbances in 128 cities, requiring 59,000 National Guard and federal troops to restore order. Worse was yet to come with the riots of 1968 following the assassination of Martin Luther King, when 76,000 troops were deployed.

By 1970, technology was racing ahead at a dizzying pace—America had just landed a man on the moon the previous year—but it was not advancing quickly enough, it seemed, to stave off impending ecological and societal calamities. People were terrified by the "population explosion" and the imminent famine it was expected to create. If overpopulation didn't spell the end of us, pollution and technological terrors such as nuclear weapons seemed sure to doom us all.

The American family was beginning to deteriorate seriously in 1970. The marriage rate had been increasing since 1959, but had begun to slow around 1970. The divorce rate had been increasing steadily since 1963, but began to escalate significantly in 1967. The year 1969 saw an increase in the divorce rate of 9% over 1968; and 1970 saw a 12% increase over 1969.

There also developed a growing "generation gap." For some obscure reason, people were divided at the arbitrary age of thirty. Those older than thirty distrusted those younger, with the feeling being mutual on the other side. This generation gap often alienated parents and children, splitting families apart.

By 1970 the world of Ozzie and Harriet was unquestionably over. B. J. Oropeza of the Christian Research Institute writes,

> The 1960s transmogrified our 1950s American dream into a nightmarish world of perpetual change. If we barely survived the 1960s, many wondered, what would happen during the 1970s?[1]

Our country seemed to be careening out of control into an unknown future. It seems fitting that the Beatles won an Oscar in 1970 for Best Musical Score with "Let It Be," which begins, "When I find myself in times of trouble . . ."

Behind the societal confusion was an attitude of radical individualism,

---

1   B. J. Oropeza, *99 Reasons Why No One Knows When Christ Will Return* (Downers Grove, IL: InterVarsity Press, 1994), 14.

of "doing your own thing." There was a desire for liberation that expressed itself in trends in clothing, life-styles, sexual mores, and moral values in general. The "liberated woman" was a hot topic in the media.

Although communes that rejected traditional culture were fashionable, the sense of community faded in the late 1960s. A spirit of romanticism and nihilism reigned that encouraged the instinctive and the impulsive. Ecstatic release, individualism, and self-gratification were celebrated, while reason, restraint, and discipline were frowned upon. Protestantism spun off a new, anti-institutional movement: the "Jesus Freaks."

Others rejected Western culture altogether and began exploring Eastern philosophies and religions. Occultism thrived with an expectation that an age was ending—the age of Pisces the Fish (representative of the Christian age)—and a new one was beginning called the age of Aquarius. This new age would usher in greater consciousness, psychic powers, prosperity, and oneness among people and "God," however vaguely defined. In a word, the age of Aquarius was the occult version of the earthly millennium. One pop group, The Fifth Dimension, released a song called "Aquarius" based on this theme.

Traditional moral and religious beliefs began to be viewed as problematic, especially among the young. Supreme Court decisions banished prayer and Bible reading from public schools. The so-called sexual revolution disconnected sexuality from the realm of marriage and procreation, with the result that teenage pregnancy and cases of sexually transmitted diseases began to rise alarmingly in the late 1960s and early '70s. There was experimentation with communal families, open marriages, and other promiscuous sexual life-styles. In 1970, America was experiencing a radical transvaluation of all values. Almost anything seemed acceptable so long as it was unacceptable according to traditional moral standards.

Although earlier in the century there had been those addicted to narcotic medications prescribed by physicians, recreational drug use was rare before the 1960s. The disintegration of moral values and the increased tolerance for a wide range of unconventional behavior, however, brought illegal drug use into vogue. Many viewed drug use in such positive terms that it was considered a virtue to "turn on" someone to drugs. The drug culture that exploded during the 1960s contributed to the rising crime rate.

In 1958, Roman Catholic philosopher Jacques Maritain wrote in his *Reflections on America*, "At each epoch of history the world was in a hopeless state, and at each epoch of history the world muddled through; at each epoch the world was lost, and at each epoch it was saved." Despite the optimism that Maritain offered, the sense of Armageddon's approach began to g ever more pronounced as society seemed to disintegrate. The worl experiencing tribulations that reverberated into individual lives, making confident predictions for the future appear both romantic and naive.

Alvin Toffler's *Future Shock,* published in 1970, affirmed what most already suspected to be true, that a strange and menacing future was crashing into our lives, leaving us overwhelmed and disoriented. The apocalyptic blurb on the book's cover said it all: "The symptoms of future shock are with us now. This book can help us survive our collision with tomorrow." Toffler started his book as follows:

> In three short decades between now and the twenty-first century, millions of ordinary, psychologically normal people will face an abrupt collision with the future. Citizens of the world's richest and most technologically advanced nations, many of them, will find it increasingly painful to keep up with the incessant demand for change that characterizes our time. For them, the future will have arrived too soon.[2]

The success of Toffler's book lay in its ability to help people make sense of the strange, new world in which America seemed to find itself in 1970. For the same reason, many such apocalyptic paperbacks were flooding the book stands at the time. Herman Kahn wrote a secular doomsday scenario in 1967 predicting the end of the world, according to the title of the book, in *The Year 2000.*

Some, however, couldn't wait till the year 2000 for Armageddon. Also in 1967, William and Paul Paddock published *Famine—1975! America's Decision: Who Will Survive?* (With such a title, elaboration on the contents seems superfluous.) Others were less concerned about the end of the world than they were about the end of—California! Curt Gentry, a California journalist, came out in 1968 with *The Last Days of the Late Great State of California*: "Oh, my God! Los Angeles has vanished! . . . Wait a minute. There's more. Orange County is gone too. And most of San Diego. And . . ."[3] Not good news for the real estate market.

In 1968, Paul Ehrlich prophesied in *Population Bomb* that by 1999 the U.S. population would plummet to 22.6 million. This would be the result of millions of Americans perishing from starvation! And not in the U.S. only, Ehrlich darkly warned, but all over the world in the 1970s hundreds of millions would starve to death from famines. The battle to feed humanity, he 'ared, was over. By September of 1979, even animal life in the oceans ` extinct. As a result of Ehrlich's book, Lester Brown of Worldwatch started predicting cataclysmic food shortages for the 1970s.

Shock (New York: Random House, 1970), 11.
yle in *The Last Days Are Here Again* (Grand Rapids: Baker Books,

Clearly, the generation that had dived under school desks in fear of the Bomb in the 1950s had come of age by 1970.

The end-of-the-world theme also became a big box-office bonanza for Hollywood around this time. The cinematic focus was frequently on nuclear holocaust, in such movies as: *The Day the Earth Caught Fire* (1962), where the earth is destroyed by an accidental nuclear exchange between the world's two superpowers; *The Planet of the Apes* (1967), where apes rule over men after humanity destroys itself in a nuclear war; and two years later the sequel, *Beneath the Planet of the Apes* (1969), wherein humanity blows itself up yet a second time with a doomsday bomb! At least in one of these films Hollywood was able to show some levity: *Dr. Strangelove, or How I Learned to Stop Worrying and Love the Bomb*, released in 1964.

These apocalyptic films could also have a religious tilt. The biggest such movie, released in 1968, was *Rosemary's Baby*. This macabre blockbuster depicted the birth of an antichrist-like child with the devil as its father. *The Omen* followed in 1976. In this film, the Antichrist was Damien Thorn, a sweet little boy destined to rise to the top of the corporate and political world. *The Omen* spawned two sequels and a number of sensational variations on the apocalyptic theme, both with and without the religious overtones. Hollywood's exploitation of apocalyptic fears continues to this very day.

A sense of impending doom also affected people's taste in religious literature around 1970. André Guenon, French metaphysician and author, was very influential with many college students in the 1960s. He saw modern history not as progressing to ever bigger and better things, but as plummeting into a dark age that he equated with the fourth and last age of the Hindu time cycle (*Manvantara*), called the *Kali-Yuga*. This age would end in deceptions and delusions, despite claims that we were progressing into a "golden age" of enlightenment. Fascinated with Hindu thought, Guenon translated these concepts into Christian terms for popular consumption. The *Kali-Yuga* became the apocalypse, and the widespread delusions became the final apostasy. After the *Kali-Yuga* would come the "new heavens and new earth" spoken of in the Christian Scriptures. One of the young minds influenced by Guenon was a student at Pomona College in California by the name of Eugene Rose, who later converted to Orthodoxy and became a famous monk by the name of Fr. Seraphim Rose.

The late 1960s and early '70s were the ideal time for books pedaling the apocalyptic. We are going to focus on one in particular that would have immense influence on people's expectations of the end. In fact, it would become the best selling nonfiction book of the 1970s—and it continues to influence the imaginations of millions even today.

Chapter Two

The End Is Near

Woe to you who desire the day of the Lord!
—The Book of Amos 5:18

*We are so constituted that we believe the most incredible things;
and, once they are engraved upon the memory, woe to him who endeavors to erase them.*
—Goethe, *The Sorrows of Young Werther* (1774)

A BOOK THAT especially helped Americans come to terms with their world back in the early 1970s was Hal Lindsey's *The Late Great Planet Earth*, which appeared at the same time as Toffler's *Future Shock*. As America was traditionally a Protestant country, the appeal of Lindsey's book lay in the fact that it drew from the Bible to put the modern world into some kind of context. Moreover, as *The Late Great Planet Earth* was a book about the apocalyptic, it resonated superbly with the mood of the times. So far, it has sold more than 25 million copies and has been printed in over thirty languages.[1]

According to Russell Chandler, former religion writer for the *Los Angeles Times*, Hal Lindsey started out as a Mississippi River tugboat captain in New Orleans before going into seminary. Then,

> Lindsey traveled with the Campus Crusade for Christ evangelistic ministry for eight years, honing his persuasive and speaking skills through open-air preaching at colleges and universities. Later Lindsey launched his own prophetic ministry, now called Christian Associates, with headquarters near the UCLA campus.[2]

---

1   Kyle, 115. The latest edition published by Zondervan, though, claims only 15 million copies sold. Zondervan perhaps is claiming sales only of its edition of the book.
2   Russell Chandler, *Doomsday* (Ann Arbor, MI: Servant, 1993), 250.

The Late Great Planet Earth drew from newspapers and magazines to create a picture of a world frighteningly out of control, matching these news reports with passages from the Bible that seemed to predict the very events portrayed in the media. The image Lindsey painted was of a world that was destined to get worse and worse until it hit rock bottom with Armageddon. Not a pretty picture, but one that rang true to many in 1970.

Yet it would be unfair to depict *The Late Great* as only a potboiler of doom and gloom. Out of the mix of apocalyptic horrors that Lindsey brewed, there was a happy ending: Jesus was returning soon to save us from ourselves and lead us into a millennial Paradise. In fact, "born-again" believers could look forward to being "raptured" off the planet just as the world hit bottom with the appearance of the Antichrist. Moreover, Lindsey's "gospel" gave people a mission in life:

> As we see the world becoming more chaotic, we can be "steadfast" and "immovable," because we know where it's going and where we are going. We know that Christ will protect us until His purpose is finished and then He will take us to be with Himself. . . . So let us seek to reach our family, our friends, and our acquaintances with the Gospel with all the strength that He gives us. The time is short.[3]

On the whole, in attempting to draw some hope out of a world that looked irreversibly bound for Armageddon, Lindsey's book was both a product and a sign of the times. Since Hal Lindsey's book was to have such an impact on the American religious psyche, we must examine it in some depth in order to understand our contemporary end-of-the-world phenomenon.

The Bible According to Lindsey

"In this book I am attempting to step aside and let the prophets speak," Lindsey proclaims with all seeming sincerity in his introduction. No doubt he truly believes he is a faithful emissary of the Prophets; but sometimes in "stepping aside," he stumbles over himself while clarifying what the Prophets are actually "saying."

What Hal Lindsey does in *The Late Great Planet Earth* is to take current events and pour them into a prefabricated apocalyptic mold. Basically, he interprets the Scriptures with the daily newspaper for a commentary, an approach that leads him to announce at the beginning of the book, "Some of the future events that were predicted hundreds of years ago [in the Bible] read like today's newspaper." [4] At times, the effect can be impressive—and to the unwary, even convincing.

---

3   Hal Lindsey, *The Late Great Planet Earth* (New York: Bantam, 1970), 176–177.

4   Lindsey, *Late Great*, 10.

Consider how Lindsey treats the following verse, Ezekiel 38:2 (Amplified Version), which reads, "Gog, of the land of Magog, the chief prince of Rosh, of Meshech and Tubal." Lindsey explains, "Gog is the symbolic name of the nation's leader and Magog is his land. He is also the prince of the ancient people who were called Rosh, Meshech, and Tubal." [5] So who is Gog? The answer happens to be the title of this particular chapter in Lindsey's book: "Russia is a Gog." From the name "Rosh," Lindsey extrapolates the name "Russia," and from "Meshech" the name "Moscow," [6] an idea popularized in the old *Scofield Reference Bible.*

Although imaginative, such an interpretation of the inspired text leaves something to be desired. The Hebrew *rosh* translates better as "head" than as a place name, and there is no evidence that a country named "Rosh" ever existed. Nevertheless, Lindsey is convinced the Prophet was talking about the Soviet Union as the descendants of "Rosh." [7] (More on this verse from Ezekiel in a later chapter.)

In another attempt to discover a modern communist nation in the Bible, in a chapter entitled "The Yellow Peril" Lindsey turns to Revelation 16:12, which describes the "kings of the east" crossing the Euphrates. He is convinced this could only be a reference to Red China. Lindsey goes back to the original Greek to find that the word "east" is a translation of *anatoles heliou,* which can be rendered literally, "the rising of the sun." In this, Lindsey imagines the Bible is referring to the Land of the Rising Sun, the Far East. [8]

In reality, even the most basic lexicon or expository dictionary—such as *Vine's Expository Dictionary of New Testament Words,* a standard reference since 1940—reveals that *anatoles heliou* simply means "east," not necessarily China. Thus, nineteenth-century prophecy forecasters often believed the "kings of the east" were the Turks or the lost tribes of Israel. Indeed, no reputable modern translation of the Bible would ever render Revelation 16:12 as the "kings of the Chinese," or the "kings of the Orientals," or even the "kings of the Far East."

Contrary to the way Lindsey approaches this passage in Revelation 16, most reputable commentators on Revelation understand it in terms of Old

---

5   Lindsey, *Late Great,* 52.
6   Lindsey, *Late Great,* 52–54.
7   In connection with the other names mentioned in Ezek. 38:2, Douglas Stewart observes: "We know quite a bit about their history . . . We know, then, that Meshech has nothing whatever to do with 'Moscow' or Tubal with 'Tobolsk,' but are simply distant, fierce, warlike nations that are mentioned in the Bible to signify the forces opposed to the Lord's people." *Ezekiel,* The Communicator's Commentary, Vol. 18 (Dallas: Word Books, 1989), 355.
8   Lindsey, *Late Great,* 70.

Testament imagery: the Euphrates River was believed to be the ideal eastern border between Israel and its pagan neighbors (see Gen. 15:18), whom God would send against Israel when the Jews neglected the Mosaic covenant. These conquests by foreign powers from the east were consequently seen by the Old Testament Prophets as just punishments for Israel's sins. The intention of the author of Revelation was therefore to evoke an image of divine chastisement using well-known prophetic language, not to allude cryptically to a twentieth-century communist nation.

Not stopping at interpreting "the kings of the east" as the Red Chinese, however, Lindsey then interprets Revelation 9:16, which speaks of a 200-million-man cavalry, as referring to the modern Chinese army: "In fact, a recent television documentary on Red China, called 'The Voice of the Dragon,' quoted the boast of the Chinese themselves that they could field a 'people's army' of 200 million militiamen." [9] If the Chinese could ever manage such a feat, it would be impressive indeed. Both the Allied and Axis powers together at their peak during World War II totaled only 70 million men. Even assuming China *could* field such an unbelievably gigantic army, including the horses mentioned in Revelation 9:17, Lindsey doesn't offer any compelling reason why China would bother actually to do so. Two hundred million men entering the open expanses of the Middle East on horseback would be little more than targets for any well-trained, modern army.

In this case, though, Lindsey does not consider the Greek text of "200 million," *dismyriades myriadon*, which can also be translated simply as "two myriads of myriads" (i.e., 2 x 10,000 x 10,000). Commentators on Revelation such as G. R. Beasley-Murray, David Chilton, and Robert Mounce note that the expression "two myriads of myriads" goes back to Old Testament sources that number the angels who serve the Lord around His throne as "a thousand thousands" (Dan. 7:10), and that the Lord's chariots are "twenty thousand, even thousands of thousands" (Ps. 68:17). In Revelation itself, the angels around the throne number "myriads of myriads" (Rev. 5:11).

In context, the figure 200 million refers to angels rather than Chinese soldiers. But the 200 million angels in Revelation 9:16 are not of heavenly origin. Rather, when we look at the actual description of the army in Revelation 9:16, 17, it strongly resembles something from the pit of hell. Consequently, most reputable commentaries interpret this army as being of demonic origin. Rather than "reduce this expression to arithmetic," to borrow Mounce's phrase, we should accept the "two myriads of myriads" of Revelation 9:16 as an incalculable number of demons coming from

---

9 Lindsey, *Late Great*, 75.

"the east," from whence traditionally came the judgment of God.[10]

Lindsey is not the first, though, to apply mathematics to the Book of Revelation. Poking fun at Lindsey's "Red Chinese army" understanding of Revelation 9:16, David Chilton in his excellent commentary on Revelation compares Lindsey's interpretation with that of a commentary written in 1873 by J. L. Martin. In quintessentially Lindseyan fashion, Martin interpreted the 200-million-man cavalry as the fighting force of the whole world as of 1870:

> We have a few more than one billion inhabitants on the earth. . . . But of that billion about five hundred millions (one-half) are females, leaving an average population of male inhabitants of about five hundred millions; and of that number about one-half are minors, leaving about two hundred and fifty millions of adult males on earth at a time. But of that number of adult males about one-fifth are superannuated—too old to fight. These are statistical facts. This leaves exactly John's two hundred millions of fighting men on earth. And when we prove a matter mathematically, we think it is pretty well done.[11]

To clinch this interpretation, Martin noted that the description of the huge army in Revelation 9:17–19 perfectly matched the state of military technology in the nineteenth century:

> [The Apostle] John is pointing to the modern mode of fighting on horseback, with the rider leaning forward, which, to his sight, and to the sight of one looking on at a distance, would appear as the great mane of the lion; the man leaning on his horse's neck. He would, in fighting with firearms, have to lean forward to discharge his piece, lest he might shoot down his own horse that he was riding. In John's day the posture was very different. . . . Now, I want to ask my friendly hearers if it is not as literally fulfilled before our eyes as anything can be? Are not all nations engaged in this mode of warfare? Do they not kill men with fire and smoke and brimstone? . . . Do you not know that this is just ignited gunpowder? . . . Could an uninspired man, in the last [half] of the first century, have told of this matter?[12]

Whether you interpret the "fire and brimstone" of Revelation as gunpowder, like Martin, or as the radioactive fallout wrought by thermonuclear weapons, like Lindsey,[13] the interpretive methodology is the same. Both men believe the Apostle John had their own day specifically in view when the

---

10 See G. R. Beasley-Murray, *Revelation*, The New Century Bible Commentary (Grand Rapids: Eerdmans, 1974), 164–165; David Chilton, *The Days of Vengeance* (Ft. Worth, TX: Dominion Press, 1987), 251; and Robert Mounce, *The Book of Revelation*, The New International Commentary on the New Testament (Grand Rapids: Eerdmans, 1977), 201–202.

11 Chilton, *Vengeance*, 12.

12 Chilton, *Vengeance*, 12–13.

13 Lindsey specifically interprets Rev. 9:18 as a description of thermonuclear war in his commentary on Revelation, *There's a New World Coming* (New York: Bantam Books, 1973), 126–127.

Book of Revelation was penned. Rather than consulting competent biblical scholars or the writings of the Church Fathers, Lindsey sees Scripture as a puzzle to be deciphered using the *New York Times* as the prophetic key, prompting more than one theologian to characterize Lindsey's approach to the Bible as "newspaper exegesis."

The highly dubious interpretations of Scripture noted above simply litter Lindsey's book, straining the reader's credulity when a third of the way through Lindsey claims, "We are not attempting to read into today's happenings any events to prove some vague thesis. . . ." No? "All we need to do is know the Scriptures in their proper context and then watch with awe while men and countries, movements and nations, fulfill the roles that God's prophets said they would." [14]

Even more disturbing are the occultic overtones to Lindsey's book. At the very beginning of *The Late Great Planet Earth*, Lindsey dwells on the way people today are consulting palm readers, fortune-tellers, augurs, and soothsayers. Lindsey also mentions the popularity of astrology, spiritualism, Edgar Cayce, and Jeanne Dixon. Throughout history, Lindsey observes, people have wanted to peer into the future, even reading omens from the entrails of chickens.

Yet Lindsey is certain the Bible is at least as reliable a tool for fortune-telling as the entrails of a chicken: "The Bible makes fantastic claims; but these claims are no more startling than those of present day astrologers, prophets and seers." [15] This attitude toward the Bible runs through the entire book to the very last chapter, which is characteristically called, "Polishing the Crystal Ball." There he sets forth what he believes is in store for the world based on his reading of the Bible, beginning with the caveat, "Don't get the idea that I think that I am infallibly right in the same way that a Biblical prophet speaking under the direct inspiration of God's Spirit was." [16]

From beginning to end of *The Late Great Planet Earth*, Lindsey approaches the Scriptures like a deck of tarot cards in an effort to second-guess the future. "We believe that a person can be given a secure and yet exciting view of his destiny by making an honest investigation of the tested truths of Bible prophecy." [17] This is not to suggest that there is no difference between Lindsey and a carnival fortune-teller; nevertheless, Lindsey's attempts to predict the future using the Bible do smack of the divining arts. Unfortunately, too many today take Lindsey's methodology seriously and consequently

---

14 Lindsey, *Late Great*, 65–66.
15 Lindsey, *Late Great*, 7.
16 Lindsey, *Late Great*, 170.
17 Lindsey, *Late Great*, 8.

attempt to peer into the Bible to glean details of the future, as though divine revelation were some sort of crystal ball.

Lindsey attempts to clarify his thoughts on how the Bible ought to be interpreted on page 40 of his book. There he simply quotes approvingly from David Cooper's book, *When Gog's Armies Meet the Almighty in the Land of Israel*, an apocalyptic potboiler written back in 1940:

> "When the plain sense of Scripture makes sense, seek no other sense; therefore, take every word at its primary, ordinary, usual, literal meaning unless the facts of the immediate context, studied in the light of related passages and axiomatic and fundamental truths, indicate clearly otherwise." This is the method which this writer [Lindsey] has diligently sought to follow.[18]

How this "literal interpretation" of the Bible works itself out in practice we will now see.

The End-Times Scenario

Everything for Lindsey hinges on the establishment of the state of Israel in 1948, when the prophetic countdown to Armageddon supposedly started ticking. He notes that since the Reformation there have always been those who, by studying biblical prophecy, foresaw the coming Israeli state. "These men held this position in spite of mocking and ridicule on the part of the majority of Christendom," Lindsey proclaims.[19] You can sense that Lindsey is proud to be counted as a member of this elite coterie of visionaries.

After indulging in a bit of hagiography for certain of his heroes, Lindsey adds, "The great contribution of these men who stood against the prevailing religious opinion of their day is obvious. They prove that these prophetic passages are clear and could be understood if taken literally." [20] It is uncertain, though, how these "literal" interpretations could be so clear when the "prevailing religious opinion" has consistently maintained they aren't.

Based on his belief that the establishment of the modern state of Israel is the linchpin for the interpretation of biblical prophecy, Lindsey proceeds to announce the imminent end of the world—not, however, before decrying the practice of "date setting." Lindsey states plainly in his introduction that he makes "no claim of knowing exactly when the world is going to end. In fact, I have never taken to the hills with my possessions and loved ones to await Doomsday." Later, in the chapter he devotes to outlining the future of Israel, he adds:

---

18 Lindsey, *Late Great*, 40.
19 Lindsey, *Late Great*, 39.
20 Lindsey, *Late Great*, 40.

THE END IS NEAR

Many Bible students in recent years tried to fit the events of World War I and II to the prophetic signs which would herald the imminent return of Christ. Their failure discredited prophecy. The people who have fled to the mountains to await the end of the world haven't had the faintest idea about the truths in Bible prophecy. It is because of these unscriptural attempts at calculating dates that some eyebrows rise when we speak of Bible prophecy today.[21]

So what follows hard upon this? What many disgruntled followers of Lindsey have characterized as "date setting."

Ten pages after making the above declaration, Lindsey goes to what is called the Olivet Discourse in the Gospel of Matthew. Lindsey focuses on the parable of the fig tree (Matt. 24:32–34), which he interprets as a symbol of Israel. After declaring that "the most important sign in Matthew [of the Second Coming] has to be the restoration of the Jews to the land of Israel," Lindsey makes a point of stating that the "fig tree," Israel, set forth its first leaves when it became a nation again on May 14, 1948. He then cites the crucial verse, "Truly I say to you, *this generation* will not pass away until all these things take place" (emphasis his).

What generation? Obviously, in context, the generation that would see the signs—chief among them the rebirth of Israel. A generation in the Bible is something like forty years. If this is a correct deduction, then within forty years or so of 1948, all these things could take place. Many scholars who have studied Bible prophecy all their lives believe that this is so.[22]

Got it? "Forty years or so" from May 14, 1948, that is, *around May 14, 1988*, Christians could expect to see the final windup. True, Lindsey didn't specifically set a date. Just the same, Lindsey's followers made all the necessary cognitive connections for him and were setting their hopes accordingly.

But then again, maybe not *all* his followers were exactly on board. The publishers of the 1977 edition of *The Late Great Planet Earth* placed a recommendation on the dust jacket that people not make plans for 1985—just in case some readers failed to catch on to the subtle mathematics of the fig-tree prophecy.[23] For those still a little slow on the uptake, though, Lindsey ushered in the 1980s with a book entitled, *The 1980s: Countdown to Armageddon*. Presumably this cleared away any lingering doubts in the minds of his readers.

The number of people taken in by Lindsey's reasoning on the fig-tree parable is astounding, and merits our pausing a moment to look at it. Jesus is

21 Lindsey, *Late Great*, 33.
22 Lindsey, *Late Great*, 43.
23 Chandler, *Doomsday*, 251.

reported in Matthew 24:32–34 as saying:

> Now learn this parable from the fig tree: When its branch has already be-
> come tender and puts forth leaves, you know that summer is near. So you
> also, when you see all these things, know that it is near—at the doors!
> Assuredly, I say to you, this generation will by no means pass away till all
> these things take place.

First of all, nowhere in the parable or in the whole chapter of Matthew
24 is a restoration of national Israel promised. Is Israel alluded to under the
symbol of a fig tree? It is doubtful that the fig tree in itself has any special
significance in this passage. The Mount of Olives where Jesus told the parable was famous for its fig trees, so Jesus simply refers to a fig tree to help
illustrate His point. In the parallel account in Luke 21:29, Jesus says, "Look
at the fig tree, and *all the trees*" (emphasis added). What Jesus is saying in
both versions of the parable is that when you see the signs of springtime in
the leaves of the trees, you know summer is near. Similarly, when you see the
signs that He has given (and the restoration of national Israel wasn't one of
them), then you know the time "is near—at the doors."

Fig trees can symbolize a number of different things in the Bible. In
1 Kings 4:25 and Micah 4:4, the fig tree is not a symbol of Israel, but of
prosperity. In fact, there is only one place in the Bible where the fig tree
clearly does represent Israel, Luke 13:6–9.[24] Here Jesus states that if the tree
doesn't bear fruit then it should be cut down—which is precisely what happened to Israel in A.D. 70. We might also point out that nowhere in this
passage in Luke is there a suggestion that Israel would be restored again as a
nation.

The next step in Lindsey's scenario for Israel is the rebuilding of the
Jewish Temple in Jerusalem. When Jewish sacrifices are resumed in the
newly constructed Temple, Lindsey states, the Antichrist will enter the Temple
and proclaim himself God. This is the "abomination of desolation" that is
spoken of in Daniel 9:27.

---

24 Jer. 24 comes close in using good figs and rotten figs to symbolize two groups of Jews: the
    good figs represent those God acknowledged, who were deported to Babylon "for their
    own good" (v. 5); the rotten figs include Zedekiah and those left behind in Judea or who
    had resettled in Egypt, thus comprising all those God had "given up" (v. 8). Another pas-
    sage in the Bible where a fig tree is thought to represent Israel is Matt. 21:18–22, where
    Jesus curses a fig tree. However, the fig tree is here probably not a symbol of national
    Israel, but of the Temple. (See William Telford's book that appeared in 1980, *The Barren
    Temple and the Withered Tree*.) This is more obvious in Mark's account (Mark 11:11–25),
    where the cursing of the fig tree is interwoven with Jesus' cleansing of the Temple. In
    Matthew, the cleansing of the Temple immediately precedes the cursing of the fig tree
    (Matt. 21:12–17). Thus Jesus was cursing the fruitlessness of Judaism and predicting the
    destruction ("withering") of the Temple.

Lindsey then turns his attention to Russia. As stated earlier, Lindsey is certain Russia has a central place in Bible prophecy. Drawing from Ezekiel 38:5, 6, he lists those who will be aligned with the Soviets in World War III, which will culminate in the battle of Armageddon. These are Iran, "Ethiopia" (the sub-Saharan African nations), "Libya" (the North African nations), "Gomer and all its hordes" (the Warsaw Pact nations), "Togarmah and all its hordes" (southern Russia and the Cossacks), and others. This great Soviet alliance is said to come from the "uttermost north" in Ezekiel 38:6, 15 and 39:2. This "king of the north" (see Dan. 11), Lindsey claims, will lead an assault on Israel that will trigger the final conflict.

Another geopolitical alignment will be Egypt and the Arab nations, collectively dubbed the "king of the south" from Daniel 11. These Arab countries, led by Egypt, will be so consumed with liberating Palestine from the Jews that they will enter a pact with the "king of the north," the Soviets and their allies. This great mass of military potential will all be aimed against tiny Israel, God's chosen people.

The third politico-military alignment is what we have seen Hal Lindsey term, "the Yellow Peril." This is the Far East, led by China and her army of 200 million men. Though Hal Lindsey details the nuclear potential of China, he sees the Oriental contribution to the Battle of Armageddon as primarily an overland human-wave assault, across the Euphrates and into Israel. Lindsey writes, "In this day of H-bombs and super weapons, it seems incredible that there could ever be another great land war fought by basically conventional means, yet the Chinese believe that with a vastly superior numerical force, they can absorb devastating losses and still win a war." [25] Nonetheless, Lindsey assures us that the Orient will be beaten badly—but not without a fight: "John says that the Eastern force alone will wipe out a third of the earth's population (Revelation 9:15–18)." [26] How this can be done "by basically conventional means"—meaning military force other than weapons of mass destruction—Lindsey doesn't explain.

Finally, we arrive at Lindsey's fourth and final world power block: the West, having the dubious distinction of being headed by the Antichrist. Lindsey is convinced that the West will revive the Roman Empire in a ten-nation European confederacy. "We believe that the Common Market and the trend toward unification of Europe may well be the beginning of the ten-nation confederacy predicted by Daniel and the Book of Revelation." [27] The

---

25 Lindsey, *Late Great*, 155.

26 Ibid.

27 Lindsey, *Late Great*, 83.

Antichrist heading this revived Roman Empire (first from Rome and then from Jerusalem) will seem to solve all the world's problems, and thus become a popular leader.

Having set the political and military stage for the final countdown to Armageddon, Lindsey now sets the spiritual stage. He believes the world will soon adopt a single religion, a combination of astrology and other unsavory elements added to the watered-down version of Christianity served up by the ecumenical movement. The World Council of Churches and the National Council of Churches both have an important part in Satan's plan for mankind, Lindsey reveals. The apostate Christian church is a part of this one-world religion called the "Whore" and "Mystery, Babylon." Lindsey begins the chapter entitled, "Revival of Mystery Babylon," by stating, "The prophecies of the Bible are a vital part of God's Word, but should not be used for sensationalism." [28] At this point, though, one wonders who can read such a statement with a straight face.

According to Lindsey, with the proper alignment of the political, military, and spiritual forces, everything is in place for the final phase of the world, a seven-year period called the "Great Tribulation," characterized by the rule of the Antichrist and the judgments of God. It will be a time too terrible to contemplate. Certainly, Lindsey reasons, God wouldn't allow His people to suffer such hardships. He therefore confidently asserts that God will snatch the Church off the earth before the Tribulation:

> Someday, a day that only God knows, Jesus Christ is coming to take away all those who believe in Him. He is coming to meet all true believers in the air. . . . God's Word tells us that there will be one generation of believers who will never know death. These believers will be removed from the earth before the Great Tribulation—before that period of the most ghastly pestilence, bloodshed, and starvation the world has ever known. Examine the prophecies of this mysterious happening—the "Rapture." Here is the real hope for the Christian, the "blessed hope" for true believers (Titus 2:13–15).[29]

Lindsey cites Titus 2:13 to back this notion of the rapture. Paul writes to Titus that we are to be "looking for the blessed hope and glorious appearing of our great God and Savior, Jesus Christ" (Titus 2:13). The word "appearing" translates the Greek word *epiphaneia*, "to become visible" and "to shine forth." In other words, Paul is telling us we await the visible manifestation of the glory of Jesus Christ that will occur at the Second Coming. This is how

---

28 Lindsey, *Late Great*, 103.
29 Lindsey, *Late Great*, 126–127.

this verse has been interpreted by Christians for two thousand years.[30] In fact, as we will see later in this book, the word *epiphaneia* is used in many other places in the New Testament for the Second Coming (e.g., 1 Tim. 6:14; 2 Tim. 4:1, 8).

According to Lindsey, however, the rapture is supposed to be something different. The rapture, he explains, is an invisible return of Jesus Christ distinct from the Second Coming:

> Another reason why we support the idea that the Rapture and second coming are separate events is that the second coming is said to be visible to the whole earth (Revelation 1:7). However, in the Rapture, only the Christians see Him—it's a mystery, a secret.[31]

This "secret" rapture will, like a celestial vacuum cleaner, suck up all true Christians into heaven, leaving the rest of the world to suffer the horrors to come. Thus for St. Paul and Orthodox Christians, our "blessed hope" mentioned in Titus 2:13–15 is Christ's visible Second Coming in glory, the "glorious *epiphaneia*." On the other hand, for Lindsey and his followers, it's a secret snatch!

After the Church has been raptured off the earth, Lindsey continues, the seven-year Tribulation commences and the Antichrist is revealed. At first, things will go along smoothly under the reign of the Antichrist. Admittedly, the sudden disappearance of several million Christians off the face of the earth in the rapture will cause some confusion, but that will be only temporary. The Antichrist will have a plausible explanation for this, whatever that might be.

Then, three and a half years after the beginning of the Tribulation, the Antichrist decides to move his headquarters to Jerusalem and declare his divinity in the newly constructed Temple. This diabolical world leader will control all economic activity within his realm and will persecute those who refuse to acknowledge his divinity. Those who acknowledge the Antichrist will receive a tattoo (or some other mark) on the forehead or on the hand. The mark will consist of the number of the Antichrist, 666, and is known as the "mark of the beast." Those who do not have this mark won't be able to buy or sell anything, or even hold a job.

At the heart of Lindsey's end-times scenario is the intricately complex Arab-Israeli conflict. He believes the Antichrist will solve this problem and

---

30 See, for example, Cyril of Jerusalem's *Catechetical Lectures* (15:2), written around A.D. 350, where he explicitly states that the "blessed hope" is the Second Coming. Titus 2:13 is read during the Liturgy for Epiphany (also called "Theophany") on Jan. 6 in the Orthodox Church.

31 Lindsey, *Late Great*, 131.

create a temporary peace in the region. Part of this solution will involve making a pact with Israel, guaranteeing its national security.

> According to Daniel's prophetic chronology, the minute the Israeli leader and the Roman leader [the Antichrist] sign this pact, God starts His great timepiece which has seven allotted years left on it. This event marks the beginning of the period of Biblical history previously noted as the Tribulation.[32]

Even though the Christian Church has been raptured, Lindsey concedes there will still be Christians on earth during the Great Tribulation. These are people who become Christians after the rapture, and they will be heavily persecuted because they refuse to take the 666 tattoo. At this point in Lindsey's book, things start picking up. World War III commences and Lindsey has included two maps to help us follow the various battles leading up to the final conflagration in the Valley of Megiddo. This valley opens onto the Israeli port city of Haifa, and is the site of Armageddon (from the Hebrew *Har Megiddo*, "Mount Megiddo"). How does the end of the world begin?

> The Arab-African confederacy headed by Egypt (King of the South) launches an invasion of Israel. This fatal mistake spells their doom and begins the Armageddon campaign. . . . Russia and her allies use this occasion to launch an invasion of the Middle East, which Russia has longed to do since the Napoleonic wars.[33]

But after sweeping through Israel, the Soviet bear doesn't stop. The Soviets continue into Egypt, double-crossing the Arabs and taking the entire Middle East. Lindsey then cites Daniel 11:44 to the effect that the Russian military commander will hear "rumors" that "the Yellow Peril" and the West headed by the Antichrist are mobilizing against him.

> The Russians will be alarmed at the news of the Roman Dictator [the Antichrist] mobilizing forces around the world to put down this breach of peace. Apparently it will surprise the Russian leader who underestimated the revived Roman Empire's will to fight. It is conjecture on this writer's part [!], but it appears that the Oriental powers, headed by Red China, will be permitted to mobilize its vast army by the Roman Dictator, thinking that they would be loyal to him against Russia. However, the Orientals will eventually double-cross him, and move a 200 million man army against the Antichrist.[34]

So Russia double-crosses the Arabs after taking the Middle East, prompting the Antichrist to form an alliance with the Chinese, who in turn double-cross him, so that we are left with a double double-cross. Any questions?

---

32 Lindsey, *Late Great*, 141.
33 Lindsey, *Late Great*, 142.
34 Lindsey, *Late Great*, 147.

Russia's fate is none too pretty. Lindsey states that, based on Ezekiel 38:18–22 and 39:3–5, the Soviets may well meet their end by tactical nuclear weapons. Lindsey then ponders the role the United States may be playing during all this, since "it is clear that the U.S. cannot be the leader of the West in the future." [35] He believes that America will be aligned with the Antichrist and, in an unlikely interpretation of Ezekiel 39:6 ("And I will send fire on Magog and on those who live in security in the coastlands"), Lindsey suggests we will be the victims of the cataclysmic nuclear holocaust that is to be visited on the planet.

But all this death and destruction is merely the preview for the main event. Next comes the final battle of Armageddon:

> With the United Arab and African armies neutralized by the Russian invasion, and the consequent complete annihilation of the Russian forces and their homeland, we have only two great spheres of power left to fight the final climactic battle of Armageddon: the combined forces of the Western civilization united under the leadership of the Roman Dictator and the vast hordes of the Orient probably united under the Red Chinese war machine. [36]

So here's the scene: A 200-million-man Oriental army is marching across the Euphrates while the Antichrist and the Western powers are preparing to meet them in the Holy Land. The final clash comes in the Valley of Megiddo, Armageddon. This does not mean, Lindsey darkly observes, that the death and mayhem will be restricted to this area. According to Revelation 9:15–18, he claims, all the cities of the world will be destroyed. "Imagine cities like London, Paris, Tokyo, New York, Los Angeles, Chicago—obliterated!" [37]

Amidst all the radioactive fallout, Lindsey perceives a ray of grace: At this point will occur something of a Jewish revival. "Zechariah predicts that one-third of the Jews alive during this period will be converted to Christ and miraculously preserved." [38] How will they be "miraculously preserved" from all the carnage going on around them?

Lindsey, of course, has an answer. Christ will return at this point, while the Antichrist and the Chinese are fighting it out in Megiddo. Jesus will descend from the sky and His foot will touch down on the Mount of Olives. Based on Zechariah 14:4, Lindsey believes the Mount of Olives will cleave in two, forming a crevasse running from east to west. Coincidentally, Lindsey adds, an oil company has "discovered a gigantic fault running east and west precisely through the center of the Mount of Olives. The fault is so severe

---

35 Lindsey, *Late Great*, 150.
36 Lindsey, *Late Great*, 151.
37 Lindsey, *Late Great*, 155.
38 Lindsey, *Late Great*, 156.

that it could split at any time. It is awaiting 'the foot.' " [39] So what does this
have to do with these "Jews for Jesus," you ask?

> Zechariah predicts a strange thing with regard to the ensuing split in the
> earth. The believing Jewish remnant in Jerusalem will rush into the crack
> instead of doing the natural thing of running from it. They will know this
> prophecy and realize that this great cavern has opened up for the Lord to
> protect them from the terrible devastation that He is about to pour out upon
> the godless armies all around. It will be used as a type of bomb shelter.[40]

What forces will Jesus unleash against these armies once He hits ground
zero? Lindsey cites Zechariah 14:12, "Their flesh shall dissolve while'they
stand on their feet, their eyes shall dissolve in their sockets, and their tongues
shall dissolve in their mouths." Lindsey observes: "A frightening picture isn't
it? Has it occurred to you that this is exactly what happens to those who are
in a thermonuclear blast? It appears that this will be the case at the return of
Christ." [41]

But this unpleasantness is of short duration. After bringing to a swift
conclusion the Battle of Armageddon, Christ separates the surviving believers from the unbelievers; and the unbelievers are promptly dispatched to weep
and gnash their teeth. Now begins what the world has been waiting for: the
thousand-year reign of Christ from His international capital in Jerusalem.
This is the millennium, an idyllic age characterized by peace and tranquility.
It will be a time of prosperity with two cars in every garage:

> All men will have plenty and be secure. There will be a chicken in every
> pot and no one will steal it! The Great Society which human rulers through-
> out the centuries have promised, but never produced, will at last be real-
> ized under Christ's rule.[42]

Because Christ returns before the commencement of the millennium,
what Hal Lindsey is teaching here is known as "premillennialism," the prefix
"pre-" meaning Christ returns "before" a literal thousand-year millennium.
Even though everyone will seemingly have everything during this millennium, including immortality, yet at the end of the thousand years there
will be a nasty little coup attempted by some malcontents, "the children of
the believers who started in the kingdom." But not to worry, "Christ will
bring swift judgment upon them before the rebellion reaches the actual fighting stage (Revelation 20:7–10)." [43] Lindsey cites Revelation 20:7–10 as his

---

39 Lindsey, *Late Great*, 163.
40 Ibid.
41 Lindsey, *Late Great*, 164.
42 Lindsey, *Late Great*, 165–166.
43 Lindsey, *Late Great*, 166.

THE END IS NEAR

source for this idea. Actually, this passage of Scripture talks about a battle between Christ and Gog and Magog led by Satan. It appears that Lindsey has suddenly changed his mind about the identity of Gog and Magog. Whereas before they were the Russians fighting the Antichrist, now they are "the children of the believers" fighting Christ!

In any event, whoever Gog and Magog are supposed to be, Christ vanquishes them at the end of the millennium. After this, the Lord creates a new heaven and a new earth, and everyone lives happily ever after.

What is unmistakable after reading Lindsey's book is that he found the world of 1970 very depressing and he wanted very badly to believe Christ was coming soon to "rapture" him out of it. He wanted to believe prophecies of the Second Coming were currently being fulfilled; and, unsurprisingly, he interpreted them in that way. Ironically, the citation at the head of the first chapter of Lindsey's book is from Demosthenes: "We believe whatever we want to believe." In the final analysis, Demosthenes' observation is what the discerning reader takes away from *The Late Great Planet Earth*.

After 25 Years, It's Later Than You Think

Whatever its shortcomings, Hal Lindsey's *Late Great Planet Earth* was such a commercial success that the *New York Times* declared it the bestselling nonfiction book of the 1970s. However, much has changed since Hal Lindsey wrote *Late Great*. There's been a lot of water under the prophetic bridge and we no longer live in the same world we did in 1970. The year 1988 came and went and we're all still here waiting for the rapture.

During this time, Lindsey moved to upscale Pacific Palisades in Southern California, pastored his Baptist church, and started Hal Lindsey Ministries, which distributes his literature and tapes. Lindsey has also led countless "prophetic pilgrimages" to the Holy Land, hosted innumerable prophecy conferences, done television and radio appearances, and started a monthly newsletter, *International Intelligence Briefing,* that presents "little-known, but significant news events. The information is then studied and analyzed by Hal Lindsey and his staff to uncover its Biblical significance." [44] The newsletter later became a full-fledged television program of the same title, "International Intelligence Briefing."

In 1976, *Late Great Planet Earth* was made into a full-length movie narrated by the somber voice of Orson Welles. Lindsey has gone on to write a number of other books, including such cheery titles as: *The Road to Holocaust, Satan is Alive and Well on Planet Earth, The Terminal Generation,*

---

44 From an advertisement for the *International Intelligence Briefing.*

The 1980s: Countdown to Armageddon, and *The Rapture*. He has also published a commentary on the Book of Revelation, called *There's A New World Coming.*

A quarter of a century after writing *Late Great*, Lindsey decided it was time for a follow-up. With the demise of the old Soviet Union—and with it the demise of the Cold War—and the start of the Madrid peace talks between the Arabs and Israel (followed by the Oslo Accord signed in Washington in 1994 between Israel and the PLO), there were many developments to be explained. At first glance, current events didn't seem to be fitting into the prophetic scenario envisioned by Mr. Lindsey. He responded in 1994 with a book called *Planet Earth—2000 A.D.*, which had the ominous subtitle, *Will Mankind Survive?* The question is rhetorical, of course.

Lindsey immediately starts out by trying to extricate himself from his less-than-successful interpretation of Jesus' fig-tree parable in *The Late Great Planet Earth*. The answer is a more elastic definition of the word "generation":

> The Jewish people declared the rebirth of their nation in 1948. They recaptured Jerusalem in 1967. A biblical generation is somewhere between 40 and 100 years, depending on whether you take the example from Abraham's day or from the discipline of Israel in the Wilderness of Sinai. In either case, you do the arithmetic folks. No matter how you cut it, there's not much time left.[45]

But Lindsey instinctively knows this isn't going to cut it with many people. Only a couple of pages later, he protests:

> I also said that *"if"* a generation was 40 years and *"if"* the generation of the "fig tree" (Matthew 24:32–34) started with the foundation of the State of Israel, then Jesus *"might* come back by 1988." But I put a lot of ifs and maybes in because I knew that no one could be absolutely certain.[46]

Later, Lindsey tries to downplay the significance of the 1948 date by focusing instead on the year 1967, the year East Jerusalem was captured by the Israelis: "My recent study of Daniel 9:24–27 has convinced me that the capture of Jerusalem in 1967 may be a more prophetically significant event than the rebirth of the nation." [47] Wisely, he doesn't explicitly argue that "this generation" ought to be dated from 1967 rather than from 1948. However, during an interview for a local California radio station on August 4, 1992, Lindsey did suggest dating the end forty years from 1967, giving the world

---

45   Hal Lindsey, *Planet Earth—2000 A.D.* (Palos Verdes, CA: Western Front, 1994), 3.

46   Lindsey, *Planet Earth—2000 A.D.*, 6. Emphasis in original.

47   Lindsey, *Planet Earth—2000 A.D.*, 144.

until 2007.[48] Still, when pressed by the talk-show host, Lindsey went so far as to give us till 2048. If Christ hasn't come by that point, Lindsey would then be willing to admit his prophecy system had serious problems.

Lindsey apparently didn't feel he was quite successful with *Planet Earth— 2000 A.D.* in fully explaining how events since 1970 fit into his prophetic vision. Thus he returned in the following year, 1995, with *The Final Battle.* On the cover, seeming to proceed from the title, a menacing blood-red mushroom cloud rises against a white background.

The Final Battle is largely a mediocre analysis of current events, and almost seems to be coauthored by Joseph de Courcy, Jr., the editor of *Intelligence Digest.* Quoting constantly from an interview he had with de Courcy, Lindsey is intent on demonstrating that he and the secular intelligence community are singing off the same page of the hymnal. Though Lindsey quotes other sources, there are no formal citations; indeed, there isn't a single footnote or endnote in the entire book. However, most of the material seems a rehash from *Planet Earth—2000 A.D.*, which does contain some formal citations.

It would seem that Lindsey is still receiving criticism despite his attempts to explain Christ's failure to return by 1988. In *The Final Battle,* he further refines his position on "this generation":

> Many biblical scholars have pointed to the fact that 40 years is generally regarded as a generation in the Bible. Some people have said that a generation has passed and nothing has happened. But note carefully, Jesus said the generation would not "*pass away* until all was fulfilled." In other words, many who saw the signs begin to come together *would not die* before their climactic fulfillment. Life expectancy today in the U.S. is about 76 years.[49]

Lindsey appears to have stolen a move from the Jehovah's Witnesses' playbook. The Witnesses believe the prophetic countdown commenced in 1914 and, like vultures, are watching the last few members of that generation "pass away" in expectation of the end. Compare what Lindsey has written above to the reasoning of the Jehovah's Witnesses, who cite the very same parable of the fig tree:

> After drawing attention to the many things that have marked the period from 1914 onward, Jesus said: "This generation will by no means pass away until all these things [including the end of this system] occur." (Matthew 24:34, 14) Which generation did Jesus mean? He meant the generation of people who were living in 1914. Those persons yet remaining of

---

48 Chandler, *Doomsday,* 251.
49 Hal Lindsey, *The Final Battle* (Palos Verdes, CA: Western Front, 1995), 263. Emphasis in original.

that generation are now very old. However, some of them will still be alive to see the end of this wicked system. So of this we can be certain: Shortly now there will be a sudden end to all wickedness and wicked people at Armageddon.[50]

The reasoning used by both Lindsey and the Witnesses is identical; only the dates are different. Once Lindsey joined the Jehovah's Witnesses on the deathwatch of an entire generation, he should have known that he'd made a theological wrong turn somewhere. In any event, by placing Christ's return 76 years from 1948, that is, to the year 2024, Lindsey has pushed whatever fallout may result from another false prognostication well beyond his lifetime.

Clearly the demise of the Soviet Union proved to be another problem for Lindsey's end-times vision. How does he explain away this incongruity in his prophetic scenario?

> Let me answer that this way. I am not a prophet. I have never claimed to be. In fact, over and over again I have tried to explain that I am simply a student of the Bible. What I know about the future is limited to what I can glean from the pages of a book whose predictions have proven to be 100 percent accurate [i.e., the Bible]. So, of course, I could never have imagined the precise scenario that led to the end of the Soviet Union.[51]

Nevertheless, based on Russia's political instability after the fall of communism, Lindsey manages to find a sufficiently frightening role for the new Russia in his revised vision of the future. He still insists there will be an alliance between Russia and the Muslim nations to invade Israel. It's a little difficult, however, for the reader to imagine how Russia will be able to undertake such an ambitious military expedition anytime in the immediate future. Unpaid, demoralized, lacking basic supplies, the Russian army ultimately proved incapable of subduing separatist rebels when it invaded tiny Chechnya in December of 1994 in order to topple Chechnyan leader Dzhokhar Dudaev. After mounting casualties and defections, the Russian army was finally forced to withdraw. The readiness of the army has only deteriorated in the years since. It is probably fair to say that Hal Lindsey has more faith in the Russian military at the moment than Russia's generals do.

Lindsey also continues to believe that China and the Orient will march a 200-million-man army into the Middle East to attack a weakened West led by the Antichrist. "Why would China attack?" he asks. Lindsey has an answer:

---

50 *You Can Live Forever in Paradise on Earth* (Brooklyn, NY: Watchtower Bible and Tract Society of New York, 1989), 154.
51 Lindsey, *Planet Earth—2000 A.D.*, 191.

But I have my own theories about why—no matter what—China will be
unable to resist the notion of someday soon marching its 200-million-strong
army off to war. . . . Well, my friends, China doesn't have a shortage of
very many things but it does have a shortage of women. . . . What all this
means in the geo-strategic sense is that China will soon have a "marriage
gap." By the year 2000, men of marriageable age, 22 to 31, will outnumber
their female counterparts so that 6 men of every 100 will be left partnerless.[52]

So what is the significance of this?

Let me just add that this problem won't just cause national instability [in
China], but *international*, as well. Just consider how bad the situation is
already. The 1990 census figures showed that there are 205 million single
Chinese over the age of 15. Of those, men outnumber women by 3 to 2. It
gets worse: Of the 8 million people in their 30s who are single, men outnumber women by nearly 10 to 1.[53]

Lindsey's point isn't immediately apparent. Is he implying that 200 million desperate Chinese men are going to invade Israel in search of women?
What Lindsey has in mind becomes clearer five pages later: "In effect, China
will have an excess population of men—a 'disposable' wealth that could be
invested in a desperate and opportunistic grab for total world power."[54]

Much of the rest of *The Final Battle* is of the same order. Lindsey will
exploit any piece of information he can find to make it fit into his idea of
what the near future should be like "according to the Bible." Even general
technological progress heralds Armageddon: "We've witnessed an explosion
of knowledge in the last half-century with the advent of jet planes, space
travel, atomic power, miracle drugs and computer technology. The prophet
Daniel saw these days coming, 'But as for you, Daniel, conceal these words
and seal up the book until the time of the end; many will go back and forth
and knowledge will increase.' (Daniel 12:4)."[55] True, the twentieth century certainly did witness a grand advancement in knowledge, particularly
in science and technology. One suspects, however, that any technological
progress beyond the horse-and-buggy stage would have elicited similar apocalyptic pronouncements from Mr. Lindsey.[56]

---

52 Lindsey, *Final Battle*, 201–202.
53 Lindsey, *Final Battle*, 202.
54 Lindsey, *Final Battle*, 207.
55 Lindsey, *Final Battle*, xvii.
56 In an age dominated by science and technology, it is instructive to note how modern proph-
    ecy pundits like Hal Lindsey assume the "knowledge" referred to by Daniel is scientific
    and technological in nature. The early Christians, on the other hand, believed that the knowl-
    edge was spiritual. St. Irenaeus of Lyons (130–202), for example, cites Daniel 12:4, 7 as
    prophesying a fuller spiritual knowledge of the Incarnation that had been pointed to in Old
    Testament types and parables (*Against Heresies* 4:26:1). Thus Irenaeus believed the knowl-
    edge spoken of by Daniel found its fulfillment in the first century.

In 1997, Lindsey released a phenomenal best-seller called *Apocalypse Code*. Much of it is similar to his previous books, beginning with a long recital of the world's woes (war, starvation, disease, etc.). If one properly "decodes" the Book of Revelation, Lindsey explains, one discovers that the Apostle John describes things like jet aircraft with "smart" weapons, modern battle tanks, ICBMs with nuclear MIRV (Multiple Independently Targeted Reentry Vehicles) capability, neutron bombs, biological and chemical weapons, space stations and satellites, lasers, aircraft carriers, nuclear submarines, and "the new super secret HAARP weapon system (High-frequency Active Auroral Research Program) that can change weather patterns over whole continents, jam global communications systems, disrupt mental processes, manipulate the earth's upper atmosphere," and so on.[57]

Evidently someone has pointed out to Lindsey that the Chinese army only has three million men in active service, not 200 million. This fact would seem to rule out the current Chinese army as the fulfillment of the prophecy in Revelation 9:16. Lindsey, though, is not one to give up easily: "But add to that [i.e., the three million on active duty] the number of militiamen under arms and you have an armed force of more than 200 million—the size of the army prophesied in the Apocalypse."[58] Unfortunately Lindsey offers no source for his assertion that China happens to have 197 million armed militiamen ready for active duty. The reader is left with nothing but Lindsey's word on it.

However, Lindsey has had second thoughts concerning the parable of the fig tree in Matthew 24. While not coming out and admitting he might have been wrong in his previous explanation of the parable, he does offer a somewhat modified interpretation:

> Just as we can tell that the general time of summer is near when we see the first leaves on the fig tree, so we will be able to tell the general time of His [Christ's] return when we see all the prophecies of His return coming together and increasing in frequency and intensity. He said that the general time would be this: the generation that sees the prophecies come together in concert will live to see their final fulfillment (see Matthew 24:32–34).[59]

Although Lindsey still believes the creation of Israel is one of those "prophecies of [Christ's] return," he appears to be moving toward what we believe is a more sober interpretation of the parable. The fact that for once he didn't specifically link the parable to Israel is a hopeful sign.

Since the publication of *Apocalypse Code*, Lindsey has continued

---

57 Hal Lindsey, *Apocalypse Code* (Palos Verdes, CA: Western Front, 1997), 36–37.
58 Lindsey, *Apocalypse*, 295.
59 Lindsey, *Apocalypse*, 26.

cranking out books to scare the credulous. To date, the most recent is *Planet Earth: The Final Chapter*, which adds nothing new to what Lindsey has said before. The title and cover may change, but the message is always the same: The end is nearer than the last time I said the end was near.

The "Unsealed" Prophetic Word

We have spent a lot of time on Hal Lindsey for two interrelated reasons: (1) Hal Lindsey is literally known as "Mr. Prophecy" in millenarian circles; and (2) despite variations in detail, Lindsey's end-times scenario has provided the basic model from which nearly all of today's end-times speculation starts. In one form or another, much of what has been briefly laid out above is "imminent reality" for millions.

But we ought not to think of Hal Lindsey as the "church father" of millennial mania. In fact, he himself readily acknowledges his dependence on others throughout *The Late Great Planet Earth*. After citing Daniel 12:4 ("O Daniel, shut up the words, and seal the book. . ."), he sketches what he thinks is the history of prophetic speculation in the following passage:

> Christians after the early second century spent little time really defining prophetic truth until the middle of the nineteenth century. Then there seems to have been a great revival of interest in the prophetic themes of the Bible. Today, Christians who have diligently studied prophecy, trusting the Spirit of God for illumination, have a greater insight into its meaning than ever before. The prophetic word definitely has been "unsealed" in our generation as God predicted it would be.[60]

Lindsey didn't produce his nightmarish vision for the end of the world *ex nihilo*. He had predecessors, as he himself admits, though it certainly isn't true that the prophetic passages of the Bible were sealed and ignored until they were "unsealed" and turned into a playground for the paranoid in the nineteenth century. Lindsey's greatest contribution to millenarianism is not as an original thinker, but as a popularizer. To uncover the sources of what Lindsey is popularizing requires a journey into the history of millennial mania.

---

60 Lindsey, *Late Great*, 170.

Chapter Three

A Historical Survey of the End of History

See, I have told you beforehand. Therefore if they say to you, "Look, He is in the desert!" do not go out; or "Look, He is in the inner rooms!" do not believe it.
    —The Gospel According to St. Matthew 24:25, 26

What's past is prologue.
    —William Shakespeare, *The Tempest* (1611–12)

"CHRISTIANS AFTER the second century spent little time really defining prophetic truth until the middle of the nineteenth century," Hal Lindsey told us at the end of our previous chapter. This is actually a half-truth. "Prophetic truth" for Lindsey is, of course, millenarianism, and that certainly existed in the second century (though not in the form Lindsey propagates).

It is also true that dispensational millenarianism, which is the specific theological system from which Lindsey spins his end-times scenarios, had its genesis in the nineteenth century. It is patently untrue, however, that millenarianism simply languished in the long period in between. To demonstrate this, we need to review in the next few chapters some of the millenarian/ end-of-the-world crazes that have periodically plagued the Church. We want to stress, however, that we will only hit the highlights, as a thorough examination of the phenomenon would require whole volumes.

The Theology of Talking Grapes

The earliest proponent of millenarianism (or "chiliasm," from *chilias*, the Greek word for "thousand") comes from someone not otherwise noted for being particularly attached to Orthodox Christianity. His name was Cerinthus, and he flourished in Asia Minor (modern Turkey)—an area that would become a hotbed for millenarianism—around the end of the first century. His teachings combined the heresies of the Ebionites[1] with the strange speculations of Gnosticism.[2]

In particular, he taught that the world was created by a perverse angel that held his creation in bondage. Christ was not born of a virgin, according to Cerinthus. Instead, Jesus was the son of Mary and Joseph, a mere man who had attained an extraordinary knowledge of God, and not the eternal Son of the Father in the flesh. Cerinthus' God chose Jesus to preach to the world so that all could achieve this higher knowledge and know freedom. God consequently sent "Christ" onto Jesus at His baptism to help Him in His mission. At His crucifixion, this "Christ" left Jesus, who then died and rose again. Jesus will return, according to this "gospel" of Cerinthus, to inaugurate a millennium of sensuous pleasure before the final judgment.[3] The Apostolic Church naturally condemned Cerinthus' bizarre teachings. St. Polycarp, a disciple of the Apostle John and the bishop of Smyrna, related that John once went into a public bath in Ephesus—only to run out immediately, exclaiming, "Let us fly, lest even the bath-house fall down, because Cerinthus, the enemy of truth, is within." [4]

Thus the earliest proponent of millenarianism appears to have come from outside the Church. The earliest proponent of millenarianism *within* the Church

---

1   The Ebionites were a Jewish-Christian sect created after the fall of Jerusalem in A.D. 70. They exalted the Mosaic Law and rejected Paul's epistles. They also believed Jesus was the son of Mary by Joseph and was elected the Son of God at His baptism, when he was united to the eternal Christ. Jesus is considered higher than the angels, but not divine. This eternal "Christ" was believed to have appeared in the guise of various Old Testament figures from Adam on, and was seen more as a teacher figure than as a savior. The Ebionites should be distinguished from the Nazarenes, a basically orthodox Jewish-Christian group. Origen distinguished between these two groups of Jewish-Christians in the early third century, though he refers to both as "Ebionites": "Let it be admitted, moreover, that there are some who accept Jesus, and who boast on that account of being Christians, and yet would regulate their lives, like the Jewish multitude, in accordance with the Jewish law,— and these are the twofold sect of Ebionites, who either acknowledge with us that Jesus was born of a virgin [likely meaning the Nazarenes], or deny this, and maintain that He was begotten like other human beings [the heretical Ebionites]. . ." (*Against Celsus*, 5:61).

2   Gnosticism is a term covering a wide variety of religious movements that stressed salvation through a secret knowledge revealed from heaven. Gnostic belief was based on a radical dualism between a transcendent God and an inferior demiurge who is the creator of the material universe. The material world is basically evil, though certain individuals contain a potentiality for divinity that can be nurtured. God sent Christ (understood in Docetic terms) to reveal this secret knowledge, which enables the initiated to realize their salvation.

3   G. L. Carey, "Cerinthus," *The New International Dictionary of the Christian Church*. J. D. Douglas, ed. (Grand Rapids: Zondervan, 1978), 207. See Eusebius of Caesarea, *Ecclesiastical History*, 3:28:1–6.

4   Related by Irenaeus, a native of Smyrna who, as a boy, was a student of Polycarp. See Irenaeus' *Against Heresies*, 3:3:4.

is Papias of Hieropolis in Phrygia, Asia Minor (i.e., the same neighborhood as Cerinthus). Papias was born sometime before A.D. 80 and composed a book consisting of five treatises, called *The Interpretation of the Oracles of the Lord*, unfortunately no longer extant except in citations from later writers. In the preface of the work, as reported by Eusebius of Caesarea (A.D. 260–340), Papias states:

> And I shall not hesitate to append to the interpretations all that I ever learnt well from the presbyters and remember well, for of their truth I am confident. . . . I inquired into the words of the presbyters, what Andrew or Peter or Philip or Thomas or James or John or Matthew, or any other of the Lord's disciples, had said, and what Aristion and the presbyter John, the Lord's disciples, were saying.[5]

Notice that Papias mentions both a John who is one "of the Lord's disciples" and a presbyter named John. Is this one and the same person, the Apostle John? Or is Papias referring to two separate individuals?

More to the point, did Papias receive his teaching of an earthly millennium from the Apostle John, the author of Revelation? Eusebius commented on this question as follows: "The Papias we are now treating confesses that he had received the words of the apostles from their followers, but he says that he actually heard Aristion and the presbyter John. He often quotes them by name and gives their tradition in his writings."[6] Eusebius maintained that Papias is talking about two separate individuals and that it was John "the presbyter" who actually wrote the Book of Revelation that mentions a thousand-year reign of Christ. The idea that Papias received his teaching of the millennium from the Apostle John, Eusebius argues, is a mistake made by one of Papias' later followers, St. Irenaeus of Lyons. It wasn't the Apostle John from whom Papias derived his teaching, but some presbyter named John.

Eusebius' refusal to believe that Papias had actually received his teaching from the Apostles is due to the strange nature of some of those teachings. According to Eusebius:

> The same writer [Papias] adduces other accounts, as though they came to him from unwritten tradition, and some strange parables and teachings of the Savior, and some other more mythical accounts. Among them he says that there will be a millennium after the resurrection of the dead, when the kingdom of Christ will be set up in material form on this earth. I suppose that he got these notions by a perverse reading of the apostolic accounts, not realizing that they had spoken mystically and symbolically. For he was

---

a man of very little intelligence, as is clear from his books. But he is responsible for the fact that so many Christian writers after him held the same opinion, relying on his antiquity, for instance Irenaeus and whoever else appears to have held the same views.[7]

What sort of things did Papias write to give Eusebius such a low opinion of his intellectual capacities? We have a sample of Papias' ideas preserved for us by his student, Irenaeus (A.D. 130–202), who was raised in Smyrna in Asia Minor and who later became bishop of Lyons in Gaul:

When, too, Creation, once made new and liberated, will produce an abundance of food of every kind from the dew of heaven and the fertility of the earth. This is in accord with what presbyters who saw John, the Lord's disciple, remember having heard from him, namely, what the Lord taught concerning those times when he said: "A time is coming when vineyards spring up, each having ten thousand vines, and each vine ten thousand branches, each branch ten thousand shoots; and on every shoot will be ten thousand clusters, and in every cluster ten thousand grapes, and every grape when pressed, will yield twenty-five measures of wine [i.e., 262.5 gallons!]. And when anyone of the saints takes hold of one of their clusters, another cluster will cry out, 'I am better. Take me; use me to bless the Lord.' In like manner a grain of wheat will grow ten thousand heads, and every head will contain ten thousand grains, and every grain will yield ten pounds of clear, pure flour; but the other fruit trees, too, as well as seeds and herbs, will bear in proportions suited to each kind; and all animals, feeding on these products of the earth, will become peaceable and friendly to each other, and be completely subject to man." To this state of things Papias, too,—a man of the primitive age, a hearer of John and companion of Polycarp—bears written testimony in the fourth of his books; actually, there are five books composed by him. And then he adds: "These things are believable to believers." And when Judas, the traitor, refused to believe and asked, "How, then, will such growths be brought about by the Lord?" the Lord, he says, replied: "Those will see who will then be living." [8]

If talking grapes exemplify Papias' vision of the Kingdom of God, it's easy to see why Eusebius had such a low opinion of his intelligence. It is a very materialistic conception of the Christian hope, a precursor to the Koran's description of Paradise as simply the uninterrupted indulgence of sensual pleasures.

Aside from Papias and Irenaeus, both hailing from Asia Minor, the only other Church figure from the second century known to have such millennial views is St. Justin Martyr (A.D. 100–165), known to the Orthodox as Justin "the Philosopher." Unsurprisingly, he also received the Christian faith in Asia Minor (in Ephesus). His exposition of the millennium is found in his

---

7   Eusebius, 3:39:11–13.
8   Irenaeus, 5:33:3, 4.

Dialogue with Trypho, where he explains:

> A man among us named John, one of Christ's apostles, received a revelation and foretold that the followers of Christ would dwell in Jerusalem for a thousand years, and that afterwards the universal and, in short, everlasting resurrection and judgment would take place.[9]

It is unclear from this statement alone whether the millennium is supposed to happen before or after the Second Coming, though probably he believed it to be after. Significantly, Justin earlier admitted in his *Dialogue* that, concerning an earthly millennium, "there are many pure and pious Christians who do not share our opinion."[10] The fact of the matter is that nearly *all* did not share Justin's opinion.

Irenaeus in the second century wrote at length on the coming Tribulation and millennium at the end of his famous work, *Against Heresies*. After Irenaeus moved from Asia Minor to become bishop of Lyons in Gaul, he wrote his *Against Heresies* and helped establish millenarian views in the West. Irenaeus in this work was writing mostly against the heresy of Gnosticism, and his lengthy tome was a major contribution to the Church. However, as the Church moved decisively against millenarianism in the third century, the millenarian part of Irenaeus' work was suppressed. Hippolytus, in writing his *On the Antichrist* at the beginning of the third century, borrowed heavily from Irenaeus, but Irenaeus' millenarianism is conspicuously absent from the work.[11] It wasn't until 1575 that a copy of *Against Heresies* was discovered containing the original millenarian chapters.

What Papias and his two later followers, Justin Martyr and Irenaeus, have in common is, of course, that they all hail from Asia Minor, which is probably the birthplace of the millenarian teaching. Unlike today's brand of millenarianism, these early teachings contain no hint of the doctrines of dispensationalism (which we shall describe later). Papias and his later followers held that the Christian Church is the true remnant of Israel, and there is no teaching of a rapture. In these and other ways, the millenarianism of the second century is different from (and less spiritually destructive than) the millenarianism espoused by Hal Lindsey and others today.

Even if Papias, Justin Martyr, and Irenaeus believed exactly the same things as the modern heralds of Armageddon, this would still not be enough to legitimize modern millenarian doctrines as "apostolic." Simply because a

---

9   Justin Martyr, *Dialogue with Trypho*, 81.
10   Justin Martyr, *Dialogue*, 80.
11   Many competent scholars, though, believe Hippolytus was a millenarian based on certain passages in his *Commentary on Daniel* and his *On the Antichrist*. E.g., J. N. D. Kelly, *Early Christian Doctrines* (San Francisco: HarperSanFrancisco, 1978), 469.

few ancient writers espouse a belief doesn't mean they are reflecting the accepted beliefs of the ancient Church. St. Vincent of Lérins, in his renowned work entitled *The Commonitories* (Latin for "Memoranda"), written around A.D. 434, penned what became a famous dictum for establishing the orthodoxy of a teaching: "Moreover, in the catholic Church itself, all possible care must be taken that we hold that faith which has been believed everywhere, always, and by all." [12]

In other words, according to St. Vincent, the true Faith speaks with one voice across both time and space in order to set forth what has been handed down by the Apostles. True doctrine must have the marks of being: (1) the *universal* teaching of the Church; (2) the consistent teaching of the Church since *antiquity*; and (3) the teaching held by the *consensus* of the Church. It is therefore not enough merely to gather a few quotes from the early Church in order to legitimize the teaching of an earthly millennium. If such a teaching hasn't been held "everywhere, always, and by all," then a few quotes appearing to bolster the doctrine serve only to highlight its novelty. Why is it that *only a few* citations can be produced to establish what was supposedly proclaimed as orthodox teaching throughout the Church?

Moreover, not every ancient text cited as "evidence" that the early Church was millenarian can be taken at face value. Sometimes the modern prophets of doom point to the pseudonymous *Epistle of Barnabas,* written sometime after Barnabas' death (probably between A.D. 96 and 131), as espousing millenarianism. The author of this work, inspired by the first chapter of Genesis, concluded that since the world was created in six days, world history would last only six thousand years. The seventh day corresponded to a millennial Sabbath rest that would be initiated when Christ returns.

This "seventh day," however, would not be superseded by the eternal state, as in premillennialism. Rather, as in rabbinic literature, *Barnabas* sees this period as identical with the eternal Kingdom itself. This conclusion is strengthened when it is noted that *Barnabas* mentions only a single resurrection of the dead, not two as in classic premillennialism: one at the Second Coming and another after the millennium. Therefore, the *Epistle of Barnabas* is not an example from the early Church of millenarianism, as is commonly believed by today's pundits of prophecy. In addition, it might be observed that *Barnabas* also applies to the Church the Old Testament promises given to Israel, thus seeing the Church as the New Israel—a historic Christian teaching that does not sit well with the Hal Lindsey crowd.

---

12 Vincent of Lérins, *The Commonitories*, 2:3. The famous phrase in the original Latin is *quod ubique, quod semper, quod ab omnibus creditum est.*

The End of the World for Millenarianism

Though the Church was basically tolerant of millenarianism in the second century, the overwhelming majority of Christians rejected such beliefs. Instead, they believed that Christ's "kingdom is not of this world" (John 18:36), but is heavenly. Hegesippus, a Middle Eastern Jew who converted to Christianity in the second century, reports an incident regarding the grandsons of Judas, a relative of Jesus of Nazareth (see Mark 6:3). Emperor Domitian (A.D. 81–96), having heard garbled reports of the Second Coming of Jesus Christ, supposedly developed a "Herod complex" and, fearing for his crown, decided the way to handle the problem was to wipe out the entire line of David. The grandsons of Judas, by that time the only living relatives of Jesus Christ, were brought before the emperor and asked whether they were in fact of the house of David. After his prisoners admitted that they were, Domitian inquired into their properties and how much money was in their possession. It turned out that they had little cash and just over nine acres of land, on which they farmed to make a living and to earn enough money to pay taxes. Domitian then inspected their hands to see whether they spoke the truth, and discovered them to be hardened from incessant work. Hegesippus adds that Domitian then

> asked concerning the Christ and His kingdom, its nature, origin, and the time of appearance, and [the grandsons of Judas] explained that it was neither of the world nor earthly, but heavenly and angelic, and it would be at the end of the world, when He would come in glory to judge the living and the dead and to reward every man according to his deeds.[13]

Apparently satisfied that these peasant farmers posed no threat to his rule, Domitian had them released. Thus, according to these last known living relatives of Jesus, the Kingdom to come after Christ returns will not be earthly, but "heavenly and angelic." This was the predominant belief of the Church, which the millenarianism of Papias and Irenaeus was challenging.

Later, during the second century, again in Asia Minor, the heresy of Montanism arose, also known as the "New Prophecy Movement." It was started in Phrygia around A.D. 156 by a man named Montanus, who appeared as a reformer calling the Church to a higher moral standard. Initially, the thrust of Montanism was more rigoristic and pietistic than theological; it was more a protest against moral laxity in the Church. Montanus quickly went beyond all reasonable limits, however, and fell into ascetical fanaticism, going so far as to impose celibacy on all his followers, including married couples.

---

13   As reported by Eusebius, 3:20:2–7.

Even worse, he began claiming to be the voice of the Holy Spirit. As the official representative of the "Spirit of Truth," he spread his dreams and visions as "divine revelation" all over Asia Minor. He naturally gathered around him a respectable number of followers, promising them that he could impart the prophetic gift. In particular, there were two women in the movement who claimed divine inspiration and began babbling ecstatic utterances. The two prophetesses, Priscilla and Maximilla, left their husbands to follow their new vocation. These two became leaders of the movement along with Montanus. After a while these dreams and visions began to be collected and called the "Third Testament."

Montanus declared the New Jerusalem was about to descend from heaven and land—where else?—at his little hometown of Pepuza in Phrygia. Then would commence the long-awaited millennium. In anticipation of the event, he renamed Pepuza and Tymion (another little town nearby) the "New Jerusalem." Montanus invited all the saints to gather in Phrygia for the blessed event. Though Montanism's ascetical demands were stringent, the movement nonetheless caught on. The persecutions that Christians in general endured starting in A.D. 177 helped spread the Montanist movement out of Asia Minor and into Africa, Rome, and as far west as Gaul.

The followers of Montanus took seriously his claim to represent the Holy Spirit on earth. An inscription as far away from Asia Minor as Numidia reads: "Flavius, grandsire of the household. In the name of the Father and the Son [and] of the Lord Muntanus [*sic*]. What he promised, he performed." [14] It seems that Montanism developed a modalistic theology wherein the Father, Son, and Holy Spirit were three modes or manifestations of a single divine Person in God. [15] Consequently, just as God acting as the "Son" could be manifested in human form as Jesus, so the "Spirit" could incarnate Himself in Montanus.

Predictably, the Orthodox Church did not take well to Montanism. The movement was condemned in A.D. 230 when the Synod of Iconium refused to recognize the validity of Montanist baptism, effectively excommunicating the movement. Pope Eleutherius (A.D. 174–189) opposed Montanism the moment it showed its face in Rome, and apologists like Miltiades and Apollinarius early on took up the quill in order to defend Orthodoxy. Sadly,

---

14 Cited by Jaroslav Pelikan in *The Emergence of the Catholic Tradition (100–600)* (Chicago: University of Chicago Press, 1971), 103.

15 Hippolytus, at the beginning of the third century, writes that many Montanists fell into the heresy of the Noetians, asserting the Father is the Son (*Refutation of all Heresies*, 8:12; 10:22). Similarly, Didymus "the Blind" of Alexandria at the end of the fourth century quotes Montanus as prophesying: "I am the Father and I am the Son and I am the Paraclete" (*On the Trinity*, 3:41:1).

around A.D. 207 the movement seduced the Church's first great Latin theologian, Tertullian of Carthage (which is why the Church has never referred to him as "St." Tertullian).[16]

Montanism was ultimately undone by its own failed prognostications for Armageddon. Epiphanius of Salamis, writing between A.D. 374 and 377, reports Maximilla as saying, "After me, she says, there will be no more prophets, but [only] the consummation."[17] Such pronouncements obviously did little to ensure the future survival of the movement.

Eusebius of Caesarea in his *Ecclesiastical History* quotes some interesting material from a treatise against Montanism written by a certain Asterius Orbanus around the year 232.[18] The Montanist prophetess Maximilla—exactly like today's doomsday evangelists—was predicting imminent wars and revolutions. Eusebius cites Orbanus' response to these predictions:

> Has it not been made obvious already that this is another lie? For it is more than thirteen years today since the woman died, and there has been in the world neither local nor universal war, but rather, by the mercy of God, continuing peace—even for Christians![19]

The parallel between Maximilla's botched predictions of impending war and those of Hal Lindsey given in the previous chapter is obvious: the Russian invasion of Israel, and the other military adventures described in Lindsey's book, have yet to materialize, decades after he predicted them. The student of history can only shake his head and mumble the old platitude, "The more things change, the more they remain the same: 'That which has been is what will be, that which is done is what will be done, and there is nothing new under the sun' (Eccl. 1:9)."

The sight of Montanus' followers in white robes converging on the mountaintops of Phrygia to await the descent of the New Jerusalem did not do much to recommend millenarianism to the majority of Christians. From

---

16 This may be an appropriate point to observe that not all of the early Christian writers that will be cited in this book are considered "Church Fathers." Tertullian, who will be cited in other contexts later, is certainly not considered a Father of the Church. Neither are Clement of Alexandria and his student Origen, whose attempts at combining Christian teaching with neoplatonism later caused controversy in the Church. Nevertheless, their writings offer an invaluable insight into the early centuries of Christianity, and much of what they wrote is perfectly orthodox. Their writings are cited in this book merely for specific, evidentiary purposes.

17 Epiphanius of Salamis, *Against all Heresies*, 48:2:4.

18 Nothing is known about Asterius Orbanus, and there is even some question whether Orbanus is the author of the work. Some think Orbanus was actually a Montanist apologist to whom the author of the treatise was trying to respond. In any event, Eusebius apparently believed that Orbanus was the author of the treatise.

19 Eusebius, 5:16:19.

the third century on, millenarian views like those expressed by Papias and Irenaeus were no longer tolerated in the Church. This attitude was ultimately voiced in the official expression of the Orthodox Faith: the Nicene-Constantinopolitan Creed.

The original Nicene Creed read, "We believe . . . in one Lord Jesus Christ . . . [who] ascended into heaven, and is coming with glory to judge the living and the dead." At the Council of Constantinople in 381, the Fathers added to the original Nicene Creed the words, "and of His kingdom *there will be no end*" (emphasis added). The Council Fathers were inspired by the Psalmist, who proclaimed, "Your kingdom is an everlasting kingdom, and Your dominion endures throughout all generations" (Ps. 145:13). Many Church Fathers also cited Luke 1:33 to the same effect: "And He [Christ] will reign over the house of Jacob forever, and of His kingdom there will be no end." In other words, the Council declared emphatically that the Kingdom is eternal, not just for a thousand years. The next ecumenical council, the Council of Ephesus in 431, characterized the idea of a thousand-year earthly reign of Christ as superstition.

Still, it could not be denied that Revelation 20:4–6 spoke of a thousand-year reign of Christ with the saints. Many Church Fathers of the third and fourth centuries nevertheless interpreted Revelation in an orthodox manner, such as Hippolytus of Rome, St. Cyprian of Carthage, St. Ambrose of Milan, St. Athanasius of Alexandria, St. Cyril of Jerusalem, and Augustine of Hippo. However, the reaction of some in the Eastern Church to the millennial interpretation of Revelation was to declare the book a spurious work, possibly heterodox and certainly not written by an Apostle of Christ. Eusebius of Caesarea, as we've seen, argued passionately that the Apostle John didn't write Revelation, but that it was written by a certain presbyter named John.

The West was inclined to acknowledge the Johannine authorship of Revelation and eventually accepted it into the canon of the New Testament, interpreting the thousand-year reign as a metaphor for Christ's reigning in the Church. In time, the East unreservedly accepted Revelation as canonical as well, but never altered its lectionary to include readings from the book. To this day, though accepting the Book of Revelation as inspired Scripture, the Eastern Church does not read from Revelation in the Divine Liturgy. This is not from any lingering doubts as to the book's canonicity, but from a desire to avoid apocalyptic speculation. After all, readings from the lectionary are intended to be interpreted in the homily, and Revelation is a notoriously difficult book to interpret.

Despite the highly negative reaction to millenarianism by the Orthodox

Church, there continued to be individuals who were looking for the thousand-year earthly reign, though these were exceptions in the Church. As Stanley Grenz relates:

> The most outstanding exception was Lactantius, tutor to [Emperor] Constantine's son, Crispus. His views concerning the physical pleasures to be enjoyed during the millennium paralleled those of Irenaeus: "The rocky mountains shall drip with honey; streams of wine shall run down, and rivers flow with milk." But he moved beyond the tradition in linking the thousand years to anticipations of a golden age articulated by pagan thinkers, who, he declared, had obtained some inklings of true doctrine: "In short, those things shall then come to pass which the poets spoke of as being done in the reign of Saturnus." [20]

It is fair to say that the desire for a "golden age," to see better times just around the corner, is inherent in all of us. Who would not like to see the world—and our own personal world in particular—become more idyllic? However, as the world entered the Middle Ages, the pursuit of the millennial dream frequently became a nightmare.

---

20 Stanley Grenz, *The Millennial Maze* (Downers Grove, IL: InterVarsity Press, 1992), 41–42.

Chapter Four

The Quest for the Millennium

You know how to discern the face of the sky, but you cannot discern the signs of the times.
—The Gospel According to St. Matthew 16:3

He that would know what shall be must consider what hath been.
—Thomas Fuller, M.D., *Gnomologia* (1732)

DOOMSDAY MOVEMENTS didn't simply fade away along with the classical world. Quite the opposite: they positively flourished. As the Middle Ages dawned with its various social stresses, the world was actually entering a millennium of rampant millenarianism, a gloomy apocalyptic age lasting from the fall of ancient Rome right up till the Renaissance.

Millenarianism During the Middle Ages

Apocalyptic fantasies throughout history, like the ones we see today, have usually been nurtured by the social and political situation of the times. More often than not, they are connected to periods of social crisis. A particularly interesting (and, until recently, largely unexplored) manifestation of millenarianism developed in the Christian East as a result of the crisis of the initial Islamic conquests in the seventh century. An elaborate apocalyptic tradition revolving around the idea of the "last Roman emperor" developed in the Eastern Empire at that time.

Though the legend has roots in much earlier ideas, the genesis of the "last Roman emperor" tradition lies in a document called *Pseudo-Methodius,* written between 644 and 678, probably in 656. It was written in Syriac in the region of Singara in northern Mesopotamia (present-day northwest Iraq), an area directly affected by the Islamic conquests. The work is ascribed by the real author to the fourth-century bishop-martyr Methodius of Patara (who happened to be a millennialist). It starts out by giving a general overview of world history from the creation in Genesis to the conquests of Alexander the Great.

Pseudo-Methodius tells a convoluted story of how Alexander the Great's mother, Cusheth, returned to her father Pil, the king of Cush (Ethiopia), after the death of her famous son. Cush was then attacked by the army of Byzas, the king and mythical founder of Byzantium. Byzas then sent one of his generals, Germanicas, to king Pil of Cush with a peace treaty. The mission was successful and Pil signed the peace treaty with Byzas. King Byzas then married Cusheth, who bore him a daughter named Byzantia. The young Byzantia then married Armalaos, king of Rome, who gave Byzantia the city of Rome as a bridal gift. The point the author is arriving at is that the great empires of Greece, Rome, and Rome's later continuation in Byzantium are all descended from the same mother, Cusheth, of the land of Cush. This point is important later on in *Pseudo-Methodius*.

The account then leaps to the seventh century, when Islam has broken out of the deserts of Arabia to conquer everything from India to Egypt and beyond. The Muslims, called "Ishmaelites," persecute the Church because of the sins of the Christian people. The Ishmaelites kill priests, destroy churches, pillage holy relics, and cause many to apostatize. For Pseudo-Methodius, this time of tribulation is undoubtedly the fulfillment of 2 Thessalonians 2:3, the falling away that will eventually reveal the Antichrist, the Son of Perdition. The Ishmaelite oppressors then speak blasphemously: There is no savior for the Christians.

> Then suddenly there will be awakened perdition and calamity . . . and a king of the Greeks will go forth against them in great wrath.[1]

This is the last Roman emperor, and he will ride out to defeat the infidels. Their servitude will be a hundred times worse than what they inflicted upon their Christian subjects—a fit payment for their aggression. The last Roman emperor will also punish those Christians who denied the Faith. Then will come a millennial paradise, when the world will be at peace and the Church will prosper:

> The earth will be at peace . . . and men will multiply like locusts . . . and there will be peace on earth the like of which had never existed, because it is the last peace of the perfection of the world. And there will be joy upon

---

1 An English translation of the Syriac *Pseudo-Methodius* can be found in Paul Alexander, *The Byzantine Apocalyptic Tradition* (Berkeley and Los Angeles, CA: University of California Press, 1985), 36–51. This citation is from p. 48.

the entire earth, and men will sit down in great peace and the churches will arise nearby, and cities will be built and priests will be freed from the tax, and priests and men will rest at that time from labor and tiredness and torture . . . and when they eat and drink and rejoice and are merry, there is no wickedness and no thought of wickedness and no fear and trembling in their hearts.[2]

Though the original Syriac is silent on the length of this "millennial" reign, later Greek apocalypses give time spans of 32, 112, or 120 years. Then the Gates of the North, made by Alexander the Great himself, will be opened to release the nations of Gog and Magog, the "unclean peoples" whom Alexander the Great had imprisoned. Now loosed, Gog and Magog commit the most horrible atrocities against the Christians. They are, however, destroyed "in one hour" in the plains of Joppa by an angel of the Lord. After this, the last Roman emperor will go to Jerusalem and reside there for "a week and a half" (which, in apocalyptic terminology, is ten and a half years).

Then is revealed the Antichrist, who will be of the tribe of Dan, as prophesied in the Septuagint version of Genesis 49:17, 18. Immediately after the appearance of the Son of Perdition, the last Roman emperor will ascend Golgotha to the True Cross, which is standing on top of the hill as it was during the Crucifixion, and place his crown upon it. Pseudo-Methodius adds, "For there is no people or kingdom under heaven that can overpower the kingdom of the Christians as long as it possesses a place of refuge in the life-giving Cross, which is set up in the center of the earth and possesses its power over height and depth." He will then stretch his hands to heaven, handing over the kingdom to God the Father, and die. The Cross and the crown will then ascend to heaven in order to precede Christ at His Second Coming.

Behind this act lie several interesting interpretations of Scripture that we should explore before continuing the narrative. One is the idea that the empire would somehow continue until the end of the world in order to allow the emperor to hand over the kingdom to the Father. Pseudo-Methodius writes: "As long as this kingdom which possesses an abiding place of refuge is the center, the Son of Perdition will not be revealed, for that something which is in the center is the priesthood and the kingship and the Holy Cross." Pseudo-Methodius seems to have in mind 2 Thessalonians 2:7—which according to the Syriac text reads, "that which restrains at present is removed from the middle"—and interprets "that which restrains" the Lawless One as the Roman Empire. That which is in "the middle" is the emperor, the priesthood, and the True Cross, which will not be removed before the end of the age.

Pseudo-Methodius was by no means the first to advance the idea of the

---

2   Alexander, *Byzantine*, 49.

permanence of the empire. It was commonplace among the Fathers of the Church to identify the Roman Empire as the power "restraining" the Antichrist in 2 Thessalonians 2:7. As we will see in a later chapter, the idea that the empire would last until the Second Coming can also be found in such early writers as St. Irenaeus, Hippolytus, Tertullian, and St. Cyril of Jerusalem.

Another interesting feature of *Pseudo-Methodius* is the idea that the emperor must hand over the kingdom to the Father. As we saw, Pseudo-Methodius took great pains to show that the Greek and Roman empires were descended from Cush. Twice in the work, Pseudo-Methodius alludes to Psalm 68:31 ("Ethiopia will quickly stretch out her hands to God"), and interprets it as follows: "Cush [i.e., Ethiopia] will hand over the hand [i.e., dominion] to God [see Ps. 68:31], because it is the son of Cusheth, daughter of King Pil of the Cushites, who will be raised to heaven, and the king of the Greeks will give up his soul to his Creator." Thus Psalm 68:31 was interpreted in medieval Byzantium as pointing to the Eastern Roman Empire, just as certain scriptures are interpreted today as pointing to modern nations.

Another verse that is used in connection with handing the kingdom to the Father is 1 Corinthians 15:24, which speaks of Christ handing over His Kingdom to the Father once the last enemy, death, is defeated. The reasoning in *Pseudo-Methodius* is by analogy: Christ reigns until "all dominion, authority, and power" have been subdued and His mission is fulfilled, at which point He hands over the Kingdom to the Father. In like manner, the emperor, having vanquished all the temporal enemies of the Christians, has fulfilled his purpose, and now the earthly kingdom can give way to the Kingdom of God. The surrender of this temporal power can be accomplished only by the head of all temporal power in the empire, the emperor.

After the emperor gives the empire to the Father and dies, "immediately every leader and every authority and all powers will cease." Then the Antichrist takes control of events and seduces the multitudes to his error. He performs many miracles and, if it were possible, would lead all astray. But Christ returns with the Cross and the crown of the Roman emperor going before Him, and the Antichrist is "delivered to Hell-fire and to outer darkness."

Translated into Greek soon after its composition in Syriac, *Pseudo-Methodius* radically and permanently influenced the Orthodox apocalyptic tradition in the Eastern Empire. Though *Pseudo-Methodius* drew from other sources, it creatively adapted that material to the then-contemporary crisis in the empire, making it immensely popular. It thus became the mother of the medieval apocalyptic tradition in the East. Dorothy deF. Abrahamse,

Professor of History at California State University in Long Beach, California, writes:

> Byzantine apocalypses were indeed written for consolation in times of trouble, and they reflected the hopes and despairs of contemporaries in very concrete historical events. The localization of these texts shows how often apocalyptic hopes arose in the fringes of Byzantine society, where the threats of invasion were greatest.[3]

Pseudo-Methodius would be redacted and changed over the following centuries to bring current crises into the prophetic tradition to help people see the hand of God in contemporary events. This same pattern of revising earlier prophetic interpretations to fit current events is easily seen in modern apocalyptic writers like Hal Lindsey.

In the West, the tradition of the last Roman emperor appeared in a treatise written by the tenth-century Burgundian abbot of Montier-en-Der, Adso, entitled *The Book of the Origin and Times of the Antichrist* (*Libellus de ortu et tempore Antichristi*). The situation in the West was quite volatile, so millenarianism was especially rife. There were self-proclaimed christs wandering around the countryside gathering believers and sometimes even assembling militias, much like David Koresh, who headed the Branch Davidians in our own time.

In fact, even as early as the time of Sulpitus Severus (363–420), there was an interesting incident involving one such self-proclaimed messiah. Severus personally knew St. Martin of Tours, and in his biography of St. Martin we read about a young man in Spain who had convinced himself and others that he was Elijah come to herald Christ's Second Advent. When he had gathered a sufficiently large following, he went on to promote himself as no less than Christ Himself returned. He was apparently so persuasive that he even managed to convince a certain bishop named Rufus, who, Severus claims, actually worshiped the imposter, and for that was deposed from office.[4]

Such a self-styled messiah also was Eon of Brittany in the eleventh century, who proclaimed himself christ and set up his own church with bishops and archbishops. He terrorized the locals, raided churches, destroyed monasteries, and murdered hermits in their huts. Death and starvation inevitably followed in the path of Eon and his followers, while Eon lived in luxury as he thought would befit the King of kings. He was eventually captured and quickly died in prison, and his followers later rounded up and ordered to deny their error or suffer execution. Most chose execution. William of

---

3   Alexander, *Byzantine*, 8.
4   Sulpitus Severus, *Life of St. Martin*, 24.

Newburgh relates that one of the condemned called out for the judgment of his executioners as he was being burned at the stake, crying, "Earth, divide thyself!" William of Newburgh soberly observed, "For such is the power of error when once it has taken hold of the heart." [5]

We need to be careful, however, not to exaggerate the scope of millennial obsession during this period, as is often done when describing the end of the first Christian millennium. Some students of doomsday, for example, point to the evening of December 31, 999, and paint a picture of people supposedly running around hysterically, and even dying of fright. There is no doubt that the year 999 was one of dread throughout much of Europe, with numerous sermons on the coming Armageddon being preached in (and outside of) the churches. A total eclipse of the sun in 968 also fueled people's apprehensions as they recalled Christ's words in Matthew 24:29 about the sun being darkened. The eclipse so terrified the army of Emperor Otto I that soldiers hid under carts and dove into wine barrels.[6] As the turn of the millennium approached, people wrote wills with openings like, "The end of the world drawing nigh, I hereby . . ." But such wills, Russell Chandler points out, are hardly indicative of the societal psyche at the time, for the openings were rather standard.[7] In fact, why bother making out a will at all if you're really convinced everything is scheduled to end in the near future?

Records from the tenth century are scanty at best, and there are only a dozen or so documents describing what occurred at the turn of the first millennium—and only half of these tell of widespread hysteria. Most of the accounts of mass panic are based, either directly or indirectly, on the *Histories* of Raoul Glaber, a Benedictine monk from Burgundy born in the late tenth century. Glaber—a mystic with the amusing nickname of "Baldpate"— wrote his *Histories* between 1025 and 1030, and his description of the doomsday delirium leading up to the year 1000 was so colorful it became the medieval version of a best-seller. However, Glaber's account lacks any corroborating evidence, and many scholars today question his objectivity.

Because of the scanty corroborating evidence, many historians today doubt Europe went completely berserk in 999. After all, such historians wonder, in the midst of the Middle Ages with its widespread social disorder, famines, plagues, massacres, lootings, rapes, rampaging armies, and other miscellaneous outrages, why should everybody get into such a tizzy over New Year's Eve, 999? [8] In any event, those who had preached doom for the

5   Norman Cohn, *The Pursuit of the Millennium* (New York: Oxford University Press, 1970), 44–46.

6   Chandler, *Doomsday*, 51.

7   Chandler, *Doomsday*, 54.

8   Chandler, *Doomsday*, 53–54.

year 1000 quickly forgot their failed prediction and turned their oratorical skills to proclaiming Armageddon for 1033—the supposed millennial anniversary of the Crucifixion. Glaber likely wrote his *Histories* with the idea of sobering people up before 1033 arrived.

What seemed to motivate people in Europe at that time was less fear of tribulation than hope for something better, that is, an earthly millennium. Many hopes in the West of such a millennium were based on the legend of Charlemagne. It was believed that he never really died, but was only sleeping in a mountain or in his crypt in Aachen. Someday toward the end of the world, he was supposed to return and overthrow the Islamic infidel and usher in the millennial age. It is easy here to see the influence of *Pseudo-Methodius,* and preachers of the Crusades used these millennial beliefs about Charlemagne to persuade peasants to join the effort. Lowly foot soldiers even placed these sorts of messianic hopes in the actual leaders of the Crusades, like Godfrey of Bouillon and Raymond of Saint-Giles. As Norman Cohn has so ably shown in his *The Pursuit of the Millennium*, the Crusades were imbued with apocalyptic and millennial overtones.

One of the landmarks in Western apocalyptic/millenarian thinking was a twelfth-century Cistercian monk (and later abbot) named Joachim of Fiore (1145–1202). Joachim was 48 years old when he began having visions, which led him to start publishing some innovative theological ideas. Winning international acclaim, he was even encouraged in his work by Pope Lucius III. Joachim was fascinated with the prophetic significance of numbers, and decided that human history was to be expressed by a threefold division. Time manifested the Trinity, Joachim reasoned, so an examination of history would reveal the Trinitarian relations.

The first age was that of the Father and was characterized by the Old Testament law. The age of the Son was the age of grace, which Joachim seemed to believe would last for forty-two generations of thirty years each. The age of the Spirit was to be an age characterized by spiritual knowledge, a sort of Sabbath rest when all men would be contemplative monks.

But to enter this new age of the Spirit, the world would first need to go through the Tribulation and suffer the Antichrist. To help the Church through this Tribulation, there would arise two new religious orders to evangelize and minister to the Church in the hour of need. All of this he "found" in the Bible. The symbols of Revelation were speaking about contemporary events in the twelfth century, Joachim believed, and this convinced him that the third age was ready to burst upon the world. While Joachim's teaching was not intended to challenge the authority of the Roman Church, it inspired reform groups, like the Spiritual Franciscans, to see their revolutionary aims in millenarian terms. Ultimately, they came to see themselves as the spiritual elites who were preparing the world for the "age of the Spirit."

Though Joachim didn't predict a date when the present age would end, a certain disciple of his, a young friar named Gerardo of Borgo San Donnino, in 1254 did set a date: The age of the Holy Spirit would commence in 1260. This date was supposedly arrived at through an interpretation of Joachim's major works. In particular, Gerardo arrived at the year 1260 from Revelation 11:3 ("And I will give power to my two witnesses, and they shall prophesy *one thousand two hundred and sixty* days . . .") and Revelation 12:6 ("Then the woman fled into the wilderness . . . *one thousand two hundred and sixty* days"). Since the "woman" of Revelation 12 had traditionally been interpreted as a type of the Church, he concluded the Church would be in the "wilderness" 1,260 years.

Gerardo thought that he had at last decoded the Book of Revelation and discovered the future. He made an even more imprudent blunder when he declared that in the new age the Church would be abolished and both the Old and New Testaments would be replaced by the writings of Joachim of Fiore! Naturally the year 1260 came and went, Gerardo wound up spending the remainder of his life in prison, and the world continued leisurely on its way.

Millenarianism and Protestantism

There were sundry millennial sects throughout the Middle Ages—like the Free Spirits, for example—but since the Reformation, Protestantism has seemed to be an especially congenial home for millenarianism. This was true from the beginning of the Reformation, even though the Reformers themselves and nearly all the denominations connected with them espoused amillennialism (that is, not believing in a future, earthly reign of Christ lasting a thousand years). Millenarianism characterized the Taborites in the early fifteenth century, a pre-Reformation sect that espoused many of the ideas later associated with Protestantism.

The Taborites were a radical branch of the Hussite movement in southern Bohemia, but they didn't really reflect the teachings of Jan Huss. They were more influenced by John Wycliffe, wishing to base their beliefs solely on what they could find in the pages of the Bible. They rejected many Roman Catholic tenets like transubstantiation, purgatory, the intercession and veneration of saints, the use of relics, and any distinction between priests and laity. The Taborites got their start in July of 1419 when 40,000 people congregated on a hill that was renamed "Mount Tabor." This was inspired by a strange belief that the mountain on which Jesus foretold His Second Coming, from which He ascended into heaven, and to which He is supposed to return, was Mount Tabor.

After this meeting on their Bohemian "Mount Tabor," the Taborites strove to impose their particular idea of the Kingdom of God on the country. Their agenda included apostolic poverty, a radical moral purity, and a total ecclesiastical break with Rome. The rest of Bohemia did not share this vision for the future and attempted to suppress the Taborites. Starting in November of 1419, the suppression of the Taborites became especially intense, with the predictable result that the apocalyptic fantasies of the Taborites grew beyond all rational bounds. In fact, the Taborites became violent.

> No longer content to await the destruction of the godless by a miracle, the preachers called upon the faithful to carry out the necessary purification of the earth themselves. One of them, a graduate of Prague University called John Capek, wrote a tract which is said to have been "fuller of blood than a pond is of water" and in which he demonstrated, with the help of quotations from the Old Testament, that it was the inescapable duty of the Elect to kill in the name of the Lord. This work served as a polemical armory for other preachers, who used its arguments to urge their hearers on to massacre. No pity, they declared, must be shown towards sinners, for all sinners were enemies of Christ. "Accursed be the man who withholds his sword from shedding the blood of the enemies of Christ. Every believer must wash his hands in that blood." The preachers themselves joined eagerly in the killing, for "every priest may lawfully pursue, wound and kill sinners." . . . But the most extreme amongst the Taborites went still further and maintained that anyone, of whatever status, who did not actively help them in "liberating the truth" and destroying sinners was himself a member of the hosts of Satan and Antichrist and therefore fit only for annihilation.[9]

While this "cleansing" of Bohemia was going on, Christ was supposed to descend to Earth. He would celebrate the "wedding feast" upon His return, after which He would boot Emperor Sigismund off his throne and rule Europe in his place. Then Christ would establish the millennium, returning the world to the innocence of that first Paradise in Eden. The institutional Church would disappear and women would conceive without sexual intercourse. What could be better?

The Taborites set about constructing a theocratic society in their territory in southern Bohemia. In theory, there was to be no human authority, for all were brothers and sisters. Of course, the theory was "modified" somewhat to allow for the necessity of government. The older brothers obviously needed to look after their younger siblings. It was also supposed to be a classless society, and a primitive version of communism was attempted. Private property, rents, taxes, and dues were abolished. Peasants from all over

---

9   Cohn, *Pursuit*, 212–213.

Bohemia and Moravia sold all their worldly possessions to contribute to the common purse. In the first part of 1420, chests were set up by the Taborite clergy in which the people were expected to deposit all their money. But here, too, reality didn't always conform to theory. The leadership concentrated so much on common ownership that they took no thought of motivating people to produce anything.

Rather than constructing a functioning economy for their newly established Kingdom of God, the Taborites turned to simple banditry whenever the communal chests were empty. As the people of God, they reasoned, they had a right to all of God's wealth found on the earth. Conversely, those who were not of the people of God, that is, all who were not Taborites, had no claim to the resources of the earth. Thus raids on the property of non-Taborites were rationalized and became common.

According to Taborite plans, after all of Bohemia was subjected to Taborite control, the purification of the rest of the world would follow through conquest and domination. This belief was deeply ingrained in the Taborite movement. Norman Cohn writes:

> As late as 1434 we find a speaker at a Taborite assembly declaring that, however unfavorable the circumstances might be at present, the moment would soon come when the Elect must arise and exterminate their enemies— the lords in the first place, and then any of their own people who were of doubtful loyalty or usefulness.[10]

This 1434 meeting was a full year after the Battle of Lipany, when the new Taborite leader, Procopius, was killed and the whole Taborite movement was effectively destroyed.

The millennial obsession of the Taborites and other pre-Reformation sects continued into the Reformation period in Western Europe. After Luther "officially" inaugurated the Reformation proper on October 31, 1517, the Anabaptists were the most conspicuous in their enthusiasm for millenarianism. After the advent of the Anabaptist movement in 1523 in Zurich, there existed some forty independent Anabaptist groups, each led by a charismatic leader. Sometimes these leaders claimed to be apostles or prophets. One of these was Hans Hut, who, claiming to be a prophet, preached that Christ was to return on Whitsuntide, 1528. Then the "saints" (i.e., Hut's followers) would hold judgment on priests, pastors, nobles, and all others for whom Hut didn't much care. The slaughter of Hut's enemies would usher in the millennium. Although not all of these Anabaptist sects taught millenarianism, many did. It was one of these millennial Anabaptist groups that took over the German town of Munster.

---

10 Cohn, *Pursuit*, 216.

Munster, like the rest of northwest Germany, was experiencing great economic pressure in the early 1530s, in part because of a new tax levied by the German emperor to finance resistance to frequent Turkish invasions. The town had only recently adopted Lutheranism when it was deluged in 1532 with Anabaptist preachers kicked out of the neighboring Duchy of Julich-Cleves. Melchior Hoffman, an Anabaptist preacher who was preaching in the Anabaptist stronghold of Strasbourg, arrived in Munster with his disciples the following year. His preaching had received only a lukewarm reception in Strasbourg, but it bore fruit in Munster. Hoffman taught that the millennium was to commence in Strasbourg in 1533, which was the fifteenth centenary of Jesus' crucifixion. This idea became a virtual obsession in Munster. Hoffman was later imprisoned in Strasbourg and spent the rest of his life inside a cage in a tower.

A self-styled messiah named John Matthys, claiming to be Enoch preparing the way for the Second Advent of Christ, afterward gained control of the millennial movement in Munster. Whereas Hoffman had taught that the Anabaptists were to await the Second Coming peacefully, Matthys was a revolutionary. Thus, in February, 1534, the Anabaptists staged an armed takeover of the town hall and marketplace. Word was sent to neighboring communities of Anabaptists to come to Munster —and to bring their families and their weapons. They were told that the earth was to be judged before Easter, and that only Munster would be saved since it was the New Jerusalem. Lutherans and Catholics quickly started evacuating the town with their goods. With the new influx of Anabaptists streaming into Munster, the annual election for the town council held on February 23 resulted in an Anabaptist takeover of the town. The following several days witnessed the looting of churches and monasteries, as well as the destruction of paintings, sculptures, and books.

All power was then concentrated into the fanatical hands of Matthys, aided by a man named Jan Bockelson. Matthys established a form of communism and started rewriting the laws of Munster. He planned to make Munster a city of the Elect, and those who resisted rebaptism were forced to flee the city or be executed. All non-Anabaptists who were unable to flee because of age, infirmity, or some other reason were forcibly rebaptized in the marketplace. These rebaptisms continued over a period of three days, and afterwards it became a capital offense to be other than an Anabaptist. From then on all were to address each other as "Brother" or "Sister."

Then the "Terror" commenced. Anyone voicing dissent was publicly executed, usually by Matthys himself. To ensure that the Anabaptist leadership controlled all thought, in March of 1534 all books except the Bible were banned. The Bible was Matthys' weapon to control the thinking of the people, and banning all possible sources of alternative interpretations of the Bible assured his control.

Then Matthys began to suspect that those who had been baptized at the time of the general expulsion might be something less than "true believers." Therefore, one day they were herded together and informed that they would be killed by the "swords of the righteous" unless God the Father chose to forgive them. They were then locked inside a church to await their fate. After a while, Matthys entered with a band of armed men that looked prepared to massacre the group. The terrorized people crawled on their knees to Matthys and implored him to pray to the Father on their behalf. He agreed to do this and left. After a long and agonizing suspense, he returned and informed his victims that the Father had allowed them to be considered among the Elect. Such were the tactics employed to govern the "New Jerusalem."

After intimidating everyone in town into submission, Matthys announced that the Father desired to eliminate the private ownership of wealth. All money was to be surrendered on pain of execution as an unbeliever. And executions did take place. Within two months, private ownership of money was a thing of the past.

After the expulsion of all Lutherans and Catholics, the prince-bishop who governed the large ecclesiastical state of Munster laid siege to the city, and, on Easter of 1534, Matthys' dictatorship came to an end. Claiming divine revelation, Matthys was convinced that an attack by him and a select handful of followers would route the besieging army. Instead, it was Matthys and his little band who were cut down. This allowed Jan Bockelson, Matthys' associate, to don the prophetic mantle from the fallen leader.

In May, Bockelson ran naked through town in a frenzy and then lapsed into a trance for three days. Afterwards, he called everyone in town together and announced that God had revealed that the town constitution needed to be replaced. The model for the new constitution was to be the ancient government of Israel. The move eliminated many of the old power structures of the town, most predating the Anabaptist takeover, and ensured Bockelson's total control. A new law code was also promulgated that, besides the normal capital punishment for capital crimes, applied the death sentence to cases of lying, slander, avarice, and quarreling.

Polygamy was eventually legislated. After all, Genesis commanded the human race to "increase and multiply," and polygamy would ensure this divine precept was kept. There was, moreover, the example of Old Testament figures like David and Solomon. Bockelson soon had fifteen wives, nearly all of whom were under twenty years of age.

Another law was promulgated that forced all women above a certain age to marry. The law was simply intended to ensure the growth of the harems, since the women were not willingly buying into polygamy. The marriages of Anabaptist women to non-Anabaptists were considered invalid, and so these women, whose husbands had fled town, were considered eligible. Refusal to remarry into a harem was of course punishable by death and, again, some executions did take place. Once these harems were formed, tensions naturally arose between the wives. A law was then passed that made quarreling between wives subject to the death sentence. However, not even the death penalty could keep the women from bickering, and eventually divorce laws were relaxed. Even the marriage ceremony began to be dispensed with in time. With polygamy and easy divorce in place, marriage soon degenerated into what might be euphemistically called "free love."

At the end of August, 1534, the city beat off a major attack so decisively that the besiegers were in disarray, and some of the mercenaries and vassals even deserted the bishop. The thing for Bockelson to do, from a military perspective, would have been to lead a mission to capture the bishop's camp. However, Bockelson's popularity was up, so he decided the time was opportune to have himself crowned king.

In October, "His Highness" King Bockelson published some pamphlets that laid out his apocalyptic fantasy for public consumption. Like Joachim of Fiore, Bockelson saw the history of man as consisting of three ages. The first was the age of sin, which lasted until the Flood. The second was the age of persecution and the Cross, which was ongoing. The last would be the age of the triumph of the saints (read Anabaptists), which would culminate in the final vengeance of God on the enemies of the Anabaptist community. Christ had tried to initiate this last stage in the first century, but the Church had quickly apostatized. From about the year A.D. 100 till the Reformation, Christianity had been exiled into spiritual "Babylon"; but now that banishment was drawing to a close. Christ was returning soon, and was preparing the seed of His New Jerusalem in Munster with Jan Bockelson as the new King David. The task of the saints in Munster was to enlarge God's Kingdom by helping to purge the earth of the unrighteous. When the purge was completed, when all who had not the "sign" of the Anabaptists were massacred "without mercy," then Christ would return and establish the millennium.

Anabaptists elsewhere were inspired by their comrades in Munster. In January of 1535, a thousand Anabaptists in the province of Groningen, armed and led by someone claiming to be Christ, marched toward Munster to join forces with Bockelson. They were quickly defeated by the Duke of Gelderland, but this didn't deter others from trying again.

In March, some eight hundred Anabaptists captured a monastery in West Frisia and held it against a force of mercenaries under the Imperial Stadtholder until, after heavy bombardment and repeated assaults, they were exterminated. At the same time three ships full of Anabaptists were stopped on their way up the river Ijsel and sunk with all their occupants. In March too an Anabaptist at Minden put himself at the head of the poorest section of the population and attempted to establish a communistic New Jerusalem after the model of Munster.[11]

At the end of 1534, the bishop received more troops and supplies to bring Munster into submission. The siege around the town consequently tightened with the aim of starving the population into surrender. Undoubtedly, someone of Bockelson's fanatical temperament would have held out to the last man; however, two men escaped Munster and informed the besiegers of certain weak points in the defenses. A surprise attack was launched on the night of June 24, 1535, and the town was taken after a couple hours. Tragically, a massacre of the citizens of Munster followed, lasting several days.

Nevertheless, the end of Munster didn't mean the end of the Anabaptist movement, even in its more extreme manifestations. In 1567, Jan Willemsen gathered around himself 300 hard-core Anabaptists and attempted to reestablish New Jerusalem in Westphalia. They even managed to reinstitute polygamy; they also formed robber bands and stole for a living in the tradition of the Taborites. This lasted some twelve years before they were finally caught and executed. However, as time went on, these more radical aspects of Anabaptism fell out of favor.

The Genesis of the Apocalypse

As we have seen, there have always been groups obsessed with the coming apocalypse who have seen in contemporary events signs of the imminent coming of Christ. These groups tended to see themselves as the uniquely elect of Christ who would survive the coming devastation and inherit an earthly millennium. The historic Church, typically viewed as full of "sub-Christians," was branded by these sects as the Whore of Babylon mentioned in the Book of Revelation. Characterizing the Church as a corrupt institution in league— either wittingly or unwittingly—with the forces of darkness enabled these sects to legitimize themselves as the only authentic continuation of Christianity. While historically these apocalypticists didn't believe they would escape the coming Tribulation through a "rapture" (for that matter, neither did the Church), each group still held the belief that its own small sect

---

11 Cohn, *Pursuit*, 277.

(Montanists, Taborites, etc.) constituted all "true" Christians on earth, who would escape the judgment to come.

It can be seen from our brief survey that these groups did not have a particular belief that Israel needed to exist as a national entity before the Second Coming would occur. Whereas the seeds of an incipient "Christian Zionism" were planted in the sixteenth century (we will look at this in a later chapter), it wasn't until the rise of nationalism in the nineteenth century that such a belief would begin to flower. It is in the nineteenth century, particularly in Great Britain and the United States, that most of the peculiar beliefs of modern millennial mania have their genesis. This will be the subject of our next chapter.

Chapter Five

That Old-Time Religion

For thus says the Lord of hosts, the God of Israel: Do not let your prophets and your diviners who are in your midst deceive you. . . . For they prophesy falsely to you in My name; I have not sent them, says the Lord.
    —Jeremiah 29:8, 9

Prognostics do not always prove prophecies,—at least the wisest prophets make sure of the event first.
    —Horace Walpole, *Letter to Thomas Walpole* (Feb. 19, 1785)

W E HAVE SO FAR briefly looked at millenarianism at the start of the Christian era, its quick condemnation by the early Church, its manifestations during the Middle Ages in both the Eastern and Western churches, and its appearance in the Protestant Reformation. We are a little better prepared now to understand millennial mania as it appears today in the United States. While Hal Lindsey may claim that "the prophetic word definitely has been 'unsealed' in our generation," the truth is that nearly every generation in American history has thought it had "unsealed" the prophetic word—usually the very same prophetic word over and over again. More often than not, this prophetic word is some passage in the Book of Daniel.

Millennial Mania American Style

One famous example of this "unsealing of the prophetic word" concerns a Yankee farmer, William Miller, from Low Hampton, New York, who started studying his Bible regularly in 1816 after being converted from deism. After fourteen years of study, he concluded the world would end in 1843. The key, he came to believe, lay in the eighth chapter of Daniel, which relates a vision about a ram and a goat. There Miller read about an angel foretelling the des-ecration and eventual cleansing of the Temple in Jerusalem. His attention was caught particularly by verse 14, which in the King James Version reads: "And he [the angel] said unto me [Daniel], 'Unto two thousand and three hundred days; then shall the sanctuary be cleansed' " (Dan. 8:14 KJV).

The "cleansing" must mean the purification of the world by fire at the Second Coming, Miller thought. Understanding the "days" as apocalyptic language for "years," Miller concluded the angel was telling Daniel the world would end in 2,300 years. But 2,300 years from when? And which calendar should he use in his calculation? Miller decided to use the Hebrew calendar; then, after studying other passages of Scripture, he concluded he should be-gin his countdown from the year 457 B.C. This meant the Second Coming was scheduled for the year 1843. This was in the very near future! Moreover, Miller believed he saw signs in the heavens.

Friends persuaded Miller to publicize his findings, and by 1831 his be-lief that the world was scheduled to end in 1843 had become general knowl-edge. Miller began receiving invitations to lecture on his theory and to preach in local churches. In 1833, he was licensed as a Baptist preacher. He spread his views still further in 1836 when he published his book, *Evidence from Scripture and History of the Second Coming of Christ, About the Year 1843, and of His Personal Reign of 1000 Years*. Through the publicity work of a certain Joshua Himes beginning in 1839, Miller managed to start a real move-ment. Himes arranged for extensive evangelistic tours, camp meetings, and newspaper publicity. By 1842, thousands would attend camp meetings to listen to "Prophet Miller," as he was by then being called. In fact, the move-ment boasted having tents seating up to four thousand, the largest in America.[1]

Soon Miller was in control of a movement estimated at anywhere from thirty to a hundred thousand, most of which were drawn from mainstream Protestant churches. The mainstream clergy, as might be imagined, were less than pleased with having their members siphoned off by a person they viewed as a crass sensationalist, and they attacked Miller and his date setting. Miller shot back by labeling his opponents disciples of the Antichrist and their churches the Whore of Babylon.

After further studying the Jewish calendar, Miller became convinced the end would occur between March 21, 1843, and March 21, 1844. This time frame was too broad for many, however, so a rumor started going around that the Second Coming would occur a week after Easter, on April 23, 1843. Wisely, Miller never endorsed the date; so when April 23 came and went, he

---

1   Kyle, *Last Days*, 89.

could credibly assert that his calculations allowed for eleven more months.

Excitement steadily increased during those eleven months until the entire United States was watching Miller's countdown. Even people in foreign countries heard about Miller's prediction. After eleven months elapsed, however, it became evident that Christ was not going to arrive on schedule. When March 21, 1844, came and went, Miller must have been humiliated; nevertheless, he doggedly continued to insist that the end was near: "I confess my error and acknowledge my disappointment; yet I still believe that the day of the Lord is near." [2] He did not, however, propose any new dates—at least, not right away.

On August 12, 1844, one follower of Miller by the name of Samuel Snow argued at a camp meeting near Exeter, New Hampshire, that Miller was off by only a few months and that the end would occur October 22. And so millennial mania was off and running again. Around two hundred full-time traveling preachers and several thousand lay preachers went about spreading the news, sometimes to crowds of four thousand and more. According to Russell Chandler, "Some Millerites quit their jobs, boarded up their businesses, abandoned their crops and animals, and sold their farms. Others confessed to unsolved crimes and gave away their goods to the poor." [3] At first Miller was reluctant to endorse the date, but, only sixteen days before the day, Miller leaped in with both feet and was again preaching to large audiences.

By October 22, approximately 50,000 Americans had left their denominations for Miller, ready and waiting for the coming apocalypse. When October 23 dawned, however, Miller's movement evaporated.

In fact, Miller himself dropped out of the movement in 1845 and died only four years later in Low Hampton. However, although Miller may have disclaimed his own apocalyptic fantasies, the Seventh Day Adventist churches still claim Miller as one of their founders. When one considers that Seventh Day Adventism has spun offshoots like the Branch Davidians (of Waco, Texas, infamy) and the Jehovah's Witnesses[4] (whose propensity for setting dates for the Second Coming is legendary), then one begins to realize what a dramatic impact Miller's idle speculation on the Second Coming ultimately had. Unfortunately, it did little to discourage date setting in a nascent movement we today call fundamentalism.

---

2   Cited by Kyle, *Last Days*, 90.
3   Chandler, *Doomsday*, 82.
4   The founder of the Jehovah's Witnesses, Charles Taze Russell (1852–1916), was heavily influenced as a young man by the Adventist preacher Jonas Wendell. Later, another Adventist preacher, Nelson Barbour of Rochester, New York, would contribute to Russell's views. Russell predicted Christ's return for 1874 and then for 1914.

The Fundamentals of Doom

Fundamentalism was originally a conservative movement that arose in response to liberal "modernist" tendencies within mainline Protestant denominations. In particular, it was a protest movement against both nineteenth-century biblical criticism, which challenged the integrity of the Bible, and the "social gospel," which deemphasized doctrine in place of "doing good" for society in general.

The roots of nineteenth-century modernist theology lay in the exaltation of reason promoted by the eighteenth-century Enlightenment. Enlightenment *philosophers*, such as Jean Jacques Rousseau, David Hume, and Voltaire, made human reason the ultimate arbiter of truth. In their defense of classical Protestantism, the antimodernists (the forerunners of modern fundamentalists) advocated a conscious return to the scholastic theological methodology of the Reformers, particularly that of John Calvin. The irony is that the scholastic methodology itself was based on the same rationalism that gave birth to the theological liberalism they were fighting. Consequently, modernism and the fundamentalist reaction are not so much opposite extremes as they are two sides of the same rationalist coin. In the words of Orthodox author Clark Carlton, fundamentalism represents "the rationalist reaction to rationalism."

In the United States, the leading members of the antimodernist movement published in 1910 an encyclopedic series of articles under the title of *The Fundamentals*. The movement was henceforth identified with its advocacy of a return to the "fundamentals" of classic Reformation theology (the Virgin Birth, the Resurrection and deity of Christ, the inerrancy of the Bible, the substitutionary atonement, etc.). In the mid-1920s, the movement also became identified with its opposition to the teaching of evolution. The term "fundamentalist" was coined in 1920 by Curtis Lee Laws, the Baptist editor of the *Watchman-Examiner*, who proposed the name for the antimodernist faction within the Northern Baptist Convention. That same year in a conference in Buffalo, New York, Laws and some fellow conservatives adopted the title "The Fundamentalist Fellowship" for their party. The name stuck and has referred to the movement as a whole to this day. The term "fundamentalist" now encompasses a wide range of church groups, including conservative evangelicals, Pentecostals, and, of course, the more doctrinaire Baptist denominations.

In their struggle against modernism at the beginning of the twentieth century, fundamentalists found close allies among those calling themselves dispensationalists, who also were staunch supporters of the "fundamental" beliefs of evangelical Protestantism. Fundamentalists were less than welcoming of the dispensationalists' end-times beliefs, which included pre-millennialism and a secret rapture of the Church. In time, however, many fundamentalists were won over to these beliefs as well as many other end-times beliefs peculiarly associated with dispensationalism. The dispensationalists would, over the course of the twentieth century, become a powerfully influential subculture within the fundamentalist subculture of evangelical Protestantism. To enter the heart of today's millennial obsession, we must tell the story of dispensationalism and its founder—John Darby.

John Darby and Dispensationalism

The early nineteenth century was a time of great apocalyptic expectation in America, as we've just seen with the movement William Miller so easily started. At the same time, a self-proclaimed prophet named Joseph Smith, Jr., was weaving bizarre fantasies into a book known as the *Book of Mormon*, published in 1830. Joseph Smith, Jr., gave his group of followers, whom people were calling Mormons, the apocalyptic-sounding name of the Latter Day Saints. Also, 1830 is the year that a man by the name of John Nelson Darby (1800–1882) took complete control of a somewhat obscure sect of Protestants in England known as the Plymouth Brethren.

Darby was born in Ireland and was a lawyer until, at the age of twenty-five, he was ordained in the Anglican Church. He did not stay with the Anglican Church long, however, and in 1827 joined the Plymouth Brethren, quickly influencing Brethren teaching in radical ways. The two distinctive characteristics of the Brethren were (1) the ecumenicity of their movement and (2) their desire to do away with an ordained clergy and anything resembling organization within the local church. Darby would ultimately alter both of these traits.

Darby's abandonment of the established Church of England was the result of his conclusions that it lacked catholicity, that it was subservient to the state, and that it was riddled with clericalism. This dissatisfaction with the Anglican Church corresponded with his developing distinction between the Church and national Israel. (Historically, the Christian Church had always proclaimed itself the spiritual continuation of Israel.) According to Floyd Elmore, a modern disciple of Darby, "Darby came to his distinction between Israel and the church very early in his Christian ministry, and he later confessed that this opinion never changed throughout his career. . . . His parting of the ways with the established church [of England] corresponded with his new understanding of the division between Israel and the true church."[5]

---

5   Floyd Elmore, "J. N. Darby's Early Years," *When the Trumpet Sounds*, Thomas Ice & Timothy Demy, eds. (Eugene, OR: Harvest House, 1995), 128–129.

Elmore later goes on to observe that "Darby's belief in eschatology [the doctrine of future things] grows out of his ecclesiology [the doctrine of the nature of the Church]." [6]

In 1845, Darby clashed with another leader of the Brethren movement, Benjamin Wills Newton, on issues of prophecy and church structure. This led in 1848 to a schism in which the Brethren were divided into Open and Exclusive Assemblies. Newton led the Open Assemblies and Darby formed the Exclusives. Darby's group claimed that where the Exclusive Assembly of Brethren met was the only true manifestation of the Christian Church in that area. In other words, Darby's group was the only divinely recognized Church on earth. This was the source of the name "Exclusive Assembly," and the claim effectively eliminated the first principle of the Brethren, ecumenicity. Darby then organized his group into a federation of assemblies with a Central Meeting, eliminating the second principle of Brethrenism, the absence of a hierarchical organization.

Darby seemed to despise history, at least as it related to Christianity. Elmore writes, "[Darby] is equally clear in his disdain for the fathers of the church and past scholarship. He asserted, 'None are more untrustworthy on every fundamental subject than the mass of primitive Fathers.' " [7] In other words, Darby believed he had a clearer insight into the Scriptures than all who came before him, especially the early Church—which had the preaching of the Apostles still ringing in its ears.

Darby actually seemed to revel in the novelty of his doctrines, which he frequently characterized as "rediscovered truths." True Christianity had been lost within the first generation or two of the Church, Darby argued; thus, he and his followers were merely reestablishing original Christianity after a lapse of about eighteen hundred years! Darby's historical obscurantism led to a tradition among his later followers of boasting that their teachings represented a radical departure from the "manmade" doctrines developed over the course of Church history. This disdain for Church history, though, was hardly unique to Darby during the nineteenth century.

Darby's teachings have been systematized into a theology known as "dispensationalism." The term "dispensation" is found in the King James Bible in 1 Corinthians 9:17; Ephesians 1:10; 3:2; and Colossians 1:25. It translates the Greek word *oikonomia*, which the Orthodox usually render into English as "economy." *Oikonomia*, as the word is used in the New Testament, is defined as "management, direction, order, or plan." The New Testament uses

---

6   Elmore, "J. N. Darby," 131.
7   Elmore, "J. N. Darby," 139.

the word for the divine administration of the Church (see 1 Cor. 4:1; 9:17; Col. 1:24, 25; Titus 1:7—Greek text), as well as for the divine plan of salvation (Eph. 1:9, 10; 3:2, 3—Greek text). For the dispensationalist, the history of mankind is divided into different "dispensations," or eras, whereby God establishes different covenants with His people.

The main outline of dispensationalist teaching can be summarized by the following five points:

(1) The Jews will eventually accept Jesus as their Messiah and be saved through repentance; they will consequently make up God's earthly people for eternity.

(2) The Gentiles, who comprise the "Church," will be saved by faith and will be taken to heaven at the rapture, there constituting God's people in heaven.

(3) The Christian Church is a "parenthesis," or an interruption, in God's overall plan centering on national Israel; the final end of this Christian "parenthesis" is full-scale apostasy.

(4) There is a sharp distinction between the "Kingdom of heaven" and the "Kingdom of God," the first being the Davidic kingdom of the Jews and the latter being the universal Church of the Gentiles.[8]

(5) God deals differently with mankind according to different dispensations.

Some have argued that Darby's teachings would have met with a well-deserved oblivion had it not been for the work of another lawyer, Cyrus Ingerson Scofield (1843–1921) of St. Louis. He was a follower of Darby and popularized his teachings in many books. He is almost exclusively remembered today for his *Scofield Reference Bible*, published in 1909. This was simply a King James Bible to which Scofield added notes on each page elucidating the dispensationalist interpretation. Though an ordained Congregational minister, Scofield composed his reference Bible with no formal theological training.

Before Scofield published his Bible, it had been an understood convention among Protestants that the Bible should be published with no

---

8   Interestingly, St. Maximus the Confessor (580–662) also discussed the possibility of seeing a distinction between the Kingdom of heaven and the Kingdom of God, though, to be sure, it bore no resemblance to John Darby's rigid separation between Israel and the Church. Maximus specifically states that the Kingdom of heaven and the Kingdom of God "do not differ in their actual natures, but merely in our conception of them." For Maximus, the two Kingdoms represent stages in how Christians perceive the created order as they grow in grace. See Maximus the Confessor's *Two Hundred Texts on Theology and the Incarnate Dispensation of the Son of God. Written for Thalassios*, 2:90–93. G. E. H. Palmer, Philip Sherrard, Kallistos Ware, trans., *The Philokalia*, Vol. II (London: Faber and Faber, 1981), 161.

explanatory notes on the same page as the sacred text. Scofield's commentary, by ignoring this convention, often acquired in the minds of its readers the authority of the Prophets, Evangelists, and Apostles with whom it shared the page. In the minds of many simple people at the turn of the century, Scofield's notes became virtually identified with Scripture because they were "in the Bible." In fact, one former dispensationalist believes that had Scofield written his notes as a separate Bible commentary, his ideas would never have gained the prominence they ultimately did.[9] As it turned out, Scofield's Bible became for many a virtual Talmud. The *Scofield Reference Bible*, revised in the mid-1960s and republished as the *New Scofield Reference Bible*, remains popular among fundamentalists to this day.

In 1914, Scofield helped establish the Philadelphia School of the Bible, and a man named Lewis Sperry Chafer (1871–1952) joined the school as a professor. Chafer afterward moved to Dallas, Texas, in 1923 and was pastor of the Scofield Memorial Church (until 1927). In 1924, Chafer founded Dallas Theological Seminary and served as its president until his death in 1952. Dallas Theological Seminary is today the mecca of dispensationalism and counts among its alumni none other than Hal Lindsey.[10] John Walvoord served as president of the seminary, as well as professor of systematic theology, from 1952 to 1986. Walvoord is universally recognized as the current patriarch of end-of-the-world dispensationalist theology, and has produced a prodigious number of books on the subject.

One of Scofield's many contributions to dispensationalism is the division of salvation history into seven specific "dispensations." These are the Age of Innocence (before the Fall of Adam and Eve), the Age of Human Government (from Noah to Abraham), the Age of Promise (from Abraham to Moses), the Age of Law (from Moses to Christ), the Age of Grace (from Christ to the rapture of the Church), and the Age of the Kingdom (the thousand-year earthly rule of Christ, starting with the Second Coming). The end of the millennium then commences the Eternal State. Neither the Tribulation nor the millennium is really a part of God's plan for the Church; both are intended primarily for national Israel.

From the above outline it can be seen that dispensationalists are necessarily "premillennialists," that is, they believe Christ will return before

---

9   William Cox, *An Examination of Dispensationalism* (Phillipsburg, NJ: Presbyterian and Reformed Publishing, 1963), 14.

10 Other prominent evangelists of the dispensationalist gospel such as Dwight L. Moody, Billy Sunday, and Reuben Torrey also started Bible schools, the best known today being Chicago's Moody Bible Institute and the Bible Institute of Los Angeles (commonly known as Biola).

("pre-") the millennium. William Cox, a former dispensationalist, elaborates on the dispensationalists' conception of the millennium:

> Dispensationalists go on to teach that, after seven years, the church will be returned to earth, where it will take part in an earthly millennium. During the millennium, according to dispensationalists, the church will have a position inferior to that of Israel. They teach that, after the millennium, the church will be returned to heaven the second time, there to spend eternity while Israel remains forever on the earth.[11]

The dispensationalist characterization of the millennium is indeed very "Jewish." One prominent dispensationalist, Charles Ryrie, states with assurance that the "news media of the Millennium will carry Jerusalem datelines for many of their stories."[12] Although the millennial rule of Christ will result in the "utopian state which men have dreamed of setting up through politics, spending, and legislation,"[13] not everyone will be happy. There will be many who won't accept Jesus' spiritual claim on them, though they will of necessity accept His political rule. In Old Testament fashion, those who get out of line may suffer the death penalty. According to Ryrie, "But all who live in this period must accept, outwardly at least, the authority of the King, or else they will be punished with even physical death."[14] Imagine it: executions in the "kingdom of heaven"!

Dispensationalists generally conceive the millennial kingdom as a re-creation of the idealized, golden age of the Davidic monarchy. Though Christ rules as the legitimate descendant of David, some dispensationalists argue that King David himself will actually rule with Christ as a sort of vice-regent. This is based on their interpretation of Jeremiah 30:9, which reads, "But they shall serve the Lord their God, and David their king, whom I will raise up for them." Because the earthly millennium is characterized as primarily a political order, dispensationalism winds up taking our Lord and Savior Jesus Christ and reducing Him to a mere politician wielding temporal power.

Though the premillennialism of Papias, Justin Martyr, and Irenaeus in the second century had no expectation of a future hope for Israel outside of the one Christian Church, such is not the case with dispensationalism, as we have seen. Rather than making a radical distinction between Israel and the Church, the premillennialists of the second century simply believed in a thousand-year reign of Christ on earth after a resurrection of all the just at the

---

11 Cox, *Dispensationalism*, 9.
12 Charles C. Ryrie, *The Final Countdown* (Wheaton, IL: Victor Books, 1982), 114.
13 Ryrie, *Countdown*, 116.
14 Ryrie, *Countdown*, 115.

Second Coming. It would be an idyllic age in which the righteous would be rewarded and Satan would be bound. At the end of the thousand years, the unrighteous would be resurrected and punished. In this there is a sharp difference between Papias, Justin Martyr, and Irenaeus on the one hand and the dispensationalists on the other.

A number of conservative Protestant denominations, particularly the Baptists, have adopted most of the central features of dispensationalism. To the apocalyptic climate that has defined so much of the twentieth century goes the credit for the prominence of modern dispensationalism in many churches. In fact, as we've seen, this apocalyptic climate allowed Hal Lindsey to make premillennial dispensationalism popular with an entire generation.

Dispensationalism's "Literal" Interpretation

In a previous chapter, we observed Hal Lindsey's literal method of interpreting Scripture. This method is characteristic of classical dispensationalism, and is passionately defended by such dispensationalist luminaries as Charles Ryrie and John Walvoord. They stress that the words of each verse from the Bible ought to be understood at face value unless there is an obvious and compelling reason to the contrary. They argue that the prophecies of Christ's First Advent were fulfilled literally; therefore, the safest approach to the prophecies of Christ's Second Coming would be a literal interpretation as well.

Orthodox Christians, though, view the dispensationalist approach to Scripture as simplistic and ill-conceived. For one thing, the New Testament itself often doesn't interpret the Old Testament "literally." Consider Peter's interpretation of Joel's prophecy in Acts 2:15–21 (see Joel 2:28–32). The context of the second chapter of Joel quoted by Peter is the future restoration of the nation of Israel under the Messiah. In this prophecy, there is reference to unusual cosmological occurrences and signs on the earth: ". . . blood and fire and vapor of smoke. The sun shall be turned into darkness, and the moon into blood" (Acts 2:19, 20). Yet Peter says that Joel's prophecy finds its ultimate fulfillment in the Church on the Day of Pentecost, thus identifying the establishment of messianic Israel with the establishment of the Church. Did the moon literally turn into blood on Pentecost? Was the sun darkened? While there were tongues of fire manifested, where was the blood and vapor of smoke? The fact is that none of this literally occurred at Pentecost. Peter was interpreting Joel spiritually.

Again, the Book of Acts (15:14–18) records James as citing the prophecy of Amos (2:11, 12), which speaks of the reestablishment of the Davidic monarchy. James interprets the prophecy in a nonliteral manner and applies it to the Gentiles coming into the Church. In Galatians, Paul refers to the Genesis account of Isaac and his older brother Ishmael, which account Paul interprets in a nonliteral fashion, saying, "these things are symbolic [Gr. *allegoreo*, that is, an allegory]" of the two covenants (Gal. 4:24).

In Paul's First Epistle to the Corinthians, we have another example of a nonliteral interpretation of the Old Testament. Paul cites Deuteronomy 25:4, which states that an ox is not to be muzzled as it treads grain, and asks rhetorically, "Is it oxen God is concerned about? Or does He say it altogether for our sakes?" (1 Cor. 9:9, 10). He then interprets the verse as meaning that clergy should be given material support so as to be free to sow a spiritual crop (1 Cor. 9:10, 11).

Jesus Christ Himself often didn't interpret the Old Testament literally. In John 3:14, He interprets the brazen serpent mentioned in Numbers 21:8, 9 as a type foreshadowing salvation through the Cross. Again, in Matthew 12:40–42 the story of Jonah in the belly of a large fish is interpreted by Jesus as an allegory of His three days and three nights in the tomb. If Christ teaches that the Old Testament prophecies can have nonliteral, spiritual fulfillments, are we not then obligated to look for them?

In fact, one of the most common mistakes people made in Jesus' own day was to interpret what He said in an earthly, literal manner instead of spiritually. Let's look for a moment at the Gospel of John. When Jesus said, "Destroy this temple, and in three days I will raise it up," the Jewish leaders thought He meant the Temple of Herod the Great, whereas Jesus "was speaking of the temple of His body" (John 2:19–21). In the next chapter, Nicodemus misunderstands Jesus' teaching on the New Birth as referring to a literal birth ("Can [a man] enter a second time into his mother's womb and be born?"), but Jesus meant a spiritual birth from above (John 3:3–7). In the next chapter, Jesus offers a Samaritan woman "living water," meaning the gift of the Holy Spirit and eternal life; however, she misunderstands Jesus as offering her running water (John 4:7–14). Later Jesus tells the Jewish leaders that He is the bread of life, and that they must eat His flesh and drink His blood to have eternal life (John 6:48–58). In a classic example of literalism, Jesus' hearers thought He was proposing cannibalism ("How can this man give us his flesh to eat?"). Later, we will see that the literal approach to the Bible frequently leads to some interpretations of Scripture no less bizarre than those recorded above from the Gospel of John—such as interpreting the cosmological phenomena mentioned in Matthew 24:29 as referring to modern UFO sightings!

Moreover, the very multiplicity of different "literal" interpretations of a single passage ought to give the serious Bible reader pause. For example,

Revelation 9:3–12 is interpreted by Hal Lindsey as describing both Cobra helicopters spraying nerve gas and nuclear missiles fired from a space station.[15] Salem Kirban, who started America's first toll-free prophecy hotline in 1981, interpreted the same passage as depicting African "killer bees." [16] John Walvoord interprets Revelation 9:3–12 as referring to demons.[17] Which, if any, of these "literal" interpretations is correct? Is it any wonder that such an approach doesn't inspire a great deal of confidence?

There is an especial danger when these "literal" interpretations are absolutized and prefaced with, "The Bible says that . . ." We need to remember that the "Bible scholars" of Jesus' day, who also tended to take the prophecies of the coming of the Messiah "literally," didn't see in Him the fulfillment of prophecy because He didn't fulfill the prophecies in the ways they expected (or rather, wanted) them to be fulfilled. In order to help avoid absolutizing personal opinions as the "literal truth," it is always important to consult the Apostolic Tradition of the Church. As the Apostle Peter said, "knowing this first, that no prophecy of Scripture is of any private interpretation" (2 Pet. 1:20).

Hal Lindsey, on the other hand, makes "private" interpretation the key to his teaching on prophecy. In *Apocalypse Code*, he says the Apostle John "was transported 2000 years into the future" to our century and commanded to write what he saw in the Book of Revelation. Thus the Apostle was "a time traveler" [18] who went through a "great time warp" and described modern weapons using first-century language.

Revelation is therefore a literal description of the twentieth century that is "encoded" (from the twentieth-century perspective) in first-century language. Lindsey explains, "The encoded prophecies can be understood only when we prayerfully seek to decipher what in today's vast arsenal of technical marvels fits best John's 1st century description of them." [19] Thus John wrote encrypted prophecy that could be decoded only by the last generation on earth—us! In Lindsey's words: "It [Revelation] was written to be understood by the generation that was near the fulfillment of the astounding

---

15 See Lindsey, *New World Coming*, 124; *Apocalypse Code*, 41–43; and Chandler, *Doomsday*, 255.

16 William Alnor, *Soothsayers of the Second Advent* (Old Tappan, NJ: Revell, 1989), 88; Chandler, *Doomsday*, 255.

17 John Walvoord, *The Revelation of Jesus Christ* (Chicago: Moody Press, 1966), 160–163.

18 "It was there [on the isle of Patmos], under extremely difficult conditions, where John wrote down in a scroll all that 'he saw and heard' during what must have been an experience of *time travel* to the beginning of the 21st century." Lindsey, *Apocalypse*, 31. Emphasis in original. Also on p. 67: "Like a time traveler, he [John] was physically transported 2000 years into the future and was commanded to write an accurate eyewitness account."

19 Lindsey, *Apocalypse*, 37.

things predicted to immediately precede the Coming of Jesus the Messiah. I believe we are that generation." [20]

So, according to Lindsey, the Book of Revelation is a private, encrypted message sent specifically to us: no one throughout Christian history was ever able to properly decode it before now. Remember 2 Peter 1:20 cited above? Lindsey's approach to prophecy is precisely that kind of "private interpretation" that Peter warned us about. No book of the Bible is a private, encoded message sent to a single group of people that can be understood only with some kind of secret decoder ring. All Scripture was given to all people in all parts of the world in all generations throughout all history. Scripture is a public revelation intended to enlighten all mankind.

Ironically, as we've already had opportunity to observe, those who interpret Scripture in a strictly "literal" manner more often than not arrive at interpretations more strange and arbitrary than any nonliteral interpretation. Hal Lindsey, for instance, "decodes" Revelation 6:2—which describes the first horseman of the apocalypse carrying a bow—in the following manner: "But the bow was a long-range weapon that could hurl a missile a long way. This is a code for long range weapons like ICBMs." [21] Identifying a primitive bow with an ICBM is supposed to be the *literal* interpretation of Revelation 6:2? Under what definition of "literal" might this be?

While hunting for oblique references to modern marvels like ICBMs, lasers, and space stations in the Bible via a "literal" interpretation, the reader usually misses the message of the inspired book. He remains as unedified after reading Scripture as he was before picking up his Bible. In this regard, the Bible becomes a closed book. The late biblical scholar William Hendriksen observed in his commentary on Revelation:

> Do these symbols [in Revelation] refer to specific events, single happenings, dates or persons in history? For if they do, then we may as well admit that we cannot interpret them. Because among the thousands of dates and events and persons of history that show certain traits of resemblance to the symbol in question, who is able to select the one and only date, event, or person that was forecast by this particular symbol? Confusion results. We get thousands of "interpretations", but no certainty. And the Apocalypse remains a closed book.[22]

Though dispensationalists are known for being breathtakingly self-assured in their knowledge of the Bible—frequently to the point of deprecat-

---

20 Lindsey, *Apocalypse*, 67.

21 Lindsey, *Apocalypse*, 72.

22 William Hendriksen, *More Than Conquerors* (Grand Rapids: Baker Book House, 1967), 40–41.

ing genuine Bible scholars—the reality is that the Bible has, in many respects, become a closed book to them because of an obtuse literalism. The temptation of literalism has been a perennial problem among Christians. The sixth-century Christian author who went by the pseudonym Dionysius the Areopagite (see Acts 17:34) also warned of how a rigidly literal understanding of Scripture robs the words of their meaning:

> In my opinion, it would be unreasonable and silly to look at words rather than at the power of the meanings. Anyone seeking to understand the divine things should never do this, for this is the procedure followed by those who do not allow empty sounds to pass beyond their ears, who shut them out because they do not wish to know what a particular phrase means or how to convey its sense through equivalent but more effective phrases. People like this are concerned with meaningless letters and lines, with syllables and phrases which they do not understand, which do not get as far as the thinking part of their souls, and which make empty sounds on their lips and in their hearing.[23]

Dionysius' exhortation to search for the meaning of Scripture beyond the verbiage has been echoed by all the Spirit-filled Fathers of the Church in every century for the past two thousand years. We today would do well to heed their wise counsel. As Paul tells us, the gospel preached is "in words taught by the Spirit, expressing spiritual truths in spiritual words"; thus he who contemplates the words in a natural or "literal" manner "cannot understand them, because they are spiritually discerned" (1 Cor. 2:13, 14 NIV).

---

23 Dionysius the Areopagite, *The Divine Names*, 4:11.

Chapter Six

The Israel of God

For in Christ Jesus neither circumcision nor uncircumcision avails anything, but a new creation. And as many as walk according to this rule, peace and mercy be upon them, and upon the Israel of God.
—The Epistle of St. Paul to the Galatians 6:15, 16

But they who pursue these things ["the new things of grace," the Gospel] shall enjoy peace and mercy and may properly be called by the name of Israel, while they who hold contrary sentiments, although they be descended from him [Jacob] and bear the appellation [circumcision], have yet fallen away from all these things, both the relationship and the name itself. But it is in their power to be true Israelites who keep this rule, who desist from the old ways and follow after grace.
—John Chrysostom, *Commentary on Galatians* (386–392)

A S DISTURBING as the thought may be, dispensationalist eschatology plays a significant role in American foreign policy—particularly with regard to Israel, which is seen by many as the key to the end times. In large measure because of unquestioning American support, the state of Israel has been free to commit the same crimes which, in Bosnia and Kosovo, elicited sharp moral outrage around the world. Consider that even while under Islamic domination for over thirteen centuries, Jerusalem's Christian population was always substantial. Today, however, as a result of constant Israeli pressure, there are barely two thousand Orthodox Christians left in Jerusalem. Most Palestinian Christians have fled either to the countryside or to the West.

The picture is just as bleak in the rest of the Holy Land. The cities of Ramallah and Bethlehem were 90 percent Christian in 1948, but are today less than 20 percent Christian. According to Timothy Morgan in a 1996 article in *Christianity Today*, Christians of all stripes—Orthodox, Catholic,

82

Protestant, Oriental Orthodox—today make up a mere "2.3 percent of the 5.6 million people in Israel and the 2.4 million in the West Bank and Gaza." [1] The change, however, has been particularly dramatic in Jerusalem:

> There were 25,000 Christians in Jerusalem in 1948, the high point in modern times. That number fell to 10,800 in 1967. Since then, Jerusalem's Christian population [including Orthodox, Catholics, Protestants, and Oriental Orthodox] has grown to about 16,000. However, the Christian influence in Jerusalem, with a total population of 584,500, has been greatly diffused by the explosive growth since 1967 of the Jewish population, increasing 200 percent, and the Muslim population, up 40 percent.[2]

Israeli sources report that there are 4.2 million Jews in the Holy Land, 1.6 million Muslims, and only 150,000 Christians, less than two percent of the population (churches there claim the figure is more like 130,000). And the Christian presence is continuing to drop.

On average, a Christian leaves the land where Christ founded His Church every eight hours (three Christians per day), so that in 75 more years Christianity will be extinct in the land of its birth. To sum up: The Patriarchate of Jerusalem, the mother church of every other Christian church in the world, is slowly being exterminated.

"Christian" Zionism and Armageddon

The plight of the Christian Church in the Holy Land rarely enters the consciousness of the prophecy "experts." It's not that they are unaware of the existence of native Christians in the Holy Land. Many of them travel to Israel every year, and they operate any number of ministries in the country. They regularly visit Orthodox shrines—such as the Church of the Holy Sepulcher in Jerusalem—and are at least vaguely aware that there exists an indigenous Church having historical roots extending back to the Day of Pentecost. No, it's not that the prophecy gurus are completely unaware of the Christians of the Holy Land—it's just that these Christians seem to hold little significance for them.

From their perspective, far more important than the Christians of the Holy Land are the Jews of the Holy Land, for they see the presence of the Jewish state in the Holy Land as nothing less than the fulfillment of biblical prophecy. Indeed, they see these times with a restored Israel as pregnant with prophecies of the rise and fall of nations and empires. In early 1980, one millenarian group met in Jerusalem to celebrate their first Feast of Tabernacles

---

1   Timothy Morgan, "Jerusalem's Living Stones," *Christianity Today*, May 20, 1996, 59.
2   Ibid., 60–61.

as a public affirmation of their belief that biblical prophecy was being ful-filled through Israel. As they see it, to support the Israeli state is to support God's will in these latter days.

Such a perspective often leads modern doom-sayers to an extreme form of Zionism rivaling that held by many Jews themselves. There is even a well-financed organization in Jerusalem called the International Christian Embassy–Jerusalem that does little other than promote radical Zionism and the dispensationalists' concept of Israel's role in end-times prophecy. The Christian Embassy also has close ties with Israel's militant Likud party, which has traditionally opposed Palestinian self-determination. During the Christ-mas season of 1995, when Bethlehem was coming under the control of the Palestinian Authority, the Christian Embassy called for a boycott of Christ-mas celebrations in Bethlehem—much to the amazement of the Holy Land's Arab-Christian population.

This ardent Zionism is not limited to millenarians operating in Israel. Browsing through the "prophecy" section of most Protestant bookstores in America quickly reveals that a preoccupation with Israel's connection to end-times prophecy is inherent in conservative Protestantism itself. On the shelves one finds books like televangelist John Hagee's *The Beginning of the End*, which interprets the assassination of Yitzhak Rabin according to Hagee's scenario for Armageddon. More recently, Hagee has published *Final Dawn over Jerusalem*, which again insists that biblical prophecy cannot be prop-erly understood apart from the modern Israeli state. Usually in close proxim-ity to Hagee on the bookshelves is Dave Hunt's *A Cup of Trembling*. The subtitle of Hunt's book claims it is about "Jerusalem and Bible Prophecy," though Hunt also wanders to such topics as extraterrestrials.

Mike Evans, head of an organization called Bridge of Love, came out in 1997 with *Jerusalem Betrayed: Ancient Prophecy and Modern Conspiracy Collide in the Holy City*. As the title suggests, the book purports to reveal how powerful forces in the highest echelons of the world's governments are conspiring against "God's chosen people" in Israel. Evans looks askance on American efforts to negotiate an Israeli withdrawal from the West Bank, be-lieving that America has "cut deals with the Arab sheiks" who "have set out to humiliate and destroy the people of God." [3] Evans is so pro-Israel that he accepts every criticism of America coming from the Israeli government as unquestionably true. Even more extreme, he calls Palestinians and other op-ponents of Israeli policy the "enemies of God." [4] Even those "whose motives

3   Mike Evans, *Jerusalem Betrayed* (Dallas: Word, 1997), xiv.
4   To select randomly one passage from among many, Evans writes, "Until that day of re-demption arrives [i.e., the Second Coming] we must not succumb to complacency and we

are essentially benign" in trying to forward the peace process are in reality dupes manipulated by the "prince of darkness." [5] Evans states his reason for writing *Jerusalem Betrayed* is:

> to warn those who will listen that events unfolding in the Middle East could push Israel into a catastrophe of immense proportions and bring the judgment of God on America for our role in manipulating this explosive international situation. Can we wait and watch the destruction of Israel without lifting a hand or crying out? Can we just sit idly by? [6]

By no means will Evans sit idly by. As he is well connected politically in both this country and Israel, he influences those who shape American and Israeli foreign policy. Such easy access to top Israeli officials by Christian Zionists like Evans is not unusual. Menachem Begin, when Prime Minister of Israel, gave the Jabotinsky Prize to Moral Majority leader Jerry Falwell and called him a "defender of Jerusalem." Also, Prime Minister Benjamin Netanyahu and other important figures in his government have appeared on Pat Robertson's Christian Broadcasting Network (CBN).

Israeli politicians have taken great care to cultivate the support of conservative Protestants for Israeli government policies. These efforts have yielded many benefits, not excluding direct financial assistance. In 1997, Christian Zionists, through the International Fellowship of Christians and Jews, gave over $5 million to the United Jewish Appeal founded by Orthodox Rabbi Yechiel Eckstein. Eckstein claims that Christian donations in 1997 to the United Jewish Appeal through his International Fellowship were double the previous year's. [7] Rabbi Eckstein's International Fellowship, which has an office in Washington, D.C. (Eckstein regularly delivers opening prayers at

---

dare not compromise with *the enemies of God*. . . If we desire God's blessing, then we must bless his people [i.e., the Jews], the People of the Book, with unconditional love. We must stand not only with God's people, but with his city, Jerusalem." (Evans, *Jerusalem*, 288. Emphasis added.) Evans never calls the Palestinian Christians "God's People," though the New Testament itself calls Christians "a holy nation, His [God's] own special people" (1 Pet. 2:9). While Evans occasionally acknowledges the suffering of the Palestinian people in his book, he never asks his readers to "stand" with them, to "bless them," or to offer them "unconditional love." One strongly suspects that Evans' definition of "unconditional love" with respect to Israel simply means unconditional support of Israeli state policy, right or wrong.

5   Evans, *Jerusalem*, 281–282.

6   Evans, *Jerusalem*, xvi–xvii.

7   The information in the above paragraph is taken from a Moaz newsletter (Feb. 1998), which in turn cites the *Jerusalem Post* (Jan. 13, 1998) for some of its information. Moaz is an international messianic Jewish organization headquartered in Israel whose goal is to evangelize Jews to Protestant fundamentalism. The organization publishes the *Moaz Israel Report*, which, according to its promotional literature, provides a "spiritual perspective" on the unfolding drama in the Middle East; a "prophetic insight into Israel, comparing current events with the Bible"; and "on the spot information to counteract the bombardment of biased news media," i.e., biased against Israel.

sessions of Congress), has an annual budget of $13–14 million and is supported by some ninety thousand followers. One of the projects that the organization runs is the "On Wings of Eagles" program that has flown large numbers of Russian Jews to the Holy Land, a program in large part funded by churches and individual believers. Of course, the International Fellowship of Christians and Jews is not the only avenue by which Christian Zionists donate money to the state of Israel. There are any number of organizations through which they fund the Jewish state, a very high percentage of the money eventually being directed into the conservative Orthodox Jewish community of the Holy Land.

Israel has also profited politically from its relationship with conservative American Protestants. One might think that those like Mike Evans, who hold such extreme views regarding Israel, would make for an insignificant and powerless special interest group within American politics. However, one must recall that the membership of most special interest groups in this country is relatively small (especially in proportion to the influence they wield), and many powerful special interest groups hold extreme views, either to the right or to the left of the political spectrum.

Moreover, the recent resurgence of conservative Protestantism as a potent sociological force (surveys conducted in the 1990s regularly indicate that evangelicals form 34 to 46 percent of the American population) has not been lost on politicians, who have either embraced them or vilified them as the "religious right." For instance, Arab American Institute President James Zogby, an Arab Christian, explained in a newspaper interview that for a political candidate during the 1996 presidential nominations "to get the endorsement of the Christian Coalition, you had to be anti-Arab and pro-Israel." [8]

Given this scenario, it comes as no surprise that an organization like the International Fellowship of Christians and Jews can host its national conference in September, 1998, at the Watergate Hotel in Washington, D.C., with such prominent invited guests as: Secretary of State Madeleine Albright, Senator Dan Coates (who is also co-chairman of the Fellowship's Center for Jewish and Christian Values and a speaker at the conference), Senator Joseph Lieberman (speaker), Dr. William Bennet, Elliot Abrams (speaker), Bill Kristol, Dr. Marvin Wilson, David Aikmann, and of course the Israeli Ambassador, Zelman Shoval. [9] The list is literally a *Who's Who* of the well-connected in Washington.

---

8   Joan Lowy, "Evangelical Support of Israel Weighed," *The Orange County Register*, April 29, 1998, World–18.

9   Information taken from an IFCJ flyer/registration form promoting the conference scheduled for Sept. 13–14, 1998.

Let there be no mistaking it: the Armageddon crowd constitutes an influential special interest group, both in this country and internationally. Mike Evans, for instance, has met with the last five prime ministers of Israel. Even more amazingly, he spoke at the Forty-Third General Assembly of the United Nations in Geneva, as well as at the Middle East Peace Conference in Madrid. No matter to whom he speaks, his message is always clear and consistent: "The prophetic purpose of my calling and the motivation behind my ministry has been to warn the nations that those who oppose Jerusalem are opposing God's will." [10] He urges all who will listen, especially those in power, to "stand with Jerusalem's defenders against those who are trying to bring about the final betrayal of the Holy City. We who have glimpsed God's mighty purpose for Jerusalem must pray and work to see God's prophetic program fulfilled." [11] Evans isn't content merely to watch God's prophetic design work itself out in history; like other doom-sayers, he believes in *working* "to see God's prophetic program fulfilled."

And work they do. In the spring of 1992, a small army of three thousand prophecy writers, lecturers, and activists congregated in San Antonio, Texas, for the First Annual National Christian Zionist Conference. "Their goal: to sway foreign policy to support Zionism in congruity with Bible passages about Israel, the return of Christ, and the Last Days";[12] in other words, to conform American foreign policy to their end-of-the-world dispensationalist theology. And in doing this, Christian Zionists are helping to bring about what a millennium and a half of militant Islam failed to produce: the elimination of the Christian presence in the Holy Land.

If dispensationalism is at the heart of the modern millennial obsession, the distinction between the Church and national Israel is at the core of the dispensationalist system. It is no coincidence that apocalyptic fervor has risen steadily since the creation of the modern state of Israel following World War II. Charles Strozier, a professor of history and a psychoanalyst who has conducted research into fundamentalist apocalypticism, states, "It is fair to say that no other event of the twentieth century has had the same significance in the belief system of fundamentalists as the creation of the state of Israel." [13]

Modern Israel's perceived prophetic significance is largely derived from modern dispensationalism's belief that God has a separate covenant with the Jews. Since antiquity, the argument goes, the Jews have been the focus of

10 Evans, *Jerusalem*, 284.
11 Evans, *Jerusalem*, 281.
12 Chandler, *Doomsday*, 217.
13 Charles Strozier, *Apocalypse: On the Psychology of Fundamentalism in America* (Boston: Beacon Press, 1994), 200.

God's attention, and the Church age is but an interruption, a "parenthesis," in God's plan resulting from Israel's rejection of the Messiah. In a sense, the Church is a sort of divine Plan B, since Israel rejected Plan A, the messianic kingdom under Jesus. Classic dispensationalism teaches that after the rapture of the Church, God will again turn His attention to the Jews during the seven-year Tribulation period. During the Tribulation, apostate Jews will sign a covenant with the Antichrist; however, God will lead a remnant to Christ (the 144,000 mentioned in Revelation), who will in turn convert their brethren. The Antichrist will eventually turn and persecute these Jewish Christians and then, when things appear hopeless, Christ will return to establish the millennium, which will be a worldwide Jewish empire run by Jesus. Plan A will finally be realized.

The dispensationalists' obsession with national Israel arises from their denial of the Church as spiritual Israel. In a sense, Israel takes the place of the Church. (Hence their indifference to the Church in the Holy Land in contrast to their idealization of the Jews in the Holy Land.) The significant date marking the consummation of God's dealing with mankind is consequently not Pentecost and the birth of the Church, but May 14, 1948, and the establishment of national Israel. As this distinction between Israel and the Church is foundational to today's millenarian beliefs concerning the end times, we need to examine this distinction in some depth.

The Jewish Schism

The historic teaching of the Christian Church, as opposed to the dispensationalist scheme summarized above, is that the Church was originally formed of God's remnant of faithful Jews (remember, the Church in its first decades was composed almost entirely of Jews), to which Gentiles were later "grafted" in, to borrow Paul's phraseology (Rom. 11:11–24). Jesus did not start a new "religion"; rather, there was a schism within Judaism in the first century between those Jews who accepted Jesus of Nazareth as their Messiah and those who did not. Each group considered itself the "faithful remnant" of Israel and the other group the "apostates." Orthodox Christians naturally say it was those Jews who had accepted Jesus as their Messiah—the Church—who were the true remnant of Israel. Thus, the history of the early Church found in Acts is basically a continuation of the story of Israel from the Old Testament.

Perhaps without fully realizing the implications, modern dispensationalists in essence deny that those first Jewish Christians constituted faithful Israel. Indeed, such a denial would seem to be essential if the 1948 establishment of the Israeli state is to have any meaning. William Alnor, for one, violently rejects the idea that the Church is the remnant of Israel in his book *Soothsayers of the Second Advent.* Immediately before citing verses "prophesying" a 1948 restoration of Israel, he excoriates what he calls "replacement theology":

> For centuries many scholars scoffed at the idea of the Jews returning to their homeland and becoming a nation again. They ignored the clear teachings of Scripture—and the teachings of Jesus Himself—when they denied Israel would be reborn. (It is indeed interesting that Jesus said, ". . . Jerusalem will be trampled on by the Gentiles until the times of the Gentiles are fulfilled" [Luke 21:24].) *Because of the lie called "replacement theology," which zoomed into prominence in the Middle Ages,* some believed the Jews would not return to their homeland. This idea says God is through with Israel forever and that He replaced her with the church. But throughout history, some studious men and women divided the Word of God carefully and knew God's promises to Israel were meant to last forever.[14]

To appreciate how deeply Alnor believes that modern Israel has special prophetic significance, note his citation of Luke 21:24. As cited by Alnor, the verse says that Jerusalem will be trampled until the times of the Gentiles are fulfilled. Then what happens after the "times of the Gentiles are fulfilled"?

To Alnor, it is presumed to be self-evident that Israel will be restored as a nation—despite the fact that the Lord says absolutely nothing about the creation of an Israeli state after the "times of the Gentiles are fulfilled." Unsurprisingly, earlier commentators on the Gospel of Luke, like Cyril of Alexandria[15] (380–444) and Theophylact of Ochrid[16] (*ca.* 1055–1108), understood Jesus' words without Alnor's dispensationalist presuppositions.

---

14 Alnor, *Soothsayers,* 48–49. Emphasis added. Though Alnor claims that "throughout history" there have been those who "knew God's promises to [national] Israel were meant to last forever," he doesn't attempt to document this alleged "fact." He only cites James J. Brookes, writing in 1878, "predicting" the rebirth of the nation of Israel. Of course, by 1878 dispensationalism had captured much of Protestant evangelical thinking through the preaching of Dwight L. Moody, the Billy Graham of the nineteenth century. Brookes himself was a mentor of C. I. Scofield. Moreover, in 1878, when Brookes was writing, the Zionist movement was in full swing. (By 1897, Theodor Herzl would organize the first World Zionist Congress; and by 1917, Zionists would succeed in gaining the famous Balfour Declaration that promised a Jewish national homeland in Palestine.) Brookes may have been reading the signs of the times concerning the emergence of a national Israel, but these signs weren't necessarily derived from the Bible.

15 Cyril of Alexandria, *Commentary on the Gospel of Saint Luke,* Homily 139. Cyril cites Luke 21:20 and then adds, "And afterwards again He [Christ] transfers His words from this subject [the destruction of Jerusalem in A.D. 70] unto the time of the consummation [of the world]." See the translation by R. Payne Smith (Studion Monastery, NY: Studion Publishers, 1983), 556.

16 *The Explanation by Blessed Theophylact of the Holy Gospel According to St. Luke* (House Springs, MO: Chrysostom Press, 1997), 274. Theophylact cites Luke 21:24 and adds, "To this point He [Christ] has been speaking of the captivity [of Israel]. Now He turns to the events of the end of the world."

After the times of the Gentiles are fulfilled, explain Cyril and Theophylact, the end times simply commence. It really can't be argued that Jesus says anything more than this.[17] Nevertheless, Luke 21:24 becomes for Alnor an example of the "clear" teaching of Jesus that "Israel would be reborn" in 1948. What leads him to such a strained interpretation of this verse is his denial that the Church is the remnant of true Israel, forcing him to find allusions to a future national Israel in the New Testament.

What is most astounding of all is Alnor's bald assertion that " 'replacement theology' zoomed into prominence in the Middle Ages." First of all, "replacement theology" is not an accurate description of the Orthodox teaching. The Church didn't "replace" Israel; the Church *is and has always been the continuation of Israel*. The Church we see today comes from the faithful remnant of true Israel, that part of national Israel that accepted the Messiah. If the word "replace" can be used at all, it would have to be in the following manner: "Israel" was a name given to one man, Jacob, the grandson of Abraham. Jacob was "replaced" by twelve sons, who together became Israel. These twelve sons were then "replaced" by twelve tribes, who were afterwards known as Israel. These tribes were in turn "replaced" by a unified nation known to the world as Israel. National Israel then evolved into (or was "replaced by," if you will) a worldwide community, the Church.

Moreover, Alnor doesn't bother to cite any source to substantiate his claim that this "lie [that the Church is spiritual Israel] . . . zoomed into prominence in the Middle Ages." Those of us who might disagree with Alnor would like to see some documentation of this "zoom" into the official doctrine of the Church at this late point in history. Alnor doesn't offer any evidence, because his assertion is wholly unfounded. From the Orthodox perspective, it is the dispensationalist teaching that "zoomed" in from out of nowhere late in Church history, during the nineteenth century.

What did the early Church teach? Among competent Church historians of all stripes, Catholic, Protestant, or Orthodox, the issue isn't even

---

17 Dispensationalists appear to be misled by the word *until* in Luke 21:24, "And Jerusalem will be trampled by Gentiles until [Gr. *achri ou*] the times of the Gentiles are fulfilled." The word "until" doesn't mean here that Jerusalem will be ruled by the Gentiles until the end times, and then it will be ruled by the Jews. In the Bible, the preposition "until" (in Greek, the synonyms *achri* and *eos*) often means only that something occurs up to a certain point, without suggesting that it does not occur after that point. For example, Paul writes, "For He must reign till [*achri ou*] He has put all enemies under His feet" (1 Cor. 15:25). Are we to assume that Christ will no longer reign after He has defeated all His enemies? Similarly, when Jesus said, "Lo, I am with you always, even to [*eos*] the end of the age" (Matt. 28:20), He didn't mean to imply that He wouldn't be with us after the end of the age! While the preposition "until" can, and often does, indicate a change of action or status in Greek, such is not always the case.

controversial. One of the most respected Protestant Church historians, J. N. D. Kelly, principal of St. Edmund Hall at Oxford and an international authority on patristic Christian thought, writes:

> Alternatively (and this conception harks back to the New Testament) the Church is regarded as the new, authentic Israel which has inherited the promises which God made to the old. So Clement of Rome [writing in A.D. 95] sees in its election the fulfillment of the prophecies that Jacob should become the Lord's portion and Israel the lot of His inheritance. Justin [writing in the mid-second century] puts the claim forcibly to the Jew Trypho, and of course it is the presupposition underlying the Christian appropriation of the Hebrew Scriptures.[18]

In Justin Martyr's *Dialogue with Trypho* (composed between A.D. 155 and 161), after Justin cites half a dozen Old Testament scriptures concerning the restoration of Israel that he applies to the Church (including Is. 14:1 and Ezekiel 36:12), Justin's Jewish opponent, Trypho, asks incredulously, "Do you mean to say that you are Israel, and that God says all this about you?" Justin takes this question as merely a desire to quibble, since he thought he had made himself sufficiently clear.[19] And indeed, earlier Justin had come right out and proclaimed, "We have been led to God through this crucified Christ, and we are the true spiritual Israel, and the descendants of Judah, Jacob, Isaac, and Abraham, who, though uncircumcised, was approved and blessed by God because of his faith and was called the father of many nations." [20]

Irenaeus in the late second century also believed the Church is the true seed of Abraham: "For [Abraham's] seed is the Church, which receives the adoption to God through the Lord, as John the Baptist said, 'For God is able from the stones to raise up children to Abraham.' . . . Thus, then, they who are of faith shall be blessed with faithful Abraham, and these are the children of Abraham." [21] A little later Irenaeus quotes the Old Testament prophecies concerning the regathering of Israel, including passages from Ezekiel 37 and 38 (which modern doom-sayers apply to the 1948 establishment of Israel). Irenaeus applies these biblical passages not to the reestablishment of national Israel, but to the gathering of the Church, spiritual Israel, out of the nations: "Now I have shown a short time ago that the Church is the seed of Abraham; and for this reason, that we may know that He who in the New Testament 'raises up from the stones children unto Abraham,' is He who will gather,

---

18 Kelly, *Early Christian Doctrines*, 190.
19 Justin Martyr, *Dialogue*, 123.
20 Justin Martyr, *Dialogue*, 11:5.
21 Irenaeus, *Heresies*, 5:32:2.

according to the Old Testament, those that shall be saved from all the nations." [22]

We have purposely cited Justin Martyr and Irenaeus because these are the two Church Fathers that the prophecy "experts" cite in support of their premillennial teachings.[23] Unlike Justin's and Irenaeus' doctrine of the earthly millennium, though, the doctrine of the Church as the true remnant of Israel never created any controversy in the Church.[24] This is simply because the doctrine was the universally accepted teaching of early Christendom.

This ought to be sufficient evidence to dismiss as absurd any notion that the doctrine that the Church is the continuation of Israel simply "zoomed into prominence in the Middle Ages." We could go on to cite much more evidence from the third and fourth centuries, but the point should already be clear. And, as J. N. D. Kelly correctly stated, this teaching "harks back to the New Testament."

The Teaching of the Gospels

When we look at the Gospels, we learn that it is not enough merely to be able to claim biological descent from Abraham, for "God is able to raise up children to Abraham from these stones" (Matt. 3:9). In one of Jesus' confrontations with Israel's leaders, Jesus acknowledges that they are Abraham's descendants; nevertheless, they are not Abraham's children because they do not "the works of Abraham" (John 8:37–39). On the contrary, because they sought to kill Him, Jesus says to them, "You are of your father the devil, and the desires of your father you want to do. He was a murderer from the beginning, and does not stand in the truth" (John 8:44).[25] Clearly it is not enough to depend on genealogical descent from Abraham to be a child of Abraham. It is not a question of biology, but of spirituality.

---

22 Irenaeus, *Heresies*, 5:34:1.

23 See Chapter 3, "A Historical Survey of the End of History," for the millennial views of Justin Martyr and Irenaeus.

24 It won't do simply to dismiss the witness of Justin Martyr and Irenaeus as the product of early Christian "anti-Semitism," for there is no evidence of anti-Semitism in either Justin or Irenaeus. In fact, Justin's *Dialogue with Trypho* was likely an actual two-day dialogue in Ephesus with the learned Rabbi Tarphon, who is mentioned in the Mishna. This would make the cordial exchange between the two one of the world's first Jewish-Christian ecumenical dialogues.

25 This passage from the Gospel of John is echoed in the Revelation of John, where it is stated, "I know the blasphemy of those who say they are Jews and are not, but are a synagogue of Satan" (Rev. 2:9). Compare also Rev. 3:9, where Jesus says to the church at Philadelphia, "Indeed I will make those of the synagogue of Satan, who say they are Jews and are not, but lie—indeed I will make them come and worship before your feet, and to know that I loved you."

In the Gospels, Jesus tells the parable of the vineyard (Matt. 21:33–46). A landowner (the Father) planted a vineyard on His land (Israel), and entrusted it to vinedressers (the religious leaders of Israel). The vinedressers, though, abused their trust and consumed the fruit for themselves. The landowner therefore sent servants (the Prophets) to collect what was owed to him from the vineyard, but the vinedressers either beat or killed the servants. Undeterred, the landowner sent his own son (Christ) in the hope that they might at least respect him. Yet they even killed the landowner's son.[26]

The point of Jesus' parable is that Israel had killed and rejected God's messengers, and will even kill God's only-begotten Son Himself. Therefore, God is more than justified in rendering a final judgment. Jesus asks the chief religious leaders the question, "What will he [the landowner] do to those vinedressers?" They reply, "He will destroy those wicked men miserably, and lease his vineyard to other vinedressers who will render to him the fruits in their seasons" (Matt. 21:40, 41). On account of their persistent infidelity to the Law and their rejection of Jesus' claims, the Lord then declares to the rulers of Israel, "The kingdom will be taken away from you and given to a nation [Gr. *ethnos*, literally "people"] bearing the fruits of it" (v. 43). And the Pharisees and chief priests "perceived that He was speaking of them" (v. 45).

Jesus is announcing that the "kingdom" is to be taken away from the unbelieving Jewish religious establishment and given to a different "people" bearing the fruits of the kingdom, meaning believing Jews and Gentiles (*ethnos* is one of the Greek words in the New Testament for Gentiles). Nevertheless, though a different *ethnos* will replace those Jews who will not believe, it is still the same kingdom promised in the Old Testament—the kingdom is messianic Israel. Jesus therefore is proclaiming that messianic Israel will include believing Gentiles as well as Jews.

With the intent of establishing messianic Israel, Jesus gathers the remnant of true, spiritual Israel. Though "He came to His own, and His own did not receive Him" (John 1:11), yet some Jews did receive Him: "But as many [Jews] as received Him, to them He gave the right to become children of God, to those who believe in His name: who were born, not of blood, nor of the will of the flesh, nor of the will of man [i.e., not mere genealogical descent from Abraham], but of God" (John 1:12, 13). In other words, their spiritual standing was not to depend upon being born of Jewish ancestry, but on being born of God.

---

26 Jesus' parable seems deliberately to echo the "Song of the Vineyard" in Is. 5: "For the vineyard of the Lord of hosts is the house of Israel . . ." (Is. 5:7). The vine itself was also a common metaphor for Israel (see Ps. 80:9ff; Jer. 2:21; Ezek. 15:1ff; Hos. 10:1). Compare Jesus' declaration in John 15:1–8, "I am the true vine, and My Father is the vinedresser."

Jesus gathered twelve disciples who were to be the patriarchs of this remnant, just as the twelve sons of Jacob became the original twelve tribes of Israel (see Gen. 35:22b–26). He took one of them, Simon bar Jonah, and renamed him, even as Abram's name had been changed to Abraham (see Gen. 17:5; John 1:42; Matt. 16:18). Simon's new name was Kepha (Peter), Aramaic for "rock," just as Abraham was called "rock" in rabbinic literature as well as in Isaiah 51:1, 2.

Jesus then gathered seventy followers and appointed them to be sent into all the cities of Israel where the Lord intended to go (Luke 10:1). They were to prepare the way so that all true Israelites would receive their Messiah. According to Exodus 1:1–5, seventy descendants of Abraham went into Egypt and formed the seed of the future nation of Israel. Later, after Israel had left Egypt, God instructed Moses to gather seventy officers and elders from among the people. The Lord then filled them with the Holy Spirit so that they prophesied (Num. 11:16–25), a foreshadowing of the Pentecost event when the Holy Spirit fell upon the Apostles. These seventy elders also accompanied Moses to the holy mountain to affirm Israel's covenant with the Lord (Ex. 24:1). This council of seventy elders later served as the model for the Sanhedrin, the highest tribunal that ruled the civil and religious affairs of the Jews. By selecting the seventy, Jesus was forming the new government of the remnant of true spiritual Israel to come out of "spiritual Egypt," that is, unbelieving Israel.

Jesus is also presented in the Gospels as the new Moses of this reconstituted Israel in fulfillment of Deuteronomy 18:18 ("I will raise up for them a Prophet like you"). As all newborn Jewish boys were slaughtered at the time of Moses' birth (Ex. 1:15—2:10), so after Jesus' birth there was a similar slaughter of innocent children (Matt. 2:16). Just as Pharaoh was characterized as hard of heart (Ex. 4:21), so also does Jesus characterize the leaders of Israel (Matt. 19:8), drawing a parallel between the unbelieving Israelites and Egypt. And as Moses gave the Law to old Israel from a mountain, so Jesus gives His new Law to the Church in His Sermon on the Mount, the Beatitudes forming a symbolic parallel to the Ten Commandments.[27]

Moreover, in the Gospel of Matthew, Jesus' sermons can even be divided into five major discourses paralleling the five Books of Moses (called the Pentateuch), leading some to call the Gospel of Matthew the "Christian Pentateuch" fulfilling the one given by Moses.[28] Jesus even duplicates and

---

27 The Gospel of John expresses the same idea: "For the Law was given through Moses, but grace and truth came through Jesus Christ" (John 1:17).

28 B. W. Bacon in his *Studies in Matthew* (1930) divides Matthew into five "Books" with a Preamble (chs. 1; 2) and an Epilogue (chs. 26—28). Book One, called Discipleship,

surpasses Moses' miracle of feeding the people manna in the desert (John 6:1–14, 22–35). In short, just as Moses led the people of God out of the corruption and slavery of Egypt and into the Promised Land, so Jesus frees us, the New Israel, from bondage to corruption and leads us to the promised land of heaven.

The first-century Church had no doubt that Jesus was the Prophet described in Deuteronomy 18 (see John 6:14; 7:40; Acts 3:22, 23; 7:37). This section of Deuteronomy ends with a menacing warning from the God of Israel to those Jews who would reject His message: "If anyone does not listen to my words that the prophet speaks in my name, I myself will call him to account" (Deut. 18:19 NIV). Divine judgment, not divine favor, awaited those Israelites who willfully rejected the Messiah predicted by Moses.

The Teaching of Paul in Romans 9–11

The Apostle Paul also makes clear that Christ reconstituted Israel from a faithful remnant. In his Epistle to the Romans, Paul starts by declaring that someone "is not a Jew who is one outwardly, nor is that circumcision which is outward in the flesh; but he is a Jew who is one inwardly, and circumcision is that of the heart, in the Spirit, and not in the letter [of the Law]" (Rom. 2:28, 29). To be a Jew is a question of spirituality and not of physical circumcision and an ethnic attachment to the Torah. Consequently, Paul argues that "they are not all Israel who are of Israel," since not all live up to their spiritual calling. Only those who have faith in the Messiah, Jesus, "are of Israel" (Rom. 9:6). On this premise, Paul goes on in Romans 9—11 to explain Israel's general rejection of the Messiah in God's overall plan of salvation. This passage is the longest, most complete presentation of Paul's thinking on Israel in the New Testament. His reasoning in this passage is tight and intricate. He quotes many passages from the Old Testament, particularly Isaiah and Deuteronomy, in order to reason with his Jewish adversaries.

Romans 9—11 explicitly contrasts Israel "according to the flesh" with the Church. For Paul, the Church is the remnant of Israel, "a remnant according to the election of grace" (Rom. 11:5). It is Israel "according to the election of grace," not Israel "according to the flesh," which is the true heir to the promises of the Old Covenant. Paul asserts that it would be incorrect to

---

comprises chs. 3—7 (narrative 3–4, discourse 5–7); Book Two, Apostleship, chs. 8—10 (narrative 8–9, discourse 10); Book Three, The Hiding of the Revelation, chs. 11—13 (narrative 11–12, discourse 13); Book Four, Church Administration, chs. 14—18 (narrative 14–17, discourse 18); Book Five, The Judgment, chs. 19—25 (narrative 19–22, discourse 23–25). Bacon's outline has weaknesses (e.g., describing the narrative of the Passion, death, and Resurrection of Christ as an "epilogue"!), and has consequently been modified by later scholars like D. W. Gooding.

believe that God has "rejected Israel," however, for he himself is an Israel-ite—and he certainly hasn't been rejected. In other words, as in Elijah's time when God had a remnant of seven thousand Israelites, so now, Paul says, there is a faithful remnant of Jews who have accepted their Messiah.

But where do Gentiles fit into this "faithful remnant" of Israel? Paul explains the presence of Gentiles in the Church by using the analogy of the olive tree, which represents God's people. Like any tree, this one occasion-ally needs pruning. The dead weight that needs to be cut off from time to time represents unbelievers. Thus, to be "pruned" is the fate of those Jews who have rejected their Messiah. God has cut them off from Israel and grafted believing Gentiles into their place. Thus Israel continues, Paul argues, but with Gentiles taking the place of those Jews who have rejected the Messiah.

The fact that Israel now consists of Jews and Gentiles doesn't mean that there are two kinds of believers, a sort of caste system in the Kingdom of God. Jews cannot look upon Gentiles as "pseudo-Jews"; nor can Gentiles point to the great number of apostate Jews in order to justify treating Chris-tians from a Jewish background as second-class citizens. Jews and Gentiles are equal in the Kingdom. In fact, the existence of unbelieving Jews serves a purpose in God's saving plan: "For God has committed them all [unbelieving Jews] to disobedience, that He might have mercy on all" (Rom. 11:32).

Paul concludes by hinting that ultimately those Jews who have rejected their Messiah will someday come to be reconciled with Christ—even as he himself, who had once rejected the Messiah, has now been reconciled. Com-menting on Romans 11:11 ("I say then, have they [unbelieving Jews] stumbled that they should fall? Certainly not!"), St. John Chrysostom wrote in the fourth century: " 'When the fullness of the Gentiles,' he [Paul] says, 'shall have come in, then shall all Israel be saved' (Rom. 11:25), at the time of His sec-ond Coming, and the end of the world." [29]

To summarize, Paul sees Jews like himself, who have accepted Jesus as their Messiah, as the faithful remnant of Israel, which he describes meta-phorically as an olive tree. Jews who have rejected their Messiah are branches that have been severed from the tree, and their place is being taken by believing Gentiles. The Gentiles are wild branches grafted onto the olive tree, becoming an organic part of Israel. Israel, therefore, is de-scribed by Paul as a community of faith, composed of both the faithful remnant of Israel and believing Gentiles. Paul rejects a concept of Israel

---

29 St. John Chrysostom, *Homilies on Romans*, Homily 19 on Romans 11:11. Chrysostom
    elsewhere mentions the conversion of the Jews to Christ during the end times as a result of
    the preaching of Elijah, who "will indeed come and will restore all things" (Matt. 17:11).
    See Chrysostom's *Homilies on Matthew*, Homily 57:1.

based on race or biological descent from Abraham (see Rom. 2:29; 9:6).

However, the Apostle doesn't turn his back on his unbelieving brethren, for he is convinced that God Himself hasn't turned His back on them. Unbelieving Israel has a place in God's economy, for the severing of unbelieving Jews has made possible the salvation of the Gentile world. Though severed from the tree, unbelieving Israel will continue as a people; and once the full number of Gentiles has been grafted onto true Israel, the unbelieving Jews will be grafted back on, "so all Israel will be saved." [30] In Jewish literature, "all Israel" was a common phrase referring to Israel as a whole, not necessarily to every single Jew. Paul is therefore saying that a day will come when Jews as a whole will accept the gospel. St. Cyril of Alexandria explains in his commentary on Romans 11:26, 27:

> Although it was rejected, Israel will also be saved eventually, a hope which Paul confirms by quoting this text of Scripture [see Is. 59:20, 21]. For indeed, Israel will be saved in its own time and will be called at the end, after the calling of the Gentiles.[31]

From the perspective described by Cyril of Alexandria, it is perfectly correct to say that unbelieving Israel has a bright future in God's loving economy. Israel has not been completely rejected, though for the time being it has rejected the Messiah.

Paul's Other Writings

While Romans 9—11 is Paul's most comprehensive analysis of the role of old Israel in the New Testament, there is more elsewhere that we should look at briefly. In Paul's other writings, we also find the distinction between racial

---

30 Irenaeus of Lyons in the late second century interpreted "Israel" in Rom. 11:26 as referring to the Jewish people (*Against Heresies*, 4:2:7). Another interpretation of this verse understands "Israel" as the Church. In this interpretation, Paul means that when the full number of the elect among the Jews and Gentiles have come to believe, then "all Israel [i.e., the Church] will be saved." See, e.g., the commentary in *The Orthodox Study Bible* on Rom. 11:25–27 for this interpretation (Nashville: Thomas Nelson Publishers, 1993), 365–366. However, with all due respect to *The Orthodox Study Bible*, I find this interpretation rather strained. Indeed, if Paul is merely declaring the self-evident truism that "all the elect will be saved," as *The Orthodox Study Bible* suggests, then Paul's whole argument in Romans 11 seems to end in a resounding anticlimax! I believe Irenaeus' understanding of Israel in this passage has a firmer basis in the text. The preceding verse unambiguously defines "Israel" as Old Israel ("blindness in part has happened to Israel"), and there is no reason to suspect that Paul has suddenly redefined the word in v. 26. Moreover, the connecting phrase "and so" in v. 26 (Gr. *kai outos*) means "in this manner" (see Rom. 5:12, Greek text), implying an elucidation of what was said in v. 25 concerning Old Israel. There is consequently no reason to believe that Israel means one thing in Rom. 11:25 and something else in v. 26.

31 Cyril of Alexandria, *Explanation of the Letter to the Romans* (Migne, *Patrologia Graeca*, 74 col. 849).

Israel, "Israel after the flesh" (1 Cor. 10:18), and the Church, "the Israel of God" (Gal. 6:16). The Church is made up of those who are spiritually a "new creation," physical circumcision consequently becoming superfluous (Gal. 6:15). The new Israel, the Church, consists of those who have the "true circumcision" in Christ: "For it is *we* who are the circumcision, *we* who worship by the Spirit of God, who glory in Christ Jesus, and who put no confidence in the flesh" (Phil. 3:3 NIV, emphasis added).

In Colossians 2:11, 12, Paul identifies "the circumcision of Christ" as Christian baptism. And through baptism, even Gentiles can enter into Israel's covenants. The Gentiles, Paul says, who were once "aliens from the commonwealth of Israel and strangers from the covenants of promise, . . . who once were far off, have been made near by the blood of Christ" (Eph. 2:12, 13). They are now part of the commonwealth of Israel and heirs of the "covenants of promise." Thus Paul can say to "Gentile" Christians at Corinth, "You know that you *were* Gentiles [implying they are such no longer], carried away to these dumb idols, however you were led" (1 Cor. 12:2, emphasis added). Like the term "Jew," Paul gives the term "Gentile" a specifically spiritual connotation that is associated with paganism.

In Galatians, Paul states very succinctly that Christians are the true heirs of Abraham: "Therefore know that *only those* who are of faith are sons of Abraham. . . . So then those who are of faith are blessed with believing Abraham" (Gal. 3:7–9, emphasis added). The blessings of Abraham have come upon the Gentiles through faith (Gal. 3:14). Again, "And if you are Christ's, then you are Abraham's seed, and heirs according to the promise" (Gal. 3:29). Because Christians are the true descendants of Abraham, those who walk according to the Christian "rule" are "the Israel of God" (Gal. 6:16). Racial Jews without faith in Christ are, according to Paul, not sons of Abraham. To become children of Abraham once again, they must accept their Messiah. Paul knows of no covenant blessing, whether it be land or anything else, outside of a relationship with Jesus Christ.

As we've already seen, Paul sees the Church as "the Israel of God"—as opposed to Israel "after the flesh," which is characterized by its insistence on fleshly circumcision. In Galatians 6:16, Paul writes, "And as many as walk according to this rule, peace and mercy be upon them, and [Gr. *kai*] upon the Israel of God" (Gal. 6:16). It is sometimes argued that Paul is distinguishing between Christians, those who "walk according to this rule," and national Israel, thus blessing both together. This interpretation not only runs contrary to Paul's practice of labeling unbelieving Israel as "Israel after the flesh" (why would Paul say that apostate Israel is "of God"?), it also runs against the context of the passage, which condemns those Judaizers who "boast in the flesh" (i.e. boast of circumcision and genealogical descent from Abraham).

Nor does the grammar require the interpretation given Galatians 6:16 by dispensationalists. Many modern translations render the word "and," *kai* in Greek, as epexegetic (that is, as introducing an additional, explanatory clause). Thus, the New International Version translates the verse, "Peace and mercy to all who follow this rule, *even to* the Israel of God." This understanding of the verse seems likely, since it would make no sense for Paul to bless a national Israel that is openly hostile to Christ, in effect blessing unbelief. Therefore, the interpretation of Galatians 6:16 by St. John Chrysostom given at the opening of this chapter is the soundest: It is the Church that is the Israel of God and that receives Paul's blessing.

A Holy Nation and a Holy Temple

Peter has the same concept of the Church as Paul. Peter in his first epistle lifts terms from the Old Testament used to describe Israel and applies them directly to the Church:

> But you are a chosen generation, a royal priesthood, a holy nation, His own special people, that you may proclaim the praises of Him who called you out of darkness into His marvelous light; who once were not a people but are now the people of God, who had not obtained mercy but now have obtained mercy (1 Peter 2:9, 10).

Compare Peter's declaration to Exodus 19:6, where Moses says of national Israel, "You shall be to Me a kingdom of priests and a holy nation"; and also Isaiah 43:20, 21 in the Greek Septuagint translation commonly used during the first century: "My chosen generation, My special people." [32]

In the same epistle, Peter calls on Gentile Christian wives in Asia Minor to submit to their husbands "like Sarah, who obeyed Abraham and called him her master" (1 Pet. 3:6 NIV). He then immediately adds, "You are her daughters [Gr. *tekna*, "children"] if you do what is right and do not give way to fear." The second part of the verse is better translated as "you have become her children," the verb being in the aorist tense. The fact that they "have become" children of Sarah probably points to their baptism, when these women had abandoned their pagan ways to become members of the new Israel. Peter in this verse echoes Isaiah 51:2, where Abraham and Sarah are together described as uniquely the parents of the Jewish people. Like Paul, therefore, Peter believes that those who imitate the faith of Abraham and

---

32 Compare Peter's *laos eis peripoiesin* to the Septuagint's rendering of Isaiah 43:21, *laon mou on periepoiesamen*. See J. Ramsey Michaels' commentary on 1 Peter in the Word Biblical Commentary, Vol. 49 (Waco, TX: Word Books, 1988), 109.

Sarah are the offspring of Abraham and Sarah and thus members of Israel, even if they are racially Gentiles.

The Epistle to the Hebrews, after listing all the great saints of old Israel, reveals that these Old Testament saints have not yet received their promised rewards, for they are not to "be made perfect apart from us" (Heb. 11:40). The Church is one, and neither the saints of the Old Testament nor the saints of the New Testament will be perfected separately. Thus the New Jerusalem that is the reward promised in the Book of Revelation has both the names of the twelve tribes of Israel inscribed on its twelve foundations, and the names of the Twelve Apostles inscribed on its twelve gates. Israel and the Church are in reality one and the same, together comprising the one people of God. As a result of the Church's identity with Israel, Christian assemblies in apostolic times were sometimes called "synagogues" (e.g., James 2:2—the word rendered either "assembly" or "meeting" in modern translations is actually *synagogein* in Greek).[33]

In the four Gospels and in the writings of Peter and Paul, Jewishness is not simply a racial characteristic. In fact, Jewishness in the Scriptures has never been a mere question of blood. If it were, Jews would never have been able to make converts. Indeed, Jews wouldn't be able to make Jewish converts any more than Hispanics could make "Hispanic converts." Yet Jews have always made converts, in some instances rivaling even Christian evangelism efforts (e.g., the conversion of the whole Khazari people to Judaism in the eighth century). Recall what Jesus said to the scribes and Pharisees in Matthew 23:15, that they would travel land and sea to win just one proselyte.

Behind the New Testament insistence that "Jewishness" is a matter of faith lies the Old Testament witness that, historically speaking, many notable "Jews" were never descendants of the original Twelve Tribes. In the Old Testament, a Jew was anyone who accepted the Mosaic covenant and, if male, underwent circumcision. Abraham circumcised not only his blood relatives into the covenant, but all his servants and his 318-man militia (Gen. 14:14;

---

33 It seems this custom of referring to local church communities as "synagogues" continued for quite some time. Some examples: Ignatius of Antioch wrote to Polycarp of Smyrna in A.D. 110, "Let the meetings [Gr. *synagogai*] be more numerous" (*Ignatius to Polycarp*, 4:2). In a mid-second-century work written in Rome, *The Shepherd of Hermas*, the author three times describes the local church as "a meeting [*synagoge*] of righteous men" (Mandate 11:9, 13, 14). We find in the writings of Dionysius the Great, Bishop of Alexandria from 247–265, frequent references to the church as a synagogue. In a letter to Fabius, the Bishop of Antioch, Dionysius writes about those who had lapsed during the persecution of Emperor Decius being received back to "the worship of the Church [*synagogon*]" (Eusebius, *Ecclesiastical History*, 7:42:5). In his treatise *On Baptism*, Dionysius in one passage twice uses the Greek word *ecclesia* for the Church and the word *synagoge* for the local congregation: "the members of the congregation [*synagesthai*] . . . admitted them to the congregation [*synagogen*]." (Eusebius, *Ecclesiastical History*, 7:7:4).

17:10–14). Abraham's son Isaac, and Isaac's son Jacob, each in turn inherited this large household.

There was even racial intermarriage by the twelve sons of Jacob. Judah married Shua, a Canaanite woman, and had by her three sons, Er, Onan, and Shelah (Gen. 38:2–5). Judah took another Canaanite woman, Tamar, as a wife for his son Er (Gen. 38:6). Joseph, after being appointed vizier of Egypt, took to wife Asenath, "the daughter of Poti-Pherah, priest of [the god] On" (Gen. 41:45). From this union with the daughter of a pagan Egyptian priest were born Manasseh and Ephraim, who fathered two of the tribes of Israel (Gen. 41:50–52; 46:20).

According to Exodus 1:5, only seventy descendants of Jacob entered into Egypt, yet so many "nonracial" Israelites (i.e., without any blood ties to Jacob) were in the entourage that the entire land of Goshen was occupied by them (Gen. 46:34). It was this Israel of mixed racial ancestry that Moses (whose own son Gershom was born of Zipporah, his Midianite wife!) led out of Egypt.

In fact, in the very genealogy of our Lord, there are "Jews" who were not descendants of Jacob at all. In the genealogy of Matthew 1:1–17 we find such prominent Gentile names as Tamar, Rahab the Canaanite harlot (whose faith is celebrated in Heb. 11:31; see Josh. 6:22–25), and Ruth. Ruth, of course, was a Moabite woman who became an Israelite through marriage. If being Jewish were merely a racial privilege, then Ruth's declaration to her Jewish mother-in-law, Naomi, becomes meaningless: "Your people shall be my people, and your God, my God" (Ruth 1:16b). Though unrelated to any one of the Twelve Tribes, she married Boaz (who was himself descended from Rahab the Canaanite harlot) and became the great-grandmother of David.

Despite this, there have been few Jews in history who have questioned the "Jewish" ancestry of King David. David himself had many notable "Israelites" in his service whose ancestry was something less than purely "Jewish." Yet who would question the loyalty of soldiers like Uriah "the Hittite" to the nation of Israel? Was he not an Israelite also? He was among David's top thirty soldiers, though not alone among the thirty in being non-Jewish according to the list in 2 Samuel 23:23–30 (see 1 Chr. 11:26–47). Uriah's wife Bathsheba would have a son by David, the future king Solomon, who would be a prominent ancestor of Jesus Christ. Yet, interestingly, Bathsheba isn't named in the genealogy in Matthew—Uriah the Hittite is! "David the king begot Solomon by her who had been the wife of Uriah" (Matt. 1:6).

The nation of Israel was always an ethnically mixed group, perhaps not unlike America today. Mixed marriages between Israelites and their neighbors frequently occurred (the marriage between Uriah and Bathsheba, the daughter of Eliam, was probably one), though this was at times discouraged because it often resulted in the importation of paganism. It will be recalled that after the return from Babylon, Ezra had the people put away their pagan wives (see Ezra 10); but it is clear that the reason these marriages were improper was not that the wives were Gentiles, but that they were pagan. (The same idea underlies the Church's ancient canons forbidding intermarriage with non-Christians, i.e., marriages outside of "Israel.") No doubt it was as a result of discouraging marriages with pagan foreigners that Jewishness, and its concept of the "people of God," degenerated into the racial exclusivity challenged by Christ and the Apostles.

Even today, the Jews living in Israel range from blond-haired, blue-eyed Jews of European descent to black Jews from Ethiopia, all of whose genealogical descent from Abraham is at best tenuous. There are Jews in Israel today who are either converts or the descendants of converts, and whose genetic link to Abraham is nonexistent. Likewise, there are many Christians in the Church who are of Jewish descent, so the Church isn't purely "Gentile" either. Many Jews over the centuries have accepted Jesus as their Messiah, and their many descendants are a part of the Church to this day.

Therefore, on a purely racial basis, the Church and the Jewish nation are both mixed groups. We are therefore left with the question, "Who are the real Jews? Which is the true Israel?" The only possible answer is the one given in the New Testament: "He is a Jew who is one inwardly, and circumcision is that of the heart, in the Spirit, and not in the letter" (Rom. 2:29); "And if you are Christ's, then you are Abraham's seed, and heirs according to the promise" (Gal. 3:29). To be a real Jew and an heir to the promises of the Old Testament requires us to be in Christ. As Fr. Basile Sakkas, an Orthodox priest, explains: "Carnal descent from Abraham can be of no use to us if we are not regenerated by the waters of Baptism in the Faith of Abraham. And the Faith of Abraham was the Faith in Jesus Christ, as the Lord Himself has said: 'Your father Abraham rejoiced to see My day; and he saw it and was glad' (John 8:56)." [34]

Fr. Sakkas goes on to explain what it means to belong to "the posterity" of Abraham and to possess Abraham's inheritance:

> Who then are the *posterity* of Abraham? The sons of Isaac according to the flesh, or the sons of Hagar the Egyptian? Is Isaac or Ishmael the posterity of Abraham? What does the Holy Scripture teach by the mouth of the divine Apostle? 'Now to Abraham and his seed were the promises made. He

---

34 Basile Sakkas, "The 'Monotheistic' Religions." Included in Fr. Seraphim Rose, *Orthodoxy and the Religion of the Future*, 4th ed. (Platina, CA: St. Herman of Alaska Brotherhood, 1996), 4.

saith not, And to seeds, as of many; but as of one, And to thy seed: which is Christ (Gal. 3:16). 'And if ye be Christ's, then ye are Abraham's seed, and heirs according to the promise' (Gal. 3:29). It is then in Jesus Christ that Abraham became 'a father of many nations' (Gen. 17:5; Rom. 4:17). After such promises and such certainties, what meaning does carnal descent from Abraham have? According to the Holy Scripture, Isaac is considered as the *seed* or *posterity*, but only as *the image of Jesus Christ*. As opposed to Ishmael (the son of Hagar; Gen. 16:1ff), Isaac was born in the miraculous "freedom" of a sterile mother, in old age and against the laws of nature, similar to our Saviour, Who was miraculously born of a Virgin. He climbed the hill of Moriah just as Jesus climbed Calvary, bearing on His shoulders the wood of sacrifice. An angel delivered Isaac from death, just as an angel rolled away the stone to show us that the tomb was empty, that the Risen One was no longer there. At the hour of prayer, Isaac met Rebecca in the plain and led her into the tent of his mother Sarah, just as Jesus shall meet His Church on the clouds in order to bring Her into the heavenly mansions, the New Jerusalem, the much-desired homeland.[35]

As Fr. Sakkas explains, any understanding of "Israel" apart from Israel's Messiah, Jesus Christ, is necessarily flawed. Only by possessing the faith of Abraham and being transformed into a new creation in Christ—that is, becoming an icon of Christ—can a person be considered a member of Israel. Regardless of racial background, no one can rightly claim citizenship in Israel without first bowing the knee to Israel's legitimate king, the Lord Jesus Christ, "the son of David, the son of Abraham" (Matt. 1:1).

The Charge of Anti-Semitism

Perhaps the objection to this Orthodox teaching that is most troubling to people is the assertion that the identification of Israel with the Church leads to anti-Semitism. In this connection are usually raised the haunting specters of pogroms and the horrors of Auschwitz. The label of anti-Semite is an ugly one, and no sane person wants to be associated with Nazis. This is essentially an *ad hominem* objection ("It's people who think like you who are responsible for things like the Holocaust!" is usually the unspoken accusation), and quite naturally the temptation in the face of such an ugly charge is capitulation.

While this is perhaps the most disconcerting argument, it is also the most vacuous, deriving its strength from pathos rather than reason. Nazi anti-Semitism was hardly based upon any conviction the Nazis had that they were the "real" Jews. Adolph Hitler and his followers fancied themselves members of a mythological Aryan superrace, and would rather have died than call

---

35 Rose, *Orthodoxy*, 4–5. Emphasis in original.

themselves Jews, spiritual or otherwise. To the Nazi, it was the Aryan race that was the "chosen people."

It is an exercise in understatement to say that Nazism was not inspired by Christian teaching. In fact, Hitler once described Christianity as one of the worst tricks the Jews had ever played on humanity. This attitude toward the Christian Faith led the Nazi hierarchy in 1942 to try to supplant Christianity in Germany with their own brand of neopaganism, replacing the Bible in churches with copies of *Mein Kampf*, the cross with the swastika, and Christ with Wotan and other Germanic deities. No doubt they would have succeeded eventually had not the exigencies of the war refocused the Third Reich's attention elsewhere. If one wants to discover the roots of Nazism and the Holocaust, one must look to German Romanticism, unrestrained nationalism, the influence of Friedrich Nietzsche's philosophical nihilism, and other such "isms," rather than to Christian teaching.[36]

If people claiming to be Christians have killed Jews, it was because of bigotry, not the theology of the Church. This cannot be said too forcefully: Orthodox teaching is directly opposed to anti-Semitism. In a truly inspired sermon delivered by the late Metropolitan Antony Khrapovitsky of Kiev (April 20, 1903), which was prompted by a pogrom in Kishnev during Easter, the Metropolitan condemned those who shielded their crimes "under the thin guise of zeal for the faith":

> O brethren, I wish to make you . . . comprehend that even today the Jewish tribe is dear to God's heart, and realize that God is angered by anyone who would offend that people. . . . Do not suppose that this [Jewish] blood was sacred only in the past, but understand that even in the future reconciliation to the divine nature awaits them [2 Pet. 1:4], as Christ's chosen vessel [the Apostle Paul] further testifies [quotes Rom. 11:25–27]. . . . How sinful is enmity against Jews, based on an ignorance of God's law, and how shall it be forgiven when it arises from abominable and disgraceful impulses. The robbers of the Jews did not do so as revenge for opposition to Christianity, rather they lusted for the property and possessions of others. Under the thin guise of zeal for the faith, they served the demon of covetousness. They resembled Judas who betrayed Christ with a kiss while blinded with the sickness of greed, but these murderers, hiding themselves behind Christ's

---

36 The Nazis had developed their own religion based on pagan Germanic mythology (even adopting the myth of Atlantis), the occult (Rudolf Hess was obsessed with astrology, the prophecies of Nostradamus, etc.), an eclectic borrowing from Hinduism (Himmler traveled with a copy of the Bhagavad-Gita and believed in reincarnation) and other religions, and of course the teachings of Hitler himself. The Nazis had their own religious calendar with holy days, their own martyrology (e.g., the 16 Immortals), and their own symbols (Nordic runes, the Swastika, etc.) and religious ceremonies (including Nazi "baptism" and marriage ceremonies performed in Nazi shrines). Nazism was influenced by many things, but the gospel was certainly not one of them.

name, killed His kinsmen according to the flesh in order to rob them.[37]

Metropolitan Antony concluded with the dry remark: "Let us overcome unbelief and impiousness among Christians first, and then concern ourselves with the Jews." Metropolitan Antony not only preached against anti-Semitism, but strove to obtain governmental action to put a stop to pogroms in Russia. On at least one occasion, while bishop of Volyn, he even physically placed himself between a synagogue and a mob intent on violence, reproaching the entire lot of them. Metropolitan Antony is but one example among many proving that authentic Orthodoxy is antithetical to bigotry and anti-Semitism.

It is true that bigots in the past have twisted Christian teaching to mean that the Jews are now cursed by God and should be abused for their Jewish heritage. These bigots have even gone so far as to blame all Jews for the crucifixion of Christ, calling them "Christ-killers." But this is not Orthodoxy, just a religious rationalization for evil. If one wants to talk about "blame" for Christ's crucifixion, then we must say that all of us, Jew and Gentile alike, are responsible for the death of Christ. He died for the sins of both Jews and Gentiles, so we are all in some respects "Christ-killers." [38]

The fact that a doctrine can be corrupted in no way justifies abandoning the doctrine. Indeed, what doctrine hasn't been perverted in the Church's long history? Our response to doctrinal corruption must never be to compromise the gospel, but to assert more vigorously doctrinal orthodoxy. The same holds with regard to the Christian doctrine that the Church is true Israel. Neither Hitler nor any other bigoted minion of Satan can be allowed to alter "the faith which was once for all delivered to the saints" (Jude 3).

One suspects there is a certain amount of Freudian self-projection behind the charge of anti-Semitism that dispensationalists level at other Christians. According to their scenario for Armageddon, when Christ comes for "His people" at the rapture, it isn't the Jewish people for whom He comes. In classic dispensationalism, there is a sort of doctrinal apartheid where the Jews

---

37 Delivered in the Cathedral of Zhitomer. I am greatly indebted to Fr. A. James Bernstein for sending me a copy of this truly inspiring sermon.

38 The fact that both Jews and Gentiles together were responsible for the crucifixion of Christ is stressed in the Gospels themselves: the Jewish authorities initiated Christ's execution and the Roman authorities willingly carried it out (even while knowing Jesus was guiltless). However, on the Cross Jesus exonerates all who were responsible by praying, "Father, forgive them, for they do not know what they do" (Luke 23:34). If Christ Himself forgave those responsible, how can His followers do any less? Moreover, so far as the ultimate "responsibility" for the crucifixion is concerned, Jesus claims this for Himself: "I am the good shepherd. The good shepherd gives His life for the sheep. . . . Therefore My Father loves Me, because I lay down My life that I may take it up again. No one takes it from Me, but I lay it down of Myself" (John 10:11, 17, 18). Given Jesus' own witness in the Gospels, it is ridiculous to lay "blame" on anyone today for the crucifixion.

are eternally God's "earthly" people while the Church is God's "heavenly" people. At the rapture, the Jews are left on earth with the heathen and all others who reject Christ. The Jews consequently suffer the wrath of God during the Great Tribulation. Prophecy mongers will even cite Zechariah 13:8, 9 to argue that God plans to slaughter two-thirds of the Jewish population during the end times! And they accuse the Orthodox of anti-Semitism?

Fundamentalist anti-Semitism has even been the focus of some interesting psychiatric research. Charles Strozier, a professor of history and a practicing psychoanalytic psychotherapist, did an interesting study of fundamentalists in New York City. Strozier spent several years visiting fundamentalist churches in the city, doing fifty-four taped interviews of twenty-five different persons. The result was a book published in 1994 entitled *Apocalypse: On the Psychology of Fundamentalism in America*. His book contains an entire chapter on fundamentalist attitudes toward Jews.

According to Strozier, fundamentalists view the Holocaust, and all the persecution of the Jews over the last two thousand years, as God's judgment against the disbelieving Jews. The ultimate purpose behind the Holocaust, according to the fundamentalists he talked to, was to drive the Jews to reestablish their homeland in Palestine and forward biblical prophecy. Strozier explains, "[The Holocaust] created the historical conditions necessary for the founding of the state of Israel. Hitler served God's purposes, as fundamentalists generally understand it." [39]

Fundamentalists argue that this ingathering of the Jews to Palestine will eventually lead to the Jews' conversion to Christ. Since the Jews aren't raptured when God comes for "His people," they suffer terribly during the Tribulation. However, before Christ returns to end their suffering, 144,000 must convert to Christianity. "The ingathered Jews who survive the violence of tribulation and the false peace engineered by Antichrist *must* all convert before Jesus returns to rule over his millennial kingdom." [40] When Christ does return, He will destroy all unbelieving Jews before establishing His millennial Kingdom.

Strozier chillingly observes, "The instrumentality of the Jews for fundamentalists is, in general, based on a lack of understanding or concern for the other and can carry within it the potential for violence." [41] He recounts an interview with a pastor who blandly described Israel's destruction during the Tribulation. Strozier then concludes: "But why does Israel need to be destroyed? The easy answer, that biblical prophecy foretells its destruction,

---

39 Strozier, *Apocalypse*, 197.
40 Strozier, *Apocalypse*, 201. Emphasis in original.
41 Strozier, *Apocalypse*, 204.

fails to satisfy even the fundamentalists themselves, who uneasily combine abstruse points of theology with old-fashioned prejudice." [42]

Strozier then makes his final evaluation of fundamentalist attitudes toward Jews, which is worth citing at length:

> Generally, then, fundamentalism is theologically pro-Jewish and at the same time anti-Semitic. Jews are special targets [of proselytism], something that is clear in the theology, as well as in the minds of ordinary believers, and their [i.e., the Jews'] suffering rounds out a history of God's wrath from the Exodus to the Holocaust. Theologically, one might say, God saves Israel for Jesus while at the same time he destroys the Jews. . . . Fundamentalists, in the end, have little empathy for Jews. They talk about "them" in the abstract and move quickly from discussing the seed of Abraham to Antichrist. It is important in this context to distinguish blatant anti-Semitism from the more subtle and pervasive forms of ambivalence and confusion about Jews that exist in the theology and in the minds of ordinary Christian believers. Fundamentalist writers themselves often react with sarcasm to the charge of anti-Semitism, stressing that they are "ardent supporters" of Israel and the Jewish heritage. . . . But as we have seen, the fundamentalist support for Jews and the state of Israel is much more complicated. For nearly all fundamentalists, instrumental images of the Jewish contribution to the end times make them and their state of Israel worth support only to fulfill apocalyptic visions. In the last analysis, fundamentalists find little of spiritual merit in contemporary Judaism, and most have in their minds a notably derogatory and devalued view of Jews as people.[43]

He ends by making the damning observation that "ordinary believers often seem almost unconscious of their contradictions as they espouse a great love for Jews while talking numbly of their annihilation in the end times." [44] This is, he repeats, because Jews aren't seen as real human beings: "Jews tend to be either idealized or debased but seldom perceived as people." [45] The paradoxes are striking: Protestant fundamentalists idealize Jews as uniquely God's people, yet they have appointed the Jews to destruction and damnation unless they become "born-again" fundamentalists like themselves. Fundamentalists claim to love the Jews more than any other group on earth, yet they have debased the Jews to a faceless *dramatis personae* in their script for Armageddon.

What ought to be the attitude of Christians toward Jews? We must love Jews not merely as objects for conversion or as props in some apocalyptic drama, but as real human beings created in the image and likeness of God. Also, Christians should have an authentic appreciation for all that is good in

---

42 Strozier, *Apocalypse*, 205.
43 Strozier, *Apocalypse*, 206–207.
44 Strozier, *Apocalypse*, 208.
45 Strozier, *Apocalypse*, 207.

the Jewish community. Does this mean, then, we are not to evangelize people from a Jewish background? Of course not, but Jews are not to be "special targets" of evangelism; rather, both Jews and Gentiles together are invited to "come and see" the Lord Jesus Christ (John 1:46). Let us not forget that, ultimately, it is not we who lead anyone to faith; it is the grace of the Holy Spirit acting in the heart of the unbeliever that gives birth to the Christian convert.

It goes without saying that anti-Semitism is wholly inimical to the gospel. Bigotry in any form is nothing less than hatred for one's fellow man, and is inspired by the common enemy of man, Satan. Whenever we are tempted by anti-Semitism, we should remember the example of the Apostle Paul. Though the majority of his fellow Jews rejected his message, Paul never expressed anger or resentment—much less hatred. Instead he expressed sorrow at the loss of his coreligionists: "I have great sorrow and continual grief in my heart" (Rom. 9:2). Paul did not refer to unbelieving Jews with hateful epithets, but called them "my brethren, my kinsmen according to the flesh" (Rom. 9:3). Paul declared that he wished he himself might be forever cut off from Christ if only Israel after the flesh would come to a saving knowledge of the gospel (Rom. 9:3). Paul loved his countrymen, and rather than dehumanizing them as special "targets" for conversion or as fodder in some end-times massacre, he desired only that they might know the blessings of the Messiah, the Lord Jesus. What selfless love, to wish oneself cut off from the Lord if only it would result in one's own people turning to the Messiah!

This is the attitude all Christians must have toward our unbelieving neighbors, whether Jew or Gentile—one of selfless love. This means extending to our Jewish and Gentile friends every Christian generosity and benevolence, wishing them well in every way while expecting nothing in return. In this way we truly introduce them to the love of Jesus the Messiah.

Since Christianity is the fulfillment of Judaism, Jews are our closest spiritual neighbors. Anyone with even the most rudimentary knowledge of Christianity knows what Christ taught about loving our neighbors (e.g., the Parable of the Good Samaritan). St. Anthony, the great Egyptian Father of monasticism, is reported to have said, "Our life and death is with our neighbor. If we gain our brother, we have gained God; but if we scandalise our brother, we have sinned against Christ." [46] This is the Orthodox teaching on relations with our neighbors, whether they are Jews or of any other race, religion, or ethnicity.

---

46 Benedicta Ward, trans., *The Sayings of the Desert Fathers* (Kalamazoo, MI: Cistercian Publications, 1975), 3.

Chapter Seven

Israel's Eternal Covenant

For where your treasure is, there your heart will be also.
—The Gospel According to St. Matthew 6:21

If a man own land, the land owns him.
—Ralph Waldo Emerson, *The Conduct of Life* (1860)

BACK IN 1990, a group of Israeli settlers moved into St. John's Hospice in the Christian Quarter of Jerusalem. These settlers had bought the hospice from Patriarch Diodoros I of the Orthodox Church of Jerusalem. Located between the ancient Church of the Holy Sepulcher and the Greek Convent of St. John, the hospice had been owned by the Orthodox Church for many, many centuries. The takeover of the hospice sent shock waves throughout the Christian world.

Choosing the Orthodox Holy Week as the time to move in, 150 Jewish settlers took over the premises on Great Thursday and covered the Christian symbols on the face of the building with Israeli flags. The settlers seemed intent upon provoking Christian sensibilities by moving in right before Easter and covering Christian symbols; but they could afford such bold affronts as they had the Israeli army standing guard while they took possession of the property. Understandably, when the traditional Orthodox procession wound its way down the street to the Church of the Holy Sepulcher, Christians tried to remove the flag covering the cross. In response, the Israeli army shot teargas at the crowd (at a concentration too toxic to be legal in this country). The international community was outraged, and the Church of the Holy Sepulcher was closed during Easter for the first time since it was built by Emperor Constantine the Great in the fourth century.

Patriarch Diodoros and several members of the Holy Synod went to the hospice to make a protest, but "were roughed up by soldiers and teargassed in front of television cameras." [1] The Patriarch claimed he had no idea he was selling the property to the government to allow for a Jewish settlement in the Christian part of the city.

Gary Burge, an evangelical New Testament scholar, was in Jerusalem while all this was occurring. He reported seeing what looked like sheets over the Christian symbols on the building and the star of David "spray-painted generously on the walls." While at the site, he had a conversation with two teenage settlers:

> "We have bought what is ours anyway, and how we did it doesn't matter," they said.
>
> I [Gary Burge] asked if it were not true that the Greeks [Orthodox Christians] had owned this property for hundreds of years—maybe even a thousand years.
>
> "It doesn't matter," they answered. "God gave us this country and this city, and the Jews can live anywhere."
>
> I reflected on the fact that Greek Christians could not buy land in the Jewish Quarter.
>
> "We are only taking what is ours by right. These people [the Christians] have no right to be in this city," they replied.
>
> This last thought enticed me. And so I pursued this idea of "rights" with these seventeen-year-old zealots.
>
> "God gave this land to Abraham, and we are his descendants. It belongs to us. Everything that happened in between simply doesn't matter. The Palestinian Christians should just get out."
>
> The conversation struck me as odd because these boys were American. They were from New York and had been in the country only a few years. And here they were ejecting an ancient Christian community that could trace its history to this bit of real estate for more than a thousand years. [2]

What is even more odd to Orthodox Christians is that many calling themselves Christians would agree with these two American Jewish boys. Indeed, today's prophecy pundits emphatically assert that God forever gave the land to Israel; and, in 1948, He not only renewed the lease but also set the prophetic clock ticking on the last days. They arrive at this conclusion by (1) seizing upon the promise of the land to Abraham in Genesis; (2) selectively citing and then twisting passages in the rest of the Old Testament; (3) leapfrogging over the New Testament altogether; and finally, (4) identifying the modern secular state of Israel as the fulfillment of those Old Testament promises.

---

1 Gary Burge, *Who Are God's People in the Middle East?* (Grand Rapids: Zondervan, 1993), 56.
2 Burge, *God's People*, 57.

Unfortunately, this uncritical support of Israel encourages anti-Christian activity in the Holy Land. Three years after the St. John Hospice incident, during Easter of 1993, there was even more blatant anti-Christian persecution. In Bethlehem, police beat and abused Christians as they gathered to await the flame from the Church of the Holy Sepulcher during Easter services. At the same time in Beit Jalla, over four thousand people awaiting the Easter fire were teargassed by Israeli soldiers in front of Santa Maria Church. As the bells of the church rang at the approach of the light, soldiers began shooting at the bells, the clock on the steeple, and the cross itself. The Christians themselves were gassed and many were arrested on trumped-up charges. Despite the unswerving devotion of "Christian Zionists" to the state of Israel, the Israelis clearly want Christians—including Christian Zionists—out of "their" land.

The Abrahamic Covenant

Much of the notion of an eventual restoration of national Israel—as well as a future Jewish millennium with Jesus seated as a political king in Jerusalem—comes from the dispensationalist understanding of the covenant God made with Abraham and his progeny. The prophecy gurus argue that the covenant, including the promise of the land, is unconditional and perpetual: "For all the land which you [Abraham] see I give to you and your descendants forever" (Gen. 13:15; compare 17:8). They conclude from this promise that the Abrahamic covenant is earthly, unconditional, and can find its ultimate fulfillment only in a final restoration and millennial kingdom still to come.

The prophecy "experts" of necessity assert that the "descendants" mentioned in the promise are the biological descendants of Abraham through Isaac and Jacob, and not, as Paul taught in Galatians 3:29 and elsewhere, Abraham's descendants through faith in Christ. This "biological descent" interpretation of the Abrahamic covenant is the one expressed above by the New York teenager when he reasoned, "God gave this land to Abraham, and we are his descendants. . . . The Palestinian Christians should just get out."

The irony is that Palestinian Christians could just as easily claim Jewish descent from those first Jewish converts in Jerusalem at Pentecost. Acts 2:11 specifically includes Arabs as among those pilgrims in Jerusalem who accepted faith in Christ during Pentecost.[3] These were Arab Jews, for the entire

---

3   F. F. Bruce notes that the term "Arabs" within the Roman Empire generally indicated the Arabs of the Nabataean Kingdom that stretched from the Red Sea to the Euphrates. In the year of the Church's birth, it was ruled by Aretas IV (9 B.C. – A.D. 40), and was annexed by Rome in A.D. 106. That there was a Christian community among the Arabs early on (likely those Arabic Jews converted to Christianity mentioned in Acts 2:11) is *(cont.)*

group converted by Peter's preaching are said to be "Jews . . . from every nation under heaven" in Acts 2:5. Unless faith in Christ somehow invalidates one's Jewish background, the Palestinian Christians have just as good a claim to Jewish "descent" as a couple of New York teenagers of European extraction.

The Orthodox, on the other hand, see the Abrahamic covenant as already fulfilled. The word in Genesis 13:15 translated as "descendants" (that is, those descendants who are to receive the land) can literally be translated, "seed." The Apostle Paul gives us the definitive interpretation of Genesis 13:15 when he writes, "Now to Abraham and his Seed were the promises made. He does not say, 'And to seeds,' as of many, but as one, 'And to your Seed,' who is Christ" (Gal. 3:16). According to Paul, Christ is the ultimate descendant in whom the promises of Genesis 13:15 find their fulfillment. St. John Chrysostom (347–407) summarized Paul's understanding of the Abrahamic covenant in Galatians 3:16 as follows: "It was promised to Abraham that by his seed the heathen should be blessed; and his seed according to the flesh is Christ." [4]

In Romans, Paul tells us that the promise made to Abraham was "that he would be the heir of the world" (Rom. 4:13). Thus Abraham's "descendants" who were to be blessed would not simply be ethnic Israel, but Gentiles as well (in Chrysostom's words just quoted, "the heathen"). A few verses later, Paul quotes Genesis 15:5 and interprets Abraham's "descendants" as the "many nations" (Rom. 4:18). Finally, assuming that Paul is the author of Hebrews, Paul explains that the land promised to Abraham refers to our "heavenly country" (Heb. 3:7—4:11; 11:13–16; compare 11:8–10).[5]

Consequently, the Church's understanding of the Abrahamic covenant is that it is fulfilled in Jesus Christ; and the beneficiaries are ultimately all those, both Jews and Gentiles, who are in Christ (the "many nations"). Moreover, the land promised to Abraham is not merely some real estate in the Middle East, but a heavenly home with the Father. When the covenant is interpreted spiritually, God's promises to Abraham are truly seen as eternal. Ironically, when the prophecy pundits see the promises as being fulfilled in an earthly millennium, they make the promises finite, since the millennium, they say, will also pass away after a thousand years.

(note 3 cont.) suggested by the fact that Paul chose to seek refuge in "Arabia" after being chased out of Damascus (see Gal. 1:17). See F. F. Bruce, *The Acts of the Apostles: Greek Text with Introduction and Commentary*, 3rd ed. (Grand Rapids: Eerdmans, 1990), 118.

4   St. John Chrysostom, *Commentary on Galatians*, 3:16.

5   Even Hal Lindsey comments on Heb. 3:7—4:11 that "entering the promised land of Canaan is a picture of God's people entering His rest and conquering through faith." *Apocalypse Code*, 289.

The Orthodox do not deny that actual land was given to Abraham and his immediate descendants through Isaac and Jacob. However, strictly speaking, Israel never "owned" the land. Leviticus 25:23 explicitly states that it is God who owns the land and who merely allowed Israel to live in it: "The land shall not be sold permanently, for the land is Mine; you are strangers and sojourners with Me." Because the land belongs to God, He could always cast Israel out and give the land to another. Consequently, simply because Scripture declares that Israel will have the land "forever" (Gen. 13:15) as an "everlasting possession" (Gen. 17:8) doesn't mean that God can't later punish the Jews with exile—or even kick them out altogether. God's promises to Abraham of a national homeland were conditional (see Gen. 15:6; 17:9). This fact may at first be somewhat difficult to grasp, so let us take a moment to look at it.

In Orthodoxy, there is a concept called *synergy*, meaning that God allows us to participate in the covenants He makes with us. For example, Jesus says, "Behold, I stand at the door and knock. If anyone hears My voice and opens the door, I will come in to him and dine with him, and he with Me" (Rev. 3:20). The Lord extends the invitation, and we respond by either opening the door or barring it. This is synergy, which literally means "working together," that is, working with God to achieve His purpose in the world.

Synergy is the basis for all of God's covenants with mankind. God makes the offer (e.g., the offer of the land of Canaan), but the promises contained in the covenant are qualified by fidelity to the conditions of the covenant. When God called Abram and promised to make of him a great nation (Gen. 12:1–3), the promise was qualified by several conditions, one being that Abram leave his country and kindred and travel to the land of Canaan. Yet what if Abram had refused the Lord and just sat fat and happy at home in Ur of the Chaldees? Would God have nonetheless fulfilled his promise of a great nation to Abram? No, to receive the promise Abram was required to do something, to meet a condition. Thus in Genesis 26:5 we read that God renewed the covenant with Isaac "because Abraham obeyed my voice and kept my charge." This obedience is characterized in Hebrews 11:8–10 as having been performed "by faith."

There are always qualifications to God's promises, even when they aren't directly stated. Consider the well-known example of Jonah. The Lord told Jonah, "Arise, go to Nineveh, that great city, and preach to it the message that I tell you" (Jon. 3:2). So Jonah entered the city and cried out, "Yet forty days, and Nineveh shall be overthrown!" (Jon. 3:4).

No hint of ambiguity there. In forty days the city would be no more. Period. No conditions are mentioned whereby the city might escape judgment; the message is straightforward: the city is doomed. Yet we learn that Nineveh was ultimately spared the judgment because the king called a fast and the city repented. "God relented" (Jon. 3:10) because the people met an unspoken condition: the judgment wouldn't be carried out if they repented.

This aspect of God's dealing with us must be kept in mind when reading scriptures that seem to make an unconditional promise. Though they are unspoken, there are conditions behind even seemingly absolute promises. With regard to the Abrahamic covenant, Israel had to be faithful to its end of the covenant in order to remain in the land. Israel as a nation couldn't turn to idolatry and then say to the Lord, "You can't permanently evict us from the land; you promised to maintain us here forever."

God certainly could evict them permanently. Consider a precedent: God created Eden specifically for Adam and his wife Eve to live in forever; yet when they rebelled, God didn't hesitate to bar them from the Garden *permanently*. Israel didn't somehow get a better deal with Palestine than Adam and Eve did with Paradise! Whether a nation stands or falls is determined by its relationship with God. The idea is outlined explicitly in Jeremiah 18:8–10:

> If that nation against whom I have spoken turns from its evil, I will relent of the disaster that I thought to bring upon it. And the instant I speak concerning a nation and concerning a kingdom, to build and to plant it, if it does evil in My sight so that it does not obey My voice, then I will relent concerning the good with which I said I would benefit it.

This held for Israel just as much as for Gentile nations. Consider, for example, a verse like Exodus 14:13, where the Lord states a seemingly unconditional promise to Israel through Moses: "For the Egyptians whom you see today, you shall see again *no more forever*" (emphasis added). This sounds like an unconditional promise never to punish Israel by sending it back to Egypt. Now compare Deuteronomy 28:68, where the price of disobedience to the covenant is described:

> And the Lord will take you *back to Egypt in ships*, by the way of which I said to you, "You shall never see it again." And there you shall be offered for sale to your enemies as male and female slaves, but no one will buy you (Deut. 28:68, emphasis added).

We see in the above example that there was an unspoken condition to the seemingly unconditional promise given to Israel in Exodus 14:13. Israel had to be faithful to the Lord and the covenant.

Again, in Exodus 3:8 the Lord is speaking to Moses and declares that He will bring Israel into the Promised Land: "So I have come down to deliver them out of the hand of the Egyptians, and to bring them up from that land to a good and large land, to a land flowing with milk and honey." There appear to be no binding conditions on the promise. God is going to bring them into the Promised Land. Yet note what God declares later when the Israelites begin murmuring:

> The carcasses of you who have murmured against Me shall fall in the wilderness, all of you who were numbered, according to your entire number, from twenty years old and above. Except for Caleb the son of Jephunneh and Joshua the son of Nun, you shall by no means enter the land which I swore I would make you dwell in. But your little ones, whom you said would be victims, I will bring in, and they shall know the land which you have despised. But as for you, your carcasses shall fall in this wilderness (Num. 14:29–32).

Though God swore to bring these people into the Promised Land, He lets them die in the desert instead because of their lack of faith. It is the children of the original people who actually enter the land.

Finally, when Joshua had brought the Israelites into Palestine, he warned them at the end of his life: "If you forsake the Lord and serve foreign gods, then He will turn and do you harm and consume you, after He has done you good" (Josh. 24:20). The land was given to Israel on strict conditions. Israel's residence in the land was dependent upon the people's standing with God. If the Israelites fell into apostasy, they would be evicted from the land and not permitted to return until they repented. If they fell into permanent apostasy, they would be permanently removed from the land.

Yes, God promised the land to Israel forever, but "forever" in the Bible isn't always used in an absolute sense. For example, "forever" can simply mean lasting the allotted time of something's intended purpose. When Solomon dedicated the Temple in Jerusalem in the tenth century B.C., the Lord appeared to him and said, "For now I have chosen and sanctified this house, that My name may be there *forever*; and My eyes and My heart will be there *perpetually*" (2 Chr. 7:16, emphasis added). Yet the first Temple lasted only from 960 to 586 B.C., roughly 374 years. A second Temple was afterwards built that lasted until A.D. 70. What happened? Did the Lord make an idle promise when He promised to dwell in Solomon's Temple "perpetually" and "forever"? Or did He somehow fall down on the job?

Neither, actually. What the Lord meant by "forever" and "perpetually" was that He would make His home in the Temple in Jerusalem *so long as* the Mosaic Covenant continued. After Christ established the New Covenant, the Jerusalem Temple was leveled, never to be rebuilt as God's abode as it was in the days of Solomon. As Peter says, we are the stones that are being built into a "spiritual house," a new spiritual Temple in which lives the glory (the *shekinah* in Hebrew) of the Lord (1 Pet. 2:5).

Along the same lines, consider the Aaronic priesthood described in Exodus 40:15 and Numbers 25:13 as "everlasting." On the surface, this implies that the Aaronic priesthood will continue into eternity. Yet we know from the Epistle to the Hebrews and other places in the New Testament that the Aaronic priesthood that slaughtered goats and bulls has ceased (Heb. 7:11—8:6; 10:1–18). Did God contradict Himself? No, and upon examining Exodus 40:15 and Numbers 25:13, we discover there is an elucidation as to what "everlasting" means: the priesthood "shall surely be an everlasting priesthood *throughout their generations*" (Ex. 40:15, emphasis added). In other words, it was to last as long as the line of Aaron lasted. The line of Aaron has disappeared along with the need to offer animal sacrifices.

From the above examples, we learn that we need to be careful about assigning absolute meanings to words like "forever" and "perpetual." We ought not to read the words of the biblical covenants in a legalistic manner. Covenants have to do with interpersonal relationships. God did not enter into a real estate contract with legal stipulations when he entered into the covenant with Abraham; rather, He instituted a loving relationship wherein He swore to care for Abraham and his descendants.

In the Old Testament, this covenant relationship between God and His people is often described in terms of the relationship between a husband and a wife. The analogy is apt, since most marriage rituals in most cultures involve some "perpetual" commitment of the spouses to each other. Yet marriages do not always last forever. Human imperfections can sometimes destroy the covenant. What destroys a marital covenant between a couple is not just the technical violation of the legal terms of the marriage contract, but the severing of the personal relationship—in a word, sin. The aim of all God's covenants with man in the Bible is to overcome precisely this problem of human sin. Therefore, we should understand the biblical covenants in the light of the interpersonal dynamics of God's love and man's sin.

If we think of the covenant in terms of a personal, synergistic relationship, instances where God appears to "break" His promises begin to make sense. For instance, in another interesting example of "forever" having a more nuanced meaning than the prophecy gurus are generally willing to recognize, there is the case of a priest named Eli.

Eli was a good priest, yet the Lord became displeased with him because he had allowed his two sons to run rampant and commit sacrilege. Thus the Lord told Eli:

Therefore the Lord God of Israel says: "I said indeed that your house and the house of your father would walk before me *forever*"; but now the Lord says: "Far be it from Me; for those who honor Me I will honor, and those who despise Me shall be lightly esteemed" (1 Sam. 2:30, emphasis added).

The prophecy against Eli goes on to state that, though the Lord had promised that Eli's family would walk before Him "forever," Eli's family would be cut off and "there shall not be an old man in your house forever" (1 Sam. 2:32). Because of sin, Eli's family lost the blessing that had been promised "forever."

Consequently, when we come across verses like Genesis 13:15 that promise the land to Abraham and his descendants "forever," we must restrain ourselves from jumping to simplistic conclusions based upon Webster's definition of the English word "forever." Actually, the Hebrew word translated "forever" in Genesis 13:15, *ad owlam*, has subtle nuances of meaning. Yes, it can correspond to the metaphysical idea of eternity, but this meaning is not the primary one. Indeed, the word usually means just "a very long time," sometimes in the distant past as in Isaiah 42:14 ("I have held my peace a long time [*ad owlam*]"). More often, though, it refers to future time, in such a manner that the actual length of time is always determined by the nature of the thing itself. When the word is applied to individual men, it commonly signifies a lifetime. Elsewhere it is used of a whole race or ruling dynasty and comprehends all the time until its destruction. This is the definition of "forever" used in connection with God's covenant with the Israelites, the laws given to them, and *the possession of the Holy Land*. In all these instances, the length of "forever," *ad owlam*, is determined by the nature of the thing itself.

The provisional nature of the Abrahamic covenant must be understood in relation to all the other covenants in the Bible, especially to Christ's New Covenant. The various covenants of the Bible have the practical aim of restoring humanity's relationship with God. To do this, the problem of sin first has to be overcome. Each successive covenant between man and God is built upon the previous ones in order to overcome sin and to reestablish the divine-human relationship. This process finally culminates in the New Covenant of Jesus Christ. The Abrahamic and Mosaic covenants have been subsumed, and in many respects superseded, by this New Covenant of Christ. Therefore, we must understand the Abrahamic covenant in relation to its ultimate goal: our covenant with Christ—and not the other way around, by interpreting our covenant with Christ in terms of the Old Testament.

The prophecy pundits, on the other hand, resist this understanding of the Abrahamic Covenant. They often assert that the Jewish people have a perpetual claim to the land of Palestine by arguing that the covenant ritual in

Genesis 15:9–17 implies an unconditional covenant. In this passage, God reaffirms His promise to Abraham of numerous descendants and a homeland in Palestine; then, to solemnly affirm the promise, God and Abraham literally "cut an oath" (Hebrew: *b'rith*) by sacrificing certain animals. The animals are then cut in two and the parts are placed opposite each other.[6]

After the sacrifice was prepared, the Bible says, "a deep sleep" overcomes Abraham and "horror and great darkness fell upon him" (Gen. 15:12). While Abraham is in this state, God relates to him what will befall his descendants in Egypt and how they will be delivered. After dark, God Himself descends as "a smoking oven and a burning torch that passed between those pieces [of the sacrificed animals]" (v. 17). God then makes the covenant of the land and outlines its boundaries (vv. 18–21).

It is sometimes noted that, by passing between the pieces of the sacrificed animals, God was personally taking upon Himself a curse if He should fail to fulfill the covenant. This is a possible interpretation, though by no means a certain one. Victor Hamilton in his commentary on Genesis has published the texts of many ancient covenant rituals, some of which involved the slaughtering of an animal and a symbolic curse, and some of which merely involved the slaughtering of an animal. He believes the covenant ritual in Genesis 15 is the latter type: "The absence of these emphases in Gen[esis] 15 [associated with covenants which include a symbolic curse] has moved many commentators to the position that Gen[esis] 15 is not concerned with God placing himself under any kind of potential curse at all. Instead, what one finds here is that the slaying and arrangement of the animals is simply a sacrificial practice by means of which a covenant is ratified." [7]

How do the prophecy gurus see in this covenant ritual an unconditional promise to Abraham and his descendants? Charles C. Ryrie, a prominent dispensationalist famous for his *Ryrie Study Bible*, draws the following conclusions from Genesis 15:

> God could not have shown more clearly that the keeping of this covenant was reaffirmed to Abraham's son, Isaac, and to *his* son Jacob (Gen. 26:2–4; 28:13–15). No conditions were attached in either instance, and the reaffirmation was made on the basis of the oath with which God made the covenant with Abraham. Abraham sinned during the years between the making of the covenant and its confirmation to Isaac, so if God viewed the

---

6   Joyce Baldwin points out that normally, in this type of ritual, the animals were partly burned as an offering to the deity and a portion of the meat was used for a communal feast. See Joyce G. Baldwin, "The Message of Genesis 12—50," *The Bible Speaks Today* (Downers Grove, IL: InterVarsity Press, 1986), 53.

7   Victor Hamilton, *The Book of Genesis Chapters 1—17,* The New International Commentary on the Old Testament (Grand Rapids: Eerdmans, 1990), 432–433.

covenant as conditioned on obedience, He would have had ample reason for abrogating His promise. Instead He reaffirmed it. This is further evidence that the covenant was unconditional as far as involving any human responsibility.[8]

Let's look at the Abrahamic Covenant in Genesis 15 a little more closely to see if Ryrie's assertions stand up.

Genesis 15:1 begins with a dialogue between Abraham and God in which the latter promises Abraham an "exceedingly great reward." God had been promising Abraham an heir for a long time, yet Abraham had seen no evidence that God's promise would ever amount to anything. Abraham promptly betrays his fear that God won't accomplish all He promised, saying to the Lord, "I go childless" (v. 2). In the next verse, the fear is expressed as an accusation: "Look, you have given me no offspring" (v. 3). The Lord reaffirms the promise that Abraham's descendants will be numerous, "and he [Abraham] believed in the Lord, and He accounted it to him for righteousness" (v. 5). The Lord then repeats the promise to give Abraham all the land of Canaan as an inheritance. Nevertheless, Abraham needs to have something concrete upon which to hang his faith, and asks God, "Lord God, how shall I *know* that I will inherit it?" (v. 8, emphasis added). Abraham's question is thoroughly human.

Therefore, in response to Abraham's need for a tangible sign of God's faithfulness to His promise, the covenant ritual is celebrated, a sign Abraham understood and appreciated. The fact that the Lord alone passed between the pieces of the sacrifice probably indicates that it is God alone who is swearing the oath in order to reassure Abraham, vowing that He will indeed perform all He had promised. The specifics of the covenant are: (1) Abraham's descendants will be numerous (v. 5); (2) Abraham's descendants will be enslaved for four hundred years and then be delivered with great wealth (vv. 13, 14); (3) Abraham will die in peace; and (4) the land that Abraham's descendants will possess is defined as extending from the Euphrates to Wadi el-Arish on the border of Egypt (v. 18). This covenant was reaffirmed with Isaac and Jacob as well as with Moses.

As we will see below, all four of these promises were fulfilled by the time of Solomon's reign. It is therefore unnecessary to assume that the establishment of an Israeli state in 1948 was the long-anticipated fulfillment of God's promise to Abraham. God was way ahead of dispensationalism's prophetic schedule in fulfilling His promises to Abraham.

Furthermore, Charles Ryrie is simply wrong in asserting that there were no conditions attached to the Abrahamic covenant, or that there weren't

---

8   Ryrie, *Countdown*, 49. Emphasis in original.

any conditions mentioned when it was reaffirmed with Isaac and Jacob. Look, for instance, at Genesis 26:3–5, where the Lord reaffirmed the covenant with Isaac:

> Sojourn in this land, and I will be with you and bless you; for to you and your descendants I give all these lands, and I will perform the oath which I swore to Abraham your father. And I will make your descendants multiply as the stars of heaven; I will give to your descendants all these lands; and in your seed all the nations of the earth shall be blessed; because . . .

Because of what? Because the covenant with Abraham was unconditional; because Abraham's part in the covenant was irrelevant? Quite the contrary:

> . . . because *Abraham obeyed My voice and kept My charge, My commandments, My statutes, and My laws* (Genesis 26:3–5, emphasis added).

How much more explicit can it get? God was honoring the covenant because Abraham had also honored his part in the covenant.

Nor is Ryrie on track with his comment that Abraham's sins would have terminated the covenant: "if God viewed the covenant as conditioned on obedience, He would have had ample reason for abrogating His promise." Obviously the conditions of the Abrahamic covenant were not that Abraham be perfect and sinless, but that Abraham observe the specific commandments, statutes, and laws God had laid down. As we see in Genesis 26:5 cited above, Abraham was faithful to observe all these. Also, the fact that these covenant requirements were binding on Abraham's descendants is stated in Genesis 17:9, "And God said to Abraham, 'As for you, you shall keep My covenant, you *and your descendants after you* throughout their generations' " (emphasis added).

The Abrahamic covenant demanded that the people of Israel keep its provisions "throughout their generations" (Gen. 17:9). As Orthodox theologian I. M. Andreyev explains:

> The Hebrew people were the elect of God. To this people the Lord gave His original Revelation. To be selected by God means much is given, but much is also asked for in return. A great deal was given to the Hebrew people, and a great deal was to be answered for by them.[9]

Though much was given to ancient Israel, Andreyev says, much was also expected of Israel. God knows how to father His children, and He naturally has expectations of them, as does any good father. A good father often

---

9   I. M. Andreyev, *Orthodox Apologetic Theology* (Platina, CA: St. Herman of Alaska Brotherhood, 1995), 116.

gives his child gifts that are educational, and he normally places conditions on the gift to foster maturity in the child. If the child seriously misbehaves, the gift can even be taken away completely. The same holds with God's gift of the Holy Land. The gift was intended to be educational and to foster spiritual maturity in the Israelites, to raise them up as God's children so they could be witnesses of the Father to the rest of the world. Consequently, the gift of the land came with conditions. To suggest that the Abrahamic covenant was "unconditional" is to accuse God of being an irresponsible Father. Such a suggestion reveals an utter unfamiliarity with the ways of God.

National and Spiritual Promises

In the Abrahamic covenant, as is true generally with the covenants of the Old Testament, we find that God's promises to Israel had two dimensions, national and spiritual. The Church, being the spiritual remnant of Israel, has received the spiritual dimensions of the promises, and these are now being realized through her. The national dimensions of the promises received by old Israel were either fulfilled or abrogated because of unbelief.

The promise of the land of Canaan in the Abrahamic covenant, a national promise, was fulfilled after the conquest of the land. Several centuries after Abraham, Moses proclaimed to the people of Israel at the Jordan River, "See, I have set the land before you; go in and possess the land which the Lord swore to your fathers—to Abraham, Isaac, and Jacob—to give to them and their descendants after them" (Deut. 1:8). The promise given to Abraham was initially fulfilled when Joshua succeeded Moses as leader of Israel: "So Joshua took *the whole land*, according to *all that the Lord had said to Moses*; and Joshua gave it as an inheritance to Israel according to their divisions by their tribes" (Josh 11:23, emphasis added). We see that God's promise to Abraham of a nation in the land of Canaan was fulfilled when Joshua took "the whole land." This is emphasized again in Joshua:

> So the Lord gave to Israel *all the land of which he had sworn to give their fathers*, and they took possession of it and dwelt in it. The Lord gave them rest all around, *according to all that he had sworn to their fathers*. And not a man of all their enemies stood against them; the Lord delivered all their enemies into their hand. *Not a word failed of any good thing which the Lord had spoken to the house of Israel. All came to pass* (Josh. 21:43–45, emphasis added).

In describing Solomon's reign, which saw the zenith of Israel's expansion in the Middle East, 1 Kings 4:20 states, "Judah and Israel were as numerous *as the sand of the sea in multitude*, eating and drinking and rejoicing" (emphasis added). This is an allusion to the Abrahamic covenant, where the Lord promised Abraham that his descendants would be "as *the sand which is on the seashore*; and your descendants shall possess the gate of their enemies" (Gen. 22:17, emphasis added).

Did the descendants of Abraham "possess the gates of their enemies" during Solomon's reign? First Kings 4:21 adds: "So Solomon reigned over all kingdoms from the River [the Euphrates] to the land of the Philistines as far as the border of Egypt [at Wadi el-Arish]." This recalls God's promise to Abraham in Genesis 15:18: "To your descendants I have given this land, from the river of Egypt[10] to the great river, the River Euphrates."

Thus the purely temporal side of the promises in the Abrahamic covenant was fulfilled when Israel reached its apex under Solomon. Old Testament scholars like Simon J. DeVries see Solomon's reign as depicted in 1 Kings "as an ideal fulfillment of these promises [to the Genesis patriarchs]. . . . Certainly this comprised an empire far vaster than 'the land' that God had promised Abraham . . ."[11] The God of Abraham had proven faithful to Israel.

Yet, as we've seen, keeping the land was conditioned by Israel's fidelity to the Lord. When they were evil, God exiled them from the land; when they repented, God returned them (see Neh. 9:28). Israel rejected its Messiah and consequently God exiled them in A.D. 70. As Israel after the flesh remains unrepentant and continues to reject the Messiah, there is no basis for seeing the modern secular state of Israel as being ordained by God.[12]

The late Orthodox biblical scholar Georges Barrois once offered the following terse observation concerning the supposed "fulfillment" of Old Testament prophecy by modern Israel:

> The absolute demand [for holiness] made by the prophets, interpreters of the covenant, would certainly not support the contention of some Zionists that the modern Israeli state is, as such, the historical realization of the promise to the Fathers [i.e., the Patriarchs Abraham, Isaac, and Jacob]. A state operating on secularized political and economic principles may not easily claim its birthright under a covenant based exclusively on faith in the divine revelation.[13]

---

10 The "river of Egypt" is likely the "brook of Egypt" described as Israel's southern border in Num. 34:5. This would be Wadi el-Arish in northeastern Sinai.

11 Simon J. DeVries, *1 Kings*, Vol. 12, Word Biblical Commentary, 72.

12 Ultra-Orthodox Jews also reject the modern secular state of Israel for much the same reason as Orthodox Christians, i.e., because it is manmade and secular. Ultra-Orthodox Jews believe true Israel will be established in the land only when the Messiah comes.

13 Georges Barrois, *The Face of Christ in the Old Testament* (Crestwood, NY: St. Vladimir's Seminary Press, 1974), 127.

Barrois makes a valuable point: temporal restoration must not be disconnected from spiritual restoration. According to Orthodoxy, spiritual restoration always precedes physical restoration.

To summarize, the national dimensions of the promises have been either fulfilled, abrogated because of Israel's rejection of the Messiah, or subsumed into the New Covenant. We must stress that any interpretation of the Old Testament promises made without reference to the New Testament is doomed to go wrong. In speaking of the need for the New Covenant initiated by Christ, the Epistle to the Hebrews explains, "In that He says, 'A new covenant' [Jer. 31:31], He has made the first [covenant] obsolete. Now what is becoming obsolete and growing old is ready to vanish away" (Heb. 8:13). Thus we must understand that many of the features of the Old Testament, particularly the national ones, have become "obsolete" and have vanished away.

On the other hand, the spiritual blessings promised to Israel are being fulfilled in the Church. Hebrews, for example, interprets the Abrahamic covenant and the promise of the land as the Christian's heavenly hope (Heb. 11:8–16), thus giving the promise of the land a spiritual dimension. Unfortunately, this spiritual understanding of the Old Testament is sorely lacking among many modern Christians.

When God made His covenant with Abraham, He said, "In you shall all the families of the earth be blessed" (Gen. 12:3). How have all the families of the earth been blessed in Abraham? Through the Messiah—and it is the Church through which the gospel of the Messiah has been manifested to all "the families of the earth." This is worth repeating: it is the Church through which the blessings of the Messiah come. It certainly hasn't been the secular Israeli state created in 1948 that has been blessing the families of the earth with the gospel of Christ!

Unfortunately, by focusing so heavily on the national promises made to Israel, many non-Orthodox Christians have fallen into an extreme form of Israeli nationalism known as Zionism. Of course, the Christian gospel by its very nature transcends any form of nationalism. Christianity is by definition a universal message calling all of humanity—from all races, cultures, ethnicities, and walks of life—into the embrace of the one Body of Christ. To conform the gospel to the nationalism of any one people is plainly a perversion of the very essence of Christianity itself. We cannot link the gospel to Zionism without falling outside the bounds of Christianity. The ultimate tragedy of linking Christianity to any form of extreme nationalism is that it radically circumscribes Christian compassion to a single group of people—in this case, only to Jews.

Zionism

Yet what exactly is Zionism? Originally, Zionism emerged out of the various European nationalist movements of the nineteenth century. Rising nationalist sentiment inspired Jews like Moses Hess, David Luzatto, Leo Pinsker, Zvi Kalischer, and Yehudah Alkalai to attempt to raise the national consciousness of ghetto Jews in Europe. With the financial assistance of philanthropists such as Moses Montefiore, Edmond de Rothschild, and Maurice de Hirsch, a number of projects were started to help Jews return to Palestine.

Theodor Herzl turned Zionism into an effective worldwide political movement in 1897 with the first World Zionist Congress held in Basel, Switzerland. Herzl's nationalist agenda, however, did not go unopposed by other Jews, particularly Jewish fundamentalists and assimilationists. There were also internal divisions within the Zionist organization itself. At the 1905 Congress, one group left in frustration when a British proposal for establishing a Jewish homeland in Uganda was rejected. Nevertheless, the movement continued to gather momentum, and eventually secured approval from the British government to establish a homeland in Palestine, the famous Balfour Declaration of 1917. The Zionist movement continued to make political gains that finally resulted in the creation of the Jewish state following World War II.

Every nation is characterized by a certain amount of nationalism. It is natural that the Jewish people, just like other peoples, desire self-determination in a country of their own. For many Jews, Zionism is simply equated with a healthy patriotism. This is the sort of Zionism espoused by the Peace Now movement in Israel, which advocates peaceful coexistence with Arabs and a Palestinian homeland.

However, there is a danger when nationalist sentiments go unchecked. When nationalism becomes extreme, it can become xenophobic or even overtly racist. Nazism, for example, which started as a nationalist movement arising from Germany's humiliation following World War I, quickly grew into the assertion of Aryan superiority and the attempt to exterminate other racial and ethnic groups.

Many believe the brand of Zionism widely espoused by Orthodox Jews and dispensationalist millenarians borders on this racist extreme. Zionism, in the extreme form so prevalent in Israel today, excludes people on the basis of race and/or religious creed, and has resulted in the "ethnic cleansing" of the Palestinian people. Indeed, the United Nations, representing the international community, on November 10, 1975, actually declared Zionism a form of racism because of Israel's treatment of Palestinian minorities.

Dispensationalists, in their idealization of Israel, rarely consider the issue of human rights in connection with the Palestinians. In the West Bank, while it was under Israeli occupation, a Palestinian needed special permission to do such basic things as travel, build a house, or even dig a well in his own backyard. In fact, permission to dig for water was routinely denied in order to force the Palestinians off their land.

Israel issues ID cards designating whether one is a Jew or an Arab, and from what part of the country one comes. If an Arab is caught not carrying his identification card, he is automatically given six months in prison and possible deportation. (Needless to say, such a punishment does not apply to Jewish Israelis caught without their ID cards.) An Israeli prison is no place to be, not even for six months. Israeli prisons—particularly Ansar in the southern desert of Negev—are notorious for their use of torture. For the "crime" of forgetting an ID card, one can find oneself for days in a sewage-filled cell with a wet bag tied over one's head. Beatings, electric shock, prolonged sleep deprivation, and exposure to scorpions and the sun are routinely reported.

Historically, Israeli policy toward the Palestinians has been oriented not toward peaceful coexistence, but toward driving Palestinians out of the land they have known for centuries. The Israeli government has consistently confiscated Palestinian land, both public and private, so that upwards of four hundred Palestinian villages have utterly disappeared since 1948. Between April, 1948 and July, 1949, when Israel seized 23 percent of the land designated for a Palestinian state, the United Nations reported that 758,000 Arabs were driven from their homes by Israeli soldiers. Many were killed in cold blood. This policy was known as Plan Dalet (now made public through the opening of Israeli Defense Forces files), and involved the massacre at Deir Yassin, a small village near Jerusalem with no armed militia which had signed a nonaggression pact with neighboring Jewish towns. Led by the future Prime Minister of Israel, Menachem Begin, the Stern Gang took over the village and slaughtered 254 people, including women and children. Israel has as much right to exist as any other nation—but it has no right to deny existence to others.

Israel's deplorable human rights record has been well documented over the years and is readily available to anyone who cares to look. The modern state of Israel is a secular state driven by a frequently extreme form of nationalism; in no way can the modern state of Israel simply be equated with the Israel of the Old Testament, which was a theocracy built upon the Mosaic Covenant.

Those who think otherwise need to look at their Bibles again. According to the Mosaic Law, the resident alien (equivalent to today's Palestinian) had full civil rights in ancient Israel (e.g., Lev. 19:33, 34). The Prophets frequently denounced Israel for trampling on these rights. Malachi, in enumerating Israel's many transgressions of the Mosaic Law, lists the crime of "depriv[ing] aliens of justice" among sins such as sorcery and adultery (Mal. 3:5 NIV). Ezekiel also condemned the Israelites, for "the people . . . mistreat the alien, denying them justice" (Ezek. 22:29 NIV). In fact, when the Jews were returning from Babylon, Ezekiel specifically recalled the provisions of the Law concerning the resident alien. In an almost word-for-word citation of Leviticus 19:33, 34, he writes:

> "You are to distribute this land among yourselves according to the tribes of Israel. You are to allot it as an inheritance for yourselves *and for the aliens who have settled among you and who have children.* You are to consider them as native-born Israelites; along with you they are to be allotted an inheritance among the tribes of Israel. In whatever tribe the alien settles, there you are to give him his inheritance," declares the Sovereign Lord (Ezek. 47:21–23 NIV, emphasis added).

Note the resident aliens are to be considered "native-born Israelites." This means citizenship with all the rights that citizenship entails, including ownership of land. Modern Israel consistently denies these rights to Palestinians, even to those holding Israeli citizenship. Palestinians are routinely driven from their land and their homes are blown up. Entire Palestinian communities are frequently closed off so that people are unable to travel to work. Israel claims to be a Western-style democracy, yet the United States and most other democratic nations treat resident aliens far better than Israel does.

The purpose here is not to paint Israel as some sort of evil nation, which it is not. Nor can it be denied that Israelis have suffered atrocities from Arabs. However, the acute problems of social justice in Israel need to be highlighted to provide balance to the idealization of Israel as God's direct creation. Certainly there are many positive things to be said of Israel, but Israel is by no means God's shining beacon to the world for the end times.

Like any other nation, Israel has a dark side—a side glossed over or totally ignored by its zealous supporters. "Christian Zionists" tend to see the complex Israeli-Palestinian tragedy as a simple fight between good and evil, between "God's People" and implacable terrorists who indiscriminately murder innocent men, women, and children. It goes without saying that Christians are obliged to denounce terrorism (let's pray that we never see the day Christians actually debate the issue); however, while vehemently condemning the evil committed by Palestinian terrorists, today's pundits of prophecy dismiss out of hand the evil committed by Israelis. The reason is obvious: acknowledging the dark side of Israel would be inconsistent with their conception of Israel as God's end-times sign to the world. The tragic result of Christian Zionism is that it has blinded many to the oppression of the Palestinians, many of whom are our brethren in Christ.

One doesn't need to be particularly well read in the writings of the ancient Church to know that the early Christians weren't Zionists. (In fact, dispensationalists regularly castigate the Church Fathers for being "anti-Semitic.") A nascent Christian Zionism first emerges in a fifty-page English monograph entitled *Apocalypsis Apocalypseos*, written by a certain Thomas Brightman in 1585. Sir Henry Finch, a member of the British Parliament and one of Brightman's followers, gave Brightman's views more of a "biblical basis" in 1621 in a pamphlet called *The World's Great Restauration* [sic] *or Calling of the Jews and (with them) all the Nations of the Earth to the Faith of Christ.*

These ideas fermented rather slowly and became popular only during the nineteenth century—and even then, only in England and the United States. John Darby incorporated this brand of early Zionism into his theology. Darby's Zionism, in turn, influenced Lord Anthony Shaftesbury (1801–1885), British statesman and philanthropist. Shaftesbury envisioned the British empire "helping" God keep His promises to the Jews by employing British colonial might. Shaftesbury was a member of the evangelical Clapham Sect, which included other notable British statesmen.[14] As a result of Shaftesbury's influence, Zionist ideas entered into British political thinking.

The rise of Zionism during the late nineteenth century, with its goal of creating a Jewish state in Palestine, found ready allies among dispensationalists. Prominent evangelical supporters of Zionism included William Blackstone (1841–1935), author of *Jesus is Coming*, and Arno C. Gaebelein (1861–1945), who started a magazine and a press called *Our Hope* to provide literature for Jews on biblical prophecy. Such apocalyptic expectations regarding Israel were especially aroused following the Balfour Declaration in November, 1917, in which British foreign secretary Arthur Balfour declared: "His Majesty's Government views with favour the establishment in Palestine of a national home for the Jewish people, and will use their best endeavors to facilitate the achievement of this object." A month later, in December, 1917, the Turkish Ottoman Empire collapsed in the Middle East and

---

14 The Clapham Sect was a group of wealthy Anglican evangelicals who lived mostly in Clapham, England. The group was mainly concerned with asserting evangelical influence in the British government. Among its prominent members were parliamentarian and famous abolitionist William Wilberforce; Charles Grant, director of the East India Company; James Stephen, a leading barrister; Zachary Macaulay, member of the Sierra Leone Company and an abolitionist; and William Smith, dissenting member of Parliament and a Unitarian.

Palestine was in British hands. The establishment of Israel as an independent state following World War II rendered Zionism as indispensable to dispensationalism as the Nicene Creed is to Orthodoxy.

Millenarianism today is so permeated with a narrow Zionistic nationalism that pronouncements of damnation await any whose Christianity is not perceived as being properly subservient to the lordship of Israel. This is not said entirely tongue-in-cheek. So extreme can Zionism become among some that the Lord Himself often winds up elbowed off His throne as one's destiny becomes based upon a right relationship to the secular Jewish state.

While "Christian Zionists" may bristle at such a charge, their own writings confirm its truth. The International Christian Embassy–Jerusalem (ICEJ), for example, declares that "the destiny of nations, Christians, and even that of the church is linked to the way in which these groups respond to this restoration [of Israel]." [15] There it is: our destiny is said to be determined by our response to Israel, not to Christ. Similarly, Mike Evans asserts that, at the Lord's return, "Nations will be judged by whether they helped Jerusalem, or tried to destroy her, and rewarded and punished accordingly." [16] Thus, at the final judgment, our eternal reward is not decided so much by our relationship to Christ as by our relationship to Israel.

As bizarre as it may sound, many dispensationalists are firmly convinced that God blesses us or curses us depending upon our attitude toward the Israeli state. This belief is largely based on their interpretation of God's oath to Abraham in Genesis 12:3 ("I will bless those who bless you and curse those who curse you"). [17] To curse "Abraham" (meaning criticizing modern Israel) is to fall under God's curse, with all of the dire consequences which that implies. For them, our relationship to God—and, by extension, our ultimate salvation—is directly linked to our uncritical support ("blessing") of modern Israeli state policies.

All this applies to nations as well as to individual Christians. In his book

---

15 *Prepare Ye the Way of the Lord* (a brochure published by the International Christian Embassy–Jerusalem, 1991). Cited by Donald Wagner, *Anxious for Armageddon* (Scottsdale, PA: Herald Press, 1995), 104.

16 Evans, *Jerusalem*, 115.

17 While there isn't space here for a detailed explanation of this verse, commentaries usually point out that Gen. 12:3 harks back to mankind's blessing at creation (Gen. 1:28), its renewal after the flood (Gen. 9:1), and the table of nations listed in Gen. 10. The context of Gen. 12:3 makes explicit that people are not judged by their response to Abraham's person as such, but by their response to God's working in Abraham to realize the divine plan (see Ps. 72:17, 18 and Is. 19:23–25 for this interpretation of Gen. 12:3). The New Testament in Acts 3:25 and Gal. 3:8 sees the fulfillment of Gen. 12:3 in the Advent of Christ, the ultimate Seed of Abraham, in whose divine Person all the nations of the earth have been blessed. Therefore, Gen. 12:3 points to the realization of God's plan for mankind in the Person of Christ, not to an extreme form of Zionism.

The Final Battle, for instance, Hal Lindsey presents what he believes is evidence of waning support for Israel in the United States, and concludes (after somberly quoting Genesis 12:3) with the warning:

> The U.S. has been protected by God because it has been a haven for Israelites and an ally for their survival. It has been one of those great factors in our protection. Now that we are turning away, look for the "Late Great United States." [18]

Like many, Lindsey sees an uncritical Zionism as being as essential to national security as a heavily armed military—perhaps even more so.

We discussed in the last chapter how Christians are obliged to love and respect their Jewish neighbors. This means we are not to reduce them to pagan talismans by which we receive blessings and curses. Rather, we must affirm them as authentic persons to be valued in their own right. Nor must our love for our neighbor be limited to our Jewish neighbors only. Palestinians, many of whom are fellow Christians, are also entitled to our full love and respect. Moreover, Palestinian Muslims—who often know little or nothing of the gospel—need to be exposed to genuine Christian love. How can we expect them to come to a saving knowledge of the truth if they are convinced that the gospel mandates their extinction as a free people in their homeland?

The biblical adage that we can recognize a tree by its fruit is particularly relevant in connection with the dispensationalist understanding of Israel. The fruit that has resulted from the identification of national Israel with true Israel is the transmogrification of Christianity into an extreme Jewish nationalism. This alone must lead us to question the understanding of Israel according to modern end-times speculation. True Christianity never allows an earthly kingdom to usurp its commitment to the Kingdom of heaven.

Now comes the big question raised by millennialist theology: Is the existence of the modern state of Israel in accordance with biblical prophecy? Or is the reverse true: Have the doom-sayers made biblical prophecy accord with Israel?

---

18 Lindsey, *Final Battle*, 231.

Chapter Eight

1948 and the Wandering Dispensationalist

See! Your house [the Temple] is left to you desolate; for I say to you, you shall see Me no more till you say, "Blessed is He who comes in the name of the Lord!"
—The Gospel According to St. Matthew 23:38, 39

Moreover, at that feast which we call Pentecost, as the priests were going by night into the inner [court of the] Temple, as their custom was, to perform their sacred ministrations, they said that, in the first place, they felt a quaking, and heard a great noise, and after that they heard a sound as of a great multitude, saying, "Let us remove hence."
—Flavius Josephus, first-century Jewish historian, recounting in his *Wars of the Jews* the ominous signs preceding the destruction of Israel in A.D. 70

LET'S QUICKLY REVIEW the prophecy gurus' teaching on modern Israel: The Jews ceased being a nation in the land of Palestine in A.D. 70 after an unsuccessful attempt to liberate themselves from Roman rule. Jerusalem and its Temple were destroyed, and the people were afterwards scattered among the various nations of the earth, to be "wandering Jews" until the rebirth of the nation in 1948. This event was predicted through the "literal" interpretation of Scripture, say the modern soothsayers of Armageddon, and thus validates their approach to prophecy.

According to these "experts," there is a radical distinction between Israel and the Church, and God plans to deal with each separately. God's national promises to Israel are still valid and must be fulfilled once God has finished with the Church. Consequently, God is about to rapture the Church out of the world, judge the earth for its sins, and fulfill His promises to the nation of Israel during the millennium.

At the end of the previous chapter, we asked whether the pundits of prophecy read the Bible and see in its pages the creation of Israel in 1948, or whether they have looked at modern Israel and then decided the Bible must have foretold its creation. The answer is the latter. When the Zionist movement was forming among Jews in the late nineteenth century, it was natural that the movement borrow passages from the Prophets that spoke of the regathering of the remnant of Israel from exile. It was certainly not the first time that a political movement used prophecy in support of its cause. The dispensationalist movement picked up on these Zionist interpretations of prophecy and also championed the future creation of a Jewish state. When the Zionist movement ultimately achieved its aim with the creation of Israel in 1948, this was seen by dispensationalists as a vindication of their interpretation of prophecy. Since then, anything that happens concerning Israel is seen, in one way or another, as the fulfillment of some prophecy.

This belief that Israel must be reestablished just before the end was fairly common in the United States at the beginning of the nineteenth century; and if successfully predicting Israel's rebirth as a nation validates dispensationalism, then it must also validate a number of other, more bizarre theological systems.

For example, John Thomas, a British physician who immigrated to America in 1832, also looked for the return of the Jews to Palestine, linking an incipient Zionism with the coming of Christ's Kingdom. Thomas was initially a Campbellite, but later joined William Miller and his end-of-the-world craze. He eventually went off to start his own sect, the anti-Trinitarian Christadelphians (Brothers of Christ). Along with other seriously aberrant ideas—such as Jesus Christ not existing except in the mind of the Father before the Incarnation—the Christadelphians reject the immortality of the soul, a personal devil, and a "heaven beyond the skies." Salvation is through good works, and the Christian's ultimate reward is Jesus' return to reign in Jerusalem. The righteous will reign with Him and the wicked will simply be annihilated. There are still twenty thousand Christadelphians in Britain and about the same number in twenty states in the U.S.

Also at the start of the nineteenth century, the Mormon prophet Joseph Smith, Jr. (1805–1844), taught that the Jews must regather in Palestine. Then, when Christ returns, He will rule the earth from Jerusalem—and Independence, Missouri. (Perhaps as the Lord's summer home?) Joseph Smith incorporated this belief in the restoration of Israel as Article 10 of his thirteen Articles of Faith: "We believe in the literal gathering of Israel and in the restoration of the Ten Tribes." This declaration simply reaffirmed what is stated repeatedly in the Book of Mormon.[1] In 1841, believing that the "times of the Gentiles" would soon be fulfilled, Smith sent Elder Orson Hyde on a mission to Jerusalem to dedicate the Holy Land for the return of the Jews and for the rebuilding of the Temple. Mormons also see prophetic significance in the year 1948.

Charles Taze Russell (1852–1916), the founder of today's Jehovah's Witnesses, was another who expected the Jews to return soon to Palestine. An early Zionist, he included the name "Zion" in almost everything he created. In 1879 Russell launched his magazine, *Zion's Watch Tower and Herald of Christ's Presence,* and then went on to found Zion's Watchtower Tract Society in 1884. Ironically, now that there exists a state of Israel, modern Jehovah's Witnesses no longer see any significance in a Jewish return to Palestine!

"For what saith the Scripture?"

As has already been noted, there is a certain reasoning with regard to the belief about the modern Israeli nation and prophecy. The advocates of imminent Armageddon reason that their system of interpreting prophecy predicted the return of the Jews to Palestine. The Jews did return to Palestine "in fulfillment of biblical prophecy"; therefore, they conclude, their approach to prophecy must be correct.

While the advent of the Israeli nation may appear on the surface to be a confirmation of their prophetic system, still, the question remains: Did Scripture really predict the birth of Israel in 1948? After all, if someone went around arguing that the Bible "predicted" the reelection of President Bill Clinton in 1996, and that Clinton's subsequent election confirmed that person's whole system of biblical prophecy, would it not be proper to question whether the Bible actually predicted the reelection of Bill Clinton in the first place? Similarly, we need to examine whether the Bible actually predicted the creation of the state of Israel in 1948.

Before we examine some of the specific proof texts cited as predicting the creation of the modern secular state of Israel, we should first take a moment to discuss how the Fathers of the early Church approached the Bible. The Fathers were very conscious of the fact that the Scriptures were inspired by the Holy Spirit. Consequently, they believed that there was always a deeper, spiritual meaning to any text that went beyond the surface meaning. The Fathers coined the term "literal interpretation" for the surface meaning of a

---

1 See James Talmage, *A Study of the Articles of Faith* (Salt Lake City: Deseret Book Co., 1984), 301–304.

text, and they used this literal meaning as a springboard for a deeper, spiritual meaning. To arrive at this spiritual meaning, they approached the text in a variety of ways.

One approach was to find the *typical* meaning. This method finds something in the text and interprets it as a type foreshadowing something greater. Paul used this approach in 1 Corinthians 10:1–4, where he interprets the Exodus account as foreshadowing Christ, baptism, and the Eucharist. The *allegorical* approach derives a spiritual meaning from a narrative. Characters and events are interpreted as representing abstract ideas, principles, and forces. In this method, the Fathers looked for a deeper, symbolic parallel sense in the text. Paul employed this method in Galatians 4:21–31. Another way to understand the text was to find an *anagogical* meaning, whereby heavenly realities are detected in references to earthly things in the Bible. A reference to the earthly Temple might be understood as an allusion to the heavenly Temple (see Rev. 15:5—16:1), the earthly Jerusalem as an allusion to the new, heavenly Jerusalem (see Heb. 12:22), and so forth.

The proof texts brought forth as allegedly predicting the 1948 establishment of Israel (all of which are from the Old Testament) were generally interpreted by the Fathers in the spiritual fashion described above. As we will see later, the New Testament and the Fathers interpreted many of these biblical passages as applying to the formation of the Church on the Day of Pentecost, not to national Israel in 1948.

The dispensationalist millenarian, on the other hand, is appealing exclusively to what he believes is the "literal" meaning of these biblical texts. Usually without being aware of it, however, he has been heavily influenced by the presuppositions of dispensationalist doctrine and its interpretive tradition in arriving at this supposedly clear, literal meaning. The fact is, what is "clear" to him is not at all clear to most Christians—which is not surprising since most Christians aren't dispensationalists. From the Orthodox perspective, the dispensationalist interpretation of these proof texts is a novel contrivance held by a minority.

Since dispensationalist beliefs concerning Israel hinge on a literal understanding of certain prophecies, we are going to focus primarily on the literal meaning of these prophecies as determined by the text's surrounding context. The literal interpretation we arrive at will be consistent with historic Christian teaching and the exegesis (interpretation) of sound biblical scholars.

The Literal Truth?

Which scriptures supposedly predicted the formation of the Jewish state in 1948? The passages most frequently cited are from Ezekiel, particularly chapters 36 and 37. For example, Ezekiel 36:24 reads, "For I will take you from among the nations, gather you out of all countries, and bring you into your own land."

Another passage is Ezekiel 39:27, 28:

> When I have brought them back from the peoples and gathered them out of their enemies' lands, and I am hallowed in them in the sight of many nations, then they shall know that I am the Lord their God, who sent them into captivity among the nations, but also brought them back to their own land, and left none of them captive any longer.

Hal Lindsey quotes Jeremiah 23:7, 8 as a prediction of the large number of Jews who would flee to Israel after the collapse of the Soviet Union.[2] Note the reference to the "north country" that Lindsey interprets as Russia:

> "Therefore, behold, the days are coming," says the Lord, "that they shall no longer say, 'As the Lord lives who brought up the children of Israel from the land of Egypt,' but, 'As the Lord lives who brought up and led the descendants of the house of Israel from the north country and from all the countries where I had driven them.' And they shall dwell in their own land."

It is universally agreed that these verses point to a restoration of Israel after a time of exile. The problem is that, according to most reputable biblical commentaries, these verses don't address the exile that began in A.D. 70, but the exile that occurred during the ascendancy of the Babylonian Empire under Nebuchadnezzar II (605–562 B.C.). Nebuchadnezzar conquered Judea in 598 B.C. and deported many Jews to Babylon. Later, after an unsuccessful revolt by King Zedekiah, Nebuchadnezzar destroyed Jerusalem in 586 B.C., after a two-year siege, and deported an even larger group to Babylon.

Jeremiah 23:7, 8 cited above is about this Babylonian exile. One hint pointing in this direction is that the Prophet declares the imminent fall of Jerusalem to the Babylonians several verses earlier: "And I will give you into the hand of those who seek your life, and into the hand of those whose face you fear—the hand of Nebuchadnezzar king of Babylon and the hands of the Chaldeans [i.e., the Babylonians]" (Jer. 22:25). Jeremiah announces the fate of King Jehoiachin (Jer. 22:24–30)—who ruled only three months before being deported to Babylon to be held as a royal hostage until the death of Nebuchadnezzar—and then castigates Israel's religious leaders, who greatly contributed to Israel's downfall by not leading the people in the ways of righteousness (Jer. 23:1, 2). After all, it was because of the people's sin that God sent them into Babylon.

2   Lindsey, *Planet Earth—2000 A.D.*, 136.

But immediately Jeremiah promises that the Lord "will gather the remnant . . . out of all countries where I have driven them" (Jer. 23:3). The promise is to restore the nation and set up good leaders for Israel, which inspires Jeremiah to prophesy the day when the Messiah will appear and Himself lead the people (Jer. 23:4–6). Next follow the verses that Lindsey cites, which repeat the promise of the return from Babylonian captivity. So what is the "north country" referred to in verse 8? Most commentators say it refers to Assyria. Assyria had conquered Northern Israel in 722 B.C. and assimilated the ten northern tribes into the Assyrian Empire. The Babylonians conquered the Assyrians in 605 B.C. and integrated their empire into the Babylonian Empire. Jeremiah in 23:8 is contemplating a general restoration of exiles back to the Promised Land and a rebirth of the nation.

Therefore, in context, Jeremiah 23:7, 8 says nothing on the literal level about the regathering of Israel in 1948 or the migration of Russian Jews in the 1990s. The restoration spoken of by Jeremiah found its fulfillment in 539 B.C., when Cyrus the Great, the king of the Medes and Persians, captured Babylon and allowed the exiles to return home in 538. The same can be said for all the Old Testament verses that supposedly "predict" the creation of the Israeli state in 1948, including the verses from Ezekiel. Since Ezekiel is so frequently cited in this capacity, it is worthwhile to take a look at the book as a whole.

We really know very little about the Prophet Ezekiel. He was a priest and the son of a priest named Buzi. Ezekiel expected to spend his life serving in the Temple, but was exiled in 597 B.C. after Nebuchadnezzar's brief siege of Jerusalem. He settled in an area near the Chebar River at a place called Tel Abib (Ezek. 3:22–24). Four years later, in 593 B.C., God called Ezekiel to the prophetic ministry.

Though the Book of Ezekiel appears forbidding in its symbolism and extravagant imagery, the basic structure is simple and orderly. It begins with a vision of the majesty of God and Ezekiel's call to be a prophet to Israel (chs. 1—3). Then there is a long section that predicts and justifies God's wrath upon Jerusalem and its inhabitants (chs. 4—24). Then, after a section that gives God's judgments against Israel's neighbors (chs. 25—32), Ezekiel declares, "The city [Jerusalem] has been captured!" (Ezek. 33:21). This is the turning point in the book, and Ezekiel starts proclaiming another message (chs. 34—37). Ezekiel still explains the causes of Israel's ruin (e.g., irresponsible shepherds over the people), but he now begins to hold out the promise of an eventual Good Shepherd and a messianic age. That God will restore the people to the land is the theme of chapters 36 and 37, which section includes the famous vision of dry bones being resurrected. Just as the dry bones were brought back to life, so will Israel be resurrected once the Lord brings her back from Babylon. Chapters 38 and 39 look into the distant future, "after many days" and "in the latter years" (38:8), and describe in apocalyptic terms the victory of Israel over Gog and Magog, symbolizing all of Israel's enemies. Finally, the last section of the book is a detailed vision much like the one that began the book. Ezekiel describes a new Jerusalem with an ideal Temple in which God will dwell with His people forever (chs. 40—48).

Having looked at the overall layout of the book, let's turn briefly to Ezekiel, chapters 36 and 37. Chapter 36 begins by promising to return the people to the Holy Land because "the enemy" has been boasting of having conquered the land that God promised to the people of Israel (v. 2). Because of God's anger with the nations, God will bless Israel (36:1–15). Then the prophecy goes on to explain that God exiled the people "for the blood they had shed on the land, and for their idols with which they had defiled it" (v. 18). Israel was exiled to Babylon for idolatry, which was not the case with the exile in A.D. 70. This leads us to understand this section as relating to the Babylonian captivity.

But even in Babylonian exile the Jews had profaned God's name among the Gentiles, so that the restoration occurs despite Israel's reprobate nature:

> But I had concern for My holy name, which the house of Israel had profaned among the nations wherever they went. Therefore say to the house of Israel, "Thus says the Lord God: 'I do not do this for your sake, O house of Israel, but for My holy name's sake, which you have profaned among the nations wherever you went.' " (36:21, 22)

God then declares that He will cleanse Israel by sprinkling the people with water and giving them a new heart, putting His Holy Spirit within them so that they will walk in His statutes (36:25–27). This has traditionally been understood by Christians as foreshadowing Pentecost and the ultimate restoration of Israel in the formation of the Church. Again, only a few verses later, it is repeated: " 'Not for your sakes do I do this,' says the Lord God, 'let it be known to you' " (v. 32). The reason for the restoration is so that "the nations which are left all around you shall know that I, the Lord, have rebuilt the ruined places and planted what was left desolate" (v. 36). In other words, God used Babylon to exile Israel into the surrounding nations to teach Israel to fear the Lord. The Lord now returns Israel to the land and blesses it to teach the nations that all that happens is by the design of the God of Israel, "for My holy name's sake."

Chapter 37 is divided into two parts. The first part is the vision of a valley of dried bones that God resurrects into "an exceedingly great army"

(37:10). This is "the whole house of Israel" (v. 11) that had been dead in Babylon but which is being restored to national life. The first vision ends with the promise of a spiritual as well as a national restoration from Babylon, which Christians have tended to see as finding its fulfillment in the gospel: "I will put My Spirit in you, and you shall live, and I will place you in your own land. Then you shall know that I, the Lord, have spoken it and performed it" (v. 14).

In the second part, God instructs Ezekiel to find two sticks to represent both Judea and the northern kingdom of Israel (conquered by Assyria in 722 B.C.). These two sticks are to be held end to end in the Prophet's hand so that they will look like one stick: "Thus says the Lord God: 'Surely I will take the stick of . . . the tribes of Israel . . . and I will join them . . . with the stick of Judah . . . and they will be one in My hand" (v. 19). The rest of the chapter depicts a golden age when the people of Judea and the scattered people of the northern kingdom will be cleansed of all sin and united under the Messiah, "David my servant" (v. 24). This is obviously not a description of today's secular Israel.

In the last half of Ezekiel 37, the Prophet has taken an idealized past and used it as a model to describe the coming messianic age. In this messianic age there will be a new testament (or "covenant"): "Moreover I will make a covenant of peace with them, and it shall be an everlasting covenant with them; I will establish them and multiply them, and I will set my sanctuary in their midst forevermore" (v. 26). The traditional Christian perspective is that this new covenant of peace came into existence with the First Advent of Jesus Christ. As a result, all the nations, including the remnants of the northern kingdom, have been "grafted" onto Israel under the kingship of the Messiah, the Lord Jesus Christ (see Rom. 11:13–18). Thus Christians traditionally have seen this prophecy as already fulfilled in the Church.

There is no evidence that the "literal" meaning of the prophecy in Ezekiel 36 and 37 is Israel's return to Palestine in 1948. Given the overall context of Ezekiel, the evidence points to the exile in Babylon because of idolatry (see Ezek. 36:18; 37:23) rather than the exile of A.D. 70 as a result of its rejection of the Messiah. Even Ezekiel 38 offers the prophecy crowd no support. This chapter describes an attack by Gog and Magog upon Israel, which prophecy pundits like Hal Lindsey interpret as Russia invading modern Israel. However, Revelation 20 describes this as happening *at the end* of the millennium, which these same pundits believe will be after Christ's Second Coming. Thus, even by their own millenarian understanding of prophecy, the prophecy gurus' interpretation of Ezekiel 38 cannot stand.

The only possible literal interpretation of Ezekiel 36—40 points to the return from Babylon around 538 B.C., following the conquest by Cyrus the Great. The same can be said for most of the Old Testament proof texts brought forward that allegedly predict the establishment of Israel in 1948: they speak of Israel's return from Babylon in 538 B.C. Consequently, the entire end-times scenario that has the modern restoration of Israel as its prophetic cornerstone collapses right from the start.

However, it will be objected, not all of the prophecies of restoration can be ascribed to the return of the Jews in 538 B.C. Consider Amos 9:14, 15, for example:

> I will bring back the captives of my people Israel; they shall build the waste cities and inhabit them; they shall plant vineyards and drink wine from them; they shall also make gardens and eat fruit from them. I will plant them in their land, and no longer shall they be pulled up from the land I have given them, says the Lord your God.

How can this be understood as referring to the return of the Jews from Babylon, it is sometimes argued, when the Scripture says that they will "no longer . . . be pulled up from the land I have given them"? In fact, they were pulled up again from the land in A.D. 70 and weren't restored until 1948! Certainly, it is asserted, Amos 9:14, 15 must be referring to the restoration of Israel just prior to the Second Coming of Christ in our days.

Actually, this is another of those biblical passages that the Fathers interpreted as speaking of the Church. Indeed, this is also how the Apostles themselves interpreted it: Amos 9:11, 12 is cited by James in the Acts of the Apostles as already being fulfilled. In Acts 15:16, 17, James takes the passage in Amos 9 regarding the rebuilding of the tabernacle of David (i.e., the Davidic kingdom), and all the nations flocking to it, and interprets it as the Gentiles coming into the Church—and not as the restoration of Israel in 1948. In other words, the Church is the fulfillment of the Davidic kingdom. Accepting James' interpretation in the Acts of the Apostles as authoritative, the Orthodox interpret the entire passage in Amos 9:11–15 as already fulfilled.

William Alnor, whose strident comments we examined in a previous chapter, would of course hotly disagree with what has been said above. He is certain that Scripture points to a restoration of national Israel in 1948. What scriptures does he offer to support this? In his book *Soothsayers of the Second Advent*, Alnor points to Isaiah 11:11; 14:1 and, of course, to Ezekiel 37:12, 14. The prophecy in Isaiah 11:11, 12 runs:

> It shall come to pass in that day that the Lord shall set His hand again a second time to recover the remnant of His people who are left, from Assyria and Egypt, from Pathos and Cush, from Elam and Shinar, from Hamath and the islands of the sea. He will set up a banner for the nations, and will

assemble the outcasts of Israel, and gather together the dispersed of Judah, from the four corners of the earth.

Is the 1948 restoration of national Israel the likeliest "literal" interpretation of this text? Again, let's look at the context. In the immediately preceding chapter of Isaiah, chapter 10, the subject is the judgment of Assyria, which had conquered the northern kingdom of Israel. In Isaiah 10:20–34, God tells the people, "Do not be afraid of the Assyrian" (v. 24), and promises their restoration from captivity. This restoration happened with the rise of the Persian Empire, which allowed the Jews exiled by the Assyrians and the Babylonians to return to their land. Then in Isaiah 11:1–10, God promises the people their ultimate restoration in the Messiah, the "stem of Jesse."

Note that Isaiah 11:11, 12 speaks of a *second* restoration of Israel. That this is a "second time to recover the remnant of His people" points to the first recovery of God's people from captivity in Egypt (see v. 16: "as it was for Israel in the day he came up from the land of Egypt"). The Jews in Babylon frequently took encouragement from remembering their last deliverance from bondage in Egypt (see Jer. 16:14, 15; 23:7, 8; Zech. 10:10, 11). If one interprets 1948 as the fulfillment of this verse, then wouldn't we have expected to read of *the third time* God recovered "the remnant of his people" from captivity?

"Yet," it will surely be objected, "in the prophecy the exiles are brought from many different nations and even from distant islands, not just from Babylon." The exiles who were to come from the various far-off lands had been sold into slavery by the Assyrians and Babylonians, a common practice in the ancient world and one that is often decried in the Bible (Ezek. 27:13; Joel 3:7, 8; Amos 1:6–9; Rev. 18:13). These people were eventually freed under the new Persian Empire established by Cyrus. According to Isaiah 11:16, these people, "the remnant of His people," will come home upon a special "highway" (Heb. *mesillah*). The Persians are known to have developed extensive networks of highways to bind their empire together, a concept later taken up by the Romans. Therefore, the fact that the exiles come "from the four corners of the earth" in Isaiah 11:11, 12 is perfectly consistent with the return of the Jews under Cyrus the Great.

Even more dubious is Alnor's use of Isaiah 14:1, "For the Lord will have mercy on Jacob, and will still choose Israel, and settle them in their own land." This one doesn't even come close to predicting the creation of the Israeli state in 1948. The entire previous chapter of Isaiah is devoted to proclaiming judgment on Babylon (13:1–22), and the verses following Isaiah 14:1 deal with the fall of the king of Babylon (14:3–11). Moreover, after a passage dealing with the fall of Lucifer personified as the king of Babylon,

Isaiah 14:22, 23 predicts the destruction of the Babylonian Empire. What, then, are the odds that the return of Israel to "their own land" spoken of in Isaiah 14:1 is a return from Babylonian captivity? On a literal level, therefore, there is absolutely no evidence that Alnor's proof text refers to the creation of Israel in 1948.[3]

In the Latter Days

One final type of "restoration" proof text ought to be examined. In Jeremiah 30:18–24 we read:

> Thus says the Lord: "Behold, I will bring back the captivity of Jacob's tents, and have mercy on his dwelling places;" . . . The fierce anger of the Lord will not return until He has done it, and until He has performed the intents of His heart. In the latter days you will consider it.

This passage, like the other ones we've seen, could be shown to have already been fulfilled simply by looking at the surrounding context. However, what makes this passage different is that, at the end of verse 24, we have a reference to its being fulfilled "in the latter days." To many, the term "the latter days" means "today," or "our own times." In a sense, the mistake is natural since we have grown accustomed to understanding the phrase "latter days" in the sense of those days that immediately precede the end of the world.

In reality, however, the expression "the latter days" has a far wider meaning in the Bible. In the marginal cross-reference to Jeremiah 30:24 cited above, we usually find listed Genesis 49:1, which reads: "And Jacob called his sons and said, 'Gather together, that I may tell you what shall befall you in the last days." Here, "last days" simply means "in the future," the near as well as the far future.

Returning to Jeremiah, we have another example where "the latter days" refers to an event in the near future. In Jeremiah 48:47 and 49:39, the Lord passes judgment on Moab and Elam. The Lord, Jeremiah declares, will return the captives Moab and Elam acquired in the Babylonian captivity. Each time the prophecy ends by stating that this will come to pass "in the latter days" (Jer. 48:47; 49:39). Obviously, as both Moab and Elam have long ceased being nations (Moab, around 582 B.C.; and Elam sometime around 596 B.C.), and are consequently no longer holding Jewish captives, the phrase "latter days" doesn't refer to the days just prior to the restoration of Israel in 1948.

---

3   A short list of the major prophecies that allegedly "predicted" the creation of the Israeli state in 1948 would include: Is. 11:1, 2; 14:1; 27:13; 43:5–7; 60:21; Jer. 16:14–16; 31:21–40; 32:37–44; Ezek. 11:17; 20:33–38, 42; 37:21, 22; 39:25–29; and some rather obscure passages from the minor Prophets.

In Daniel 2:28 and 10:14, the expression "the latter days" is connected to visions of the demise of Babylon and the future Persian, Greek, and Roman empires, not to the turn of the second millennium A.D. We could go on, but it ought to be apparent that "the latter days" is simply a Semitic expression meaning "in the future." (Other verses where the expression refers to the near future are Num. 24:14; Deut. 4:30; 31:29; and Jer. 23:20.) In Jeremiah 30:24 cited above, the "latter days" are simply the days after the end of the seventy-year Babylonian captivity.

Dispensationalists and the Temple of Doom

Another argument for the restoration of the state of Israel in 1948 stems indirectly from 2 Thessalonians 2:3, 4, which states the Second Coming won't occur until "the man of sin [the Antichrist] is revealed, the son of perdition, who opposes and exalts himself above all that is called God or that is worshiped, so that he sits as God in the temple of God, showing himself that he is God." The Temple in Jerusalem was destroyed in A.D. 70, and today the Dome of the Rock, Islam's third holiest shrine, sits on the site where the Temple once stood. It is argued that Paul's statement in 2 Thessalonians 2:4 implies the Jerusalem Temple will be reconstructed during the Tribulation so that, just before the Second Coming, the Antichrist can then enter it and demand worship. The point is, the existence of a functioning Temple in Jerusalem could occur only if the Jews controlled the Holy Land.

There is some question whether or not Paul is talking about a literal temple in 2 Thessalonians 2:3, 4. It could be, as F. F. Bruce asserts, that Paul is talking about the Jerusalem Temple "in a metaphorical sense," [4] or even the Christian Church as "the temple of God" (see 1 Cor. 3:16; 2 Cor. 6:16; Eph. 2:21). There are actually several possibilities here, and one can just as well take Paul literally as not.

Many in the early Church believed a literal Temple would be rebuilt by the Antichrist before the Lord's Second Coming. St. Irenaeus believed that the Temple would someday be rebuilt, stating that the Antichrist "will reign for three years and six months, and sit in the Temple at Jerusalem; and then the Lord will come from heaven in the clouds." [5] Hippolytus of Rome wrote a treatise around the year 200 called *On the Antichrist*, the most comprehensive discussion of the subject of the Antichrist in early Christian literature. In large measure, Hippolytus simply expands on Irenaeus' writing on the end times. Hippolytus, after describing how the Antichrist will mimic the Lord,

---

4   F. F. Bruce, *1 & 2 Thessalonians*, Vol. 45, Word Biblical Commentary, 169.
5   Irenaeus, *Heresies*, 5:30:4.

states: "The Savior raised up and showed His holy flesh like a temple (see John 2:19), and he [the Antichrist] will raise a temple of stone in Jerusalem." [6] However, like Irenaeus, Hippolytus doesn't elaborate on the subject of a future Temple.

Origen in the third century also seemed to believe that the Antichrist would defile a rebuilt Temple.[7] St. Cyril of Jerusalem (315–386) believed the Antichrist would rebuild the Temple in order to convince the Jews that he is their long-awaited Messiah. After there is no longer any trace of the former Temple, then the Antichrist appears to rebuild it: "Then shall he come 'with all signs and lying wonders' (2 Thess. 2:9), exalting himself against all idols." [8] St. John of Damascus (675–749), in his classic *Exposition of the Orthodox Faith,* also states that the Antichrist would deify himself in a rebuilt Jewish Temple, citing 2 Thessalonians 2:3, 4.[9]

It would be a mistake, however, to conclude that all the early commentators on 2 Thessalonians 2:4 thought that there must be a rebuilt Temple in Jerusalem during the Tribulation. St. John Chrysostom (347–407), for example, understood the "temple" referred to by Paul as the Church, based on the fact that Christians had always called their churches "temples." John states that the Antichrist will proclaim his blasphemies in the church in Jerusalem, and "not that in Jerusalem only, but also in every church." [10] Chrysostom's opinion on this verse still carries great weight within Orthodoxy. Elsewhere, citing Luke 21:24 and Matthew 24:2, Chrysostom specifically states that the Temple and the sacrificial system associated with it would never be reinstated.[11]

Chrysostom's thinking was not original to him. The belief that the Church itself was the end-times temple goes back in the writings of the Fathers as far as *The Epistle of Barnabas* in the early second century.[12] Jerome (331–420), a great biblical scholar of the early Church, wrote a letter in which he interpreted the temple in 2 Thessalonians 2:3 as the Church.[13]

---

6   Hippolytus of Rome, *On the Antichrist*, 6.

7   Origen, *Against Celsus*, 46.

8   Cyril of Jerusalem, *Catechetical Lectures*, 15:15.

9   John of Damascus, *Exposition of the Orthodox Faith*, 4:26. The *Exposition* is actually the third part of a larger work called *The Fount of Wisdom*.

10 John Chrysostom, *Homily 3 on 2 Thessalonians*, 2:4.

11 John Chrysostom, *Discourses Against Judaizing Christians*, Discourse 5, 1:6. See the translation by Paul Harkins in Vol. 68, The Fathers of the Church (Washington, D.C.: The Catholic University of America Press, 1979), 99.

12 *The Epistle of Barnabas*, 16:6–10. Pseudo-Barnabas is interpreting what appears to be a free paraphrase/conflation of Dan. 9:24–27: "when the week is ended that a temple of God shall be built gloriously in the name of the Lord."

13 Jerome, Letter 121:11; written to a lady in Gaul named Algasia in 406.

Emperor Julian the Apostate made an attempt to rebuild the Temple in the year 363. Desiring to discredit "the pale Galilean," as he called Jesus Christ, he endeavored to reverse Christ's judgment on the Temple: "See, your house is left to you desolate . . . Assuredly I say to you, not one stone shall be left here upon another that shall not be thrown down" (Matt. 23:38; 24:2). With help from the local governor of the province, the guidance of Jewish leaders, and under the able supervision of Alypius, the praetorian prefect of Britain, the work of clearing the rubble and constructing the Temple commenced. Cyril, the bishop of Jerusalem, is said to have looked on impassively at the proceedings and predicted the attempt was doomed since it was impossible to reverse what Christ Himself had decreed unless the Lord willed it.

According to the account left us by Ammianus Marcellinus, a pagan historian who served in Julian's army on the Persian frontier in 363, earthquakes plagued the construction from the beginning. Nevertheless, the project was pushed on. Finally, Marcellinus relates, balls of fire burst forth from the foundation of the temple site that burned some to death and made work impossible. Julian was eventually forced to abandon the project, which John Chrysostom and other Christians saw as a great vindication of Christ's prophecy in Matthew 24:2.

Assuming Paul meant a literal temple would be rebuilt someday, which is one traditional Orthodox Christian understanding of 2 Thessalonians 2:4, is the 1948 reconstitution of the state of Israel necessary for the rebuilding of the Temple? Not at all. Some versions of the legend of the Last Roman Emperor, for instance, also incorporated the idea that there would literally be a reconstructed Temple that the Antichrist would defile—but there was never any thought that a state of Israel would be necessary to construct it. In fact, none of the early proponents of a reconstructed Temple ever dreamed that there would need to exist a state of Israel to rebuild the Temple. The belief was that it would be the Antichrist, not Israel, who would actually build and run the Temple.

Conclusion

We have seen how Hal Lindsey anchored his whole prophetic system upon the founding of the state of Israel in 1948. This restoration of an Israeli state is significant in the belief system of dispensationalism because it supposedly signals the end of a Gentile "Christian" dispensation and the commencement of the Tribulation and, following the Tribulation, the start of the Jewish millennium. The Old Testament passages that are used to "prove" the prophetic significance of 1948 are verses that historically have been understood to refer not to a modern reestablishment of Israel, but either literally to the re-gathering of Israel from Babylonian exile or spiritually to the gathering/evan-gelizing of people into the Church.

Nor are there any promises of a return of the Jews to the land in the New Testament.[14] None. When the disciples asked the Lord before His ascension, "Lord, will You at this time restore the kingdom to Israel?" (Acts 1:6), Christ did not promise them a secular—or even a theocratic—state in 1948. Instead, He tells the disciples that it was not for them to know "the times and seasons" of the Father's divine plan (Acts 1:7). As John Chrysostom correctly ob-serves, the disciples at this time "had not any clear notion of the nature of that kingdom; for the Spirit had not yet instructed them." [15] Therefore, Christ promised His disciples that the Holy Spirit would descend upon them to make them witnesses to all the nations of the earth (Acts 1:8)—suggesting the King-dom would transcend their narrow nationalistic expectations.

Under the guidance of the Holy Spirit, the early Christian Church quickly came to realize the Kingdom was not to be equated with a mere Jewish state, but would include all of mankind. Therefore, it is not sur-prising that the Fathers of the ancient Church never looked for a revived Israel in order to fulfill biblical prophecies.[16] The whole idea that the modern Jewish state is such a fulfillment must simply be rejected by the Orthodox Christian.

If it is accepted that God has two separate peoples, Israel and the Church, and different programs for each,[17] then the doctrine of the rapture of the Church before the Great Tribulation follows logically. This is how the Church "pa-renthesis" ends so God can turn His attention back to Israel for the next dis-pensation. Dispensationalism teaches that, after the rapture of the Church

---

14 Rom. 11:25–29 says nothing about the land or a future national restoration. In context, the "gifts and callings of God" refer to the fulfillment of all gifts and callings, the gospel. What Paul says is that, though a "hardening in part has happened to Israel" (11:25), nevertheless "all Israel will be saved" (11:26) eventually through the gospel.

15 John Chrysostom, *Homilies on Acts*, Homily 2 on Acts 1:6.

16 An interesting exception might be Hippolytus. In passing, he states in his treatise *On the Antichrist* that the Antichrist will raise up the kingdom of the Jews during the Tribulation (25). This is supposedly based on Daniel 7:8! One hopes that the end-times crowd doesn't take this interpretation of Daniel 7:8 too seriously. It would certainly be embarrassing for Christians of all stripes if they started proclaiming that Chaim Weizmann—perhaps the single most instrumental man in establishing the modern state of Israel—was the Anti-christ!

17 When Orthodoxy insists that God has a single economy in Christ for all mankind, includ-ing the Jewish people, it must not be thought that God has no special providential purpose for the Jewish people. While insisting there is one divine economy, the Church has always upheld the belief that God has specific plans for individuals and nations. This also applies to Israel. The Apostle Paul in Rom. 9—11 hints that God will preserve the Jewish people until the end times, when "all Israel will be saved."

from the earth, national Israel again takes center stage during the Tribulation when the Jews finally begin accepting Jesus as their Messiah. After this follows the millennium, during which the offer of the messianic kingdom rejected by Israel two thousand years ago will finally become a reality. Thus along with dispensationalism, and its separation of Israel and the Church, also arose the doctrine of the pretribulational rapture. To keep their strange doctrinal system from collapsing, the modern purveyors of the apocalypse must prove the doctrine of the pretribulational rapture—a doctrine wholly unknown to Christianity before it was invented in the nineteenth century.

Chapter Nine

The Rapture versus Scripture

I do not pray that You should take them out of the world, but that You should keep them from the evil one.
—The Gospel According to St. John 17:15

While predicting the return of Christ has always been a part of the history of the church, since the arrival of the pretribulational Rapture doctrine around 1830, the boom in doom has reached a fever pitch as we near the end of the twentieth century.
—Gary DeMar, *Last Days Madness* (1991)

WHILE THE REST OF THE WORLD awaits extermination, the Elect await evacuation. This, in a nutshell, is the doctrine known as the "pretribulational rapture." The prophecy gurus readily concede that the word "rapture" occurs nowhere in the Bible. Their explanation is that the word is derived from the Latin translation of 1 Thessalonians 4:17: "Then we who are alive and remain shall be caught up together with them in the clouds to meet the Lord in the air. And thus we shall always be with the Lord."

The word translated as "caught up" is a form of the Greek verb *harpazo*. The Vulgate, the official Latin version of the Bible used by the Roman Catholic Church, translates the Greek verb in 1 Thessalonians 4:17 as *rapiemur* (from the Latin verb *rapio*, to seize and carry off), hence the English word *rapture*. Roman Catholics frequently have fun with the fact that fundamentalists, who are quick to declare Catholicism the Whore of Babylon and the Pope the Antichrist, resort to Rome's official translation of the Bible for the source of the word "rapture."

Though the doctrine that Christ will rapture the Church from the earth seven years before the Second Coming has captured most of those who consider themselves evangelical "born-again" Protestants, opinion is by no means united on the issue. This is because the teaching of a pretribulational rapture is a fairly recent innovation within the Protestant fold. David Hunt, who has written several end-times books, complains about the reluctance of many Protestants to accept the teaching:

> Christians have no problem with two comings of Christ, if one is in the past and one in the future. He came once, and will come again as He promised. That there are yet two comings still in the future, however—the Rapture and the Second Coming—separated by seven years, is not generally accepted in the Church.[1]

Hunt wants to see the rest of the Protestant world—as well as non-Protestants, of course—brought into the rapture fold.

What Is the Rapture?

Protestants are divided into three camps on the rapture. First there is the "pretribulational" camp, which encompasses nearly all fundamentalists. This position holds that the rapture will occur at the beginning of the seven-year period known as the Tribulation. It will be a secret rapture, meaning no one will know what has happened to all the Christians who have vanished. Hunt explains, "Millions of Christians—and quite likely all infants—will suddenly vanish from earth, but how or why will not be known by the world." [2] The Antichrist, though, will have an explanation that will satisfy all who are left behind. The saints will then wait in heaven for seven years while God lets loose some rather nasty judgments on the world. They will then return to earth with Christ at the Second Coming.

The "pretrib" rapture (as it is often called in millenarian jargon) goes back to the early nineteenth century, though its exact origin is uncertain. One theory is that a young Scottish woman named Margaret MacDonald was given the pretribulational rapture doctrine through a series of trances in 1830. Be this as it may, the pretribulational rapture as an established belief can definitely be linked to John Darby and the Plymouth Brethren. The position adopted here is that the pretribulational rapture flows naturally out of dispensationalist logic; consequently, the dispensationalist system is the likely source of the doctrine.

The second view is known as the "midtribulational rapture." The "midtribulational" camp, which doesn't seem to have many prominent supporters, holds that the rapture will occur three and a half years into the Tribulation. According to this school of thought, the rapture occurs either before

---

1   Dave Hunt, *How Close Are We?* (Eugene, OR: Harvest House, 1993), 10.
2   Hunt, *Close*, 108.

or immediately after the Antichrist's claiming to be God in the rebuilt Temple in Jerusalem. This view is basically the same as the pretribulational rapture view, except that the wait of the saints in heaven has been cut in half.

Then there is the position the Orthodox Church has always held, which has recently been dubbed the "posttribulational rapture." Actually, according to Orthodox theologian Stanley Harakas, the Orthodox Church doesn't "even use the non-scriptural word 'rapture' when we do talk about the end-times." [3] With this caveat, we will nevertheless use the term "posttribulational rapture" here as a convenient and descriptive label of the Orthodox teaching that non-Orthodox Christians will readily understand.

Unlike the other two positions, the Orthodox teaching (which is also held by Roman Catholics and mainline Protestants) is not that Christians will be taken to heaven only to be returned to earth several years later. Rather, Orthodoxy asserts that Christians who are alive at the moment of the Second Coming will be caught up by Christ into the air and "changed," that is, glorified with their new bodies.

That the Body of Christ, the Church, will be gathered after the Tribulation is what Christ taught in Matthew 24:

> *Immediately after the tribulation* of those days the sun will be darkened, and the moon will not give its light; the stars will fall from heaven, and the powers of the heavens will be shaken. Then the sign of the Son of Man will appear in heaven, and then all the tribes of the earth will mourn, and they will see the Son of Man coming on the clouds of heaven with power and great glory. And He will send His angels with a great sound of a trumpet, and they *will gather together His elect from the four winds, from one end of heaven to the other*. (Matt. 24:29–31, emphasis added; compare Mark 13:26, 27)

Aside from the explicit reference to this gathering taking place "immediately after the tribulation," the description of the Son of Man "coming on the clouds[4] of heaven with power and great glory" also points to this gathering happening at the Second Coming.

---

3   Stanley Harakas, *The Orthodox Church: 455 Questions and Answers* (Minneapolis: Light and Life, 1988), 272. Harakas, though, also says, "We do not use the word 'rapture' in our theology of the last things (eschatology). . . . The Orthodox Church does not use the word 'rapture,' but *its basic meaning is not contrary to Orthodox belief*." (Ibid. Emphasis added.)

4   Clouds in the Bible signify a *theophany*, an appearance of God revealing His divinity and power. When God brought the Israelites out of Egypt, He went before them by day "in a pillar of a cloud" (Ex. 13:21). Clouds depict judgment and the glory of the Lord in many places in the Old Testament: e.g., Ps. 18:11; 104:3; Ezek. 1:4; Jer. 4:13; Dan. 7:13; Joel 2:1, 2; Nah. 1:3; and Zeph. 1:5. Jesus drew on these texts when He proclaimed to the high priest and the Sanhedrin the imminence of His coming in judgment: "Hereafter you will see the Son of Man sitting at the right hand of the Power, and coming on the clouds of heaven" (Matt. 26:64).

The Book of Revelation also indicates that Christians will be alive on earth during the Tribulation. "The ones who come out of the great tribulation" will be "a great multitude which no one could number, of all nations, tribes, peoples, and tongues, standing before the throne [of God] and before the Lamb" (Rev. 7:9, 14). The Antichrist persecutes these saints, implying that the Church is present on the earth during the Tribulation:

> So they [the people of the earth] worshiped the dragon who gave authority to the beast. . . . And it was granted to [the beast] to make war with the saints and to overcome them. . . . Here is the patience and the faith of the saints. Then I saw another beast coming up out of the earth, and he had two horns like a lamb and spoke like a dragon. . . . He was granted power to give breath to the image of the beast, that the image of the beast should both speak and cause as many as would not worship the image of the beast to be killed. (Rev. 13:7, 10, 11, 15)

Blessed Augustine of Hippo (354–430) cites Revelation 20:9, 10 to make the same point: "They went up on the breadth of the earth and surrounded the camp of the saints and the beloved city. And fire came down from heaven and devoured them. And the devil who deceived them was cast into the lake of fire and brimstone where the beast and false prophet are. And they will be tormented day and night forever and ever." Following the traditional interpretation of this verse, Augustine understands "the camp of the saints" as the Church and the fire from heaven as the Second Coming, which is followed by the Last Judgment. He comments on this verse as follows:

> Now this [passage of Scripture] refers to the last judgment; but I thought it should be quoted at this point for a particular reason: to prevent anyone from supposing that in the short time when the Devil will be let loose there will be no Church on this earth, either because he will find no Church here when he is unloosed or because he will have annihilated it by all kinds of persecutions.[5]

Advocates of the pretrib rapture resist the import of the biblical verses cited above by arguing that the "elect" and the "saints" who are alive during the persecution of the Antichrist, and who are "gathered from the four winds, from one end of heaven to the other" at Christ's return, are not the Church, but "Christianized" national Israel! So argues Dave Hunt concerning Matthew 24:29–31.[6] Indeed, the prophecy "experts" seem to have an interesting twist on every single verse in the Bible when defending their beloved doctrine of the pretrib rapture. So what is their biblical support for a secret

---

5   Augustine of Hippo, *The City of God*, Book 20, 8.
6   Hunt, *Close*, 222–223.

rapture seven years before the "Second" (or is it actually the "Third"?) Coming?

Biblical Proof Texts and the Pretrib Rapture

It is said that one day some old men, one of whom was Abba Joseph, came to see St. Anthony in the Egyptian desert. Wanting to test them, Anthony recited a text from the Scriptures. Starting with the youngest, Anthony asked each of them what it meant. Each interpreted the scripture as best he could, but to each Anthony declared, "You have not understood it." Last of all he asked Abba Joseph, "How do you explain this saying?" He only responded, "I do not know." Anthony then exclaimed, "Indeed, Abba Joseph has found the way, for he has said: 'I do not know.' " [7]

Whenever we attempt to interpret Scripture, it is good to recall this teaching from St. Anthony and try to maintain a certain reserve. The gospel cannot be interpreted according to worldly wisdom; as the Apostle explains, "the world through wisdom did not know God, [so] it pleased God through the foolishness of the message preached to save those who believe" (1 Cor. 1:21). The "literal" or "logical" meaning hardly exhausts the depth of God's revelation. In fact, in many instances, the application of human reason to Scripture can lead us astray. How many heresies have been born due to people speculating on the meaning of Scripture, and consequently elevating their erroneous opinions to the level of dogma?

This is not to say we must throw out logic when reading the Bible, but only that we must be cautious in our speculations. Following the tradition of the Church while interpreting a biblical text is the best way to avoid misinterpreting Scripture. Below we will examine the logic that the end-times augurs apply to certain proof texts for the pretrib rapture; where applicable, we will also look at examples of the early Church's interpretation of these texts. The intent is not to counter pretrib proof texts with "proof texts" of our own, but to show that the passages in question hardly necessitate pretrib conclusions.

It was stated earlier that dispensationalists pride themselves on a literal interpretation of Scripture, yet frequently overstep their own interpretive rule. Nowhere can this be more clearly seen than in their interpretation of their biblical proof texts for a pretribulational rapture, where they often resort to allegory or typology. As we examine the major proof texts, let us ask whether the pretribulational rapture doctrine is "literally" taught in the texts or whether the dispensationalist system—which demands a pretribulational rapture—leads people to see a doctrine that isn't actually present.

---

7   Ward, *Sayings*, 4.

Matthew 24:40–42. "Then two men will be in the field: one will be taken and the other left. Two women will be grinding at the mill: one will be taken and the other left. Watch therefore, for you do not know what hour your Lord is coming." It is pointed out that this passage depicts a "catching away" before the Second Coming. On this basis, it is argued that Jesus taught a pre-tribulational rapture.

This passage does teach a "catching up," but not the kind the prophecy gurus suspect. Jesus says nothing of this "catching up" occurring before the Tribulation. To the contrary, a cursory reading of the passage in context reveals that this rapture occurs at the Second Coming. In Matthew 24:29–31, Jesus describes His Second Coming in apocalyptic imagery: the sun and the moon are darkened, the stars fall, and angels gather together the Elect from the four corners of the earth at the sound of a trumpet.[8] Jesus then tells the parable of the fig tree and states that no one knows the day or the hour when the Son of Man will come (v. 36). Immediately after this, Jesus turns to the lesson of Noah: Christ's Second Coming and judgment will be as unexpected as the judgment in Noah's day (vv. 37–39). Then come verses 40–42, which speak of the "catching up" that will happen on the day when Christ returns to render judgment. In context, therefore, Matthew 24:40–42 depicts the gathering of the Elect when Christ returns after the Tribulation, not a pre-tribulational rapture.

John 14:2, 3. "In my Father's house are many mansions; if it were not so, I would have told you. I go to prepare a place for you. And if I go and prepare a place for you, I will come again and receive you to myself; that where I am, there you may be also." These two verses would seem on the face of it to be rather straightforward: Jesus promises to return and take His followers to heaven.

Note there is no mention in John 14:2, 3 of Jesus secretly visiting the earth seven years before His Second Coming and snatching the Church out of the world. Jesus only says that He will come again to take His disciples to be with Him. So how does a dispensationalist see in this verse a "proof" of a pretribulational rapture? John Walvoord explains:

> [The disciples] would meet the Lord and go to the place he was going to prepare for them, an obvious reference to heaven. The purpose of this event would be to remove believers from earth and take them to the Father's house. This is an important point in understanding the doctrine, because it makes clear that the purpose of the Rapture is entirely different from that of the Second Coming. At his second coming, Jesus will come back to

---

8   We will examine the apocalyptic imagery of Matt. 24 in Ch. 12, "Portents of Judgment."

judge and reign over the earth. In the Rapture he will come to take his own out of the world and take them to his Father's house. The two events have nothing in common except that both are referred to as a "coming." Posttribulationists are hard pressed to explain this passage with any relevance to what the passage actually says.[9]

Walvoord is simply reading too much into the text of John 14:1, 2. This is no doubt because Walvoord has steeped himself so long in dispensationalism that he can no longer even recall "what the passage actually says."

Dave Hunt is another who is amazed that so many people fail to see that Christ was teaching the pretrib rapture in John 14:1–3. In fact, he laments that Jesus' promise of the rapture has *never* been properly understood by the Church: "There has been a consistent blindness from the very beginning to the true meaning of these words [uttered by Christ in John 14:1–3]—a blindness even going back all the way to those who first heard this comforting pledge from His own lips." [10] On the rapture question, it seems not even the Twelve Holy Apostles could get it right.

The thrust of the dispensationalist argument is that Jesus promised to take His disciples to "heaven," whereas the Second Coming will witness an earthly kingdom. The problem here is the dispensationalist's underlying assumption that Jesus taught an earthly, millennial reign would be inaugurated at His Second Coming. In none of the Gospels, however, did Jesus teach an earthly millennium. Jesus instead talked about a heavenly Kingdom that will appear in its fullness at the Second Coming. We should also observe that Jesus in John 14 doesn't lay out a specific chronology for the Second Coming (i.e., rapture, tribulation, millennium); instead He is simply promising His disciples heaven when He returns. We will, of course, receive the fullness of our heavenly blessings after the resurrection and the general judgment at Christ's return.

First Corinthians 15:50–53. "Now this I say, brethren, that flesh and blood cannot inherit the Kingdom of God; nor does corruption inherit incorruption. Behold, I tell you a mystery: We shall not all sleep, but we shall all be changed—in a moment, in the twinkling of an eye, at the last trumpet. For the trumpet will sound, and the dead will be raised incorruptible, and we shall be changed. For this corruptible must put on incorruption, and this mortal must put on immortality."

The entire fifteenth chapter of 1 Corinthians is devoted to the subject of the resurrection, both that of Christ and that of those who die in Christ. In the

---

9   John Walvoord, *Major Bible Prophecies* (New York: Harper, 1991), 313.
10 Hunt, *Close*, 9.

verses cited above, Paul says that the bodies we now have cannot enter heaven; therefore, they will be instantaneously changed ("in the twinkling of an eye") at the Second Coming. Thus, simultaneously, the dead will rise and those who are living will be transformed. It must be stressed that this resurrection occurs at Christ's return in glory: "But each one [is resurrected] in his own order: Christ the firstfruits, afterward those who are Christ's *at His coming*. Then comes the end, when he delivers the kingdom to God the Father, when he puts an end to all rule and all authority and power" (1 Cor. 15:23, 24, emphasis added). Another pointer indicating that Paul is talking about Christ's Second Coming and not about some pretribulational rapture occurs in verse 52, in the "proof text" itself: the resurrection and the "change" of the living happens at "the last trumpet"—not the "*second*-to-the-last trumpet" at His second-to-the-last coming at the alleged "pretrib" rapture.

Also note what *isn't* discussed in 1 Corinthians 15. Paul doesn't say Jesus comes secretly and that only His saints will see Him. Neither does Paul say that Jesus' coming, along with the accompanying resurrection and transformation of the living, occurs before the Great Tribulation. Nor does Paul say that Jesus is going to turn around and head back to heaven for another seven years after the resurrection and the transformation of the living saints. (For that matter, we might add that Paul doesn't talk here about a millennial reign of Christ on earth before "He delivers the kingdom to God the Father.") In other words, there is no teaching of a pretribulational rapture anywhere in 1 Corinthians 15.

First Thessalonians 4:16, 17. "For the Lord Himself will descend from heaven with a shout, with the voice of an archangel, and with the trumpet of God. And the dead in Christ will rise first. Then we who are alive and remain shall be caught up together with them in the clouds to meet the Lord in the air. And thus we shall always be with the Lord." This is undoubtedly the most commonly used proof text for the pretribulational rapture.

We have just learned that Christians will instantaneously "put on incorruption" at the Second Coming (1 Cor. 15:50–53). In 1 Thessalonians 4:16, 17 we learn that we who are alive at the time will be caught up to meet Christ in the air while the Lord descends from heaven. Again, we know this is occurring during Christ's Second Coming because an archangel is blowing "the trumpet of God" and the Lord descends "from heaven with a shout" (see John 5:25, 28). This is no "secret" rapture to quietly snatch away Christians. Paul has in mind the same imagery used in Joel 2:1 and Matthew 24:31, where the Second Coming is connected with angels and trumpets. This is confirmed two verses later, in 1 Thessalonians 5:2, where Paul explicitly states that he is talking about "the Day of the Lord," that is, the Day when Christ returns in judgment (see 2 Pet. 3:10). Moreover, the word used to describe Christ's "coming" in 1 Thessalonians 4:15 is *parousia*, which, as we will see in a later chapter, is one of three Greek words used throughout the New Testament for the Second Coming.

In commenting on the "shout" with which the Lord will descend, prominent dispensationalist Charles Ryrie, Professor of Systematic Theology at Dallas Theological Seminary, explains that, "This word of command is used in classical Greek for the shout with which an officer gave the order to his troops or his crew. There is in the term a ring of authority and a note of urgency." [11] We might also add that the battle cry in ancient Israel had a religious significance, proclaiming the presence of the Lord in the battle (see Judg. 7:18, 20). In short, the shout in 1 Thessalonians 4:16 is that of a commander going into battle. This is what we would expect at the Second Coming when the Lord will descend to put down Satan and the Antichrist's diabolic reign. It is *not* what we would expect if the Lord were coming "secretly" to snatch up His followers and then quietly retreat back into heaven.

To summarize, Paul is saying in 1 Thessalonians that, at the Second Coming, Christ will descend from heaven with a shout and an archangel will blow a trumpet. Then the dead in Christ will rise and we who are alive will be caught up to meet Christ in the air, to be forever with the Lord. It is appropriate that this meeting with the Lord occurs in the air, for the air is described by Paul as the abode of Satan (see Eph. 2:2). Christ gathers His Church in the air and establishes His supremacy over the satanic realm.

Sometimes advocates of the pretrib rapture ask why we are raptured to meet Christ in the air only to turn around and come back. What's the point of the rapture then? Of course, the question could be turned around on the pretrib camp: Why should Christ come from heaven to meet us in the air only to turn around and go back to heaven? Why not simply bring us all the way to heaven, which is what happened to Enoch (Gen. 5:24) and Elijah (2 Kin. 2:1–12)? Unless the Lord and the Church are going to spend eternity "in the air," Christ's meeting of the Church at the rapture implies one party is going to "return" somewhere—and the Orthodox are pretty confident it won't be the Lord who will be turning back.

Many biblical scholars believe that, in describing Christ's meeting of His saints in the air, Paul had an ancient Hellenistic custom in mind. Writing in A.D. 398–404, St. John Chrysostom referred to this custom in his commentary on 1 Thessalonians 4:15–17. After citing verse 18 ("Comfort one another with these words"), Chrysostom asks:

---

11 Ryrie, *Countdown*, 83.

> If He [Christ] is about to descend, on what account shall we be caught up? For the sake of honor. For when a king drives into a city, those who are in honor go out to meet him; but the condemned await the judge within. And upon the coming of an affectionate father, his children indeed, and those who are worthy to be his children, are taken out in a chariot, that they may see and kiss him; but those of the domestics who have offended remain within.[12]

It was the protocol in the Apostle Paul's day to meet an arriving dignitary officially outside a city and then escort him back to the city. Cicero, in describing Julius Caesar's tour of Italy in 49 B.C., mentions the custom and even remarks that in 44 B.C. the same honor was paid to Caesar's adopted son, Octavian. When Paul was being taken to Rome as a prisoner, the Roman Christians came and met Paul at Appii Forum and Three Inns to escort Paul to Rome (Acts 28:15). In connection with the Second Coming, Jesus' parable of the ten virgins will be recalled. When the bridegroom came at midnight, the cry went out, "Behold, the bridegroom is coming; go out to meet him!" (Matt. 25:6). The virgins then went out and escorted the bridegroom back to the house. Jesus obviously intended this as a picture of what would occur at the Second Coming.

In his commentary on 1 Thessalonians, Orthodox biblical scholar Paul Nadim Tarazi describes this custom of greeting an arriving VIP at his "coming" (Gr. *parousia*, used in 1 Thessalonians 4:15):

> Now, in the Hellenistic literature contemporary to Paul, parousia in the sense of coming referred specifically either to the appearance of a deity or to the official visit of an emperor, ruler or governor, or even to the official welcome given a victorious general. The latter kind of parousia entailed an extensive paraphernalia: the preparation of the city for the joyous and glorious event, the awaiting, the clamor announcing the arrival of the visitor, the procession out of the gates to meet him, the parade bringing him into the city, his acclamation by all its inhabitants as well as his welcome, praise and glorification by the emperor. The concept and imagery of the parousia was thus readily used in the early church to render the coming in glory of the Lord at the end times, especially since Jesus combined in His person the threefold aspect of deity, ruler and victorious warrior over death.[13]

If Tarazi is correct, then this suggests that, after we meet Christ in the air, we escort Him "into the city" (i.e., to earth) as He continues His descent. Then, at His Second Coming, there follows the general judgment of humanity. After this, the saints remain forever with Christ in His eternal Kingdom.

---

12 John Chrysostom, *Homilies on Thessalonians*, Homily 8 on 1 Thess. 4:18.

13 Paul Tarazi, *1 Thessalonians: A Commentary* (Crestwood, NY: St. Vladimir's Seminary Press, 1982), 182. Tarazi's commentary on pp. 147–153 should be consulted by those wanting a good, concise examination of 1 Thess. 4:15–17.

This seems to be what Chrysostom had in mind when he wrote in one of his homilies on the Gospel of Matthew:

> And how says He [Christ] elsewhere, that "the righteous are caught up first?" Because they are indeed caught up first, but Christ being come, those others are given over to punishment, and then the former depart into the kingdom of heaven. For because they must be in heaven, but *He Himself is to come and judge all men here*;[14] having passed sentence upon these, like some king *He rises with His friends, leading them to that blessed portion*. See you that the punishment is twofold, first to be burnt up, and then to fall from that glory?[15]

Chrysostom in another of his homilies places the "catching up" of 1 Thessalonians 4:17 specifically at the Second Coming:

> Remove your thoughts from these things [i.e., earthly splendor] to things above, and to that awful day in which Christ is coming. . . . For the "powers of the Heavens," He says, "shall be shaken" (Matt. 24:29). Then is the whole Heaven thrown open, and the gates of those concaves [i.e., the "vaults" of heaven] unfold themselves, and the Only-begotten Son of God cometh down, not with twenty, not with a hundred men for His bodyguard, but with thousands, ten thousands of Angels and Archangels, Cherubim and Seraphim, and other Powers, and with fear and trembling shall everything be filled, whiles the earth is bursting itself up, and the men that ever were born, from Adam's birth up to that day, are rising from the earth, and all are caught up (1 Thess. 4:17); when Himself appears with such great glory as that the sun, and the moon, and all light whatever, is cast into the shade, being outshone by that radiance.[16]

St. John Chrysostom was (and is) one of the most celebrated expositors of Scripture in the early Church. This is because he always explicated the traditional, Orthodox understanding of a biblical text in a way that was meaningful to his hearers. The name Chrysostom ("Golden Mouth" in Greek) was given to John while he was in Antioch, on account of his eloquent preaching of the Word of God. No one, not even his enemies, ever accused him of novel or unusual interpretations of Scripture. Thus it is very significant that St. John Chrysostom never once suggested that 1 Thessalonians 4:15–17 taught a pretrib rapture.

Since this passage in 1 Thessalonians is the key pretrib-rapture proof text, let's look at another example of how the early Church interpreted it. In the following citation from the *Apostolic Constitutions*, written in Syria sometime between A.D. 341 and 400, we find an allusion to 1 Thessalonians 4:16 that places it within the overall context of the early Church's expectations of the Second Coming:

---

14 Gr. *entautha*—here in this place, i.e., earth.

15 John Chrysostom, *Matthew*, Homily 47:1. Emphasis added.

16 John Chrysostom, *Romans*, Homily 14 on Romans 8:27.

For in the last days prophets shall be multiplied, and such as corrupt the word; and the sheep shall be changed into wolves, and love into hatred: for through the abounding of iniquity the love of many shall wax cold. For men shall hate, and persecute, and betray one another. And then shall appear the deceiver of the world, the enemy of truth, the prince of lies, whom the Lord Jesus "shall destroy with the spirit of His mouth, who takes away the wicked with His lips; and many shall be offended at Him. But they that endure to the end, the same shall be saved. And then shall appear the sign of the Son of Man in heaven" (Is. 11:4; Matt. 24:13, 30); *and afterwards shall be the voice of a trumpet by the archangel* (cf. 1 Thess. 4:16); and in the interval shall be the revival of those that were asleep. And then shall the Lord come, and all His saints with Him, with a great concussion above the clouds, with the angels of His power, in the throne of His kingdom, to condemn [the devil], the deceiver of the world, and to render to every one according to his deeds. "Then shall the wicked go away into everlasting punishment, but the righteous shall go into life eternal" (Matt. 25:46), to inherit those things "which eye hath not seen, nor ear heard, nor have entered into the heart of man, such things as God has prepared for them that love Him" (1 Cor. 2:9); and they shall rejoice in the kingdom of God, which is in Christ Jesus.[17]

In the *Apostolic Constitutions*, the "catching up" of 1 Thessalonians 4:16, 17 clearly takes place at the Second Coming. First, evil grows rampant in the world, while apostasy, persecution, and "wolves" ravage the Church. Next, the Antichrist appears to deceive the world; then there appears in heaven the sign of the Son of Man. Only then does the Lord "descend from heaven with a shout, with the voice of an archangel, and with the trumpet of God" (1 Thess. 4:16). After this follows the destruction of Satan with his cohorts and the general judgment.

In another example, Cyril of Jerusalem around A.D. 350, writing in his *Catechetical Lectures*—lectures intended to instruct new converts, which consequently avoided speculative and controversial interpretations of Scripture—cites 1 Thessalonians 4:16, 17 in connection with the Second Coming of Christ, and not with a pretribulational rapture.[18] This interpretation is found wherever 1 Thessalonians is cited by the early Church Fathers. The more one looks at how the Fathers interpreted 1 Thessalonians 4:16, 17, the more obvious it becomes that it is impossible to pull a pretribulational rapture out of this passage without first having the doctrine firmly ensconced in the mind.[19]

---

17 *Apostolic Constitutions*, 7:32. Emphasis added.

18 Cyril of Jerusalem, *Catechetical Lectures*, 15:19.

19 In another example of how the Fathers generally approached this text, note the highly spiritual interpretation given 1 Thess. 4:16, 17 in St. Gregory of Nyssa's *Life of Moses,* written in the fourth century: "Reweaving this bodily nature [through acts of repentance], we should be close to what rises upwards and is light and airy, in order that when we hear the last trumpet we may be found weightless and light in responding to the voice of *(cont.)*

Second Thessalonians 2:3. "Let no one deceive you by any means; for that Day will not come unless the falling away comes first, and the man of sin is revealed, the son of perdition." Brace yourself, for the interpretive twists and turns required to pull the pretrib rapture out of this verse can only be likened to Mr. Toad's Wild Ride at Disneyland.

The argument is made based on the phrase, "the falling away," which in Greek is the word *apostasia*. In Hellenistic Greek, the word generally meant political rebellion, though it also came to mean rebellion against the law of God (see Acts 21:21). The word has been transliterated into English as "apostasy," meaning religious rebellion and defection.

Proponents of the pretribulational rapture have argued that not only can *apostasia* be understood as meaning a departure from the Faith, it can also mean a physical, spatial departure from the earth in a rapture. H. Wayne House has exhaustively argued this interpretation in an essay entitled "Apostasia in 2 Thessalonians 2:3: Apostasy or Rapture?" [20] However, even most pretribulationists don't buy this strained interpretation of the text. This may be changing, though, since a rather prominent preacher, Chuck Smith of Calvary Chapel in Costa Mesa, California—one of the biggest churches in America—has also adopted this particular interpretation of 2 Thessalonians 2:3.[21]

Orthodox Christians understand this verse in the context of the New Testament teaching that in the last days before Christ's return, lawlessness and wickedness will abound (e.g., Matt. 24:12; 2 Tim. 3:1–9). Christians are specifically warned in Scripture that there will be an increase in false prophets and false teachers who will lead us away from the Faith (Mark 13:9–13). Since Paul refers to this *apostasia* as something that the Thessalonians were already informed about as a part of Paul's general teaching ("Do you not remember that when I was still with you I told you these things?"—v. 5), it is likely that Paul had in mind this general rebellion against God during the end times that was a normal part of his teaching.

As false teaching is the immediate context of 2 Thessalonians 2:3, the usual understanding of *apostasia* appears appropriate. Paul exhorts the Thessalonians "not to be soon shaken in mind or troubled" by a false teaching that Christ's Second Coming had already taken place (2 Thess. 2:2). It is

(note 19 cont.) the One who calls us. Then we shall be borne on high through the air to be together with the Lord (1 Thess. 4:17), not drawn down to earth by anything heavy [i.e., sin]." *Life of Moses*, 2:191. See the translation by Abraham Malherbe and Everett Ferguson in *The Classics of Western Spirituality* (New York: Paulist Press, 1978), 104.

20 H. Wayne House, "Apostasia in 2 Thessalonians 2:3: Apostasy or Rapture?", *When the Trumpet Sounds*, 261ff.

21 Chuck Smith, *The Final Curtain* (Eugene, OR: Harvest House, 1991), 37.

interesting that Paul is talking about people being "shaken in mind" about a false teaching concerning Christ's Second Coming. Could the "pretrib" rapture doctrine itself be a part of this final apostasy from the Christian Faith?

In fact, evangelical Scripture scholar Bob Gundry comments that this verse actually *disproves* a belief in a rapture before the Tribulation:

> In 2 Thessalonians 2:3, Paul recognizes that seeds of "the rebellion" are already germinating ("For the mystery of lawlessness is already at work"— verse 7). But he doesn't allow for the view that the rebellion reaches a climax before the rapture and that the man of lawlessness will be revealed when he makes a covenant with Israel at the start of Daniel's seventieth week, the tribulation (as in Dan 9:27). The making of a covenant as mentioned by Daniel doesn't enter Paul's picture. He leaves it out. But he does describe in some detail the Antichrist's opposition to God, self-exaltation to the status of a deity who demands that others worship him, and so on (verses 4–12). And Paul says that this rebellion comes first, not that the rapture does.[22]

In his *Dialogue with Trypho*, written around A.D. 135, the Christian apologist St. Justin Martyr gives us a helpful allusion to 2 Thessalonians 2:3: "Two advents of Christ have been proclaimed . . . and the second [advent], in which He [Christ] will come from the heavens in glory, when the 'man of apostasy' (2 Thess. 2:3), who utters extraordinary things against the Most High, will boldly attempt to perpetrate unlawful deeds on earth against us Christians." [23] Obviously Justin Martyr, who was trying to explain the Christian Faith objectively to a Jewish rabbi named Trypho, did not believe that Christians would be raptured before the Tribulation and escape the persecution of the Antichrist.

Second Thessalonians 2:6–8. "And now you know what is restraining, that he may be revealed in his own time. For the mystery of lawlessness is already at work; only he who now restrains will do so until he is taken out of the way. And then the lawless one will be revealed, whom the Lord will consume with the breath of His mouth and destroy with the brightness of His coming." Is the "restraining" force that holds back the appearance of "the lawless one" (the Antichrist) the Church? This is what many prophecy gurus argue, suggesting that the Tribulation can't get under way until the Church "is taken out of the way," meaning raptured off the earth.

First of all, even assuming that the "restrainer" mentioned in this passage is the Church (or the Holy Spirit in the Church), Paul doesn't say it

---

22 Bob Gundry, *First the Antichrist* (Grand Rapids, MI: Baker Books, 1997), 31.
23 Justin Martyr, *Dialogue*, 110.

will be taken off the planet, but simply "taken out of the way." This is an important distinction, for an obstacle can be taken out of the way without totally eliminating its existence in the world. Second, why should we think that the Church is this restraining force to begin with? In the last two thousand years, why hasn't the Church, indwelt as She is by the Holy Spirit, prevented the rise of lesser "antichrists" who, though not as diabolical as the final Antichrist, were nevertheless hostile to Christ and His people? Why didn't the presence of the Church prevent Nero, Decius, and Diocletian from appearing? Or in this century, why didn't the Church restrain the rise of Hitler, Stalin, and Chairman Mao, all of whom fiercely persecuted Christians? If the Spirit-filled Church didn't "restrain" these precursors to Antichrist, then why think the Church is the one restraining the rise of the ultimate Antichrist?

This passage of Scripture is fraught with difficulties all around. First, the pronoun rendered "he" in this verse occurs both in the masculine personal form and in the impersonal form; in other words, as both a "he" and an "it." Consequently, that which restrains can be either an impersonal thing or a person. Moreover, the verb "to restrain" in Greek, *katecho*, can mean (1) to hold fast (see 1 Thess. 5:21), (2) to hold back (see Philem. 13), or (3) to hold sway (if intransitive). While commentators generally understand the verb in the sense of "to hold back" in this particular verse, the issue is by no means settled.

As a result of this grammatical ambiguity, opinions vary considerably on exactly what the thing/person is that holds back (or holds sway/holds fast). The early Church beginning with Irenaeus thought it was the Roman Empire or the Roman emperor that restrained "the lawless one." Thus it was believed that the fall of the Roman Empire meant the ushering in of the Antichrist and the Great Tribulation. Tertullian, writing around A.D. 197, states, "We know that the great force which threatens the whole world, the end of the age itself with its menace of hideous suffering, is delayed by the respite which the Roman Empire means for us. We do not wish to experience all that; and when we pray for its postponement [i.e., the Tribulation] are helping forward the continuance of Rome." [24]

Since the fall of the empire, others have modified the view and suggested that the "restrainer" is human government, or even simply the principle of law and order. Some modern commentators have thought Paul meant the Jewish state. Satan has been suggested and, if you don't believe that one, others have put forth God as the restraining person/force. While some dispensationalists insist it is the Church, others (like Dave Hunt) have thought

---

24 Tertullian, *Apology*, 32:1.

it is the Holy Spirit. Others say it is merely the preaching of the gospel. Another possible interpretation (the one favored by this author) connects the "restraining" in this passage to the binding of Satan in Revelation 20. Finally, one commentator, C. H. Giblin, has even advanced the position that Paul was referring to himself as the restraining force![25]

All sides need to be honest on this passage of Scripture: no one knows exactly what Paul meant, because Paul assumes his readers already know what he's talking about. As Leon Morris openly admits, "But the plain fact is that we do not know [what Paul meant]. It is best honestly to admit this and not try to force the passage into conformity with some theory we have evolved on the basis of imperfect knowledge." [26] Obviously 2 Thessalonians 2:6–8 is too cryptic a passage upon which to base a doctrine like the pretribulational rapture.

In fact, it could even be argued that Paul is here assuming that Christians will go through the Great Tribulation. In verses 3–12 of this chapter, Paul instructs the Thessalonians about the coming of the Antichrist so that they won't fall victim to his deceptions. After all, "those who perish" are deceived by the Antichrist because "they did not receive the love of the truth" (2 Thess. 2:10), not heeding Paul's warnings and exhortations. This assumes the Thessalonians will go through the Tribulation and encounter the deceptions of the Antichrist. Otherwise, why warn them if they won't be around to encounter these deceptions?

Revelation 3:10. "Because you have kept my command to persevere, I also will keep you from the hour of trial which shall come upon the whole world, to test those who dwell on the earth." The common dispensationalist treatment of this Scripture is, first, to note that the Book of Revelation begins with Christ sending seven messages to seven local churches in Asia Minor. These are then interpreted to be seven prophecies of seven Church ages, the last one being to the church of Laodicea. The church of Laodicea represents the church from 1900 to the Tribulation age, becoming the apostate Christendom that will go through the judgments of the Great Tribulation.

The message to the church in Philadelphia comes right before that to the Laodicean church, and it is the church of Philadelphia that receives the message that it will not go through "the hour of trial." This Philadelphia church, according to Hal Lindsey, covers the period from 1750 to 1925 and is characterized by great missionary zeal. "The Philadelphia type of church is still

---

25 I. Howard Marshall, *1 and 2 Thessalonians*, The New Century Bible Commentary, 196–199.

26 Leon Morris, *1 and 2 Thessalonians*, Tyndale New Testament Commentaries (Grand Rapids: Eerdmans, 1984), 131.

present in the world and it will be here until the Rapture, but it is not the dominant force in the professing Christian church today." [27] The Philadelphia church is kept from the hour of trial by means of the rapture. As we enter the third millennium, though, one wonders how much longer the Philadelphia church can bleed over into the Laodicean church.

This interpretation raises some interesting questions about Church history. For example, the church of Thyatira, which is supposed to be the medieval Church, receives higher praise from Christ than the prophecy pundits would normally grant ("I know your works, love, service, faith, and your patience; and as for your works, the last are more than the first"— Rev. 2:19). On the other hand, the Lord says to the church of Sardis, allegedly representing the Church of the Reformation, that "you have a name that you are alive, but you are dead" (Rev. 3:1). Is this how our Protestant prophecy "experts" really view the Reformation?

Also, observe how this interpretation of the seven letters to the seven churches totally abandons the principle of "literal" interpretation in order to read the rapture into this passage. The church in Philadelphia, for example, was a real, historical congregation during the first century, when the Book of Revelation was written. Why not view Revelation 3:10 as an actual message to a literal church community, instead of allegorizing this community as the Church between the years 1750 and 1925? Moreover, the text of Revelation 3:10 never explicitly mentions anything about a rapture—this must be supplied by the dispensationalist system.

In principle, there is nothing wrong in allegorizing Scripture. The Orthodox Church has a long tradition in the allegorical interpretation of the Bible. Archbishop Averky, of the Russian Orthodox Church Outside of Russia, in his commentary on Revelation also sets forth, as "an opinion," the idea that "the seven churches signify seven periods of the whole Church of Christ from its foundation to the end of the world." [28] This is fine. It is another thing, however, to set forth one's allegorical interpretation as the "literal" understanding of Scripture and then proceed to construct upon it a novel and dubious doctrine. That is unacceptable.

Another issue: Is Christ promising to keep Christians *out of* the hour of trial or to keep them from evil *through* the hour of trial? We think the latter, because of what Jesus said in John 17:15: "I do not pray that you should take them out of the world [as in a rapture], but that you should keep them from the evil one." In John 17:15, Jesus specifically excludes any secret rapture of

---

27 Lindsey, *New World*, 49.
28 Averky Taushev, *The Apocalypse in the Teachings of Ancient Christianity* (Platina, CA: St. Herman of Alaska Brotherhood, 1985), 101.

Christians during the time of trial, instead praying that God's grace will keep
them through the dark hours to come. Even the Greek constructions of Revelation 3:10 and John 17:15 are similar. If we assume that John is the author
of both the fourth Gospel and Revelation, the parallel is strengthened even
more. Because of this parallel, it is highly unlikely that Jesus' promise of
keeping the Christians of Philadelphia "from the hour of trial" in Revelation
3:10 can be interpreted as indicating a pretrib rapture.

Revelation 4:1. "After these things I [the Apostle John] looked, and behold,
a door standing open in heaven. And the first voice which I heard was like a
trumpet speaking with me, saying, 'Come up here, and I will show you things
which must take place after this.' " If this isn't the weakest proof text of all,
it comes close. Before we explain the pretrib spin on the Apostle John's mystical vision, let us ask ourselves whether it is apparent that this verse teaches
a rapture seven years before the Second Coming. If one is not already im-
mersed in dispensationalism, the pretribulational rapture isn't obvious at all
in Revelation 4:1.

The argument is that the Book of Revelation should be interpreted chron-
ologically, the messages to the seven churches being interpreted as the seven
ages of the Church, as we saw when we looked at Revelation 3:10. In the first
three chapters of Revelation, the word "church" is used nineteen times. Then,
when these messages are completed with the one to the church in Laodicea
(Rev. 3:14–22), John is taken up to witness the end times from heaven (4:1),
which is a symbol of the rapture of the Church in the person of John. The
voice from heaven is "like a trumpet," and since dispensationalists believe
the rapture will occur with a trumpet (but, as we've seen, so does the Second
Coming!), this is supposed to strengthen the symbolism. The Tribulation period encompasses chapters 4 through 18, and the word "church" doesn't appear in any of these chapters. The Church does not appear again until the
Second Coming in Revelation 19:7–14, when the Church accompanies Christ
to earth—even though the word "church" doesn't appear in this chapter either! Thus, according to this strained reasoning, the Book of Revelation supposedly teaches the pretribulational rapture.

First of all, it is completely arbitrary to see in John's mystical trip to
heaven a foreshadowing of the rapture before the Tribulation. After all, we
could just as easily argue that the catching up to heaven of the two witnesses
in Revelation 11:11, 12 represents the rapture toward the end of the Tribulation. (In fact, in v. 12 the two witnesses are said to ascend "in a cloud," which
closely parallels 1 Thessalonians 4:17: "We . . . shall be caught up together
with them in the clouds . . .")

Moreover, John is depicted in Revelation as continually ascending and descending between heaven and earth. He is back on earth watching an "angel coming down from heaven" in Revelation 10:1 (and 18:1). Also, in many other places, John finds himself on earth describing events and then returning to heaven to relate things happening there. If John is supposed to be portraying the Church, we're going to be piling up a lot of frequent-flyer mileage during the Tribulation!

What about the absence of the word "church" from Revelation 4—18? Does this prove the Church is absent from the earth during the Tribulation? This line of reasoning is plagued with insurmountable difficulties. First, while the word "church" doesn't appear between chapters 4 and 18, it is untrue that the Church isn't being referred to in that long section. The word "saints," which is a biblical synonym for the "church," occurs several times in chapters 4—18 (see Rev. 5:8; 8:3, 4; 11:18; 13:7, 10; 14:12; 16:6; 18:24). When confronted with this, however, the pretrib camp will assert that these "saints" are not the Church, but people who have become Christians after the rapture and who must be saved through martyrdom.

Yet how can one be a Christian without being a part of the Church? How can one be *in* Christ and not *of* Christ's Body? Whenever there are two or three gathered together in His name (the biblical requirement for a valid witness—Deut. 17:6; 19:15; Matt. 18:16), Christ is in their midst (Matt. 18:20), and that constitutes the witness of the Church to the world. If there are any Christians on earth witnessing to Christ during the Tribulation, that is the Church.

In any event, the question is academic since the Bible itself shows that "saints" and "church" are synonymous: "To the *church* of God which is at Corinth, to those who are sanctified in Christ Jesus, called to be *saints*, with all who in every place call on the name of Jesus Christ our Lord, both theirs and ours" (1 Cor. 1:2); "For God is not the author of confusion but of peace, as in all the *churches of the saints*" (1 Cor. 14:33); and even the prophecy gurus concede that when Paul writes that Christ will come again "with all His saints" (1 Thess. 3:13), Christ is coming with His Church.

Paul also writes, "Dare any of you, having a matter against another, go to law before the unrighteous, and not before *the saints?* . . . do you appoint those who are least esteemed by *the Church* to judge?" (1 Cor. 6:1, 5). Paul is not talking about two different groups, the saints and the Church, but about the one Body of Christ that is called both "the saints" and "the Church."

Why is the word "church" absent from Revelation 4 to Revelation 22:16? The answer lies in the way John actually uses the word. All the uses of "church" in Revelation denote a local church community (the church "in Smyrna," for example), not the whole "catholic" church universal, as we so often use the word today. In the descriptions of the Antichrist's persecution in chapters 4—18, John simply chose to use different words (like the word "saints") to describe what was happening to the universal Church. He was not hinting at any pretribulational rapture.

The pretrib interpretation of Revelation raises an interesting problem when applied to the rest of the New Testament. The word "church" occurs only once in Hebrews (12:23) and twice in 2 Corinthians (1:1; 2:14). The word "church" isn't used in Romans until the last chapter (which some consider a kind of appendix to the epistle). Ironically, the word "church" doesn't occur in any of the verses that supposedly point to the pretrib rapture of the Church. The word is also absent from Mark, Luke, John, 2 Timothy, Titus, 1 Peter, 2 Peter, 1 John, 2 John, and Jude. Yet if the Church isn't the subject of all this New Testament Scripture, then what is? The 1948 restoration of Israel?

In fact, dispensationalist semantics can cut both ways. The word "Antichrist" doesn't occur anywhere in the Book of Revelation. Are dispensationalists prepared to concede that the Book of Revelation doesn't talk about the Antichrist? Dispensationalists believe that during the period of the Tribulation covered in Revelation 4 through 18, God focuses on restored Israel. Yet the word "Israel" occurs *only once* in this whole section, in Revelation 7:4!

These word-count interpretations so popular with dispensationalists are virtually meaningless, because the method can be made to prove almost anything. If the fact that the word "church" doesn't appear in Revelation 4—18 proves the rapture, then what does the fact that the word "God" doesn't occur in the Book of Esther prove? That the author of that book was an atheist? That God was napping during the period discussed in the Book of Esther?

More to the point, Revelation 4—18 describes events occurring not only on earth, but also in heaven. According to the word-count interpretation, the Church cannot be in heaven during the Tribulation either, since the word "church" is absent from these descriptions of heaven. Are we therefore to conclude that the Church is neither in heaven nor on earth during the Tribulation? After the rapture, are we to believe Jesus leaves the Church floating in space somewhere between heaven and earth? This is absurd. It is better simply to accept the fact that John says the Church, which he calls the "saints," is on earth during the Tribulation in Revelation 4—18.

Having examined the major proof texts that are used to "prove" the rapture of the Church into heaven seven years before the Second Coming, go back and review them. Simply read the biblical texts and ask yourself whether this pretribulational rapture doctrine just leaps out at you from any of them. Is it that the pretrib rapture is clearly discerned from a literal reading of these biblical texts, and that *everyone* throughout Church history simply overlooked the clear import of all these texts until 1830? Or is it that the dispensationalist system conjured up by John Darby in the nineteenth century led people to interpret these scriptures in bizarre ways?

Chapter Ten

Enraptured with Syllogisms and Mythology

*For the wisdom of this world is foolishness with God. For it is writ-
ten, "He catches the wise in their own craftiness."*
　　—The First Epistle of St. Paul to the Corinthians 3:19

*Man has such a predilection for systems and abstract deductions
that he is ready to distort the truth intentionally; he is ready to deny
the evidence of his senses only to justify his logic.*
　　—Fyodor Dostoevsky, *Notes from the Underground* (1864)

ULTIMATELY, THE WEAK PROOF TEXTS brought forward in favor of the pretribulational rapture have not succeeded in convincing most Christians of the orthodoxy of the doctrine. In consequence, a number of arguments have been brought forward to bring people to see the "logic" of the pretrib rapture. We need to look at these arguments and then, having done that, try to uncover the real reason people are drawn to the pretrib rapture.

Will the Church Experience the Wrath of God?

One argument for the pretrib rapture is based on the nature of the Great Tribulation. How does God see the Tribulation period, the prophecy pundit asks? The Tribulation is "the great day of His wrath" (Rev. 6:17), the Day in which God's "wrath has come" to "destroy those who destroy the earth" (Rev. 11:18). God does not intend wrath for the Church. On the contrary, it is argued, Paul writes, "For God did not appoint us to wrath, but to obtain salvation through our Lord Jesus Christ" (1 Thess. 5:9). Therefore, we await God's "Son from heaven, . . . even Jesus who delivers us from the wrath to come" (1 Thess. 1:10). This deliverance, we are told, is the rapture to occur before the Tribulation, "the great day of His wrath."

This is how Chuck Smith makes the argument:

> When Peter in his second epistle warns of the judgment of God that is coming upon the wicked, he points out that in the history of God's judgment, He has spared the righteous. He spared Noah by instructing him to build the ark to take him safely through the destroying flood, and He delivered righteous Lot, who was vexed by the filthy way the wicked were living. Peter comments, "For the Lord knoweth how to deliver the godly out of temptations, and to reserve the unjust unto the day of judgment to be punished" [2 Pet 2:9].[1]

Having made his point that God takes care of the righteous while He is judging the wicked, Smith then makes his second point, that the Tribulation will be a period of incredible wrath:

> [The Prophet Isaiah] declares that God is going to punish the world for its evil, and the wicked for their iniquity, that mankind for the most part will be destroyed. The heavens will be shaken and the earth moved out of its place by the wrath of the Lord and His fierce anger. It is comforting to know that according to the Word of God spoken through Paul to the Thessalonians [1 Thess. 5:9], God has not appointed us unto such wrath. The Lord will surely deliver the Church before His day of judgment falls.[2]

Smith then cites 1 Thessalonians 4:15–18, implying that only a pretribulational rapture can keep us from the divine wrath to come.

The above argument can be laid out as follows: (1) The whole world will be subject to divine wrath during the Tribulation, and (2) the Church is exempt from divine wrath; therefore, (3) the Church must be raptured off the earth before the Tribulation. On the face of it, the argument isn't even logical. If we grant the first and second points, still the conclusion doesn't necessarily follow. True, rapturing the Church would be one way to protect the Body of Christ from the effects of divine judgment; but is it the *only* way God could protect the Church?

Let's recall for a moment Israel's captivity in Egypt. Because Pharaoh wouldn't release Israel, God's wrath came down heavily upon Egypt: Egypt's main water supply, the Nile, was turned into blood and rendered undrinkable; frogs, gnats, and flies covered the land, which utterly ruined agriculture; then there was a plague on the livestock that, together with Egypt's destroyed agriculture, totally obliterated the economy and ensured famine. And in case anything happened to survive, God sent hail and locusts to wipe out whatever remained. Finally, God struck down all who were the firstborn of Egypt. Pharaoh ultimately relented, and Israel was allowed to leave for the Promised Land.

---

1   Smith, *Final*, 26–27.
2   Smith, *Final*, 27.

Though God showered Egypt with divine wrath, Israel was obviously not the object of that divine wrath. Was it necessary that God rapture Israel out of Egypt before commencing the plagues? If Chuck Smith had been preaching in Egypt at the time, no doubt a large part of the Jewish population would have been expecting the blessed blastoff at any moment. The Book of Exodus, however, describes a different sort of providential care.

Rather than rapturing them, God protected the children of Israel in an area in the northeastern section of the Nile Delta called Goshen. Only *after* the judgment had occurred did the Lord take the Israelites out of the land of Egypt and lead them into the Promised Land. So will it be with the Church when God pours His wrath upon the earth. The Lord will preserve us through the Tribulation, and then will lead us to our heavenly Promised Land.

We can already hear the objection: "But God judged only a small geographic area when He judged Egypt, sparing Goshen where the Israelites were. During the Tribulation, God will judge the *whole* world and there will be no place to hide!"

When we look at Scripture, we find only one instance when God judged the entire world. This was in Noah's day, when God cleansed the world of its wickedness by a flood. However, God spared Noah and his family because they were righteous. But how did God spare Noah and his family from this judgment that engulfed the whole earth? Did God rapture Noah and then return him to earth when the judgment was over? No, God instructed Noah to build an ark and then preserved Noah and his family through the judgment.

The early Christians saw Noah's ark as a type of the Church, with those inside the ark being preserved from the Day of Judgment. Like the ark, the Church will be preserved through the coming Tribulation, not teleported off the planet. This is in accordance with Christ's prayer for the Church: "I do not pray that You should *take them out of the world*, but that You should keep them from the evil one" (John 17:15, emphasis added). We will not be taken out of the world by a rapture, but protected from Satan, the "evil one," and from Satan's agent, the Antichrist.

This preservation of Christians during the Tribulation can be seen quite clearly in the Book of Revelation.[3] In Revelation 16, for example, God's judgments are specifically said to fall on the ungodly, those who have "the mark of the beast and those who worship his image" (Rev. 16:2; also 14:9, 10). Divine wrath falls on those who "have shed the blood of saints and prophets" (16:6), and on those who "blasphemed the name of God . . . and . . . did not repent and give Him glory" (16:9; also v. 11). The wicked encounter the

---

3   The following examples are taken from Gundry, *Antichrist*, 51–52.

full wrath of God when they gather to fight Christ Himself at "the place called in Hebrew, Armageddon" (16:16; also 14:19; 19:15). The examples could go on and on. On the other hand, when God sends His plagues on "Babylon" (a symbol in the Bible for the nations of the world with their self-exaltation, idolatry, and rebellion), it is specifically said that God calls His people out of Babylon so that they *won't* receive His wrath: "Come out of her, my people, lest you share in her sins, and lest you receive of her plagues" (18:4). Such a warning reveals God's concern to safeguard His people during the judgment. Also, in Revelation 7:3, God's servants are sealed precisely in order to protect them during the Tribulation.

Chuck Smith argues in *The Final Curtain* that God took Lot out of Sodom before judgment fell on that city, and in like manner God will take the Church out of the world before the Tribulation.[4] The analogy, however, is rather weak. God simply sent heavenly emissaries to escort Lot and his family to a place of safety outside the city, but he was still in the plain, close enough to see the destruction (which, it will be recalled, is how Lot's wife met her demise). Lot then fled to the nearby city of Zoar while God overthrew "all the plain, [and] all the inhabitants of the cities" (Gen. 19:15–23).

Finding the rapture in this incident is not biblical theology, but pseudomysticism. It is simply arbitrary to take this one act of the preservation of Lot and give it an esoteric interpretation in order to come up with a doctrine unknown to the Church until the nineteenth century. Following Smith's reasoning, we could just as easily argue that because Rahab was saved within Jericho when the city was destroyed (Josh. 6:17), therefore the Church will be preserved on earth through the Tribulation.

However, what really throws a monkey wrench into this whole argument is that the pretrib proponents themselves concede that there will be Christians alive on earth during the Tribulation, as mentioned in places like Revelation 7 and 13. Hal Lindsey explains his understanding of these Tribulation believers:

> God has never been without a witness of His salvation on this earth. Since all believers from this present age will have been suddenly and miraculously removed by the event known as the Rapture, new witnesses must be raised up immediately.[5]

If Christians can't experience the wrath of God during the Tribulation, necessitating their complete evacuation off the face of the earth, then how do these Tribulation Christians escape God's wrath? You can't have it both ways.

---

4   Smith, *Final*, 25–27.
5   Lindsey, *Apocalypse*, 117.

You can't argue that a pretrib rapture is necessary to spare Christians from God's wrath and then say that God can protect these Tribulation Christians adequately while they remain on earth, as Hal Lindsey attempts to do.[6] Lindsey must at least be consistent and concede that these Tribulation Christians will suffer the wrath of God. Yet, Bob Gundry pointedly observes, such a double standard for Tribulation Christians makes a mockery of the gospel:

> Now here's the rub if you want to argue that the salvation of Christians from God's wrath requires their absence during the tribulation. Take those saints who come out of that period. What kind of salvation are they celebrating if not a salvation from God's wrath? Washed white in the blood of the Lamb yet suffering the wrath of God because they missed a pretrib rapture? Is that what we're supposed to think about them?[7]

Gundry goes on to protest:

> Christians have never been promised exemption from tribulation in general. On the contrary, they've been told they will suffer it (John 16:33; Acts 14:22; Rom. 5:3; 1 Thess. 3:3; Rev 1:9; 2:10). . . . So what if persecution by the Antichrist will exceed any previous persecution? In the nature of the case, one persecution is liable to exceed all others, but that fact offers no reason to exempt the church from the worst persecution and put that persecution onto later saints, the delay in whose conversion would in many cases be due to the church's failure to evangelize them before the tribulation. Some justice![8]

We may rest assured that even though God is not going to "rapture" us off the planet before the Tribulation, this does not mean we will be left helpless by God. During the Tribulation, God will see to it that angels lead the people of God to the shelter of a Goshen. And like Noah, the Church will pass through the flood and inherit a renewed Creation.

The "Imminence" Argument

The "imminence" argument is Dave Hunt's favorite. In fact, he devotes a full chapter to this argument in his book, *How Close Are We?* It's really a very simple argument when stripped of all its rhetorical embellishments. First, the reasoning goes, recall the elementary blunder of the Jews in Jesus' day. They were faced with two sets of contradictory prophecies for the coming of the

---

6   Hal Lindsey, commenting on the "woes" pronounced upon "those who dwell on the earth" in Rev. 8:13, concludes that the believers of the Tribulation are specially protected by God: "Since the woes are not addressed to the believers of this time, it implies that they are somehow specially protected. In light of the magnitude of the judgments already studied, there would not be a believing remnant left on earth apart from some kind of divine protection." *Apocalypse*, 148.

7   Gundry, *Antichrist*, 49.

8   Gundry, *Antichrist*, 50.

Messiah: one set that depicted Christ as a Suffering Servant and another that depicted Him as the conquering Anointed of the Lord who comes to vindicate Israel. The blunder was in not recognizing that these prophecies required two distinct Advents of the Messiah, the first to suffer for the sins of the world and the second as the glorious King of kings.

As the Jews faced two sets of seemingly contradictory prophecies in the Old Testament that told of two comings of the Messiah, Hunt argues, so Christians are faced with two sets of contradictory prophecies of Christ's return. One set of New Testament scriptures speaks of Christ as coming as a "thief in the night" (see Matt. 24:43; Luke 12:39; 1 Thess. 5:2, 4; 2 Pet. 3:10; Rev. 3:3; 16:15), whose coming will be unexpected (Matt. 24:44), as was the judgment in Noah's day (Luke 17:26, 27). However, another set of scriptures instructs us to watch the "signs of the times," like wars, famines, plagues, earthquakes, the coming of Antichrist, and so forth. If Christ's Second Coming is accompanied by such dramatic signs, Hunt argues, then how can it come unexpectedly, like a "thief in the night"? The answer is supposedly that there are two more comings of Christ, one that is unexpected—a secret rapture—and another preceded by dramatic signs, the coming of Christ as King of kings. Thus scriptures that speak of Christ's coming as imminent are interpreted as referring to the rapture at the beginning of the Tribulation, whereas scriptures that say Christ's Advent will be preceded by signs refer to Christ's coming at the end of the world.[9]

A variety of difficulties arises once we begin to set up such a dichotomy between scriptures that speak of Christ's unexpected and imminent coming and scriptures that speak of Christ's coming being preceded by signs. In fact, Hunt himself is conscious of a damaging inconsistency in this argument for the rapture. For Hunt's reasoning to have full force, he must stress that there

---

9   Larry Crutchfield takes this reasoning a step further in an essay entitled, "The Blessed Hope and the Tribulation in the Apostolic Fathers." Crutchfield notes that many early Fathers believed they were living in the last days and were looking daily for Christ's return; therefore, he reasons, the Apostolic Fathers planted the seeds of the pretribulation rapture! While conceding that "the position of the early fathers was a type of imminent posttribulationism" (which Crutchfield has chosen to dub "imminent intratribulationism"), and conceding "that dispensationalists today do not say that the early church was clearly pretribulational, or that there are even clear individual statements of pretribulationism in the fathers," Crutchfield nevertheless weakly concludes, "Had it not been for the drought in sound exegesis [in the early Church], brought on by Alexandrian allegorism and later by Augustine, one wonders what kind of crop those seeds might have yielded—long before J. N. Darby and the nineteenth century." What one really "wonders," however, is why Crutchfield ignores the exegetical work of the Antiochian Fathers, particularly St. John Chrysostom. The reason may be that Antioch, despite not being given to the allegorism characteristic of Alexandria, still didn't develop anything like a pretrib rapture. See Larry Crutchfield, "The Blessed Hope and the Tribulation in the Apostolic Fathers," *When the Trumpet Sounds*, 85–103.

is an absolute distinction between two sets of scriptures that speak of Christ's return. The "second" coming, meaning the rapture, cannot be preceded by signs: "There will be no signs for the Rapture, no warning that it is about to occur," as Hunt repeatedly stresses.[10]

Yet, as anyone who peruses the doomsday literature quickly learns, the current belief that the rapture can happen at any moment is not based on a merely generic doctrine of "imminence," but on the signs of Christ's return supposedly being reported each day on CNN's "Headline News" and ABC's "World News Tonight." Indeed, Hunt answers the question in the title of his book, *How Close Are We?* (referring to the imminence of the rapture), by pointing to the "signs." These are, for example, the 1948 restoration of Israel and the talk of "peace and safety" (1 Thess. 5:3) that many believe will occur before the rapture. Also, it is commonly believed among many that the gospel must first be preached in all the world for a witness to all nations before the rapture will come (Matt. 24:14).

Dave Hunt is at least consistent with his own argument. He acknowledges that it was not necessary for Israel to be back in Palestine before the rapture.[11] Therefore, Hunt is forced to argue that the restoration of Israel, the expected building of the Temple in Jerusalem, and the reinstitution of sacrifices might all have occurred in the short three-and-a-half-year period after the rapture, as improbable as that might seem. Nevertheless, Hunt can't resist seeing in contemporary events pointers to the rapture that mark our times as unique in all of history: "Thus it is not only *possible* for the Rapture to occur at any moment, as it always has been, but now it is highly *probable*—certainly more probable than at any time in history!"[12]

Conversely, more "orthodox" millenarians readily admit that no one knows the day or the hour of Christ's Second Coming in power and glory (Matt. 24:36), and will condemn date setting. They will therefore admit that there is a certain amount of unexpectedness in Christ's final return (His "third" coming) at the end of history. Hunt, though, to maintain his artificial distinction between "imminent" passages and "sign" passages in the Bible, is forced to argue that just as the date for the first coming of Christ was knowable [?], "the exact date of the Second Coming can be known as well."[13] However, by this Hunt only means that the date of Christ's return can be calculated by adding seven years to the date of the rapture, once that event occurs.

Hunt's main problem, then, is in maintaining a seeming distinction

---

10 Hunt, *Close*, 109.
11 Hunt, *Close*, 262–264.
12 Hunt, *Close*, 262. Emphasis in original.
13 Hunt, *Close*, 154.

between certain scriptures when, in fact, there isn't any. Look at how Hunt tries to respond to the problems created by this artificial distinction:

> One cannot escape the fact that Christ and His apostles gave definite signs to watch for that would herald the nearness of His return. Why give these signs if some generation at some time in the future was not expected to recognize them and know that His Second Coming was, as He Himself said, "near, even at the doors"? [14]

In other words, why would Christ leave signs to indicate the nearness of His final return in glory if the Church has been raptured off the planet and there is no one around to watch for them? Jesus surely didn't leave these signs for non-Christians, who wouldn't believe them anyway even if they happened to know them. So why leave signs and ask Christians to "watch" for them, as our Lord commands in numerous places (Matt. 24:42; Mark 13:35; Luke 21:36; et. al.)? Hunt continues:

> Yes, but if the Rapture occurs seven years prior to the Second Coming, then those signs are not for us. So it would seem. Yet Christ commanded His own to watch for His coming and warned against being caught by surprise at His return—and surprise could only apply to the Rapture. Are we faced again with a contradiction, and this time one that cannot be resolved? [15]

The answer is "yes," but Hunt isn't going down without a fight. Hunt stresses that the signs Jesus says will precede His return are like birth pangs, slowly growing in intensity until the end arrives:

> Moreover, it would seem that these signs *begin* prior to the Rapture. Then how could the Rapture come as a surprise? Because these signs when they begin, will by their very nature be phenomena which have always been known on the world scene: earthquakes, famines, pestilences, wars. [16]

In other words, Jesus told us to watch for "signs" so vague as to be virtually meaningless, leaving us without a clue as to the nearness of the rapture. Yet, according to Hunt, we know the rapture is near today because of the signs pointing to the Second Coming—but these signs are so vague and general they don't really count as "signs" of the imminent rapture. After all, these signs have always been present in the world. But how do we know then that ours is the generation that will see the rapture? Because of the signs . . . Well, the reader gets the picture. Hunt reasons in so many circles that one wants to take pity and mail him some motion-sickness pills.

Worse still for Hunt is a verse he has totally overlooked: Revelation

---

14 Hunt, *Close*, 115.
15 Ibid.
16 Hunt, *Close*, 116. Emphasis in original.

16:15, which, according to the dispensationalist's chronological interpretation of Revelation, is situated right in the middle of the Great Tribulation (after the rapture and before the Second Coming). In this verse Jesus states quite plainly, "Behold, I am coming as a thief." Jesus couldn't be referring to the rapture, which has supposedly already taken place. He must therefore be speaking of the unexpectedness of His Second Coming, which will sneak up on us like "a thief." [17] With just this one verse, Hunt's strained dichotomy between the rapture and the Second Coming completely unravels.

Moreover, many dispensationalists (like Hal Lindsey and Charles Ryrie) don't even date the Second Coming from the rapture, but from a treaty that the Antichrist is supposed to sign with Israel. In fact, Ryrie states, "Though I believe that the rapture precedes the beginning of the Tribulation, actually nothing is said in the Scriptures as to whether or not some time (or how much time) may elapse between the rapture and the opening of the Tribulation." [18] So we are left with the question: Does the seven-year countdown begin with the rapture or the signing of the covenant with the Antichrist? If the latter, then does this seven-year period start with the handshake, the public announcement, or the ceremonial signing? When exactly does the clock start ticking down seven years? If in fact this can't be determined, how can we know when Christ will return? If the time of Christ's return can't be known, then aren't we left to conclude that the specific time of Christ's final Advent will be unexpected, just as the rapture is supposed to be?

After enduring Dave Hunt's painful cut-and-paste job on the Bible, how refreshing it is to turn to the simple wisdom of the early Church Fathers! Listen to how St. John Chrysostom (347–407) explains the relation of "imminence" and "signs" to Christ's Second Coming:

> But it may be worthwhile to ask, If Antichrist comes, and Elijah comes (cf. Mal. 4:5), how is it "when they say peace and safety" (1 Thess. 5:3), that then a sudden destruction comes upon them? For these things do not permit the day to come upon them unawares, being signs of its coming. But he [Paul] does not mean this to be the time of Antichrist, and the whole day, because that will be a sign of the coming of Christ, but Himself will not have a sign, but will come suddenly and unexpectedly. For travail, indeed, you say, does not come upon the pregnant woman unexpectedly: for she

---

17 Some dispensationalists understand Jesus' coming as a thief to mean that Christ will come in "secret," as in a secret rapture of the Church out of the world. Yet as any survey of the "thief" motif in the New Testament quickly reveals, the idea is that the thief comes unexpectedly, not secretly. In Matt. 24:43, 44, for example, the thief strikes unexpectedly; we must therefore be prepared, "for the Son of Man is coming at an hour you do not expect." For another good example, see Rev. 3:3.

18 Ryrie, *Countdown*, 90–91.

knows that after nine months the birth will take place. And yet it is very uncertain. For some bring forth at the seventh month, and others at the ninth. And at any rate the day and the hour is uncertain. With respect to this therefore, Paul speaks thus [in 1 Thessalonians 5:3]. And the image is exact. For there are not many sure signs of travail; many indeed have brought forth in the high roads, or when out of their houses and abroad, not foreseeing it. And he has not only glanced here at the uncertainty, but also at the bitterness of the pain. For as she while sporting, laughing, not looking for anything at all, being suddenly seized with unspeakable pains, is pierced through with the pangs of labor—so will it be with those souls, when the Day comes upon them.[19]

Chrysostom's point is that, though we are given signs letting us know when the Second Coming is at hand, these signs do not inform us of the specific time when the event will occur. Just as a mother can know from certain signs when she will soon give birth to a child, yet not know exactly when the birth will happen, so the Church will know when Christ's return is imminent without knowing exactly when this event will happen. The Church will therefore anticipate the Second Coming based on the signs, though the exact moment of Christ's return will come unexpectedly.

Ultimately, Hunt's argument for the rapture creates more problems than it solves. All the scriptures that speak of Christ's final Advent speak of it as being both unexpected and preceded by certain general signs. Therefore, we do not need to create a complicated and artificial distinction between two groups of biblical texts. We will never know exactly when Christ will return, but we can know when His arrival is near. The answer to Hunt's allegedly "contradictory" prophecies is so simple that it's amazing he doesn't see it himself. Unfortunately, Hunt's devotion to an ill-conceived pretribulational rapture doctrine prevents him from jumping off the theological carousel that has him perpetually reasoning in circles.

The Rapture Mythology

Dave Hunt's problems don't end with the syllogistic pretzel upon which he bases his doctrine of the rapture. There is also the difficulty of the doctrine's history—or, to be more precise, the lack thereof—with which he must contend. Obviously, he doesn't admit the doctrine was conceived in the nineteenth century as a necessary cog in John Darby's dispensationalist system. Instead, Hunt attempts to find a "history" of the rapture doctrine in the Church. The story runs like this:

Once upon a time, in a land far, far away in the eastern Mediterranean, there was a small band of simple people who came together to form what

---

19 John Chrysostom, *Thessalonians*, Homily 9 on 1 Thess. 5:3.

they called the "church." These were the first Christians, and they believed that their leader, Jesus, would come again soon to rapture them from the planet. This rapture they called their "blessed hope" (Titus 2:13). Then, after seven years of divine wrath, they would return with Jesus to set up a thousand-year political order with the Lord sitting on the throne of David in Jerusalem.

Back then, everyone believed in this "blessed hope" of the rapture. However, this golden age of "orthodoxy" wasn't to last for long:

> As the weary weeks became years, however, and the years multiplied into decades, and finally centuries passed, the vast majority of those who claimed to be Christ's followers gave less and less thought to that "blessed hope." The promise of Christ's return was first neglected and then forgotten. Finally it was lost in the maze of new interpretations and heresies which began to multiply.[20]

With the Church in this weakened state, Emperor Constantine came on the scene and seduced the Church into an unholy alliance to help him rule the empire. To Dave Hunt, Constantine was to Christianity what Darth Vader was to Luke Skywalker. ("Turn to the Dark Side, Luke, and together we shall rule the empire as father and son!") According to Hunt, Christianity went down the tubes once Constantine stopped the persecution of the Christians and legalized the Church:

> Now that Christianity was recognized along with the old paganism, Constantine assumed leadership of the Christian Church. In doing so, he took the title Vicar of Christ. . . . In a moment of weakness, a Church weary of persecution accepted the same offer [of an earthly kingdom] from Satan [which Jesus had rejected in the wilderness], this time presented through the Roman emperor. It was the beginning of centuries of what would be known as the Church's "Babylonian captivity."[21]

One thing inevitably led to another and, before long, even sinners were being allowed into the Church. Alas, none of these people entering the Church without the threat of persecution was really serious about Christ: "False professions were more the rule than the exception."[22] As Hunt has no appreciation for monasticism, the fact that monastic vocations soared during this period in Church history means nothing to him as far as the vitality of the Church is concerned. Nor does Hunt seem cognizant of the fact that this

---

20 Hunt, *Close*, 95.
21 Hunt, *Close*, 97. Actually, the "Babylonian Captivity" in Church history refers to a seventy-year period in the fourteenth century when the popes resided in Avignon, France. The term originated with Dante and Petrarch, Italian patriots who felt that the papacy was under the absolute control of the French monarchy.
22 Ibid.

period was a golden age of brilliant theological achievements, as exemplified by the composition of the Nicene Creed at the first two Ecumenical Councils, not to mention the theological accomplishments of St. Athanasius of Alexandria and the Cappadocian Fathers. To Hunt, the Church simply divorced orthodoxy at this time and married a corrupt world. Inevitably, "the Church lost its hope of heaven and began to look upon itself as the replacement for God's earthly people, Israel." [23] At this point all was lost and the rapture doctrine wasn't even a distant memory.

The Reformation did nothing to "recover" the rapture doctrine, Hunt complains, and the doctrine is still denied among Anglicans, Lutherans, and the Reformed churches, such as the Presbyterians. Hunt concedes that he can somewhat understand his Protestant brethren's reluctance to adopt the rapture doctrine:

> Unfortunately, when the "blessed hope" of Christ's imminent return has been revived periodically in the last two centuries, the excitement created here and there has usually developed into date setting, causing the Rapture to become an object of derision. Voluntarily divested of their earthly possessions, cruelly deluded, white-robed zealots have more than once waited in vain on hilltop or rooftop while the promised hour came and went. Such fanatical anticipation has always subsided once again into disillusion and forgetfulness.[24]

Hunt then notes some of the recent comical attempts to set dates for the rapture, and how these have sabotaged the efforts of Hal Lindsey and others "attempting a biblical treatment of the Rapture." Hunt observes, "In the wake of such excited anticipation and then disappointment, greater disillusionment than ever has now smothered the legitimate hope of Christ's imminent return." [25] Of course, Lindsey himself contributed greatly to this general disillusionment by hinting the Second Coming would happen in 1988, implying the rapture would occur seven years earlier in 1981.

The problem with Hunt's "history" of the rapture is that it is entirely mythological. He makes lots of assertions but doesn't attempt to document any of them. In fact, there are only three footnotes in *How Close Are We?* to reference anything Hunt claims. The attitude seems to be, "Why weigh down the book with things like footnotes? What could the simple reader want with documentation anyway?" We are consequently left to accept Hunt's word that the Church originally taught the pretribulational rapture, and that the evil Constantine so convoluted Christian doctrine that it wasn't until recently

23 Hunt, *Close*, 98.
24 Hunt, *Close*, 101.
25 Ibid.

that folks like Lindsey and Hunt rediscovered the rapture teaching in the Bible.

The reason Hunt doesn't cite any evidence for his fanciful "history" is that there simply isn't any. All the evidence is on the side of the traditional teaching of the Church, which affirms that Christians will go through the Tribulation. We have already seen some passages from the writings of the early Church in the previous chapter that affirmed this belief. Let's look at a few others.

There exists a Syrian church manual that dates to as early as fifty years after the composition of the Book of Revelation. This work is called the *Didache*, and the expectation of the Second Coming is prominent throughout. Contrary to what Hunt would have us expect, the *Didache* describes Christians going through the Tribulation.[26] As a product of the sub-Apostolic Church (A.D. 100–150),[27] this work is obviously too early for the pretrib rapture to have been simply "forgotten."

There is also another interesting document from about the same period, but from a different part of the world. Written at Rome in the mid-second century, *The Shepherd of Hermas* tells those who go through the Great Tribulation: "Blessed are you, as many as endure the Great Tribulation [Gr. *thlipsin*] which is coming, and as many as shall not deny their life." [28] The Greek word for "Tribulation" used here is the same one that is used in places like Matthew 24:21, 29 and Revelation 7:14 for the Tribulation at the end of the world. The author of *The Shepherd* obviously believes that Christians (specifically, his own generation) will go through the Great Tribulation.

Later in the second century, Irenaeus tells us that, after the Antichrist accepts the kingdom from ten kings (represented by the ten horns of the beast in Revelation 17:12), he then will "put the Church to flight," [29] which would be impossible if the Church had already been raptured. We noted in the previous chapter, when we looked at pretrib rapture proof texts, that Paul writes about the Antichrist to warn his readers to beware of this adversary, obviously assuming that Christians will go through the Tribulation. Irenaeus interprets the number of the beast in Revelation 13:18 in the same way: "But he [John] indicates the number [666] of the [Antichrist's] name now, that when this man comes we may avoid him, being aware [of] who he is." [30]

26 *Didache*, 16:4–8.
27 Though the time of composition for the *Didache* is generally agreed to be between A.D. 100 and 150, some have posited a date as early as A.D. 70.
28 *The Shepherd of Hermas*, Vision 2:2:7.
29 Irenaeus, *Heresies*, 5:26:1.
30 Irenaeus, *Heresies*, 5:30:4.

Everything Irenaeus wrote concerning the Tribulation assumed the Church would be present during that time.

Tertullian, from Carthage in north Africa, wrote a treatise in Latin entitled *On the Resurrection of the Flesh* (also called *On the Resurrection of the Dead*) between the years 208 and 212. Tertullian not only states that the rapture and glorification of living Christians occur at the Second Coming after the reign of the Antichrist, but he also cites the main pretrib rapture proof text in the process:

> Now the privilege of this favor [not to suffer physical death] awaits those who shall, at the coming of the Lord, be found in the flesh, and who shall, owing to the oppressions of the time of Antichrist, deserve by an instantaneous death, which is accomplished by a sudden change, to become qualified to join the rising saints, as he [Paul] writes to the Thessalonians [Tertullian then cites 1 Thess. 4:15–17].[31]

What we have been looking at is concrete historical evidence that the early Church believed it would go through the Tribulation, encounter the Antichrist, and meet the Lord in the air in glorified bodies at the Second Coming. The evidence presented above is clear and comes very early in the life of the Church. Dave Hunt simply cannot match this because there is absolutely no evidence of a belief in a pretrib rapture among the ancient Christians. Not only are there no positive affirmations of a pretrib rapture in the early Church, there aren't even any *negative* ones. There are no ancient writings arguing against a minority belief in some sort of pretrib rapture. This is because absolutely no one ever held such a belief. Simply put, the teaching never existed in any form in the early Church.

Pseudo-Evidence for a Pseudo-History

Prophecy peddlers obviously recognize the need to show some proof that someone before the 1830s actually held to a pretribulational rapture, and consequently have left no ecclesiastical stone unturned in order to find evidence to refute their critics. One respectable attempt has recently been made by Grant Jeffrey in an essay entitled, "A Pretrib Rapture Statement in the Early Medieval Church." [32] Jeffrey, an avowed dispensationalist, was convinced "that the pretribulational rapture is taught so clearly in the New Testament that it is virtually impossible that no one ever taught this doctrine in the 18 centuries before 1830." [33] A man on a mission, Jeffrey spent a decade

---

31 Tertullian, *On the Resurrection of the Flesh*, 41.
32 Grant Jeffrey, "A Pretrib Rapture Statement in the Early Medieval Church," *When the Trumpet Sounds*, 105ff.
33 Jeffrey, "Pretrib," 108.

searching for proof from the early Church to establish once and for all that the pretribulational rapture didn't just pop up out of nowhere in the nineteenth century. In the summer of 1994, after ten long years, he finally found what he was after.

What he discovered was a sermon called *On the Last Times, the Antichrist, and the End of the World*, ascribed to the fourth-century Church Father, Ephrem the Syrian.[34] (Of the four extant Latin manuscripts, however, one ascribes the work to St. Isidore of Seville [A.D. 560–636].) The document is known to scholars as *Pseudo-Ephrem*. Whoever actually composed the sermon (it certainly wasn't Ephrem),[35] the work comes from the early Middle Ages, sometime between the fifth and seventh centuries. What got Jeffrey so excited is the following:

> Why therefore do we not reject every care of earthly actions and prepare ourselves for the meeting of the Lord Christ, so that He may draw us from the confusion, which overwhelms the world? . . . Because all saints and the Elect of the Lord are gathered before the tribulation which is to [*sic*] about to come and are taken to the Lord, in order that they may not see at any time the confusion which overwhelms the world because of our sins. (Section 2)[36]

Jeffrey has reproduced the entire text of Pseudo-Ephrem (translated from a Latin text by Cameron Rhoades of Tyndale Theological Seminary in Fort Worth, Texas) to place the above statement in its full context. So what are we to conclude from this citation? Does it prove that there were Christians during the Middle Ages who believed in a pretrib rapture? Even more provocatively, does Pseudo-Ephrem preserve something of the true Ephrem's belief in a rapture before the Tribulation?

Robert Gundry, who devotes an entire chapter to analyzing Pseudo-Ephrem in his book *First the Antichrist*,[37] observes that the passage cited

---

34 Ephrem was born in A.D. 306 in Nisibis, on the Roman–Persian frontier. After the bishop of Nisibis returned from the Council of Nicaea in 325, he appointed Ephrem to a teaching position in the prestigious theological school of Nisibis. Ephrem left Mesopotamia in 363 when Nisibis came under Persian control and went to Edessa, where he was ordained to the diaconate. When a plague broke out in Edessa, Ephrem cared for the sick. Ephrem died in the course of the plague, on June 9, 373. Ephrem is best remembered for his hymns and metrical homilies.

35 Collections of works ascribed to Ephrem exist in several languages, the largest body of texts being Greek. This Greek corpus mostly consists of ascetical literature that is today widely believed to be spurious. Nearly all the surviving texts attributed to Ephrem in languages other than Syriac and Armenian are derived from this Greek corpus, including the Latin corpus.

36 Jeffrey, "Pretrib," 110–111.

37 Gundry, *Antichrist*, 161ff. Our evaluation of Pseudo-Ephrem closely follows Gundry's analysis.

above says nothing about Christ's coming, as in Paul's description of the rapture in 1 Thessalonians 4:16, 17. Also absent is a mention of the resurrection of the dead and the glorification of living Christians, which both 1 Corinthians 15:51, 52 and 1 Thessalonians 4:16, 17 describe. Nor does the passage from Pseudo-Ephrem actually state that Christians are taken to heaven, as dispensationalists argue based on their interpretation of John 14:2–4 and Revelation 4:1, 2. In other words, what is missing from the above citation are precisely all the main elements of a pretrib rapture. Consequently, Gundry points out, there is good reason to doubt that Pseudo-Ephrem is really describing a pretribulational rapture.

Moving into the overall context of the citation, Pseudo-Ephrem describes Christians being on earth during the Tribulation period, which Pseudo-Ephrem conceives as a period lasting three and a half years (not seven). After the alleged rapture of the Church in section 2 of Pseudo-Ephrem, we read, "When therefore the end of the world comes, there arise . . . persecutions, slaughters and massacres everywhere" (section 3).[38] As a result, we learn in section 4 that the corpses of dead Christians (Orthodox Christians, as distinguished from heretics) are lying around unburied due to the horrors and anarchy of the Tribulation: "In those days people shall not be buried, neither Christian, nor heretic, neither Jew, nor pagan, because of fear and dread there is not one who buries them; because all people ignore them while they are fleeing." [39]

As a result of the horrors of the Tribulation, many Christians flee to the desert and live an ascetic life: "But those who wander through the deserts, fleeing from the faces of the serpent, bend their knees to God, just as lambs to the udders of their mothers, being sustained by the salvation of the Lord, and while wandering in states of desertion, they eat herbs" (section 8).[40] Gundry calls attention to the echo of Revelation 12:6, 13–17 in the above passage.

Section 9 then describes the "inevitability" of the suffering that falls on both the "just and unjust," though noting that the just will be "found good by their Lord." The "just" therefore are Christians whose fidelity is pleasing to "their Lord." Pseudo-Ephrem states that Enoch and Elijah will appear on earth to free them from the Antichrist's seductions: "And when the just ones [Enoch and Elijah] have appeared . . . [they will] call back the faithful witnesses to God, in order to free them from his [the serpent's] seduction." Moreover, when Christ appears at the end of the Tribulation in section 10, He destroys those who have followed the Antichrist, but the ones who didn't,

---

38 Jeffrey, "Pretrib," 111.
39 Jeffrey, "Pretrib," 112.
40 Jeffrey, "Pretrib," 114.

"the righteous ones shall inherit everlasting life with the Lord for ever and ever." [41]

If the Christians were raptured before the Tribulation, where do these persecuted Christians come from who need to be freed from the Antichrist's seductions and who are separated from the Antichrist's minions when the Lord comes in glory? Jeffrey doesn't consider this, probably because he sees these as Jews who have come to believe in Christ during the Tribulation. Consequently he wouldn't believe this poses a problem for him, even though Pseudo-Ephrem doesn't say these Christians are Jews who converted to Christianity after the supposed rapture.

However, the pretrib rapture interpretation of Pseudo-Ephrem faces even more serious problems. When the Lord's Second Coming occurs in Section 10, Pseudo-Ephrem states that He comes with "the whole chorus of the saints" and "the angelic trumpet . . . which shall sound and declare: Arise O sleeping ones, arise, meet Christ, because his hour of judgment has come! Then Christ shall come and the enemy shall be thrown into confusion . . . but the righteous ones shall inherit everlasting life with the Lord forever and ever." [42]

The parallels between this account of the Second Coming and 1 Thessalonians 4:16, 17 are clear. Both describe the angelic trumpet, which is characterized as a "voice," and dead Christians (remember the unburied Christian corpses) rise in the resurrection to "meet Christ." Even the last words in the above passage, "with the Lord forever and ever," recall Paul's concluding words in 1 Thessalonians 4:17, "and so shall we ever be with the Lord" (KJV). Pseudo-Ephrem sees the resurrection of the saints and the Second Coming of Christ with those saints as a single event. Consequently, if the resurrection of Christians described in 1 Thessalonians 4:16, 17 occurs at the Second Coming, then so does the rapture of the Church.

Significantly, in the above citation from Pseudo-Ephrem (section 10), the Latin verb for "to meet," *occurrite*, is a cognate of the noun *occursum*, "meeting," which is used in the alleged pretrib rapture proof text in section 2: "the *meeting* of the Lord Christ." [43] Therefore, the "meeting of the Lord Christ" mentioned in Section 2 should be understood to occur at the Second Coming, when living and dead Christians are explicitly said "to meet Christ." Again, this echoes Paul in 1 Thessalonians 4:17, which, translated literally, says that the living and the dead "shall be seized in clouds to a *meeting of the Lord* in [the] air." We can only conclude from this that Pseudo-Ephrem is not describing a pretrib rapture, but a rapture that occurs at the Second Coming

---

41 Jeffrey, "Pretrib," 114–115.
42 Ibid.
43 Gundry, *Antichrist*, 170.

when we meet the Lord in the air and escort him to the final judgment.

Given the above, including the fact that Pseudo-Ephrem describes Christians going through the Tribulation, we need to go back and take a second look at Jeffrey's citation that says Christians "are gathered together before the Tribulation which is to [*sic*] about to come and are taken to the Lord." Gundry observes that the Latin verb translated "are gathered," *colliguntur*, as well as the verb translated "are taken," *adsumuntur*, are in the present tense and are normally translated as an action in progress. He therefore translates the passage in question: "For all the saints and elect of God *are being gathered* prior to the tribulation that is to come, and *are being taken* to the Lord lest they ever see the confusion that is to overwhelm the world because of our sins." [44]

This translation allows us to reconcile the pretrib "proof text" with Pseudo-Ephrem's explicit description of our meeting Christ at the Second Coming. Gundry draws on the genuine writings of Ephrem to show that Ephrem frequently used the image of a Jewish pilgrimage to Jerusalem "as a symbol of all nations being gathered evangelistically and taken to the Lord in Christian conversion." [45] The "Ephremic tradition," of which Pseudo-Ephrem is a part, continued to speak of evangelization as a "gathering" of the Elect to be "taken" to the Lord. Therefore, what Pseudo-Ephrem is likely saying is that the Elect are being "gathered" and "taken" to the Lord in the sense that they are being evangelized and drawing closer to their Lord in the Church. They are spiritually preparing themselves prior to the Tribulation so that they will be able to avoid "the confusion that is to overwhelm the world" during the Tribulation. When the lures of the Antichrist begin to draw Christians away, Pseudo-Ephrem informs us that Enoch and Elijah, the two witnesses of Revelation 11, appear to call them back to Christ. The Lord then returns and rewards their fidelity. This understanding of Pseudo-Ephrem renders it consistent with the genuine writings of Ephrem, which portray evangelism as a gathering and which also describe Christians as going through the Tribulation.

However, for the sake of argument, let's say that Pseudo-Ephrem is everything Grant Jeffrey claims it to be—a clear affirmation of the pretribulational rapture by a Christian in the medieval Church. Even if we grant this, it would only mean that a single Christian formulated the basic idea of the pretrib rapture in the early Middle Ages, and that this basic idea was developed only later in the nineteenth century. Instead of a nineteenth-century innovation, then, the pretrib rapture is actually a medieval innovation. This

---

44 Gundry, *Antichrist*, 176. Emphasis in original.
45 Gundry, *Antichrist*, 183.

hardly gives the doctrine impressive credentials. Yet, on the basis of Pseudo-Ephrem alone, Jeffrey is ready to proclaim the apostolic origin of the pretribulational rapture as being firmly established! Jeffrey triumphantly declares:

> The biblical truth of the glorious rapture of the church prior to the Tribulation was definitely taught in the early church. . . . This finding of the pretribulation rapture in Ephraem's writings illustrates that the biblical truth of God's blessed hope and deliverance of the saints was upheld by a remnant of the faithful from the beginning of the church until today.[46]

There it is: after an intense ten-year quest, the medieval Pseudo-Ephrem (fifth to seventh century) is all that Jeffrey can dig up in support of a pretribulational rapture predating John Darby in 1830. Nevertheless, Jeffrey is certain the finding is earth-shaking:

> Those who have attacked the pretribulation rapture on the basis that it is some kind of innovative theory, never taught before throughout the history of the church, need to become more familiar with these important texts [Pseudo-Ephrem and a quotation from John Gills, who Jeffrey also believes—mistakenly—taught a pretrib rapture prior to the eighteenth century]. The French writer Joubert once wrote, "Nothing makes men so imprudent and conceited as ignorance of the past and a scorn for old books." [47]

One has to admire Jeffrey's spirit. With what meager evidence he has mustered, he comes as a young David before the overwhelming weight of evidence that is on the side of the historic Church. If a medieval sermon is enough to declare the pretribulational rapture no "innovative theory," then what can be said of the teaching of the Orthodox Church, the historical evidence for which reaches back to the dawn of Christianity, and, if piled together, could physically crush Jeffrey by its sheer weight? If anything, Jeffrey's possible "exception," only dug up after ten years of intense searching, actually proves the rule: the pretribulational rapture is an "innovative theory." Moreover, according to Gundry, the "exception" is actually no exception at all. In the end, all that Jeffrey has established with his research is the flimsiness of the claim that the early Church believed in a pretribulation rapture.

Orthodox theologian Georges Florovsky once observed that it isn't enough merely to quote the early Church Fathers—one must acquire the mind of the Fathers. That is, one must learn to think as the Christians of the early Church did. Anyone can quote an ancient source to "prove" anything. The

---

46 Jeffrey, "Pretrib," 125. Jeffrey's enthusiasm has gotten the better of him here. Pseudo-Ephrem is obviously not a part of real Ephrem's writings.

47 Jeffrey, "Pretrib," 122.

Jehovah's Witnesses and the Mormons do it all the time, often using the same source to buttress contradictory claims. To cite an ancient author, for example, as seemingly denying the divinity of Christ (as the Jehovah's Witnesses routinely do) is not the same as proving that the teaching of the ancient Church originally denied Christ's divinity. Even if the ancient author cited did in fact deny Christ's divinity, we must not confuse the erroneous opinion of one man with the teaching of the universal Church.

As far as learning to think like the early Christians is concerned, Jeffrey is not even close. To put it bluntly, Jeffrey uses the Fathers as a drunkard uses lampposts—for support rather than illumination.[48] This is not intended as an *ad hominem* attack upon Jeffrey. It is simply a terse observation that Jeffrey was never seeking enlightenment as to what the early Christians actually believed concerning Christ's Second Coming, but only apparent support for his pet theory. As he himself frankly admitted, he was already firmly convinced before doing any research, based upon his own eccentric reading of Scripture, that the pretribulational rapture was a teaching held by the original Christians. He then proceeded to look for any evidence that might be used to affirm what he had already decided must be true. What he found was a brief statement in an obscure medieval homily. Jeffrey found what he wanted to find—which was an apparent affirmation of his own peculiar reading of the New Testament, and not the mind of the early Church on the question of the rapture.

The Triumph of Pop Theology?

The rapture is an immensely popular teaching among contemporary millenarians, which is why people like Grant Jeffrey work so hard at producing fig leaves to cover up its more embarrassing aspects. As a sign of this popularity, one can frequently see cars on the road with bumper stickers like, "WARNING: In the event of the rapture, this car will be driverless." Or one might see T-shirts with a picture of a "Post-Rapture Milk Carton." On the side of the milk carton is a photograph of an immense crowd, with the question, "Have you seen me?" written underneath.

At the end of 1995, Tim LaHaye and Jerry Jenkins coauthored a novel called *Left Behind* that attempted to chronicle what the postrapture world would be like. The book quickly sold more than a hundred thousand copies. In the story, people vanish in an instant, leaving only their clothes and jewelry on the spot where they once stood (we aren't informed whether the elderly left dentures and pacemakers). Cars crash, planes drop from the sky, and

---

48 Simile borrowed from Scottish scholar and author Andrew Lang (1844–1912).

death and mayhem reign everywhere. In one memorable scene, CNN airs a home video of a woman in a hospital delivering a baby when the rapture hits. Suddenly her abdomen deflates and the doctor delivers only a placenta. *Left Behind* is now also a popular video.[49]

Somehow, though, an old comic book by Jack Chic called *Chaos* captures the peculiar aura of the rapture doctrine best. On the cover is a picture of a hospital nursery with all the incubators empty. A nurse is running down the hallway after a doctor, screaming, "Doctor . . . the babies . . . they're ALL MISSING!" The doctor replies, "That's impossible!"

Chaos is about "the nation's foremost authority on biblical prophecy," Dr. Harry Morse, who has been targeted by a cult for assassination. As we work our way through the story, we naturally learn from Dr. Morse that the most important sign that we are in the last days is the restoration of Israel, which was predicted in Ezekiel 38:8: "I believe the final generation began on May 14, 1948, when Israel became a nation!" However, Dr. Morse devotes most of his time to talking about the rapture.

What will the rapture be like? He describes the scene of a Boeing 747 crashing at an airport during landing because the pilot has just vanished. Immediately below a drawing of passengers being tossed about inside the cabin, panicking at their impending death, 1 Corinthians 15:51, 52 is quoted: "In a moment, in the twinkling of an eye . . ." This horrible event is followed by the hospital scene depicted on the cover, with babies and other patients disappearing mysteriously. The character to which Dr. Morse is describing all this can only respond, "Man . . . I never heard anything like that before!"

But *Chaos* is only warming up at this point. Later on, we are informed that astronomers have supposedly found "a great empty space in the north of the nebula of the constellation of Orion," reportedly more than 16 trillion miles in diameter. Dr. Morse believes this could very well be the entrance to heaven through which the saints will pass at the rapture. On the other side of this entrance, the raptured saints will all sit around a massive table in heaven. This is the "marriage supper of the Lamb," and all around the massive table are angels with trays acting as busboys and waiters.

Of course, not all the adherents to the pretrib rapture subscribe to Jack Chic's comic-book theology. But Chic aside, the marketing of such comic books, bumper stickers, T-shirts, novels, videos, and so forth testifies to the ongoing popularity of the doctrine. It is to this popularity, rather than to any compelling biblical or patristic evidence, that the pretrib rapture owes its

---

49 In fact, the success of the first book motivated the authors to produce an entire series of sequels for Tyndale Publishers. As of this writing, this series includes *Tribulation Force, Nicolae, Soul Harvest,* and *Apollyon,* published at a rate of a book a year.

continued existence. And why wouldn't the pretrib rapture be popular? Who wants to suffer through the Great Tribulation?

The problem, of course, is that the pretrib rapture is a perversion of historic Christian teaching that allows a fear of the end times to supersede the proclamation of the gospel. Consider Tim LaHaye's and Jerry Jenkins' book, *Left Behind*. LaHaye and Jenkins wanted somehow to help people left on earth after the two of them had been raptured off the planet. *Left Behind* was therefore written specifically for the people who would be "left behind" after LaHaye and Jenkins had escaped the Great Tribulation.[50]

Left Behind informs those unfortunate enough to be "on the other side" of the rapture of what to expect and how to "get saved" during the reign of the Antichrist—since the Church won't be there to help. The message to the billions "left behind" after Christ raptures the Church seems to be: "Sorry folks, you're on your own. Here's a novel you can read to help you out." [51] *Left Behind* has in turn spun off a four-part anthology called *Left Behind: The Kid's Series*. In *The Kid's Series*, according to a publicity blurb, four children, "left behind and all alone, find faith and learn to fight the evil forces that threaten their lives." What a bedtime story! It would seem no age is tender enough to be spared the horrors of Armageddon.

Is this how the Church is to minister to the world at its lowest moment, with a novel? And what about those four children who are "left behind and all alone"? Are we to believe that Christ would deprive them of the benefits of the Body of Christ simply because LaHaye and Jenkins can't imagine the Church suffering through the Tribulation? One has the impression that fear of the Tribulation is so great with LaHaye and Jenkins that such questions aren't even considered by them.

None of us desires to suffer for our witness to Christ; yet the fact remains, all who "live godly in Christ Jesus will suffer persecution" (2 Tim. 3:12). The Church in its long history has many times endured persecutions and martyrdoms, persevering in its witness of the gospel despite great hardships. Indeed, this is the Church's *raison d'être*: to point the world to Christ, even when the world largely ignores this witness. Rather than set her hopes

---

50 This is the purpose of the book as stated by Tim LaHaye in several radio interviews. Interestingly, in the novel itself there is a pastor who makes a videotape of himself explaining what will happen after the rapture and how to get "saved" during the Tribulation. The main character of the story, Rayford Steele, comes to know Christ after the rapture as a result of this tape (the pastor himself of course had been raptured). Tim LaHaye explains the idea came to him from a pastor who actually did something like this.

51 Charles Ryrie writes: "But how were these people saved [during the Tribulation]? Even though there will be no Christians on earth immediately after the Rapture, there will be Bibles, and books about the Christian faith. In other words, information will be available to give men the facts on which to find saving faith." *Countdown*, 96.

upon escaping the world's darkest hour, the Church is prepared to continue this witness to Christ right up until the day of the Lord's return.

According to the Church Fathers, the only ones who need fear anything in the last days are the enemies of Christ. In commenting on the sign of the Cross that is to precede the Lord's Second Coming (see Matt. 24:30), St. Cyril of Jerusalem writes, "The sign of the Cross shall be a terror to His foes; but joy to His friends who have believed in Him, or preached Him, or suffered for His sake. Who then is the happy man, who shall then be found a friend of Christ?" [52]

If we are genuine friends of Christ, to borrow St. Cyril's expression, then we have reason to be happy indeed. Orthodoxy, along with the Apostle Paul, vigorously contends that "God has not given us a spirit of fear, but of power and of love and of a sound mind" (2 Tim. 1:7). The Christian Faith, therefore, is not about a morbid fear of the end times; it is instead about "a sound mind," about empowerment, and, above all else, about love. "There is no fear in love; but perfect love casts out fear" (1 John 4:18)—and, along with it, the pretrib rapture.

---

52 Cyril of Jerusalem, *Catechetical Lectures*, 15:22.

Chapter Eleven

The Tribulations of Interpreting Daniel

Then the devil took Him up into the holy city, set Him on the pin-
nacle of the Temple, and said to Him, "If You are the Son of God,
throw Yourself down. For it is written: 'He shall give His angels
charge concerning you,' and, 'In their hands they shall bear you up,
lest you dash your foot against a stone' [Ps. 91:11, 12]."
    —The Gospel According to St. Matthew 4:5, 6

The devil can cite Scripture for his purpose.
    —William Shakespeare, *The Merchant of Venice* (1596–1597)

WHENEVER THERE IS WAR, the prophecy pundits immediately cry out that the end is near, citing Matthew 24:6 ("And
you will hear of wars and rumors of wars . . ."). When there is
peace and the future looks bright, the same crowd again announces the end to
be near, citing 1 Thessalonians 5:3 ("For when they say, 'Peace and safety!'
then sudden destruction comes upon them . . ."). No matter what happens in
the world, the prophecy peddlers interpret it as a sign the rapture is about to
occur and the world is about to enter a period known as the Great Tribulation.

The Tribulation in the dispensationalist's scheme of things is a seven-
year period that commences once the Church has been raptured off the planet
and the Antichrist signs a covenant with Israel. At this point, the Church
dispensation ends and God turns His attention back to the Jewish people.
Two things occur during the Tribulation: God's judgment finally comes upon
a world that has long rejected Him, and the Jewish people finally come to
recognize that Jesus of Nazareth is their Messiah.

The chronology of the Tribulation varies depending upon the "authority" you speak to, though Hal Lindsey's depiction of events as laid out in *The
Late Great Planet Earth* is more or less followed. The Antichrist comes to

power at the head of a revived Roman Empire consisting of a confederacy of ten European nations. His headquarters will naturally be in Rome, though many believe he will later move it to Jerusalem. He will establish peace in the world, solving, among other things, the complex problems in the Middle East.

The Antichrist will make it possible to rebuild the Temple in Jerusalem and reinstitute animal sacrifices. However, three and a half years into this seven-year Tribulation, the Antichrist will enthrone himself in the Jerusalem Temple and cause everyone to worship him. John Walvoord also believes that the Antichrist will proclaim himself world dictator at this point.[1]

There will be 144,000 male Jewish virgins who will be preaching the gospel during this time; they will be heavily persecuted by the Antichrist. God will then raise up two witnesses against the Antichrist (Hal Lindsey believes they will be Moses and Elijah). Though the Antichrist kills the two witnesses, leaving their bodies on display for three and a half days, they are resurrected and assumed into heaven. Then will come the series of battles between the "Roman Empire" (Western Europe) and Russia, and, later, between the Chinese and the "Romans."

Within this basic chronology imaginations run rampant, seeing all manner of fantastic, nightmarish catastrophes. Here we will limit ourselves to examining the biblical foundations of certain basic ideas common to all these scenarios, which are derived largely from the dispensationalist interpretation of the Book of Daniel. Based on their interpretation of this book, the doomsayers have no doubt we are living in the last days.

The Last Days

One thing on which the prophecy pundits and Orthodox Christians agree is that we are living in the "last days." What the two groups mean by the phrase, however, is rather different. The prophecy pundits consider the last days to be the last years of the world, including the seven-year Tribulation period. What Orthodox Christians understand by the last days is the entire messianic era, starting at Christ's First Advent two thousand years ago and ending at the Second Coming.

The latter definition of the term "the last days" is found in a common prayer Orthodox Christians say before receiving communion. The prayer, attributed to St. Basil the Great (A.D. 330–379), begins, "O Lord and Master, Jesus Christ, our God . . . who in thine exceeding love didst become incarnate

---

1 John Walvoord, *Armageddon, Oil and the Middle East Crisis*, rev. ed. (Grand Rapids: Zondervan, 1990), 158–159.

in *the latter days* . . ." According to St. Basil, the latter days began when the Son of God became flesh and dwelt among us (see John 1:14). This is the historic definition of the phrase. Sad to say, the traditional Christian understanding of the last days is wholly unknown to most contemporary Protestant Christians. Therefore, we should briefly examine it.

The Jewish view of history found in the Bible is linear, as opposed to the Greek and Eastern views of history, which saw time as circular and forever repeating. According to B. J. Oropeza, the linear concept of history held by the Jews was roughly divided into three eras: (1) before Creation; (2) between Creation and the coming of the Messiah; and (3) after the coming of the Messiah. To this view of history, the Christians added an extra era to arrive at the following: (1) before Creation; (2) between Creation and the First Advent of Christ; (3) between Christ's First and Second Comings; and (4) after Christ's Second Coming.[2]

The early Christians believed they were living in the third era between Christ's two "comings," and they called this era "the last days." This practice goes straight back to Pentecost, when Peter preached the Church's first sermon. Peter cites Joel 2:28–32 as already fulfilled: "And it shall come to pass in *the last days* . . ." (Acts 2:17). For Peter, the last days started at Pentecost. Paul also characterized the age he was living in as "the end of the ages" (1 Cor. 10:11; compare Phil. 4:5). The author of Hebrews states that we are in the "last days" (Heb. 1:2), and that Christ's incarnation took place "at the end of the ages" (9:26). John comes right out and says that "we know that it is the last hour" (1 John 2:18).

Thus Christians have always lived in a state of tension. The last days are now—still the end is not yet. The Kingdom has arrived (Matt. 12:28), yet we are still waiting for it. We enjoy the grace and blessings of Christ's reign while the full manifestation of Christ's victory is still to come. The Christian era is one of paradox: we live in the last days looking for the *last day*—which will also be the first day of eternity.

The "Revived" Roman Empire

What about this notion of the European Economic Community being a sort of revived Roman Empire? From whence is this idea derived? The prophecy gurus base this theory primarily on the Book of Daniel in the Old Testament. The second chapter of Daniel records a dream that troubled the Babylonian Emperor Nebuchadnezzar. In this dream there is a giant statue with a head of gold, chest and arms of silver, belly and thighs of bronze, legs of iron, and

---

2   Oropeza, *99 Reasons*, 28.

feet of both iron and clay. Then a stone "cut out of a mountain, without [human] hands," appears and strikes the statue on the feet of iron and clay, breaking the feet. The statue crumbles to the ground, and then the stone grows into a great mountain that fills the earth.

The Prophet Daniel interpreted this statue as four successive kingdoms. These were usually identified by the early Fathers of the Church as follows: the head of gold is the Babylonian Empire, the chest and arms of silver are the Medo-Persian Empire, the belly and thighs of bronze are the Greek Empire, and the legs of iron are the Roman Empire.[3] The feet of iron and clay suggest the Roman Empire would be divided into two parts, as actually occurred when Rome was divided into separate Eastern and Western empires. Daniel further observes of Rome: "And as the toes of the feet were partly of iron and partly of clay, so the kingdom shall be partly strong and partly fragile" (Dan. 2:41, 42).

The stone in Nebuchadnezzar's dream represents Christ, who sets up the Kingdom of God, the Church, which will be established during the Roman Empire and which "shall stand forever." According to the Prophet Daniel:

> And in the days of these kings [the emperors of the Roman Empire] the God of heaven will set up a kingdom which shall never be destroyed; and the kingdom shall not be left to other people; it shall break in pieces and consume all these kingdoms, and it shall stand forever. (Dan. 2:44)

How do the prophecy pundits come up with a "revived Roman Empire" from this prophecy of four kingdoms followed by the Kingdom of God? First, they distinguish between the legs of iron, the Roman Empire, and the feet of iron and clay, which they call the "revived Roman Empire" and which they say will appear at the end of history. Between the legs and the feet, dispensationalism inserts a Church "parenthesis" of nearly two thousand years. In other words, there is a "gap" inserted between the legs and the feet. Daniel 2:44, which speaks of the "kingdom which shall never be destroyed," is then interpreted as the supposed millennial reign of Christ on earth—despite the fact that the supposed millennial kingdom will cease at the end of a thousand

3 Rather than understanding the four empires as Babylon, Medo-Persia, Greece, and Rome, many modern scholars list them as Babylon, Media, Persia, and Greece. The problem with this modern interpretation is that Media and Persia were never actually two separate empires. While Media was a sovereign kingdom after breaking free of Assyria, it ceased being an independent nation to become Persia's first satrapy (called Mada) in 550 B.C. However, there continued to be a close relationship between Medes and Persians; in fact, it was a sort of joint empire. More importantly, Daniel himself saw the two as a single empire. He symbolizes the Medo-Persian Empire as a ram in Dan. 8:20 and refers specifically to the "kings of Media and Persia." Since Daniel himself sees the Medes and the Persians as forming a single, joint empire, I have accordingly understood Daniel's four empires as Babylon, *Medo-Persia*, Greece, and Rome.

years, according to dispensationalist teaching, and consequently doesn't "stand forever," as Daniel said it would.

This interpretation of Daniel is gratuitous, to say the least. There is absolutely no justification for inserting a gap lasting all the way from the days of ancient Rome to the dawn of the twenty-first century! Such a gap isn't even hinted at in the inspired text. How do those claiming to be biblical "literalists" explain away this inconvenient fact? They point out that some Old Testament prophecies speak simultaneously of the First and Second Comings of Christ without suggesting the actual lapse of time between the two comings; therefore, the "experts" feel free to assume that such is the case with the prophecy in Daniel 2. There are, however, two serious objections to this explanation.

First, the prophecy in Daniel speaks of four kingdoms succeeding each other with no gaps in between them (Babylon was conquered by Persia, Persia by Greece, and Greece by Rome). Even if the feet were a separate empire, we would expect it to follow immediately upon Rome as the others followed directly upon their predecessors.

Second, there is nothing to indicate that the feet are even a separate empire to begin with, "revived" or otherwise. The prophecy says that, though the fourth kingdom was strong (made of iron), yet at its base it was mixed with clay. Iron and clay don't bond together, making the composite fragile. In his explanation of this verse, Sinclair Ferguson describes this weakness of the Roman Empire:

> Inherent in the development of this empire—"in its feet"—would lie the seeds of its own decay. Although the Roman Empire possessed a longevity surpassing those empires immediately preceding it, according to Edward Gibbon's famous thesis, it was subject to a decline and fall in its moral and spiritual corruption. Historians tell us that Paul's description of the Roman world (Rom. 1:18ff.) is no exaggeration.[4]

At the height of Roman power, the Rock not cut by human hands descended from heaven to a manger in Bethlehem and smashed this pagan empire to pieces (the empire was destined to be Christian), establishing the reign of Christ on earth in the hearts of men. And, as the prophecy indicates, this new Kingdom is becoming a great mountain filling the whole earth (Dan. 2:35).

The early Church interpreted Daniel's dream of the four beasts in Daniel 7 in the same way. In this prophecy, Daniel saw four beasts rise out of a mythical, limitless sea, each beast representing an empire. The fourth beast, Rome, was "dreadful and terrible, exceedingly strong. It had huge iron teeth"

---

4   Sinclair Ferguson, *Daniel*, Vol. 19, The Communicator's Commentary (Waco, TX: Word Books, 1988), 63.

(Dan. 7:7). The Church interpreted this fourth beast as Rome as early as Irenaeus[5] and Hippolytus[6] at the end of the second century. However, there is nothing in the text of Daniel of a "revived beast," suggesting a later continuation of this empire. As in the previous prophecy in Daniel 2, we learn that "the saints of the Most High shall receive the kingdom, and possess the kingdom forever, even forever and ever" (Dan. 7:18).

Nevertheless, dispensationalists push this prophecy into the future by pointing out that the fourth beast is said to have "ten horns" (Dan. 7:7), which, they say, are "ten kings who shall arise from this kingdom" (Dan. 7:24). Since Rome never had ten kings ruling it at the same time, the reasoning goes, this must imply a revived Rome made up of ten nations (kings), which is even now coming together in the EEC (European Economic Community). Further, Daniel speaks of a "little horn" arising from the midst of the ten that overthrows three of the horns in order to rule over the others (Dan. 7:8). This is obviously the Antichrist, it is argued, that will appear during the end times, for he speaks blasphemies, persecutes the saints, and changes "times and laws"—meaning he will deify himself, for only God "changes the times and the seasons" (see Dan. 2:21).

It is not quite accurate to say, however, that there weren't "ten kings" ruling the Roman Empire along with the "little horn" when God established His everlasting Kingdom, the Church. According to Gary DeMar, president of American Vision (an evangelical educational organization), the empire was divided up into ten provinces: Italy, Achaia, Asia, Syria, Egypt, Africa, Spain, Gaul, Britain, and Germany.[7] The rulers of these provinces were sometimes called "kings," as was, for example, King Agrippa, who is mentioned in Acts 26:2. Though these rulers were called kings, they were still very much subject to the "little horn," Caesar (who is also called "king" in John 19:15).

In any event, whether or not Daniel is actually referring to the political organization of the Roman Empire, it is true that many Fathers in the early Church did, in a sense, see Daniel's "ten kings" as being in the future toward the end of the world. Writers such as St. Irenaeus, Hippolytus, St. Cyril of Jerusalem, Lactantius, and others believed that the Roman Empire, the fourth beast, would be the last empire on earth, since it is the last empire mentioned in Daniel's prophecy. This unified Roman Empire, they believed, would crumble into chaos and splinter into ten kingdoms ruled simultaneously by ten kings. The Antichrist (the "little horn") would then arise to seize the

---

5   Irenaeus, *Heresies*, 5:30:2.

6   Hippolytus interprets both the legs and the feet of iron and clay (Dan. 2:31–35)—as well as the fourth beast in Dan. 7—as the Roman Empire in his *On the Antichrist* (19–28).

7   Gary DeMar, *Last Days Madness* (Brentwood, TN: Wolgemuth & Hyatt, 1991), 205.

empire and consolidate it under his rule. He would deceive the world and persecute the saints "until the Ancient of Days came, and a judgment was made in favor of the saints of the Most High" (Dan. 7:22).

Obviously, the Roman Empire came and went hundreds of years ago. Rather than fracturing into ten kingdoms, the Roman Empire continuously shrank over the centuries as it lost territory to invaders. Nobody today can argue that it was the last world empire. The Turkish Empire that conquered New Rome (Constantinople) in 1453 was an empire no less powerful than Rome was at its height. Moreover, the only "Antichrist" to appear at the Eastern Empire's demise was Sultan Mehmet II, who marched triumphantly into Hagia Sophia, the main church of the empire in Constantinople, and claimed it as a Turkish mosque.

Although the patristic interpretation of Daniel is similar in some respects to dispensationalism's, there is a significant difference: the Fathers of the Church did not picture the ten kingdoms as a resurrected empire appearing hundreds of years after Rome's fall. Nor, we might add, did they see the Roman Empire as merely a "unified" Western Europe. In fact, Western Europe was the backwater of the empire. The Eastern Mediterranean was where the strength of the empire actually lay, and this is why the Roman emperors allowed the Western Empire to fall to barbarian invaders while they consolidated their power in the East. The ten kingdoms of Daniel's prophecy would certainly have included the Eastern Empire in the thinking of the Fathers.

Both Orthodox Tradition and the prophecy pundits agree that the little horn that speaks blasphemies, persecutes the saints, and deifies himself describes the Antichrist to come. Yet we should note that it also perfectly describes the Roman emperors as well. Didn't, for instance, Nero and Caligula speak blasphemies against the Most High? Didn't Caligula at one point attempt to erect his statue in the Temple in Jerusalem, thus attempting to proclaim himself God in the Temple? Didn't Nero persecute the Church, even martyring the Most Holy Apostles Peter and Paul? Didn't both Nero and Caligula proclaim themselves to be gods? As we will see in a later chapter, there is a close correspondence in the New Testament between emperors like Nero and the Antichrist to come at the end of the age. If the fourth beast of Daniel's prophecy speaks of the Roman Empire, then the "little horn" would be both a historic Roman ruler and, by typology, descriptive of the Antichrist to come.

The Prophecy of the Seventy Weeks

Next we come to the most abused prophecy in all of Daniel. In the ninth chapter (Dan. 9:20–27), the Prophet is praying at mid-afternoon, the hour of the evening oblation. Lamenting his exile in Babylon, Daniel was confessing his own sin and that of his people, praying toward Jerusalem and the "holy mountain" (where the Temple had been). He had been reading the Prophet Jeremiah, who spoke of the desolation of Jerusalem as lasting seventy years (see Jer. 25:11; 29:10). In response to Daniel's prayer, the Archangel Gabriel appears with a "word" (Hebrew: *dabar*) from God, "for you [Daniel] are greatly beloved" (Dan. 9:23). Then Gabriel gives Daniel a vision (Hebrew: *mar' eh*).

Gabriel says that seventy weeks (or literally, "seventy 'sevens'," as in the NIV translation) were determined for Israel and Jerusalem in order to (1) finish transgression, (2) make an end of sins, (3) make reconciliation for iniquity, (4) bring in everlasting righteousness, (5) seal up vision and prophecy, and (6) anoint the Most Holy (Dan. 9:24). Gabriel continues:

> Know therefore and understand, that from the going forth of the command to restore and build Jerusalem until Messiah the Prince, there shall be seven weeks and sixty-two weeks; the street shall be built again, and the wall even in troublesome times. And after the sixty-two weeks Messiah shall be cut off, but not for Himself; and the people of the prince who is to come shall destroy the city and sanctuary. The end of it shall be with a flood, and till the end of the war desolations are determined. Then he shall confirm a covenant with many for one week; but in the middle of the week he shall bring an end to sacrifice and offering. And on the wing of abominations shall be one who makes desolate, even until the consummation, which is determined, is poured out on the desolate. (Dan. 9:25–27)

It is generally agreed that by "seventy weeks" is understood 70 x 7 years, or 490 years, a day equaling a year. This figure is probably based on Leviticus 25:8, which speaks of the year of Jubilee as falling every seven weeks of years (7 x 7), or 49 years. The year of Jubilee was the Sabbath year when all were freed of their debts. Thus Gabriel is decreeing a great Sabbath to occur in 70 x 7 years (490 years) in order to free the people. The commencement of the seventy weeks, according to Daniel 9:25, is likely when Artaxerxes I allowed Ezra to rebuild Jerusalem, including the Temple, in 458 or 457 B.C. (Ezra 7:1–26; 9:9).[8] Taking the year 457 B.C. as our starting point, we add the first seven weeks (49 years) to arrive at 408 B.C., the year the Temple was finished. Adding 62 weeks (434 years) brings us to the year A.D. 27, the date of the beginning of Jesus' ministry generally accepted by modern scholars. This leaves us with a final "week," or seven-year period.

Daniel 9:27 states, "Then he shall confirm a covenant with many for one

---

8   Edwin Yamaguchi, *Ezra-Nehemiah*, Vol. 4, The Expositor's Bible Commentary (Grand Rapids: Zondervan, 1988), 651.

week; but in the middle of the week He shall bring an end to sacrifice and offering." Three and a half years into the final week, that is, in the spring of A.D. 30, Jesus was "cut off" (Dan. 9:26), which brought an end to sacrifices and offerings (Heb. 7—10; 1 Pet. 1:18, 19) and initiated the New Covenant that was confirmed in Christ's own blood. The "abomination of desolation" that Daniel then mentions in the last half of verse 27 refers to the destruction and defilement of the Temple in A.D. 70. This is how Jesus seems to have interpreted the verse (Matt. 24:15; Mark 13:14). Significantly, the war that culminated in Jerusalem's destruction by the Romans lasted three and a half years—the final half-week. The final half-week is symbolically used to represent the final Tribulation period in Revelation 11:2, 3; 13:5.

French biblical scholar René Laurentin in his book *The Truth of Christmas Beyond the Myths* has shown that the "seventy weeks" prophecy of Daniel was creatively interwoven into the Infancy narrative in the Gospel of Luke. The parallels between Daniel and Luke are indeed intriguing. For example, the only places the angel Gabriel is mentioned in the Bible are in Daniel and in Luke. In Luke, as in Daniel, Gabriel appears at the hour of the evening oblation (Luke 1:10, 11; compare Dan. 9:21) as a response to prayer (Luke 1:13; compare Dan. 9:20, 21). This is because Gabriel stands before God and speaks in His name (Luke 1:19; compare Dan. 9:22, 23).[9]

In the Greek Theodotion translation of Daniel 9, which was the standard text of Daniel used in the primitive Church, the Hebrew word for "vision" (*mar' eh*) is translated six times into Greek as *optasia*. This Greek word is used only four times in the New Testament, three of those times by Luke. One of those times is in Luke 1:22 after Gabriel's meeting with Zacharias. Moreover, in both Luke 1:28 and Daniel 9:23, Gabriel describes the one he addresses as "favored" by God.[10]

Luke uses the seventy weeks prophecy in a unique way in his Gospel. The seventy weeks are not 490 years, but a literal seventy weeks (i.e., 490 days). From Gabriel's annunciation to Zachariah in the Temple to the presentation of Christ in the same Temple is a period of exactly 490 days, subtly associating Jesus, the Temple, and the seventy weeks prophecy: "But what could such a parallel mean? It is a matter of transposition or concretization, according to the midrashic interpretation prevalent at the time." [11] The point of this "midrashic interpretation" is to show Jesus' First Advent to be the

9   René Laurentin, *The Truth of Christmas Beyond the Myths* (Petersham, MA: St. Bede's, 1986), 49.

10 Ibid.

11 Laurentin, *Christmas*, 65.

fulfillment of Daniel's prophecy. Luke, therefore, evidently understood the fulfillment of Daniel 9:24 to be in the angelic proclamation to Mary and in the presentation of Christ in the Temple (Luke 2:22–38).

How do the Orthodox interpret this prophecy today? The Church's interpretation of this passage in Daniel is heavily influenced by the way the Fathers of the early Church commented on it. The Fathers, in turn, were influenced by the late-first-century Jewish interpretation of Daniel 9:20–27.

The first-century Jewish historian, Flavius Josephus, wrote in his *Antiquities of the Jews* of the desolation brought upon Israel by the Romans in A.D. 70, seeing in it the fulfillment of Daniel's prophecy: "In the very same manner Daniel also wrote concerning the Roman government, and that our country should be made desolate by them." [12] Josephus' understanding of the seventy weeks as applying to the destruction of Israel came to be the standard Jewish interpretation, and this influenced the Christian interpretation of Daniel.

However, Christians also incorporated into this Jewish interpretation the fact of the First Advent of Christ. One of the earliest of these Christian interpretations of Daniel 9:20–27 was Clement of Alexandria (A.D. 150–211). After quoting Daniel 9:24–27, Clement explains:

> That the Temple [in Jerusalem] accordingly was built in seven weeks [49 years], is evident; for it is written in Ezra. And thus Christ became King of the Jews, reigning in Jerusalem in the fulfillment of the seven weeks. And in the sixty and two weeks the whole of Judea was quiet, and without wars. And Christ our Lord, "the Holy of Holies" [see Dan. 9:24], having come and fulfilled the vision and the prophecy, was anointed in His flesh by the Holy Spirit of His Father. In those "sixty and two weeks," as the prophet said, and "in the one week," was He Lord. The half of the week Nero held sway, and in the holy city Jerusalem placed the abomination; and in the half of the week he was taken away, and [emperors] Otho, Galba, and Vitellius. And Vespasian rose to the supreme power, and destroyed Jerusalem, and desolated the holy place. And that such are the facts of the case, is clear to him that is able to understand, as the prophet said. [13]

The Latin theologian Tertullian also tried his hand at Daniel's seventy week prophecy. In his *Against the Jews* (written sometime between A.D. 198 and 208), Tertullian adds up the reigns of all the rulers of the Persian and Greek empires, beginning with Darius I and ending with Augustus Caesar. Then, "in the forty-first year of the empire of Augustus, when he has been reigning for twenty-eight years after the death of Cleopatra, Christ is born." [14]

---

12 Flavius Josephus, *Antiquities of the Jews*, 10:11.

13 Clement of Alexandria, *Stromata*, 1:21.

14 Tertullian, *Against the Jews*, 8.

Tertullian believes that the period from the Persian ruler Darius I till the twenty-eighth year of Augustus' reign, when Christ was born, is the sixty-two and a half weeks of Daniel's prophecy. The remaining fifteen years of Augustus' reign till the reign of Emperor Vespasian, who destroyed Jerusalem and the Temple in fulfillment of Jesus' prophecy in Matthew 24, complete the seventy weeks.[15]

Whereas early Christians differed in how they calculated the seventy weeks (depending on their knowledge of history), they all generally agreed Daniel's prophecy found its fulfillment in the first century with Christ, the beginning of the New Covenant and the end of the Old. Jerome in the fourth century wrote in his *Commentary on Daniel* concerning the seventy weeks prophecy, "I realize that this question has been argued over in various ways by men of greatest learning, and that each of them has expressed his views according to the capacity of his own genius." [16] He then gives lengthy citations from earlier writers on Daniel's prophecy, like Julius Africanus who agonizes over which date the computations ought to start from and which calendar ought to be used in counting the years. (Should the Jewish calendar be used?)[17] One thing of which Africanus has "no doubt," the entire prophecy predicted Christ's First Advent, "for He appeared to the world at the end of seventy weeks." [18]

This view of the seventy weeks prophecy as being fulfilled in Christ's First Advent (Dan. 9:24–26) and in the destruction of the Temple in A.D. 70 (Dan. 9:26, 27) continues to be the traditional Orthodox interpretation. In Christ's First Coming, transgression of the Law was finished, an end was made to sin, a reconciliation for iniquity was achieved, everlasting righteousness was established, vision and prophecy were sealed, and the Most Holy was anointed. Consequently, the Orthodox don't look for a future fulfillment of Daniel 9:24–27; for us the fulfillment is already a glorious reality.

Dispensationalists, on the other hand, take this 490-year prophecy and arbitrarily insert their parenthesis of two thousand years between the sixty-ninth week and the last week. Where the Messiah is cut off in the sixty-ninth week, they claim, the prophecy suddenly ceases and "the Church age" begins. All prophecy then freezes until the rapture, at which point the Antichrist signs a "covenant" with restored Israel. The last week of Daniel's prophecy then commences, which they believe to be the seven-year period called the

---

15 Ibid.

16 Frank Sadowski, *The Church Fathers on the Bible: Selected Readings* (New York: Alba House, 1987), 223.

17 In the Bible, the calendar was based on a solar year of 365 1/4 days and a lunar month of 29 1/2 days.

18 Sadowski, *Fathers on the Bible*, 224.

Tribulation. Therefore, although Gabriel declared that "seventy weeks are determined" from the construction of the Temple, dispensationalists today declare that what was determined was actually seventy weeks *plus* two thousand years (or more if the Lord should tarry).

Thus, according to "gap think," in a 490-year prophecy there is a pause of indeterminate length that is several times longer than the prophecy itself! One would think that such an important part of this prophecy as a two-thousand-year "pause" would at least be hinted at in the text of the prophecy. Is there any such suggestion of a "gap" in Daniel's prophecy?

It is sometimes argued that the way the seventy weeks are arranged in Daniel 9:24–27 (seven weeks, sixty-two weeks, and the final week) makes such a gap possible because the final week is separated from the other sixty-nine. Yet if we admit this, are we also prepared to allow a gap of thousands of years between the first seven weeks and the sixty-two weeks? If dispensationalists object that such a gap is unwarranted, can't the same be said for any attempt at putting a similar gap before the final week?

Numbers have a definite significance in Scripture. In both the Old and New Testaments, the number seven signifies perfection and completeness. For example, there are seven attributes of the Lamb (Rev. 5:12), signifying the perfection of attributes that Christ possesses; and in Revelation 7:12, God is praised using seven different terms—blessing, glory, wisdom, thanksgiving, honor, power, and might—signifying perfect and complete praise.

There is a similar meaning in Daniel's prophecy of the seventy weeks (70 x 7). In fact, we are given a hint as to what seventy times seven means in Matthew 18:21, 22. There, Peter asks if he ought to forgive his brother as many as seven times, and Jesus responds, "Up to seventy times seven." Jesus was obviously not saying that we were to forgive our brother exactly 490 times, no more and no less. What Jesus meant was that we are to forgive our brother fully and completely. In the same vein, Daniel's prophecy means that, when the "fullness of the time" comes (Gal. 4:4), God will send forth His Son to complete those things mentioned in Daniel 9:24. However, before the end arrives when Christ delivers the kingdom to God the Father (see 1 Cor. 15:24), there will come a period of darkness.

This period is Daniel's "half a week," or three and a half years, which is also mentioned in Revelation (11:2, 3; 12:6, 14; 13:5). Being exactly half of seven, it represents spiritual incompleteness. As biblical scholar and translator James Moffatt once noted, this symbol of a period of spiritual darkness may have been influenced by the fact that winter was calculated in the Babylonian calendar as lasting three and a half months, Babylon itself also being a symbol of spiritual darkness. The drought in Elijah's day lasted exactly three and a half years (Luke 4:25; James 5:17), and the Maccabean revolt that plunged Israel into so much tribulation lasted from June 168 B.C. to December 165 B.C., exactly three and a half years. Thus the number three and a half is the perfect figure to represent the spiritual darkness that will reign at the end of the world.

Presaging this period of darkness will be certain signs that may be discerned by God's elect. Millennial mania, however, encourages people to interpret every natural disaster and military conflict as a portent of the Great Tribulation. An earthquake shakes a city, or a volcano erupts somewhere, and the prophecy gurus immediately rush to press with books explaining how this had been foretold long ago in the Bible as an omen of the end times. As we will soon discover, though, the ability of these "experts" to read the tea leaves at the bottom of the cup of God's wrath leaves something to be desired.

Chapter Twelve

Portents of Judgment

A fool also multiplies words. No man knows what is to be; who can tell him what will be after him?
  —The Book of Ecclesiastes 10:14

Every cloud engenders not a storm.
  —William Shakespeare, *King Henry VI, Part 3* (1590–1591)

I N A PREVIOUS CHAPTER, we looked at how William Miller predicted the end for 1843, gathering thousands of Americans into an apocalyptic frenzy. A contributing factor to this mania was a spectacular meteor shower that filled the skies for several nights in November of 1833. Rural folk, their minds full of Miller's predictions of Armageddon, remembered Christ's words in Matthew 24:29 about heavenly phenomena preceding the Second Coming. Surely, they thought, doomsday couldn't be far off. To add further fuel to the flame, a large comet streaked across the sky in February of 1843, a month before Miller's March 21, 1843, deadline for the Second Coming. Such celestial portents inspired the following Millerite hymn:

> We, while the stars from heaven shall fall,
> And mountains are on mountains hurled,
> Shall stand unmoved amidst them all,
> And smile to see a burning world.[1]

However, as Shakespeare once observed, "Every cloud engenders not a storm." Nor does every astronomical event herald the Second Coming. In the end, the breathtaking celestial displays of the early nineteenth century proved to be prophetically insignificant, and the Millerite interpretation of Matthew 24 quite mistaken.

---

1 Cited by Chandler, *Doomsday*, 87.

Interpreting Matthew 24

We ought not to be too hard on the Millerites, however. Matthew 24 has long been regarded as one of the most difficult to understand of all of Jesus' discourses. R. T. France, in his commentary on Matthew, admits: "Chapter 24 poses great problems for the interpreter. It begins by talking about a coming destruction of the Temple (which was to take place in AD 70 as a result of the Roman repression of the rebellion of AD 66), but by the end of the chapter it seems clear that the scene has moved to the parousia, the final 'coming' of the Son of man." [2]

The discourse in Matthew 24 (known as the "Olivet Discourse") is preceded by Jesus' pronouncement in Matthew 23 of seven woes upon the scribes and Pharisees in the Jerusalem Temple. The "Seven Woes" conclude with Jesus' final sentence upon the religious establishment: "See! Your house [the Temple] is left to you desolate" (Matt. 23:38).

Jesus then leaves the Temple and the disciples chase after Him, pointing out to Jesus the magnificence of the Temple buildings. How could these awesome buildings dedicated to the God of Israel, they ask, ever be destroyed?

Jesus responds, "Do you see all these things? Assuredly, I say to you, not one stone shall be left here upon another, that shall not be thrown down" (Matt. 24:2).

After this prediction of the coming destruction of the Temple (fulfilled in A.D. 70), the disciples ask Him, "Tell us, when will these things be [i.e., the destruction of the Temple]? And what will be the sign of Your coming, and of the end of the age?" (Matt. 24:3). In the minds of first-century Jews, the destruction of the Temple and the end of the age were all part of a single event. Jesus, however, intimates there would be a delay between the two.

The Lord in Matthew 24 declares that, before the destruction of the Temple and the end of the world, there will be persecution and false christs, as well as wars, famines, pestilences, and earthquakes in various places. And these all occurred before the destruction of Jerusalem in A.D. 70. We need not look very far in the New Testament itself to learn of the many persecutions and false prophets that afflicted the early Church (e.g., Acts 5:34–37; 8:1–4; 12:1–23; 13:4–12; Gal. 1:6–10; 2 Pet. 2; Jude 4). The Book of Acts records at least one severe famine in Judea itself (Acts 11:27–30; compare Rom. 15:25–32; 1 Cor. 16:1–4), and an earthquake in Philippi (Acts 16:26), both of which were "signs." There were also other earthquakes during the first century in Crete, Smyrna, Miletus, Chios, Samos, Laodicea, Hieropolis, Colossae, Campania, Rome, Pompeii, and Judea.[3]

---

2   R. T. France, *Matthew*, Tyndale New Testament Commentaries, 333–334.

3   DeMar, *Last Days Madness,* 47.

As far as wars and rumors of wars are concerned, Emperor Caligula nearly started a long and bloody conflict in Judea when he attempted to place his image in the Temple in Jerusalem. The Romans fought battles in Germany, Africa, Thrace, Gaul, Britain, and Armenia, and there were constant wars with Persia. As far as pestilences are concerned, given the primitive level of medicine during the first century, it should not be surprising to learn they were perennial. "But the end is not yet," Jesus warns. "All these are the beginning of sorrows" (Matt. 24:6, 8).

Before the end comes for Jerusalem, the gospel must first be preached "in all the world as a witness to all the nations" (Matt. 24:14). Here "all the world" likely has the same meaning it has in Luke 2:1, where Caesar's census of the Roman Empire is called a census of "all the world." At that time, the Roman Empire was considered the whole of the civilized world. Paul in his Epistle to the Romans cites Psalm 19:4 to the effect that the gospel had been preached "to the ends of the world" by the Apostles (Rom. 10:18); and to the Colossians he writes that the gospel had come not only to them, but also to all the world (Col. 1:6). In fact, he adds that it has been preached "to every creature under heaven" at the time of his writing (Col. 1:23). Thus Cyril of Jerusalem, after citing Matthew 24:14, can exclaim in the year 350, "And as we see, nearly the whole world is now filled with the doctrine of Christ."[4] Consequently, Matthew 24:14 was generally understood in the early Church as predicting that the gospel would be preached throughout the then known world by A.D. 70.

After the gospel has been preached to all the nations "as a witness," Jesus reveals that there will be a spectacular display of God's judgment on Jerusalem. The holy city will fall and the Temple will suffer the "abomination of desolation" spoken of in Daniel. The expression "abomination of desolation" denotes the profanation of the Temple, and seems to have first been used to describe the dedication of the Jerusalem Temple to Zeus in 167 B.C. by the Greek Seleucid emperor Antiochus Epiphanes. First Maccabees 1:54, written about 140 B.C., also uses the term in connection with this event. Jesus reveals, however, that the Temple will again be profaned, this time by the Romans.

Jesus says the fall of Jerusalem will be terrible: "For then there will be great tribulation, such as has not been since the beginning of the world until this time, *no, nor ever shall be*" (Matt. 24:21, emphasis added). Here Jesus hints that the fall of Jerusalem will not occur at the end of history, since He tells us that nothing that *shall come after* it will quite equal it. And in fact the fall of Jerusalem in A.D. 70 was horrible. After the capture of the city, the

---

4   Cyril of Jerusalem, *Catechetical Lectures*, 15:8.

Romans crucified Jews at a rate of 500 per day. So many Jews were executed around Jerusalem that the Romans ran out of trees—so they started nailing people to the walls surrounding the city!

Again, Jesus warned the disciples that false christs would appear. Such a warning was well taken. There is even evidence in the Acts of the Apostles of a few of these pseudo-christs who were running around stirring up trouble (e.g., Acts 5:36, 37). The first-century historian Josephus tells us that Judea was crawling with would-be messiahs and false prophets before the country fell. He recounts how an Egyptian false prophet gathered an army of thirty thousand men and threatened to take Jerusalem by force (see Acts 21:38).[5]

Josephus writes poignantly elsewhere that while the Romans were besieging Jerusalem in A.D. 70, many Jews despaired and committed suicide, while other desperate souls were heeding the vain hopes of these self-proclaimed prophets:

> A false prophet was the occasion of these people's destruction, who had made a public proclamation in the city that very day, that God commanded them to get up upon the temple, and that there they should receive miraculous signs of their deliverance. Now, there was then a great number of false prophets suborned by the tyrants [the leaders of the Jewish rebellion] to impose upon the people, who denounced this to them, that they should wait for deliverance from God; and this was in order to keep them from deserting, and that they might be buoyed up above fear and care by such hopes. Now, a man that is in adversity does easily comply with such promises; for when such a seducer makes him believe that he shall be delivered from those miseries which oppress him, then it is that the patient is full of hopes of such deliverance. Thus were the miserable people persuaded by these deceivers, and such as belied God himself; while they did not attend, nor give credit, to the signs that were so evident, and did so plainly foretell their future desolation; but, like men infatuated, without either eyes to see or minds to consider, did not regard the denunciations that God made to them.[6]

Jesus instructs His disciples to ignore such false prophets and messiahs. The final coming of Christ, Jesus says in Matthew 24:27, will be as visible and dramatic as lightning across the sky.[7] At this point in the discourse, Jesus begins to elaborate on His Advent at the end of the age.

---

5 Flavius Josephus, *The Wars of the Jews*, 2:13:5.

6 Flavius Josephus, *The Wars of the Jews*, 6:5:2–3.

7 That Matt. 24:27 refers to Jesus' Second Coming and not to His "coming" in judgment on Jerusalem in A.D. 70 is indicated, I believe, by the presence of the words *parousia* and *phaino* (the verb form of the noun *epiphaneia*). As we will see in a later chapter, *parousia* and *epiphaneia* are two words commonly used in the New Testament for the Second Coming. Arguing that these words refer only to Christ's "coming" in judgment on Jerusalem in the first century usually leads to a preterism that interprets all the passages in the NT that speak of Christ's Second Coming in judgment as having been fulfilled in the fall of Jerusalem. Indeed, there is even a radical school of preterism that interprets NT references to the

Starting in Matthew 24:29, Jesus describes His Second Coming in apocalyptic terminology. He will come with clouds and glory, angels will gather His elect, there will be a trumpet call, there will be celestial disturbances, and the "tribes of the earth" will mourn (an allusion to Zech. 12:10–12, which is referred to elsewhere in the New Testament in connection with the Second Coming).

In Matthew 24:32–35, Jesus describes the entire period between His two Advents with the parable of the fig tree (the same parable that got Hal Lindsey into trouble, as we saw in Chapter 2). Let's place the parable in context: Jesus has warned His disciples of the general course of the age, in particular the judgment about to befall Jerusalem (Matt. 24:4–28). This age will climax when Christ returns in glory (vv. 29–31). In response to the disciple's question, *"When* will these things be?" (v. 3), Jesus makes two points in verses 32–35. First, "all these things" (all that is described in vv. 4–28 concerning the fall of Jerusalem) must happen first.[8] Second, after Jerusalem falls, the Second Coming will be "near—at the doors!" (v. 33). The Second Coming is the next major event after God's judgment on Jerusalem.[9]

"This generation" that will not pass away "till all these things take place" (v. 34) does not refer to the generation alive in 1948. Nearly all biblical commentators agree that the best interpretation of "this generation" is that it is the generation to whom Christ is speaking, that is, the generation alive in A.D. 30. In the previous chapter, Matthew 23, Jesus says to the scribes and Pharisees, "Assuredly, I say to you, all these things [judgments] will come upon *this generation"* (Matt. 23:36, emphasis added), meaning that the judgments were coming upon the scribes and Pharisees themselves. The overall context indicates that it is the same generation being spoken of in both chapters. Therefore, Matthew 24:34 says that the distress of verses 4–28,

---

general resurrection (e.g., 1 Cor. 15:50–58) as merely referring to a spiritual resurrection occurring in A.D. 70!

8   In a good example of a strictly preterist interpretation of Matthew 24, R. C. Sproul in *The Last Days According to Jesus* argues that the phrase "all these things" includes all that Jesus said about His "coming" *(parousia)* in judgment, interpreting all of Matt. 24 in terms of God's judgment on Jerusalem in A.D. 70. He quotes extensively from Herman Ridderbos' commentary on Matthew that it is "perfectly arbitrary" to restrict the phrase "all these things" to the events pertaining to Jerusalem's destruction. See *The Last Days According to Jesus* (Grand Rapids: Baker Books, 1998), 63–65.

9   I have chosen to follow D. A. Carson's reasoning on the phrase "all these things": "If the words include the celestial signs *and the Parousia itself* (vv. 29–31), then vv. 32, 33 are illogical, because any distinction between 'all these things' and 'it is near' would be destroyed. . . . The more natural way to take 'all these things' is to see them as referring to the distress of vv. 4–28, the tribulation that comes on believers throughout the period between Jesus' ascension and the Parousia." D. A. Carson, *Matthew*, Vol. 8, The Expositor's Bible Commentary, 507. Emphasis in original.

including the fall of Jerusalem, will occur within the generation that heard Christ's pronouncement. Verse 34 therefore does not suggest that the Second Coming would happen in "this generation," only that the Second Coming cannot occur before "this generation" witnesses the judgment on Jerusalem spoken of in Matthew 24:4–28.[10]

This understanding of Matthew 24 is no modernist construct. Consider, for instance, how Blessed Theophylact, the Greek Archbishop of Ochrid (hierarch of Bulgaria and author of one of the standard Orthodox commentaries on the New Testament), interpreted Matthew 24 in the late eleventh century. In his commentary on Matthew, he interpreted Matthew 24:4–22 primarily as relating to the fall of Jerusalem and only secondarily as pointing to the end of the world. On Matthew 24:6, which speaks of "wars and rumors of wars," Theophylact writes that Jesus "is speaking of the wars conducted by the Romans in Jerusalem."[11] Commenting on verse 14 as to the statement that the gospel would be preached to all nations, Theophylact writes that Paul in his time already spoke of the gospel as having been "preached to every creature under heaven" (Col. 1:23; compare 1:5, 6; Rom. 10:18), and Paul was obviously writing before the destruction of Jerusalem.[12] Theophylact understands the "abomination of desolation" as a reference to the defilement of the Jerusalem Temple by the Romans,[13] and so forth right up to the end of Matthew 24:22.

Along the same line, St. Maximus the Confessor (580–662) wrote that the "abomination of desolation" occurred in A.D. 70: "That these things have already taken place in history no one, I think, who has read [the Jewish historian] Josephus will doubt."[14]

St. John Chrysostom (347–407) understood the "wars and rumors of wars" as being the wars fought by the Jews against the Romans, also citing Matthew 23:36: "Assuredly I say to you, all these things will come upon this generation."[15] "This generation" was thus the generation alive in A.D. 30. He interprets as fulfilled the preaching of the gospel to all the world (Matt. 24:14),

---

10 Many commentators instead chose to assign the fall of Jerusalem discourse to vv. 3–36 so as to include Jesus' comment that "this generation" would witness "all these things."

11 *The Explanation by Blessed Theophylact of The Holy Gospel According to St. Matthew* (House Springs, MO: Chrysostom Press, 1993), 205.

12 Theophylact, *Matthew*, 206.

13 Ibid. Theophylact writes, "The 'abomination of desolation' means the monument of the city's captor which he set up in the inner sanctuary of the temple."

14 Maximus the Confessor, *The Four Hundred Chapters on Love*, 2:31. *The Philokalia*, Vol. II, 70–71. Maximus then immediately adds, "though some say that they will also come to pass in the time of the Antichrist." He therefore doesn't appear to preclude a secondary fulfillment of Matt. 24:15 at the end of the age.

15 Chrysostom, *Matthew*, Homily 75:1. In Homily 77:1, however, Chrysostom also interprets "this generation" as all Christian believers of all times who will suffer tribulations.

understanding the words, "and then the end shall come," as the end of Jerusalem.[16] He also understands the "abomination of desolation" as the Roman defilement of the Temple, stressing that Jesus had said to the disciples, "when *you* see the abomination of desolation" (emphasis added), meaning at least some of them would live to see it occur.[17] Chrysostom concludes, "And if thou art minded to learn these things more distinctly, I mean, the famines, the pestilences, the earthquakes, the other calamities, peruse the history about these things composed by Josephus, and thou wilt know all accurately."[18]

In the early fourth century, Eusebius of Caesarea (263–340) interpreted Matthew 24 as being largely fulfilled in the Jewish war of A.D. 70, comparing what Christ had predicted with the record of Josephus. Eusebius specifically cites Matthew 24:19–21 and Luke 21:20, 23, 24 as describing "the second year of the reign of Vespasian," that is, A.D. 70.[19] Our approach to Matthew 24 is, therefore, not a modernist invention, but actually quite "traditional."

How Not to Interpret Matthew 24

Although many Fathers of the Church interpreted the first part of Matthew 24 as applying to the destruction of Jerusalem and its Temple in the first century, some Fathers also understood the passage as applying to the end of the world. This line of interpretation may have been influenced by first-century Judaism. One stream of Jewish thought believed that the Temple would disappear only with the coming of the Messiah and the end of the age, when a new Temple would be built. Jesus' description in Matthew 24 of the destruction of Jerusalem and the Temple, accompanied by famines, pestilences, and earthquakes, is closely associated with His description of the end of the world. It is not surprising, therefore, that many Fathers saw Jesus' description of the destruction of Jerusalem in Matthew 24 as foreshadowing the destruction of the world at the end of time.

As has already been discussed earlier, the Fathers were quite willing to derive a mystical interpretation from a given biblical text. However, even while seeing the end of the world as coming with wars, famines, plagues, and earthquakes in Matthew 24, the Fathers always observed a certain moderation in their writings. The Venerable Bede, writing in the early eighth century, preserves a letter in his *Ecclesiastical History of the English People* that was written by Pope Gregory the Great of Old Rome (called "the Dialogist"

16 Chrysostom, *Matthew*, Homily 75:2.
17 Ibid. See also Homily 76:1.
18 Chrysostom, *Matthew*, Homily 75:3.
19 Eusebius, *History*, 3:7.

by the Orthodox). Writing to the Christian King Ethelbert in Britain in 601, Gregory describes these signs of the imminent Second Coming:

> We would also have Your Majesty know what we have learned from the words of Almighty God in holy Scripture, that the end of this present world is at hand and the everlasting kingdom of the Saints is approaching. When the end of the world is near, unprecedented things occur—portents in the sky, terrors from heaven, unseasonable tempests, wars, famines, pestilences, and widespread earthquakes (see Matt. 24:7). Not all of these things will happen during our own lifetimes, but will all ensue in due course. There-fore, if any such things occur in your own country, do not be anxious, for these portents of the end are sent to warn us to consider the welfare of our souls and remember our last end, so that, when our Judge comes, He may find us prepared by good lives.[20]

Though describing the tempests, wars, famines, and so forth in Matthew 24:7 as characterizing the times just prior to Jesus' return, Gregory quickly reassures the king "not [to] be anxious," but to look to the welfare of his soul in order to be ready for the judgment, whenever that may come.

The Fathers of the early Church were neither strict "futurists" nor strict "preterists" (that is, interpreting Matthew 24 entirely in terms of its fulfillment in the first century). For example, whereas many early Orthodox commentators on the Gospel of Matthew, like St. John Chrysostom (e.g., *Homily 75 on Matthew*) and Blessed Theophylact, interpreted Matthew 24:7 as referring primarily to the destruction of Israel in A.D. 70, it was not uncommon for the Fathers to see in the verse a secondary fulfillment at the end of time. The destruction of Jerusalem in such an interpretation became a prototype of a greater cosmic judgment, when there would be unprecedented natural calamities.

Therefore, taking our cue from the Fathers, we ought to avoid two extremes in interpreting Matthew 24. One extreme is to interpret all that Jesus says as relating to the end of the world; the other is to interpret everything as having happened in A.D. 70, when the Romans destroyed Jerusalem and the Temple.[21]

Modern prophecy gurus routinely err on the side of the first extreme.

---

20 Bede, *The Ecclesiastical History of the English People*, Book 1, 32. Taken from Leo Sherley-Price, trans. (New York: Penguin Classics, rev. ed. 1990), p. 95.

21 A good patristic example of balance here is Cyril of Alexandria. Cyril in his commentary on Luke 21 (Homily 139) brings together both Luke's and Matthew's versions of Jesus' eschatological discourse. He cites Luke 21:10, 11 and Matt. 24:29 as signs of the end, but then immediately adds: "But in the middle the Savior places what refers to the capture of Jerusalem; for He mixes the accounts together in both parts of the narrative." Cyril then gives a brief account of the fall of the city and the persecution of the Church. See Cyril of Alexandria's *Commentary on the Gospel of Luke,* 554–557.

John Walvoord, for instance, believes that Jesus was describing the destruction of the Temple only in verse 2. The disciples' question in verse 3, he asserts, is in three parts: (1) concerning the destruction of the Temple; (2) when Jesus would return and the signs preceding it; and (3) what will be the signs of the end of the age. Walvoord states that the answer to the first question is preserved in Luke 21:5–36, but that Matthew addresses only questions two and three![22] Yet why should Matthew have preserved the disciples' question on the destruction of the Temple while not preserving Jesus' answer?

D. A. Carson, Baptist commentator and professor of New Testament at Trinity Evangelical Divinity School, has observed with regard to Walvoord's curious perspective on Matthew's Gospel:

> Granted the dispensational interpretation, Jesus' answer must have not only been opaque to his auditors but almost deceptive. Their first question concerns Jerusalem's judgment. But since a substantial part of Jesus' answer is couched in terms dealing with Jerusalem's destruction, how could the disciples think Jesus was *not* answering their question but describing a *second* destruction of the city [at the end of the world], unless Jesus explicitly disavowed their understanding? But he does nothing of the kind. So perhaps it is not surprising that the dispensational identification of vv. 15–28 *exclusively* with the Great Tribulation after the Rapture of the church, whether revealed or unrevealed, finds no exponent till the nineteenth century. The dispensational approach to the Olivet Discourse must be judged historically implausible in reference to both the history of Jesus and the history of interpretation.[23]

Contemporary scholars generally agree that Jesus talks about both the destruction of the Temple and the Second Coming in Matthew 24, as the Fathers taught. Where end-times doom-sayers frequently go wrong in Matthew 24 is in (1) not seeing the destruction of Jerusalem anywhere in the passage, and (2) indulging in fantastic interpretations of apocalyptic symbolism. Let's look at a few typical examples.

An example of the first type of error involves Matthew 24:7, which reads: "For nation will rise against nation, and kingdom against kingdom. And there will be famines, pestilences, and earthquakes in various places." Unlike the Fathers, today's celebrated "authorities" on prophecy don't bother considering the primary fulfillment of this verse in A.D. 70. Nor do they take into account the Semitic literary style of the discourse. Instead, they seize upon one of the calamities mentioned, like "pestilence" for instance, and then

---

22 Walvoord, *Major Bible Prophecies,* 293–294.
23 Carson, *Matthew,* 495. Emphasis in original.

elaborate at great length as to why today's AIDS epidemic is the literal fulfillment of Jesus' prophecy.

Yet why should we think that Jesus was specifically predicting the AIDS
epidemic in Matthew 24:7 when history has recorded the passage of many
other epidemics far worse than AIDS? The bubonic plague, known as the
Black Death, killed an estimated 100 million people in Asia, the Middle East,
and Europe during the sixth century. It struck again during the fourteenth
century, cutting the population of the Eastern Empire by a third and the population of Europe nearly in half. Entire communities were wiped out when the
plague was at its peak from 1349 to 1351. By the beginning of the fifteenth
century, 40 million Europeans had died out of a 90 million population, some
regions of Europe losing three-quarters of their population.

In certain parts of England, nine-tenths of the population had been eliminated. The population of London, which was around 50,000 people, was cut
in half, as were the populations of Florence and Venice. When the Black
Death hit Paris, 800 people a day died. According to Russell Chandler, "Multiple waves of the Black Death scourged much of the world, abating in Europe only about 1720. Virtually no city anywhere in Europe regained its 1300
population in less than two centuries." [24] The bubonic plague, a bacterium
(now called *yersinia pestis*) which many scientists believe was spread by
caravans from China's Gobi desert, has since traveled around the globe. Yet,
for all the devastation it caused, the Black Death didn't usher in the end. So
why should AIDS be so interpreted?

Even the twentieth century has known widespread epidemics that were
worse than AIDS. Hal Lindsey in *Apocalypse Code* cites a World Health
Organization report for 1996 that claims that a total of 6.4 million deaths
have been caused by AIDS. [25] Yet the great flu epidemic of 1918, known as
the "Spanish flu," killed a far greater number of people in just one year: over
20 million people around the world (the world population at that time is estimated at around 1.8 billion), and approximately 675,000 in the United
States. [26] Once the first case was reported on March 4, 1918, at Camp Funston,
Kansas, the virus spread around the globe within a matter of four months
(and this was before the advent of commercial air travel). The victims died
quickly, literally drowning as their lungs filled with their own blood. Nor did
the flu target only the very young, the elderly, and the already infirm; it hit

---

24 Chandler, *Doomsday,* 118.
25 Lindsey, *Apocalypse,* 20.
26 From Sept. 1918 through March 1919, 33,387 people died in New York City as a result of
    the Spanish flu, a little over 1% of the city's entire population. Alaska was even harder hit,
    with some Alaskan villages losing as much as 50% of their inhabitants. In Teller Mission
    (present-day Brevig Mission), Alaska, 85% of the people died within only one week!

especially hard those between the ages of 25 and 34. The comparison between AIDS and the Spanish flu of 1918 is not intended to trivialize the tragedy of the current AIDS epidemic, but to help us put AIDS into some kind of larger context.

In the same verse, Matthew 24:7, today's heralds of doom make a great deal of the "earthquakes in various places" that are "the beginning of sorrows." Often it is claimed that earthquakes today are occurring at an ever greater frequency, thus signaling the imminent rapture. A great point is made of this even though Matthew 24:7 doesn't actually say there will be an increase of earthquakes, only that they will be "in various places." [27]

Yet what about the claim that we have witnessed an unprecedented increase in earthquakes? Scientists have been gathering seismic information in a systematic manner only since 1880, the year the seismograph was invented (and, in consequence, when the science of seismology was born). Before this, history recorded an earthquake only if it occurred in a populated area. For obvious reasons, the recording of earthquakes was more a haphazard affair than a methodical and scientific accumulation of facts. Indeed, we have no records at all prior to the eighteenth century for earthquakes in the continents of North and South America, Africa, or Australia.

Today scientists use sensors and other types of equipment to monitor shifts in the earth's plates, even minor tremors in very remote regions. The World-Wide Standard Seismograph Network (WWSSN) can measure an earthquake at any one of 125 stations around the world on instruments of exactly the same characteristics. Also, there now exist large-aperture seismic arrays, and very long-period, high-gain seismographs have been developed and deployed at a few specially selected low-noise sites around the world. Now for the first time in history we are able to arrive at basic conclusions about seismic activity on our planet.

Approximately 80 percent of the seismic energy in the world is released in a belt around the Pacific Ocean, a fact that isn't likely to surprise those

---

27 The prophecy pundits derive this idea that earthquakes and other natural disasters will increase in frequency before the end from Matt. 24:8, "All these are the beginning of sorrows." The word "sorrows," *odin* in Greek, can also be translated as "birth pangs." As birth pangs increase in frequency before birth, it is reasoned, so these signs will increase in frequency before the rapture and the Second Coming. The "birth pangs" imagery stems from OT passages such as Is. 13:8; 26:17; Jer. 4:31; 6:24; and Mic. 4:9, 10. By Jesus' time, the prophetic imagery had evolved into a special term for a period of distress, "the birth pangs of the Messiah," that would occur before the Messiah came. While the phrase can encompass an increase in the frequency of natural disasters, it can also indicate a period of divine wrath without any increase in natural disasters at all. In Matt. 24:4–8, Jesus is saying that natural disasters (plagues, famines, earthquakes, etc.) only herald the beginning of a terrible period known as "the birth pangs of the Messiah," not necessarily that natural disasters will increase in frequency.

Notable Earthquakes in History

Date	Location	Remarks
373 B.C.	Helice, Greece	Reported in Strabo's *Geography*
A.D. 365	Eastern Mediterranean	Tsunami leveled the Pharos in Alexandria
A.D. 476	Rome	Destroyed Rome
A.D. 526	Syrian Antioch	250,000 deaths recorded; Antioch destroyed
Jan. 24, 1556	Northern China	Worst death toll in history; 830,000 dead
June 7, 1692	Jamaica	Destroyed city of Port Royal
Winter 1699/1700	American Northwest	Tsunami hit Japanese island of Honshu
Oct. 28, 1703	Tokyo, Japan	200,000 killed
Nov. 1, 1755	Lisbon, Portugal	60,000 killed on All Saints' Day
Feb. 5, 1783	Calabria, Italy	181 villages leveled; 30,000 people killed
Dec. 16, 1811	New Madrid, Missouri	Extremely large intraplate earthquake
Mar. 26, 1812	Venezuela	Destroyed city of Caracas
Aug. 23, 1868	Peru	Tsunami reached 3 miles inland
June 15, 1896	Honshu, Sanriku Coast, Japan	27,000 killed by tsunami whose epicenter was 93 miles off coast

Table taken, with some modifications, from *The 1996 Grolier Multimedia Encyclopedia* (©1996 by Grolier Electronic Publishing, Inc., Danbury, CT)

who live in places such as Mexico, California, Alaska, Japan, and China. Around 15 percent of the world's seismic energy is released in the Mediterranean area. It seems China holds the unfortunate record for loss of human life: in January of 1556, an earthquake in a northern province killed approximately 830,000 people.

Scientists are not only studying present seismic activity, but are now studying old earthquakes as well. Recently, researchers from both Japan and the United States have found that a 9.0 earthquake occurred in the winter of 1699 in the American Pacific Northwest, resulting in a tsunami that hit the Japanese island of Honshu on January 27, 1700, flooding coastal Japan. This earthquake was triggered by a shift in the Cascadia subduction zone, a 600-mile fault from British Columbia to Northern California, which was not previously thought capable of producing a magnitude 9.0 quake.[28]

Are earthquakes increasing in frequency? In reality, earthquakes are extremely common events. During the 1980s, scientists detected 15,436

---

28 David K. Yamaguchi, Brian F. Atwater, Daniel E. Bunker, Boyd E. Benson, Marion S. Reid, "Tree-Ring Dating the 1700 Cascadia Earthquake," *Nature* 389, no. 6654 (Oct. 30, 1997), 922–923. See also the fascinating article by Rick Gore in *National Geographic*, May, 1998 (Vol. 193, no. 5; pp. 6–37), entitled, "Cascadia," which also talks about this earthquake in some depth.

earthquakes with a magnitude 5.0 or greater. Christopher Scholz writes in
the *McGraw-Hill Encyclopedia of Science and Technology*, "Although thousands of earthquakes occur every day, *and have for billions of years*, a truly
great earthquake occurs somewhere in the world only once every 2 or 3
years." [29] While this may be true as a generalization, the specific evidence for
the twentieth century actually points to a *decline* in the number of earthquakes. B. J. Oropeza notes:

> Those who preach distorted earthquake statistics get their information from
> sources that give an incomplete picture of major earthquakes. John Milne,
> the father of modern seismology, lists a total of 4,151 devastating earth-
> quakes from A.D. 7 to A.D. 1899. In fact, more people died between 1715
> to 1783 from earthquakes (1,373,845) than between 1915 and 1983
> (1,210,597). Moreover, when we compare figures from 1900 with figures
> from 1990, both major (8.0 magnitude or higher) and shallow (7.0 magni-
> tude and higher) earthquakes have declined in number and global energy
> (energy released from earthquakes).[30]

Oropeza then quotes Charles F. Richter, inventor of the Richter Scale, as
stating:

> One notices with some amusement that certain religious groups have picked
> this rather unfortunate time to insist that the number of earthquakes is
> increasing. In part they are misled by the increasing number of small earth-
> quakes that are being catalogued and listed by newer, more sensitive sta-
> tions throughout the world. It is worth remarking that the number of great
> [that is, 8.0 and over on the Richter Scale] earthquakes from 1896 to 1906
> (about twenty five) *was greater than in any ten-year interval since.*[31]

"Information" provided by the purveyors of doom and gloom indicating
a dramatic increase in seismic activity is usually the misleading and spurious
product of an overwrought imagination. All too often there is no way of knowing whether the statistics cited by the prophecy gurus are even accurate to
begin with, since they rarely provide formal references to reputable scientific journals and periodicals. More often than not, to cite one warning of
seismic calamity, the only clue as to the possible source of the information is
something vague like: "according to the U.S. Geological society [*sic*]," or,
"One seismologist at the Scripps Research Center in La Jolla, California,
said . . ." [32] It is virtually impossible to verify such nebulous references. Can

---

29 Christopher H. Scholz, "Earthquake," *McGraw-Hill Encyclopedia of Science and Technol-
    ogy*, Vol. 5 (McGraw-Hill Book Co., 1987), 517. Emphasis added.
30 Oropeza, *99 Reasons,* 78.
31 Oropeza, *99 Reasons*, 79–80. Emphasis in original.
32 Tim LaHaye, "Twelve Reasons Why This Could Be the Terminal Generation," *When the
    Trumpet Sounds*, 439.

the reader be faulted for skepticism when the author himself appears less than anxious to have his sources examined?

Let us move on to consider Matthew 24:15–22. Jesus says:

> Therefore when you see the "abomination of desolation" spoken of by Daniel the prophet, standing in the holy place (whoever reads, let him understand), then let those in Judea flee to the mountains. Let him who is on the house-top not go down to take anything out of his house. And let him who is in the field not go back to get his clothes. But woe to those who are pregnant and to those who are nursing babies in those days! And pray that your flight may not be in winter or on the Sabbath. For then there will be great tribulation, such as has not been since the beginning of the world until this time, no, nor ever shall be. And unless those days were shortened, no flesh would be saved; but for the elect's sake those days will be shortened.

Many Church Fathers and Orthodox commentators have seen in these verses the future Antichrist defiling a rebuilt Temple. So do today's doom-sayers, but without considering the prophecy's primary fulfillment in the fall of Jerusalem.

In context, as pointed out by Chrysostom and others, the Lord in this passage is discussing the desolation of the Temple in A.D. 70. The setting is explicitly said to be in Judea. Consider the parallel passage in Luke 21:20, 21: "But when you see Jerusalem surrounded by armies, then know that its desolation is near. Then let those in Judea flee to the mountains . . ." Matthew and Luke are describing the same saying of Jesus, even down to the admonition to flee to the mountains.

In A.D. 70, Jerusalem was surrounded by armies, and the Christians of the city escaped before the Roman siege. The Temple was profaned when the Roman soldiers brought their ensigns into the Temple area, set the ensigns against the eastern gate, and offered sacrifices to them (the "abomination of desolation"). All of this is Jesus' answer to the disciples' question as to how the Temple was to be destroyed. Even John Walvoord admits that Luke 21:20, 21 describes the destruction of Jerusalem forty years after the Crucifixion. If Matthew 24:15, 16 is the parallel passage to Luke 21:20, 21, then the passage in Matthew describes the destruction of Jerusalem's Temple in A.D. 70 as well.

Sometimes the objection is raised that although the Roman soldiers did defile the Temple area, the profanation did not actually occur in the "Holy of holies"; therefore, it could not be the abomination of desolation spoken of by Jesus. It should be pointed out, though, that Jesus doesn't say that the abomination of desolation would occur in the Holy of holies in the center of the Temple, but that it would occur in "the holy place." The entire Temple area was considered "the holy place," as can be seen by the veneration that contemporary Jews show for the Wailing Wall.

The phrase "abomination that causes desolation" is taken from Daniel (9:27; 11:31; 12:1). In the Old Testament, the word "abomination" was virtually a synonym for "idolatry" (e.g. 1 Kin. 11:5–7; 2 Kin. 23:13, 24; Is. 66:3). The phrase "causes desolation" points to the desecrating effect that idolatry has on the Temple: it causes worship of the true God to cease. Whether the Roman standards were set up in the Temple precincts or in the Holy of holies itself is ultimately immaterial, since its intended aim of desecrating the Temple, rendering it unfit for true worship, was accomplished. In setting up their standards, the Romans intended to assert sovereignty over Israel by "dethroning" its God and replacing Him with the god of the conqueror, a common practice in the ancient world.

While Orthodox writers on the end times will sometimes cite Matthew 24:15 as applying to the Antichrist and a rebuilt Temple (though the Fathers more often cited Daniel or 2 Thess. 2:3 when speaking of this), nevertheless, they usually recognize the primary fulfillment of Matthew 24:15 in the destruction of the Temple in A.D. 70. This destruction is then taken as the prototype that will have its greater fulfillment when the Antichrist proclaims himself God in the Temple in the last days, the ultimate abomination of desolation.

For many, though, this is too nuanced. Hal Lindsey, for one, prefers to read the prophecy in Matthew 24:15 as though it were tomorrow's newspaper written before the fact. This includes the flight from Judea to the mountains: "The residents of Israel who believe in Jesus [during the Tribulation] will flee to the mountains and canyons of Petra[33] for divine protection, as promised."[34] Lindsey cites Matthew 24:16, "Then let those who are in Judea flee to the mountains," as well as Revelation 12:6, 14, which says, "Then the woman fled into the wilderness . . . that she might fly into the wilderness."

Yet why seek a future fulfillment of Jesus' prophecy when it was fulfilled during the Roman siege of Jerusalem in A.D. 70? Eusebius, writing early in the fourth century in his *Ecclesiastical History*, tells us that "the people of the church in Jerusalem were commanded by an oracle given by revelation before the war to those in the city who were worthy of it to depart and dwell in one of the cities of Perea which they called Pella."[35] Many commentators on Matthew have wondered whether the "oracle given by

---

33 Petra was once the capital of the Nabataean Kingdom and is located between the Dead Sea and the Gulf of Aqaba, just to the west of what is today called Wadi Musa.

34 Lindsey, *Late Great*, 142.

35 Eusebius, *History*, 3:5:3.

revelation" refers to the warning given by the Lord in Matthew 24:16 (or at least an oral tradition of the warning). In any event, the flight of the Jews to Pella, a city across the Jordan south of the Sea of Galilee (in the *mountainous* region of Perea, per Matthew 24:16), is so reminiscent of Lindsey's predicted flight of the Jews to Petra, an ancient site south of the Dead Sea, that one wonders why Lindsey doesn't just see the fulfillment of the Lord's warning in the flight to Pella.

The second type of abuse common to dispensationalist interpretations of Matthew 24 is fantastic explanations of apocalyptic symbolism. Let's look at one example. Matthew 24:29 reads: "Immediately after the tribulation of those days the sun will be darkened, and the moon will not give its light; the stars will fall from heaven, and the powers of the heavens will be shaken." As can be imagined, doomsday soothsayers are barely able to control themselves when pondering such apocalyptic imagery. In *The 1980s: Countdown to Armageddon*, Hal Lindsey imagined that these cosmic signs are connected to modern UFO sightings and the so-called Jupiter Effect.

The Jupiter Effect, it may be recalled, was an idea spread by Stephen Plagemann and John Gibbon. The theory was that in 1982 the planets were supposed to align and cause tremendous earthquakes and other natural catastrophes. Though such a "Jupiter Effect" had once before been predicted, earlier in the century (by Alberta Porta for December 17, 1919), with no doomsday occurring, Hal Lindsey and many other prophecy buffs readily bought into the new version revived by Plagemann and Gibbon. Of course, the "Jupiter Effect" in fact turned out to be quite uneventful.

What does the imagery of the sun, the moon, and the stars signify in the Bible? Actually, this imagery is used in the Bible in relation to dominion and power.[36] For example, when Joseph tells his brothers of a dream in Genesis 37:9, he says: "Look, I have dreamed another dream. And this time the sun, the moon, and the eleven stars bowed down to me."

Joseph, being the second youngest son in the family, is in subjection to his father Jacob, his mother, and his ten older brothers. In his dream, Joseph's father is the sun, his mother is the moon, and his eleven brothers are the eleven stars. When Joseph later tells his dream to the entire family, everyone immediately grasps the imagery: Joseph would have power and dominion over his family. "So he [Joseph] told it to his father and his brothers; and his father rebuked him and said to him, 'What is this dream that you have

---

36 It is interesting that in the Creation account we read: "Then God made two great lights: the greater light to rule [Heb. *menshalah*] the day, and the lesser light to rule [Heb. *menshalah*] the night. He made the stars also" (Gen. 1:16). James Strong defines *menshalah* as dominion, government, and power. Thus the sun and moon each "governs" its own jurisdiction.

dreamed? Shall your mother and I and your brothers indeed come *to bow down to the earth before you?'"* (Gen. 37:10, emphasis added). In fact, this is exactly what happened after Joseph became vizier of Egypt (see Gen. 42:6).

This kind of imagery is often used of nations and earthly government. In Judges 5:19, 20 there is a bit of Hebraic parallelism that demonstrates this particularly well. In verse 19 we read, "The kings came and fought," meaning the kings of Canaan. In verse 20 we read, "The stars from their courses fought from the heavens; the stars from their courses fought against Sisera." Here earthly kings are represented as stars battling in heaven against Sisera, one of the judges of Israel.

In the New Testament, spiritual Israel (the Church), is symbolized as being in heaven as "a woman clothed with the sun, with the moon under her feet, and on her head a garland of twelve stars" (Rev. 12:1). The Church is thus represented as having full authority and dominion from Christ (see Matt. 28:18–20). David Chilton in his excellent commentary on Revelation observes that this description of the Woman/Bride "clothed with the sun" is reminiscent of the description of her divine Husband (see Ps. 104:2; Is. 60:1, 2; Rev. 1:16; 10:1). " 'The moon under her feet' and her [the Woman's] 'crown of twelve stars' enhance the picture of glory and dominion—indeed, of her ascent from glory to glory (1 Cor. 15:41; 2 Cor. 3:18)." [37]

Returning to Matthew 24:29, Jesus says that when He returns the sun will be darkened, the moon will not give off its light, the stars will fall from the sky and "all the powers of the heavens will be shaken." In other words, when Christ returns all worldly power, authority, and glory will be brought down. Jesus will "turn out the lights" on the rulers of this world. On that day, all power, authority, and dominion will be Christ's alone; then, as Paul says, "when all things are made subject to Him, then the Son Himself will also be subject to Him who put all things under Him, that God may be all in all" (1 Cor. 15:28).

Is there any precedent for this interpretation of Matthew 24:29? As a matter of fact there is, for the imagery is common in both apocalyptic and prophetic literature. For example, Isaiah prophesied the destruction of Babylon in the following manner: "For the stars of heaven and their constellations will not give their light; the sun will be darkened in its going forth, and the moon will not cause its light to shine" (Is. 13:10). Isaiah's prophecy was fulfilled in 539 B.C. when the Persians captured Babylon, ending the Babylonian Empire. No strange, supernatural astronomical phenomena occurred in the sky at the time. The language is purely symbolic.

---

37 Chilton, *Vengeance*, 297–298.

Isaiah uses the same imagery when speaking of the judgment that was to strike Edom: "All the host of heaven shall be dissolved, and the heavens shall be rolled up like a scroll" (Is. 34:4). Edom has long since disappeared from the map, yet was the host of heaven ever literally "dissolved," or did the heavens roll up like a scroll when the Edomites ceased to be an identifiable people? No, again the language is symbolic of God's judgment on Edom.

The Prophet Ezekiel writes in a similar vein with regard to Egypt: "When I put out your light, I will cover the heavens, and make its stars dark; I will cover the sun with a cloud, and the moon shall not give her light. All the bright stars of the heavens I will make dark over you, and bring darkness upon your land" (Ezek. 32:7, 8). Here the symbolism is made more explicit as the Prophet says, "I will put out *your* light." In other words, it is Egypt that will be extinguished for not coming to Israel's aid against the rising Babylonian Empire, not the actual lights of the sun, the moon, and the stars.

Amos prophesied in the northern kingdom of Israel towards the end of the reign of Jeroboam II (785–754 B.C.). On the eve of Assyria's conquest of the northern kingdom, Amos prophesied Israel's downfall: "And it shall come to pass in that day, says the Lord God, that I will make the sun go down at noon, and I will darken the earth in broad daylight" (Amos 8:9). Like Isaiah and Ezekiel, Amos is using cosmological terminology to describe the judgment of God upon a nation.

Consequently, it is likely that when the disciples heard Jesus speaking of the Second Coming in terms of the sun and the moon being darkened and the stars falling from heaven, "and the powers of the heavens" shaken, they understood the Lord in terms of the Hebrew prophetic tradition: the Lord will put down all worldly authority at His coming.

Of course, there are other legitimate ways of interpreting Matthew 24:29. The usual patristic interpretation of the verse asserts that the brightness of Christ's glory will overpower the light of the sun, the moon, and the stars at His coming; and Blessed Theophylact interprets the shaking of the heavenly powers as the astonishment of the angels at the judgment and glorification of creation.

In the final analysis, the issue is not one of blindly accepting an official and authoritative interpretation of Matthew 24. The Church has never asserted that a single interpretation of the Lord's prophecy exhausts its meaning. However, biblical interpretation must be kept within rational limits. The key to understanding verses like Matthew 24:29 is to interpret them within the overall context of the Christian Tradition, not according to the latest findings of the Hubble telescope. The cause of Christ is not well served by professing Christians worked up into a frenzy over amateur astronomy. If we would only take the time to reflect on both the context of Scripture and the accepted teaching of the Church Fathers, we would not be nearly as prone to speculate on the end every time a meteor passes in the night sky.

Gog and Magog as Portents of the End

Buried deep within the Book of Ezekiel is a cryptic reference to the battle of Gog and Magog. Although Ezekiel is well known for his extensive use of symbolic imagery (for example, the whirling, intersecting wheels with eyes all around the rims in Ezekiel 1), many published emissaries of Armageddon have arbitrarily decided to interpret the battle of Gog and Magog as a literal military campaign.

The Armageddon scenario they have concocted is supposed to commence with a Russian invasion of Israel. This is based on a convoluted interpretation of Ezekiel 38:2, which the New King James Version renders as, "Son of man, set your face against Gog, of the land of Magog, the prince of Rosh, Meshech, and Tubal, and prophesy against him" (see also Ezek. 39:1). Since Rosh sounds like "Russia," Meshech a little like "Moscow," and Tubal like the Russian city of "Tobolsk," some interpreters, beginning in the mid-nineteenth century, began to see this verse as a hidden reference to Russia. Though this was only a minority view among Protestants, this interpretation of the verse was put forward in the old *Scofield Reference Bible* as the interpretation upon which "all agree."

With the rise of the Soviet empire in the twentieth century, this interpretation gained immense credibility even among those who otherwise might not have bought into it. This is hardly surprising. Historically, people have tended to identify Gog and Magog with their enemies, whoever that might happen to be. For instance, the Puritan minister Cotton Mather (1663–1728), who in 1690 was elected a fellow at Harvard (in other words, he was no mental midget), was convinced Gog and Magog were the American Indians!

Yet despite Scofield's confident declaration, historian Richard Kyle reveals that dispensationalists have not always been "agreed" upon the interpretation of Ezekiel's prophecy:

> But prophecy enthusiasts had long differed whether this nation would be Russia or the dreaded Turks. The Russian Revolution and the collapse of the Ottoman Empire combined to settle the issue—it would be Russia. The Soviet Union was now a godless communist state and a foreboding threat—two prominent themes in premillennial thinking for most of the twentieth century.[38]

---

38 Kyle, *The Last Days Are Here Again,* 109.

Needless to say, such an arbitrary play on the English pronunciation of Hebrew words (i.e., *rosh* = Russia) is not how biblical scholars approach this verse in Ezekiel today. The word *rosh* in Hebrew actually means "chief," and the King James along with most modern translations renders the verse, "the *chief* prince of Meshech and Tubal." [39] The alternative translation "the prince of Rosh" is generally rejected by translators because there's no historical evidence that a country or people named Rosh ever existed. Modern Russia, therefore, is not a descendant of a mythological people named "Rosh."

For the record, the name "Russia" is derived from the Scandinavian "Rus," introduced into the Ukraine during the Middle Ages when the Vikings ruled the eastern Slavs. It apparently meant either "seafarers" or "rowing." [40] Also, Meshech and Tubal do not refer to Moscow and Tobolsk, respectively, but to areas in central and eastern Asia Minor.[41] Meshech and Tubal are listed in Ezekiel 27:13 as trading partners of Tyre who "bartered in human lives"; and in Ezekiel 32:26 they are consigned to the Pit along with Egypt and other traditional enemies of Israel (see Gen. 10:2; 1 Chr. 1:5).

Ezekiel 38 and 39, according to those especially wedded to literalism, is supposed to predict a modern invasion of Israel by Russia using wooden weapons like bows, arrows, and spears. These are supposedly wielded by men on horseback. Imagine, in an age when wars are fought using "smart" bombs and troops are quickly transported with air-lifters like the C-17, many actually believe the Russians will ride into the Middle East on horseback and defeat Israel with bows and arrows!

The logic of literalism naturally leads them into such a ridiculous position. After all, it is inconsistent to assert the biblical passage predicts a literal invasion and then turn around and claim the wooden weapons and horses mentioned in the passage *aren't* to be so interpreted. B. J. Oropeza, however, highlights the insurmountable difficulty of interpreting Ezekiel 38 and 39 in such a "woodenly" literal manner:

> Do we honestly think Russia would invade Israel with horses, spears, and wooden bows and arrows (Ezek. 38:15; 39:3, 9, 10, 20)? Some have

---

39 The exceptions are the NKJV, the NASB, and the Jerusalem Bible, though the New Jerusalem Bible has changed "the prince of Rosh, Meshech and Tubal" to "the paramount prince of Meshech and Tubal." Obviously, the decision to translate Rosh as a place doesn't imply the translators of the above Bibles identified Rosh with modern Russia.

40 The etymology of the English word "Russian," according to the *American Heritage Dictionary*, is from Medieval Latin, *Russianus*, originating from the Old Russian *Rusi*, which was in turn taken from the Old Norse *rodhsmenn* (seafarers), a word derived from the Norse *rodhr* (rowing).

41 See "Meshech" in the *New Bible Dictionary*, 2nd ed., J. D. Douglas, ed. (Wheaton, IL: Tyndale House, 1982), p. 763; and "Tubal" in John McKenzie's *Dictionary of the Bible* (New York: Collier, 1965), p. 903.

convoluted the issue by claiming the Russians have made new weapons out of a wooden product called lignostone to evade radar detection. Even if this were true, it still doesn't explain away the horses or the spears, war clubs, and bows and arrows that will be used for fuel for several years [see Ezek. 39:9, 10]. Will the arrows be nuclear-tipped? Bomb-tipped arrows popularized on the silver screen are still no match for Israel's automatic weaponry, tanks and aircraft—unless, of course, every Russian fights like Rambo! It is simply ludicrous to think that Russian generals would have their forces battle with ancient weapons.[42]

Reputable biblical scholars attempting to find a literal identification for Gog and Magog agree that Gog is a person who heads the land of Magog, and that the people of Meshech (the "Muski" in Assyrian documents) and Tubal mentioned in Ezekiel 38:2 are aligned with him. Gog is their "chief prince," the preferred translation of an admittedly awkward Hebrew phrase. "Gog" has been variously identified with Gyges (*Gugu* in Assyrian), who was the king of Lydia, as well as a god called Gaga. Other identifications have been put forward as well. Magog could simply be Assyrian for "the land of Gyges" (Assyrian: *ma(t) gugu*). In general, we can conclude that Gog is a person from the region of Magog who is the chief ruler of the countries of Meshech and Tubal, areas located between the Black Sea and Caspian Sea in a region today encompassing Turkey, Georgia, Armenia, Azerbaijan, and Iran. Modern Russia is not what Ezekiel had in mind when he penned his prophecy.

We can already hear the objection: "But Ezekiel 38:15 and 39:2 state that Gog will come from the *far* north, meaning the people to the most extreme north on the globe. This can only be Russia."

Was modern Russia, stretching from Siberia to the White Sea, what our Hebrew Prophet had in mind when he wrote "the far north"? It is far more certain that Ezekiel was describing an area familiar to his readers, and the area around modern Turkey and Armenia constituted "the far north" in the world that Ezekiel and his readers knew. In Ezekiel 38:6, for example, it is stated that "the house of Togarmah" is "from the far north." What, then, is Togarmah in "the far north" to be identified with? One of the Baltic states— or perhaps Finland? No. According to reputable commentators on Ezekiel, *Beth-togarmah* (the house of Togarmah) is to be identified with the area around Armenia.[43] Therefore, we see in this instance that "the far north" means the extreme northern edge of Israel's geopolitical world—not a country that no Jew would see for many centuries to come. This same understanding of the "far north" applies to Gog and Magog as well.

---

42   Oropeza, *99 Reasons,* 100–101.
43   E.g., John Taylor, *Ezekiel,* Vol. 20, Tyndale Old Testament Commentaries, 245.

As Gary DeMar observes, the dispensationalist twist on Gog and Magog simply doesn't fly:

> The most damaging piece of evidence that Ezekiel 38 and 39 do not refer to modern Russia's invasion of Israel during the "Great Tribulation" is that there is no mention of Gog and Magog or Meshech and Tubal in Revelation 4—19, yet this is when dispensationalists tell us the battle is to take place. The Battle of Gog and Magog is *after* the millennium, and its description is quite different from Ezekiel's depiction of the battle (Revelation 20:8).[44]

In the Book of Revelation, as well as in rabbinic literature, Gog and Magog symbolize the antagonists of God and His people. In *Everyman's Talmud*, Talmudic scholar Abraham Cohen tells us the rabbis believed that, in the seventh year of a seven-year period before the Messiah would come, there would be great wars on earth: "The time of his [the Messiah's] advent will be particularly marked by political unrest, culminating in bitter warfare. . . . This strife is symbolized under the term 'wars of Gog and Magog' (see Ezek. xxxviii)."[45] At the end of the millennium, Revelation describes bitter warfare using the symbols of Gog and Magog, as in rabbinic teaching. Note that Revelation doesn't identify Gog and Magog as Russia, but as all "the nations which are in the four corners of the earth" (Rev. 20:8). Consequently, from a "plain" reading of the text, there is nothing to commend the doomsayer's narrow equation of Gog and Magog with modern Russia.

144,000 Jewish Monks

Will there be 144,000 celibate "Jews for Jesus," all male, running around the earth during the Tribulation getting folks "born again" before the Second Coming? Dispensationalists are certain of it. This notion is taken from Revelation 7:4–8, where John has a vision of the servants of God who are sealed on their foreheads, 144,000 from all the tribes of Israel, each tribe contributing 12,000 men. These 144,000 men, we are told, are distinguished from the great multitude "of all nations, tribes, peoples, and tongues standing before the throne and before the Lamb" (Rev. 7:9)—that is, Gentile believers. In Revelation 14:1–5, we learn these 144,000 are standing on Mount Zion and that they "were not defiled with women, for they are virgins . . . and in their mouth was found no deceit, for they are without fault before the throne of God."

There are more than a few problems with a literal interpretation of this passage. For one thing, as Robert Mounce points out in his classic commentary on Revelation in *The New International Commentary on the New*

---

44   DeMar, *Last Days*, 202. Emphasis in original.

45   Abraham Cohen, *Everyman's Talmud* (New York: Schocken Books, 1949), 350.

Testament, "This interpretation seriously complicates the Book of Revelation by bringing in racial distinctions which no longer exist in the N[ew] T[estament] purview." [46] In other words, this interpretation fails to take into account Paul's teaching in Galatians 3:28 that in Christ "there is neither Jew nor Greek." There aren't "Jewish" Christians and "Gentile" Christians in the Body of Christ: there are only "Christians."

Evangelical biblical scholar Robert Gundry, who taught at Westmont College for thirty-five years and is the author of *A Survey of the New Testament* (a standard textbook used in many colleges and seminaries), notes that Revelation 7 says that John only "heard" about the 144,000. Then, after listing the twelve tribes of Israel, he "looked, and behold, a great multitude which no one could number, of all nations" (Rev. 7:9). This phraseology is similar to another passage in Revelation where John "heard" about the lion of the tribe of Judah and then "saw" a Lamb (Rev. 5:5, 6). In both incidents, what is "heard" and what is "seen," though seemingly different, both describe the same thing. In Revelation 5 it is Christ, the Lion and the Lamb; and in Revelation 7 it is the Church, both Israel and the multitude of the Gentile nations.[47]

Biblical scholar Leon Morris, of Ridley College in Melbourne and the general editor of the Tyndale New Testament Commentary series, also criticizes the distinction that dispensationalists make between the 144,000 and the "great multitudes" saved from among the nations: "A strong objection is that in this case Israel is sealed for protection but a mighty multitude from all nations [Rev. 7:9] is saved without this sealing. Surely both would be sealed if they are different groups." [48] Rather than seeing the 144,000 and the great multitude as two distinct groups, scholars like Mounce and Morris see the two as being one and the same group—the whole Christian Church. Morris explains that, in the New Testament,

> The church is referred to as "the twelve tribes" (Jas 1:1; cf. Mt 19:28; Lk 22:30), and this is probably the thought when a letter is sent to "the Dispersion" (1 Pet 1:1; RSV, JB). The Christian appears to be the true Jew (Rom 2:29) and the church "the Israel of God" (Gal 6:16). Descriptions of old Israel are piled up and applied to the church (1 Pet 2:9; cf. Eph 1:11, 14). It is the church which is God's "very own" people (Tit 2:14), and "the circumcision" (Phil 3:3). Abraham is the father of all who believe (Rom 4:11); again these are Abraham's children (Gal 3:7). Many hold that Israel "after the flesh" (1 Cor 10:18; see RSV mg.) implies an Israel "after the Spirit." [49]

---

46 Mounce, *Revelation*, 168.

47 Gundry, *Antichrist*, 92.

48 Leon Morris, *Revelation*, rev. ed., Tyndale New Testament Commentaries, 111.

49 Morris, *Revelation*, 111–112.

Yet, it may rightly be asked, is this what the author of Revelation has in mind with regard to the 144,000 from the twelve tribes of Israel? Did John himself equate Israel with the Church? Morris responds:

> [John] expresses it by implication when he speaks of those "who say they are Jews and are not, but are a synagogue of Satan" ([Rev.] 2:9; cf. 3:9). He regards the new Jerusalem as the spiritual home of Christians ([Rev.] 21:2, etc.), and it has on its gates the names of the twelve tribes (21:12). There is thus good reason for seeing a reference here to the church as the true Israel. Here [i.e., Rev. 7:4] it is the church, sealed in view of the coming trials; later in the chapter it is the church triumphant and at peace.[50]

William Hendriksen, who received his Th.D. from Princeton Theological Seminary, is another evangelical scholar who has had problems with the dispensationalist interpretation of Revelation 7. Hendriksen's excellent commentary on Revelation, which has been in continuous print since 1939, points out that both the tribes of Ephraim and Dan are missing from the list given in Revelation 7:5–8. This, Hendriksen observes, ought to raise flags for the discerning reader: "Besides, if Israel according to the flesh were meant, why should Ephraim and Dan be omitted? Surely not all the people in the tribe of Dan were lost." [51]

In other words, God could certainly have found a representative number of the descendants of these two tribes if He had intended the 144,000 actually to be from Israel according to the flesh. After all, the list includes twelve thousand from such otherwise "lost" tribes as Issachar, Gad, and Naphtali—why not Ephraim and Dan as well? The fact that these tribes were excluded points to a different interpretation of this passage. (We will explore why Dan is omitted from this list in the next chapter.)

That the 144,000 are representative of spiritual Israel, the Church, is by no means a novel interpretation of this passage in Revelation. It was being interpreted this way in the earliest recorded biblical commentaries. In the early third century, for example, Origen wrote, "It appears to me that the whole people of Christ, when we regard it in the aspect of the hidden man of the heart, that people which is called 'Jew inwardly' and is circumcised in the spirit (Rom. 2:29), has in a more mystic way the characteristics of the tribes [of Israel]." [52] Origen then proceeds in the following two chapters to develop this idea based on Revelation 7.

As we've already had a chance to observe, numbers in the Bible—and particularly in apocalyptic literature like the Book of Revelation—often have

---

50 Morris, *Revelation*, 112.
51 Hendriksen, *More Than Conquerors,* 111.
52 Origen, *Commentary on the Gospel of John*, Book 1:1.

a symbolic significance. Looking at the number 144,000, we find it breaks down to 12 x 12 x 1,000. The number 1,000 in the Bible indicates an unlimited amount. To what do the two "twelves" refer?

Old Israel began with Twelve Patriarchs, and the New Israel began with the Twelve Apostles; consequently, in Revelation the New Jerusalem that descends from heaven has twelve foundations for the Twelve Apostles and twelve gates for the Twelve Patriarchs of Israel (Rev. 21:12–14). Thus we have 12 (tribes of Israel) multiplied by 12 (Apostles of the New Israel) multiplied by 1,000 (a great amount). Therefore the completion and perfection of the Church—embracing the great number saved from both Old and New Israel—is indicated by the number 144,000.

However, some suggest more may be meant by the number 1,000 in this context. Some have seen here an allusion to spiritual warfare. One thousand men, comprised of ten units of a hundred each, was the basic military division in Israel,[53] each tribe having a certain number of divisions to contribute to the common defense. For example, the Prophet Samuel said that the first king of Israel, Saul, would "appoint captains over his thousands and captains over his fifties" (1 Sam. 8:12). At the time of David's ascent to power, it is recorded that the tribe of Issachar had "thirty-six thousand troops of the army ready for war" (1 Chr. 7:4), that Benjamin could field "seventeen thousand two hundred mighty men of valor" (1 Chr. 7:11), and that Asher had twenty-six thousand men "fit for battle" (1 Chr. 7:40).

With this background in mind, some have understood John's vision of the 144,000—twelve divisions from each tribe—as a military roll call of the Lord's troops as the final battle commences between God and the forces of hell. Every "tribe" in the Church is called upon to contribute its "divisions" to the war effort; none sits on the sidelines. That the Lord's troops are "sealed" symbolizes God's protection, meaning the Church will ultimately emerge from battle triumphant. The fact that the men are described as not having been "defiled with women" points, within context, to the spiritual purity of God's warriors, not to their marital status as such.

Therefore, the consensus of Christian opinion is, and always has been, that the 144,000 refers to the Church, not to Jewish monks.

The Two Witnesses

Less controversial is the identity of the two witnesses mentioned in Revelation 11:3–12 who are to herald the Second Advent. These two witnesses appear in Jerusalem during the Tribulation and prophesy against the Antichrist,

---

53 See Num. 31:1–5, 48–54; 2 Sam. 18:1; 1 Chr. 12:20; 13:1; 15:25; 26:26; 27:1; 28:1; 29:6; 2 Chr. 1:2; 17:14–19; Ps. 68:17.

working many miracles. The Antichrist kills them, and they lie unburied in the streets of Jerusalem three and a half days while the ungodly of the world rejoice. After this, God resurrects them and they ascend into heaven. Many, like Hal Lindsey, believe these two witnesses will be Elijah and Moses, though some, like televangelist John Hagee, believe they will be Enoch and Elijah.

Orthodox Tradition also teaches that two witnesses will appear and exercise a ministry during the Tribulation. Historically, both in the Liturgy and in the writings of the Fathers, the Church has strongly identified these two witnesses as Enoch and Elijah, both of whom were assumed into heaven without tasting death (see Heb. 11:5; 2 Kin. 2:1–13).

The earliest Christian reference to the appearance of Elijah before the Second Coming is from St. Justin Martyr in the mid-second century. Apparently with Matthew 17:11 in mind, Justin writes in his *Dialogue with Trypho*,

> We have been taught . . . by our Lord Himself that this would certainly be so, namely, that Elijah also would come; and we know that this will take place when our Lord Jesus Christ will be about to come from Heaven in glory, just as the spirit of God that was in Elijah, in the person of John, who was a prophet of your [Jewish] race, after whom no other prophet has appeared among you, came forth as the precursor of His first Advent.[54]

Hippolytus, around A.D. 200, names the two witnesses as Enoch and Elijah.[55] Tertullian, writing around A.D. 210–213, also speaks of Enoch and Elijah returning to "extinguish the Antichrist."[56] The mention of the appearance of both Enoch and Elijah together before the Second Coming is also found in apocryphal works of the second and third centuries, like *The Gospel of Nicodemus*, *The History of Joseph*, the "Apocalypses" of Peter and Paul, and the *Acts of Pilate*. Archbishop Andrew of Caesarea, in his *Commentary on the Apocalypse*, a fifth-century work that largely summarizes the pre-Nicean (before A.D. 325) understanding of Revelation, also believed the two witnesses were Enoch and Elijah.

However, many modern biblical scholars make a strong case for the two witnesses being Elijah and Moses, both of whom appeared with the Lord on the Mount of Transfiguration (Matt. 17:3) and who together would represent the witness of the Law (Moses) and the Prophets (Elijah) to a world about to be judged. The selection of Moses as the second witness is also suggested by the fact that the witnesses repeat some of the miracles associated with Moses, like turning water into blood (see Rev. 11:6 with Ex. 7:17, 19, 20) and striking the earth with plagues.

---

54 Justin Martyr, *Dialogue*, 49.
55 Hippolytus, *On the Antichrist*, 43.
56 Tertullian, *Treatise on the Soul,* 50.

On the other hand, Revelation 11:3 states the two witnesses are "clothed in sackcloth," dress traditionally associated with prophets from the time of Elijah to the time of John the Baptist (2 Kin. 1:8; Is. 20:2; Jon. 3:6; Zech. 13:4; Matt. 3:4; Mark 1:6). Sackcloth symbolized the prophet's mourning over the people's apostasy. Though Moses is certainly considered a prophet, he is characterized more as the Lawgiver in the Bible.

Enoch, though, was closely associated with the Prophet Elijah in Jewish literature since Enoch was also assumed into heaven without dying. After the return of the Jews from Babylon, Enoch began to be seen as an ancient sage and was credited with inventing the art of writing. He was also said to have received heavenly revelations that he wrote down for later generations. Apocryphal writings claiming to have been written by Enoch—many of which were apocalyptic in style—were popular at the time of Revelation's composition. Thus Enoch was considered a prophet like Elijah among both the Jews and the Christians of the first century, and it is not surprising that the early Christians saw the two witnesses as Enoch and Elijah. A good case can therefore be made for the traditional Orthodox view that the second witness in Revelation 11 is Enoch.

Armageddon

As we noted in passing in Chapter 2, the word "Armageddon" is a Greek transliteration of the Hebrew *Har* (mount) *Meggedon*,[57] or "Mount Megiddo." [58] The word is found in Revelation 16:16, and has been the source of much speculation by biblical scholars. The reason for all the speculation is that, when you look for "Mount Megiddo" in your Bible atlas, you quickly discover no such mountain exists. In fact, there is no other reference to Armageddon in the Bible, nor is there any mention of Armageddon in any other ancient writing or map. In other words, there is no "Armageddon"!

Megiddo was actually a city on a plain on the north side of the Carmel ridge which commanded the crucially strategic pass from the coastal plain to the valley of Esdraelon. When John wrote the Book of Revelation, Megiddo sat upon a ten-acre mound, today known as Tell el-Mutesellim, which was then only about seventy feet in height—hardly qualifying as "Mount" Megiddo! In fact, the earliest known interpretation of the word Armageddon is "the trodden, *level* place." [59]

So what does "Armageddon" signify if it is not an actual place? This is

---

57 Zech. 12:11 renders Megiddo as *meggedon*.

58 Another possible transliteration may be the Hebrew *har migido*, meaning "His fruitful mountain." This would then be a reference to Mount Zion.

59 The reference exists only in Arabic: *'lmwd' 'wtv* (the Plain?). See "Armageddon," *New Bible Dictionary,* 83.

an open question for biblical commentators, though perhaps David Chilton offers the best explanation of what Armageddon may mean. He sees "Mount Megiddo" as a conflation of two distinct images. The nearest mountain to Megiddo is Mount Carmel, most noted in biblical history as the place where the Prophet Elijah challenged and defeated the prophets of Baal and Asherah, the deities promoted by Jezebel (1 Kin. 18—19:2). The city of Megiddo itself was the scene of a number of significant battles. Chilton notes in particular a battle wherein King Josiah fought Neco, the Pharaoh of Egypt. Though God had revealed to Josiah that he was not to face Neco in battle, Josiah went forth anyway and was killed (see 2 Chr. 35:20–25). After this defeat at Megiddo, Israel slid downhill into apostasy (see 2 Chr. 36), mourning Josiah's death till the days of Ezra (2 Chr. 35:25).

Chilton concludes that the primary meaning of the battle of "Mount Megiddo" mentioned in Revelation is the ultimate defeat of false prophets and all those who deliberately disobey God, a sort of "Waterloo" for spiritual darkness.[60] Whether this "Waterloo" will actually be a military battle in the same region between lower Galilee and Samaria is ultimately a secondary question. The issue in the final analysis is not one of topography and military tactics: Armageddon symbolizes the final resistance of evil prior to the advent of Christ's Kingdom. Unfortunately, the millenarians' preoccupation with geography and apocalyptic military battles has overshadowed the real message of Armageddon: that peace and hope are ours because of our sure knowledge of Christ's ultimate triumph over evil.

Armageddon may spell the end of things as far as this world is concerned, but it does not conclude our look at the dispensationalist scenario of the end times. We must next take a math lesson from the Antichrist.

---

60 David Chilton, *The Great Tribulation* (Ft. Worth: Dominion Press, 1987), 142–144.

Chapter Thirteen

The Antichrist According to Algebra

Here is wisdom. Let him who has understanding calculate the number of the beast, for it is the number of a man: His number is 666.
—The Apocalypse of St. John 13:18

It is therefore more certain, and less hazardous, to await the fulfillment of the prophecy [in Revelation 13:18] than to be making surmises and casting about for any names that may present themselves, inasmuch as many names can be found possessing the number mentioned; and the same question will, after all, remain unsolved.
—St. Irenaeus of Lyons, *Against Heresies* (A.D. 180)

WHEN CHANNEL-SURFING the television late some Sunday night, try checking out "Jack Van Impe Presents." It isn't a bad way to kill an hour for those who can appreciate the offbeat and the campy. The impression the program gives is that of a news broadcast, or at least a news-related program like "20/20." The opening music is similar to that associated with the evening news, and the set is basically empty except for the standard news desk used by news anchors. The lead introducing the program has a deep, somber voice, and behind the news desk sit the two hosts of the show, Jack and Rexella Van Impe.

While the show does relate current events, these are all understood vis-à-vis prophecies that are supposed to happen in the near future. In a sense, the Van Impes attempt to broadcast the news *before* it occurs. It is tomorrow's news delivered into your living room today, getting the ultimate scoop on the more established, run-of-the-mill news organizations.

Though their show doesn't give the headlines at the top and bottom of the hour like CNN's "Headline News," nevertheless CNN has nothing on Jack and Rexella Van Impe. As could be expected, the Van Impes have been regularly castigated by mainstream news organizations for inaccurate and sensational "news" reporting. The daily TV program "A Current Affair" investigated the Van Impes in the fall of 1995 and aired an exposé accusing them of extorting donations from the public through apocalyptic fear mongering.[1] According to "A Current Affair," the Van Impes declared $350,000 on their 1994 tax return. Not bad. It would seem the Van Impes intend to enter the approaching millennial kingdom with a tidy nest egg.[2]

In 1995 Jack Van Impe Ministries International produced a video called *666: The United States of Europe and the New World Order*, which can be obtained with a contribution to the ministry of $24.95. The cardboard jacket summarizes the contents of this 107-minute video:

> In the most remarkable video ever from Dr. Jack and Rexella Van Impe, you will see . . .
> — How the year 2000 is pivotal to God's end-times agenda.
> — How the diabolical New Age Movement is bringing together a one-world religion—and how mass murder figures into their plans.
> — How Satan is installing promoters of literal Satan worship in places of power across North America and around the world . . . to make ready for the rise of the Antichrist!

The video doesn't live up to its lurid promotion. Except for a few breakaway shots to illustrate Jack Van Impe's monologue, it is nearly two hours of dull lecture occasionally broken by asides from Rexella. Those who remain awake through the video learn that it is no coincidence that the state of Israel, the European Union, and the World Council of Churches were all established in the same year, 1948. That, of course, was the year God wound up His prophetic wristwatch.

Van Impe announces that Israel, the European Union (the Revived Roman Empire), and the World Council of Churches (the Whore of Babylon described in Revelation 17) will all play a vital role in the Antichrist's New World Order. Conspiracy lurks everywhere in the drive to establish Big Brother's Brave New World. Van Impe assures us that plans for this New World Order have been in the works for a long time, as witness the fact that

---

1 "A Current Affair," rebroadcast May 13, 1996.

2 The blatant exploitation of people's fears of Armageddon has recently been satirized in *Dilbert*, a comic strip by Scott Adams. One of the characters, Dogbert, is pretending to be a seer, and is seated behind a table wearing a tall, "swami" style hat with a crescent on the front. Seated across from him is a customer, to whom Dogbert says, "The end of the world is coming in year 2000. Therefore, you should give me your money before it's too late. It is written that money is evil. I'll keep your money in Dogbert's special 'Evil-be-Gone' device." Then, placing a piggy-bank on the table, Dogbert adds, "And it's completely deductible . . . [in small print] from your savings." The customer, who is feverishly writing a check, exclaims, "So I'm actually making money!" Alas, how many people are really this naive.

the words *Novus Ordo Seclorum* are beneath the All-Seeing Eye on the back of our dollar bills. Van Impe darkly reveals that this Latin phrase translates as "New World Order." (Actually, this is a mistranslation, but Van Impe is not to be stayed by the technicalities of Latin grammar.)[3] It is thus plainly evident that the conspiracy to initiate the New World Order has long been ensconced in the highest places. Time is short. Your worst suspicions are true: the Antichrist's operatives are watching you even now as you read this.

Van Impe believes that before long the rapture will occur and the Antichrist will arise, taking over this New World Order and instituting a demonic, cashless society. This new economic system will entail the insertion of a small microchip into the hand that will act as a sort of dual debit card and ID. Instead of cash or checks, transactions in the future will be handled by scanning the hand. This will be the "mark of the beast" mentioned in Revelation. Jack Van Impe points out that Prince William of England is reported to have had a tracking chip inserted into his body so British Intelligence can locate him should he ever be abducted. It is all being fulfilled before our eyes— fulfilled, that is, with a little journalistic license from Mr. Van Impe.

When "A Current Affair" contacted British journalists to confirm the Prince William story, it was discovered that there had only been rumors that tracking chips might have been sewn into the Prince's clothes, not inserted into his body! For obvious reasons, British security agencies would neither confirm nor deny the existence of tracking chips in Prince William's clothing.

Some Men Can Be Such Beasts

The coming Antichrist has always held a certain fascination for people as a mysterious figure of unspeakable evil. Most tantalizing of all, the Bible in Revelation 13:18 reveals the Antichrist's name, which is ciphered as 666. Christians have played with this numeric puzzle at least as early as the second century, when Irenaeus of Lyons came up with such names as Evanthas, Teitan, and Lateinos. More often than not, however, the figure of 666 has been the stuff of puerile mudslinging.

During the Protestant Reformation, the idea that the pope was the Antichrist was virtually an article of faith. Even today, some anti-Catholic

---

3   The Latin expression is from a phrase in Virgil's *Eclogae* (4:5), *annuit coeptis novus ordo seculorum,* which is rendered in English as, "The year of the new order of centuries." Virgil's "year of the new order of centuries" was a reference to Caesar Augustus Octavian in 40 B.C. The idea implied on our dollar bills is that the birth of the American nation in 1776 signified the birth of a new, democratic age that replaced the age of monarchies.

Protestants will add up the title of *Vicarius Filii Dei*, "Vicar of the Son of God," to total 666 in Latin. Unfortunately for them, the actual title of the pope is *Vicarius Christi*, "Vicar of Christ," not *Vicarius Filii Dei*. Moreover, the title "Vicar of the Son of God" doesn't even add up to 666, but to 661![4] Nevertheless, neither the fact that *Vicarius Filii Dei* is not the title of the pope, nor the fact that it doesn't actually add up to 666, gives these extremists pause; they are certain the pope is the Antichrist anyway.

Returning the favor, Catholics have pointed out that the name Martin Luther, when Latinized as *Martin Lutera*, tallies to 666. In fact, the Protestant Reformer Thomas Muntzer of Munster in Westphalia agreed with the Roman Catholics on this point! The Seventh Day Adventists, for their part, have consigned the whole lot of us, Catholics, Protestants, and Orthodox, to the lake of fire by identifying the mark of the beast with Sunday worship, declaring that all who go to church on Sunday instead of Saturday are a part of the Antichrist's false religious system! As one Adventist put it: "Sunday worship is the mark of the Papacy's authority. . . . Sunday worship is the 'mark of the beast!' "[5]

Nearly every despised world leader has been identified as the Antichrist. Napoleon was once declared to be the villain of the Book of Revelation, which seemed to fit as far as Catholics were concerned, since he had taken the pope prisoner. During the American Revolutionary War, King George III was identified as the Antichrist by calculating the phrase "Royal Supremacy in Great Britain" in both Greek and Hebrew and arriving at the total 666. Hitler, in his turn, was declared to be the Antichrist and Benito Mussolini was supposed to be his "false prophet" (see Rev. 13:11–17). After Hitler survived an attempted assassination, doom-sayers duly pointed to Revelation 13:3, which states the Antichrist would miraculously survive a mortal wound: "And I saw one of his heads as if it had been mortally wounded, and his deadly wound was healed."

In the early 1980s, President Reagan survived an assassination attempt as well—and each of his names, Ronald Wilson Reagan, had six letters! A fairly impressive coincidence since not even Adolph (six letters) Hitler (six letters) had three names each adding up to six. (Adolph didn't seem to have a middle name.) Even worse, the address of Reagan's California mansion was 666! This clinched the issue for a great many. Poor Ronald Reagan, who had

---

4   The total 666 is normally reached by giving the vowel "u" in *Vicarius* the value of 5, even though, according to their own system of calculation, the vowels aren't supposed to receive any value.

5   A. Jan Marcussen, *National Sunday Law* (Thompsonville, IL: Amazing Truth Publications, 1983), 47.

always been sympathetic to prophetic speculation and who even believed the Soviet Union was Gog, later had the address changed to 668.[6]

Other candidates for Antichrist have included Anwar Sadat, Henry Kissinger, and King Juan Carlos of Spain. It seems that as long as there are politicians, there will always be potential Antichrists.

Having a laugh at some of the irrational games that prophecy speculators play with numbers, B. J. Oropeza decided to see if he could do a little "end-times mathematics" with the name of doomsday date-setter Harold Camping, using Camping's own system of "prophetically significant" numbers:

> Count the vowels in the name of Harold Camping = 4.
>
> Multiply this by the total letters in Camping: $4 \times 7 = 28 = 2 \times 2 \times 7$.
>
> Subtract 11 from 28 = 17 (one of Camping's significant prophetic numbers).
>
> Now add 17 to the number of letters in Harold: $17 + \mathbf{6} = 23$ (Camping's other prophetic number).
>
> Harold = 6 letters. The numeric value of the consonants of his name is $[\text{H }(8) + \text{R }(18) + \text{L }(12) + \text{D }(4)] = 42 = \mathbf{6} \times 7$.
>
> Find the numeric value of the vowels in his first name: $[\text{A }(1) + \text{O }(15)] = 16$.
>
> Multiply the value of the consonants times the value of the vowels: $42 \times 16 = 672 = \mathbf{6} \times 112$.
>
> **Note:** there are a total of three sixes, or **666.**
>
> Find the total numerical value of his first name: $42 + 16 = 58$.
>
> Multiply this by the total numeric value of his last name, Camping: $58 \times 63 = 3654$.
>
> Split 3654 into 36 and 54: ($\mathbf{6} \times \mathbf{6}$) and ($\mathbf{6} \times 9$). Once again, there are three sixes, or **666.**[7]

While it may be amusing to poke fun at Harold Camping, the larger point that Oropeza is making shouldn't be missed: numbers can be made to say whatever the conjurer wants them to say. If someone wants a name to yield 666, he will find a way, no matter how tortuous.

The theme of the Antichrist and a coming economic system controlled by computers is especially lucrative in the publishing world, as witness Peter and Paul Lalonde's book, *The Mark of the Beast: Your Money, Computers and the End of the World,* published in 1994 by Harvest House, a major Christian publisher. Harvest House followed this up in 1996 with a book coauthored by Thomas Ice and Timothy Demy called *The Coming Cashless Society.* In fact, Mary Stewart Relfe's *The New Money System*, originally published in 1982, is still found on the shelves of major Christian bookstores

---

6   Oropeza, *99 Reasons*, 149–150.
7   Oropeza, *99 Reasons*, 54–55. Bold in original.

across America. Whoever the Antichrist may be, many are certain that the Antichrist's monetary system is ready to be put in place and will culminate in the mark of the beast. Though our currency has been changed more than thirty times since our country's founding (a standard procedure to discourage counterfeiting), prophecy buffs are sure the next change of currency will somehow be different and serve as the precursor of Antichrist.

In the nightmarish world of millennial obsession, rumors are circulating that a supercomputer exists in Brussels called—what else?—the "Beast," which will act as Big Brother as it monitors our every financial transaction. (As it turns out, the "Beast" is a fictional creation from a 1970s novel written by Joe Musser, *Behold a Pale Horse*.) Biochips, which some have inserted into their pets as high-tech dog tags, will supposedly be inserted into our hands to incorporate us into the Antichrist's diabolic system. What else could these biochips be but the mark of the beast?

It is also believed that credit cards are paving the way for the actual mark that will be on our hands and foreheads. Mary Stewart Relfe in 1981 argued in *When Your Money Fails* that "VISA" adds up to 666: "vi" is obviously the Roman numeral 6; the "zz" sound stands for the Greek letter Zeta, which is the sixth letter of the Greek alphabet; and suddenly switching to English, the letter "a" looks like a 6 when turned around. Another popular idea is that the mark will be a version of the Universal Product Code (the vertical black lines found on the back of this book) that is on nearly every item we purchase at the store.

When assaulted by such inane cognitive convolutions as the above, it is tempting to heap scorn upon the whole notion of a coming Antichrist. It can be difficult to appreciate the fact that for two thousand years the Orthodox Church has taught that a time will come before the Lord's return when the Antichrist will appear and persecute Christians at an unprecedented level. Who is the Antichrist and what does 666 really mean?

The Numbers Game

The concept of the Antichrist has its roots in pre-Christian Judaism. The figure of a great adversary of the Messiah (or of God) was a regular feature of the Jewish apocalyptic literature that was popular from 200 B.C. till the time of Jesus. The Antichrist—which literally means "against the Messiah," or "in place of the Messiah"—was usually modeled in Jewish apocalyptic literature upon Antiochus IV Epiphanes, the Greek Seleucid emperor who ruled Palestine and much of the rest of the Middle East in the second century before Christ. In December of 167 B.C., in an attempt to Hellenize Israel, Antiochus tried to establish the cult of Olympian Zeus among the Jews, even profaning the Temple by slaughtering a pig[8] on the altar. He then brutally persecuted all Jews who continued to practice Judaism. The Jews revolted against Antiochus Epiphanes and, three years later, they reclaimed the Temple in Jerusalem and returned it to the worship of the God of Israel. The cleansing and reconstruction of the Temple are commemorated to this day in the Jewish feast of Hanukkah.

Daniel 8 describes the Greek kingdom of Antiochus Epiphanes as a male goat (see Dan. 8:21—"And the male goat is the kingdom of Greece"). Antiochus himself is described as a "little horn" that "grew up to the host of heaven; and it cast down some of the host and some of the stars to the ground, and trampled them. He even exalted himself as high as the Prince of the host; and by him the daily sacrifices were taken away, and the place of his sanctuary was cast down. Because of transgression, an army was given over to the horn to oppose the daily sacrifices; and he cast truth down to the ground. He did all this and prospered" (Dan. 8:10–12).

Daniel 7:19–27 and Daniel 11:21–39 describe a despot that Christians have traditionally seen as a prototype of the Antichrist. Jesus, drawing on Daniel 9:27, also predicted an "abomination of desolation" perpetrated by an Antichrist figure, which occurred when the Romans destroyed the Temple in A.D. 70 (Matt. 24:15). In a very real sense, the Roman emperor was an antichrist, a prefiguration of the Antichrist to come.

Though the Apostle John, writing toward the end of the first century, after the destruction of the Temple, writes that the Antichrist is yet to come, nevertheless, he asserts that "even now many antichrists have come" (1 John 2:18). He writes that anyone who denies the Father and the Son is called antichrist (1 John 2:22). More specifically, anyone who denies the reality that Christ has come in the flesh is antichrist (1 John 4:3; 2 John 7). It is interesting that John is the only one in the Bible to use the term "antichrist," and he uses it in a rather generic fashion.

The Apostle Paul, being a trained rabbi, describes the Antichrist as a "man of lawlessness," the word "lawlessness" referring not to civil law (in the sense that an anarchist is "lawless"), but to God's law (*torah* in Hebrew). Paul says in 2 Thessalonians that the Antichrist is being restrained by some person or power (which we cannot identify) that will be removed, and then he will be revealed. His coming will be with signs and wonders, resulting in many being deceived and falling into apostasy. The Antichrist "opposes and exalts himself above all that is called God or that is worshiped, so that he sits as God in the temple of God, showing himself that he is God" (2 Thess. 2:4). Antichrist is not Satan, but he operates "according to the working [Gr.

---

8   Pigs are considered unclean animals in Judaism. See Lev. 11:7; Deut. 14:8.

energeian, lit. "energy"] of Satan" (v. 9). Christ will destroy him at His Second Coming (v. 8).

In the Book of Revelation, the Antichrist is simply called the "beast." Like Paul, the author of Revelation distinguishes between Satan and the Antichrist. Satan is pictured as the "great, fiery red dragon" (Rev. 12:3, 9). The beast portrayed in Revelation 11:7 and in Revelation 13 is clearly distinct from Satan, though he does the works of Satan and derives his power from Satan. The beast is a man, for his number "is the number of a man: his number is 666" (Rev. 13:18).

There is an Old Testament background to John's use of the number 666, and significantly it is in connection with a political figure—King Solomon. In 1 Kings 10:14 (also 2 Chr. 9:13) we learn that at the height of Solomon's glory and power he received an annual income of 666 talents of gold, not including the income derived from traders, the kings of Arabia, and from district governors. To grasp the astronomical wealth this represents, it must be understood that a "talent" weighed anywhere from 45 to 130 pounds. We are looking at an annual income of around *twenty-five tons* of gold! As a result of this dizzying wealth, Solomon ultimately succumbed to the associated temptations of riches and started down the road to eventual apostasy, as David Chilton points out:

> One by one, Solomon breaks the three laws of godly kingship recorded in Deuteronomy 17:16, 17: the law against multiplying gold (1 Kings 10:14–25); the law against multiplying horses (1 Kings 10:26–29); and the law against multiplying wives (1 Kings 11:1–8). For the Hebrews, 666 was a fearful sign of apostasy, the mark of both a king and a kingdom in the Dragon's image.[9]

Not only the ancient Hebrews, but the ancient Christians as well understood the number 666 as the sign of ultimate apostasy. Within a hundred years of the composition of the Book of Revelation, St. Irenaeus wrote in his *Against Heresies* that 666 is the "summing up of the whole of that apostasy which has taken place during six thousand years [of human history]."[10]

Who did John have in mind when he wrote that the number of the beast is 666? While no solution is entirely without difficulties, the consensus among biblical scholars today is that 666 stands for the Roman Emperor Nero Caesar. Why is Nero today considered the likeliest candidate for 666?

The first thing to realize is that ancient written languages such as Hebrew, Greek, and Latin didn't have separate characters for numerals as we

9   Chilton, *Vengeance*, 350.
10   Irenaeus, *Heresies*, 5:28:2.

do. Consequently, the letters in their alphabets also doubled as numbers.[11] We are all familiar with Roman numerals, wherein the letter "I" also stands for 1, "V" stands for 5, "X" for 10, "L" for 50, "C" for 100, and so forth. Therefore, since letters also stood for numbers, someone's name could be said to have a numerical equivalent.

Riddles like the one in Revelation 13:18 were popular at the time when John wrote, which was around A.D. 95. These were called *isopsephia* in Greek; in Hebrew they were called *gematria*, from the Hebrew word for "mathematical." An example of this kind of cryptogram was unearthed in the excavations of Pompeii, which was buried in the volcanic eruption of A.D. 79. An interesting bit of graffiti was discovered that read: "I love her whose number is 545." The passing stranger wouldn't know the name of the girl, since many names add up to 545; however, the girl herself would likely recognize her name when she chanced upon it. Another example is taken from a Christian source, the *Sibylline Oracles* (*ca.* 150), which gives the numerical equivalence of the Greek *Iesous*, Jesus, as 888. As Jesus rose on the day after the Sabbath, popularly referred to as the "eighth" day, it seemed fitting that Jesus' name should be associated with the number eight.

Gematria was also used in popular poetry and political satire. The Roman historian Suetonius records some particularly biting political commentary posted on the city walls. Nero himself was the butt: "Count the numerical values / Of the letters in Nero's name, / And in 'murdered his own mother' / You will find their sum is the same."[12]

Political satires used *gematria* since it was possible to lampoon those in power while at the same time not actually naming names. A similar motive appears to be behind the use of *gematria* in Revelation as well. John wants his readers to understand that 666 is not merely an abstract symbol, so he stresses that 666 is the specific name of a specific man. Revelation 13:17 tells us 666 is, literally, "the name of the beast or the number of the name of it [Gr. *tou onomatos autou*]." John has an actual name in mind, but he doesn't want to state it explicitly.

Moreover, to help his readers understand who was being discussed, John provides a general description. The beast is portrayed as a persecutor of the Christians who believes himself to be divine, which accurately describes the Roman emperor. Keeping in mind that John is Jewish, it should not surprise us therefore that "Nero Caesar" adds up to 666 in Hebrew rather than Greek

---

11 The use of the Hebrew alphabet as a numerical system does not exist prior to the Maccabean period around the second century B.C., when we find Hebrew letters representing numbers on Maccabean coins.

12 Suetonius, *The Twelve Caesars*, "Nero," 39.

(Hebrew: *nrwn qsr*). Though Revelation was written in Greek, it nevertheless is one of the most "Hebraic" books in the New Testament. John translit-
erates Hebrew into Greek in other places in Revelation, like "Abaddon" (Rev.
9:11), and "Armageddon" (Rev. 16:16). Moreover, Asia Minor, to which
Revelation is addressed and which had one of the highest concentrations of
Christians in the empire at the time, was well populated with Jews, including
Christians of Jewish background.

What really clinches the beast/Nero theory for many scholars is that,
within a hundred years of Revelation's composition, a variant reading appeared that gives the number in Revelation 13:18 as 616. Though not many
manuscripts give the 616 number, there were enough for Irenaeus of Lyons
to call attention to it in A.D. 180, stating that the correct number is 666,
which is "found in all the most approved and ancient copies." [13] Top textual
critic Bruce Metzger observes, "Perhaps the change was intentional, seeing
that the Greek form of *Neron Caesar* written in Hebrew characters . . . is
equivalent to 666, whereas the Latin form Nero Caesar . . . is equivalent to
616." [14] Metzger notes that the difference between the two is only one Hebrew character.[15] It would thus appear that the textual variant appeared early
and reflects a deliberate transliteration in order to make the name of the beast
discernible to those who were familiar only with Latin. This would provide
strong support for identifying the beast as Nero.

By the time of St. Irenaeus, however, it seems that the Hebraic *gematria*
of Revelation 13:18 was lost on the then predominantly Greek Christian reading public. Irenaeus notes that there were numerous names floating around
as possible candidates for 666. He himself offers, as we mentioned above,
the following three possibilities: *Evanthas*, which is a name no longer identifiable; *Lateinos*, "Latin One," which is obviously allusive of the emperor and
the Roman Empire; and *Teitan*, the Titans in Greek mythology being those
who rebelled against the gods. Coincidentally, as Kenneth Gentry points out,
"Titan" was used as a divine name for the sun by the Romans, and the sun
was the deity that Nero most tried to emulate in his own career as a "deity." [16]

However, even as late as the time of St. John Chrysostom (347–407),
there were still Christians who remembered Nero as an Antichrist figure.
Speaking on the necessity of hell, Chrysostom writes:

13 Irenaeus, *Heresies*, 5:30:1.

14 Bruce Metzger, *A Textual Commentary on the Greek New Testament*, 2nd ed. (Stuttgart:
    United Bible Societies, 1994), 676.

15 In Hebrew, the Greek "Neron Caesar" is קסר נרון (666); the Latin form "Nero Caesar" is
        (616). In the Greek text of Revelation, the difference is   (666) and   (616).

16 Kenneth Gentry, *Before Jerusalem Fell* (Tyler, TX: Institute for Christian Economics, 1989),
    206–207.

Do you not hear St. Paul saying, "Who shall suffer everlasting punishment from the face of the Lord" (2 Thess 1:9)? Do you not hear what Nero's character was, whom Paul even calls the Mystery of Antichrist? For "the mystery of iniquity," he says, "already worketh" (2 Thess 2:7). What then? Is Nero to suffer nothing? Is Antichrist to suffer nothing? or the Devil nothing? Then he will always be Antichrist, and so the Devil.[17]

Those scholars who hold that Nero Caesar is 666 stress that the general description of the beast in Revelation fits the emperor very well, and he was obviously someone all first-century Christians knew. Nero's life was characterized by an unreasoning violence. He murdered his own family members, even kicking his pregnant wife to death. His life was also characterized by an unreasoning deviancy, as when he married a young boy he had castrated.

It is unsurprising, then, that Nero was often called a "beast" by his contemporaries. He is called the "great beast" in the *Sibylline Oracles*; and he is called a beast even by non-Christians like Apollonius of Tyana, who likely wrote before the composition of Revelation. In a passage reminiscent of the language used by John, who describes the beast as having seven heads (Rev. 13:1), Apollonius says of Nero, "this beast, that is commonly called a Tyrant, I know not how many heads it has, nor if it be crooked of claw, and armed with horrible fangs . . ."[18] Even the red color of the beast (see Rev. 17:3) recalls Nero's legendary red beard.

In Revelation, the beast is associated with Satan, who in turn is described as a serpent (Rev. 20:2). Of course, Satan has been identified with the serpent since the Garden of Eden. Nero was also associated with a serpent—even from the tender age of three! The early Roman historian Suetonius writes:

> At the age of three Nero lost his father and inherited one-third of the estate. . . . And it transpired later that Claudius' wife Messalina, realizing that Nero would become a rival to her son Britannicus [for the throne], had sent assassins to strangle him during his nap. They were driven away in terror, people said, by a snake which suddenly darted from beneath Nero's pillow; but this was a mere surmise based on the discovery of a sloughed snakeskin in his bed near the pillow. Agrippina [Nero's mother] persuaded him to have this skin set in a golden bracelet, which he wore for a long time on his right arm. Later he threw it away because it reminded him too vividly of her [Nero had had her murdered]; but when his situation grew desperate, hunted for it in vain.[19]

Another early Roman historian, Tacitus, relates a popular myth that in Nero's infancy serpents had watched over him, but that Nero himself used to

---

17 John Chrysostom, *Romans*, Homily 31 on Romans 16:16.
18 Philostratus, *Life of Apollonius*, 4:38. Cited by Gentry, *Jerusalem*, 214.
19 Suetonius, *The Twelve Caesars*, "Nero," 6.

say that only one snake had been seen in his room.[20] In Book 5 of the *Sibylline Oracles*, a Jewish work (with Christian interpolations) written in Egypt around A.D. 100, there is language similar to that found in Revelation used to describe Nero, specifically calling him a "terrible snake."[21]

Just as the beast in Revelation demands cultic worship, so did Nero. In fact, both Nero and his immediate successor Caligula even demanded worship while they were still alive. Kenneth Gentry writes:

> That Nero actually was worshiped is evident from inscriptions found in Ephesus in which he is called "Almighty God" and "Saviour." Reference to Nero as "God and Savior" is found in an inscription at Salamis, Cyprus. In fact, [citing H. H. Scullard] "as his megalomania increased, the tendency to worship him as ruler of the world became stronger, and in Rome his features appeared on the colossus of the Sun near the Golden House, while his head was represented on the coinage with a radiate crown."[22]

Finally, there is the manner of Nero's death as it seems to be reflected in the Book of Revelation. In Revelation 13:3, we read, "I saw one of his heads as if it had been mortally wounded, and his deadly wound was healed." And in verses 12 and 14 we have, "whose deadly wound was healed. . . . the beast who was wounded by the sword and lived." In June of A.D. 68, a rebellion against Nero's rule had succeeded in driving him from the throne. Fearing public execution, Nero took his own life in a private villa outside of Rome. With the help of his secretary, Epaphroditus, he drove a sword through his throat. Nero died in infamy at the relatively young age of 31.

Nero's reputation was such that, especially in the empire's eastern provinces, many found it difficult to believe that one so evil could ever simply die. A rumor began and persisted till the end of the first century that Nero had recovered from his wound (or had even risen from the grave) and was in the neighboring Parthian Empire of Persia awaiting his chance to return at the head of a vast army to wreck vengeance on Rome.[23] In the twenty years after his death, several individuals arose claiming to be Nero, two of whom were

---

20 Tacitus, *The Annals of Imperial Rome*, 11:11.

21 *Sibylline Oracles*, 5:28–30.

22 Gentry, *Jerusalem*, 272.

23 This idea can be found, for instance, in the third, fourth, and fifth books of the *Sibylline Oracles*. Also, a North African bishop known as Commodianus around A.D. 240 wrote a work called *The Instructions*, in which he states that Nero will appear again as a pagan Antichrist, conquer Rome, and again persecute the Christians for three and a half years. He in turn will be defeated by a Jewish—the real—Antichrist, who will then be accepted by the Jews as the Messiah. This Jewish Antichrist will then be destroyed by Jesus at His Return. The Lord will then establish His millennium in Jerusalem. Besides millenarianism, Commodianus also subscribed to the heresy of Monarchianism. Nevertheless, Commodianus' incorporation of the Nero *redivivus* legend is interesting.

even accepted as such in the Parthian Empire! Thus in the minds of many, though Nero's "head" had been mortally wounded, he lived on.

However, the portrayal of Nero in Revelation as a type of the Antichrist is not "pure." Characteristics associated with other emperors have been added to fill out the picture. The beast in Revelation is also closely associated with the Whore of Babylon. To readers of the Bible, the name Babylon immediately brings to mind the world's first dictator, Nimrod (Gen. 10:8, 9; Mic. 5:6), and Nebuchadnezzar (605–562 B.C.), ruler of the Neo-Babylonian Empire who conquered Jerusalem and carried the Jews into captivity in 587 B.C.

The "image of the beast" that people are compelled to worship in Revelation 13:14, 15 recalls Daniel 3, in which the Babylonian Emperor Nebuchadnezzar erected an image of himself. While priests of the cult of the Roman emperor set up images of the emperors throughout the empire, especially in Asia Minor, the Apostle John probably wasn't alluding to Nero so much as to another Caesar.[24]

Nero's predecessor Gaius Caesar, known to history as "Caligula" (A.D. 37–41), seems more likely to have been in John's mind when he wrote Revelation 13:14, 15. Caligula one day decided that his pretensions to divinity required that a gigantic statue of himself be erected in the Temple in Jerusalem. He therefore promptly sent two huge legions into Judea to accomplish the task, little caring that such an action would instigate an uprising of every last Jewish man in the empire. The expedition was met at Ptolemais by a deputation of Jews who tried to persuade Publius Petronius, the legate of Syria and leader of the expedition, to urge Caligula to reconsider. Luckily, Herod Agrippa was able to stall Caligula until the latter's assassination during the winter of A.D. 40–41 resolved the situation. New Testament scholar F. F. Bruce describes the impact of the incident on the minds of Jews and Christians alike:

> The terror of those weeks when it seemed that nothing could prevent him [Gaius Caesar] from carrying out his threat to set up his statue in the temple at Jerusalem was not quickly forgotten, and in the minds of some apocalyptists Gaius's attempt, together with the outrage perpetrated by Antiochus Epiphanes in the second century B.C., provided a pattern of what might be expected in the great distress of the end-time.[25]

Therefore, to summarize what we know of the Antichrist from the Book

---

24 The Roman Senate in fact commissioned a hundred-foot statue of Nero in A.D. 55 that was erected in the temple of Mars in Rome—Nero's statue being the same size as Mars'! See *The Annals of Imperial Rome* by Tacitus (13:8:1), Michael Grant, trans. (London: Penguin Books, 1971 rev. ed.), 287.

25 F. F. Bruce, *New Testament History* (New York: Doubleday, 1969), 256.

of Revelation, he is the epitome of all emperors and leaders who have set themselves against God, from Nebuchadnezzar and Antiochus Epiphanes to Caligula and—above all—Nero Caesar. The Antichrist to appear before the Second Coming will therefore embody all the qualities of those "antichrists" that have gone before: he will be a despotic megalomaniac who asserts his own divinity and, in consequence, cruelly persecutes the saints to force them to apostatize. The number 666 will epitomize the Antichrist because he will be the ultimate Nero, totally consumed with fantasies of his own divinity and demanding of illicit worship.

Along with the identity of the Antichrist, end-times speculators have also been preoccupied with the mark of the beast. They tend to see it as some form of electronic identification similar to supermarket bar codes or ATM cards. The "mark of the beast" spoken of in Revelation that is placed on the hands or forehead (see Rev. 13:16, 17) has been variously explained by biblical scholars. David Chilton observes:

> The "mark of the Beast," of course, is the Satanic parody of the "seal of God" on the foreheads and hands of the righteous ([Rev] 3:12; 7:2–4; 14:1), the mark of wholehearted obedience to the Law in thought and deed (Deut. 6:6–8), the mark of blessing and protection (Ezek. 9:4–6), the sign that one is *HOLY TO THE LORD* (cf. Ex. 28:36).[26]

Religious tattooing was common at the time the Apostle John wrote. Adherents to particular gods would often have themselves branded, marking themselves as "slaves" to their god (branding being a way to identify the owner of a slave, the same reason we brand cattle today). During the Greek rule of Israel, Ptolemy Philopator branded Jews who apostatized with an ivy leaf, which was the mark of Dionysian worship. The Jews in a sense "marked" themselves with the custom of wearing phylacteries (a small leather box containing four miniature scrolls with passages from the Torah) on the left hand and on the forehead (Deut. 6:8). The miter of the Jewish high priest, according to Exodus, had engraved on it, "Holiness to the Lord," adding, "So shall it be on Aaron's forehead . . ." (Ex. 28:38). In this way the high priest was set apart as distinctively *the* servant of God. The early Christians anointed converts with the sign of the cross on the forehead and hands, which is still done in the Eastern Orthodox rite of chrismation.

All of this likely lies behind the reference in Revelation to the "mark of the beast." Revelation 22:4 says that all the saints will have Christ's name "on their foreheads," meaning that after the general judgment we will belong exclusively to Him. Similarly, those who have the name of the beast on their foreheads belong exclusively to the Antichrist and are forever damned with him.

---

26 Chilton, *Vengeance*, 342.

Revelation 13:17 states that "no one may buy or sell except one who has the mark [Gr. *charagma*] or the name of the beast, or the number of his name." In order to ensure fidelity to the empire, citizens were required to offer sacrifice to the emperor. Upon completion of this duty, the worshiper was given an imperial mark or certificate. The Greek word *charagma* used in Revelation 13:17 is the technical term for the official mark or documentation. Seán Kealy in his commentary on Revelation writes, "Obviously, refusal to worship had economic consequences no matter what the social category of the person involved." [27] Many therefore understand Revelation 13:17 as expressing the economic hardship endured by Christians as a result of their "outlaw" status. Smyrna, one of the seven churches mentioned in Revelation 2 and 3, is an example of a persecuted church enduring grinding poverty (see Rev. 2:9).

Hippolytus of Rome around the year 200 also connected the "mark of the beast" to the *charagma* given after offering sacrifice to the emperor, seeing the mark mentioned in Revelation as still in the future:

> For being full of guile, and exalting himself against the servants of God, with the wish to afflict them and persecute them out of the world, because they give not the glory to him [the Antichrist], he will order incense-pans [i.e., sacrificial tripods] to be set up everywhere, that no man among the saints may be able to buy or sell without first sacrificing; for this is what is meant by the mark received upon the right hand. And the word—"in their forehead"—indicates that all are crowned, and put on a crown of fire, and not of life, but of death.[28]

Hippolytus then adds that this is like what Antiochus Epiphanes did when he issued a decree against the Jews commanding them to set up pagan shrines and sacrifice, as well as march in procession in honor of Dionysius while waving chaplets of ivy. The "mark" on the right hand and forehead signify for Hippolytus the economic (the "hand") and spiritual (the "forehead") ramifications of this ultimate apostasy. He thus sees the mark placed on the right hand and the forehead symbolically, which is quite reasonable given the highly symbolic nature of Revelation.

Today most biblical scholars, for many of the reasons presented above, conclude that 666 must have originally been a reference to Nero, and the "mark of the beast" a reference to the imperial cult. The Antichrist to come will be the ultimate "Nero" and will establish a similar cult. G. R. Beasley-Murray expresses the scholarly consensus on John's description of the Antichrist in Revelation:

27 Seán Kealy, *The Apocalypse of John* (Wilmington, DE: Michael Glazier, 1987), 179.
28 Hippolytus, *On the Antichrist*, 49.

It must be emphasized, however, that John did not look upon the reigning emperor as the antichrist; rather he viewed the emperor cult as preparing the way for an antichrist who would exploit it to the full, in a comparable manner as Paul in 2 Thessalonians 2:7 spoke of "the mystery of lawlessness" as already at work in the world. More precisely, John applied the dragon symbol to Satan (Rev 12), to the antichrist (Rev 13) and to the city and empire over which he ruled. But John goes further in that he conjoins the antichrist concept with the contemporary expectation of the return of Nero to Rome. . . . By his presentation of antichrist as another Nero, John has made it clear that the cult of the emperor is a projection of what will take place when the seeds of its beginning reach their full harvest.[29]

Certainly this understanding of the beast in Revelation is preferable to the one offered by dispensationalism, which tries to shoehorn the names of twentieth-century political figures into 666. It is, after all, difficult to believe that the Apostle John had Ronald Reagan (or some other contemporary world leader) in mind when he wrote that, using "wisdom" (Gr. *sophia*), the readers of his day would be able to understand the number 666. What sort of wisdom, short of psychic clairvoyance, could John's first-century readers possibly have had to figure out Ronald Reagan, an American president, from 666? Or that the mark of the beast is actually a VISA card?

Still, no doubt, there are some reading this who are still asking themselves, "Who is the Antichrist that will appear at the Tribulation?" The answer is that we cannot know until he appears and demands illicit worship. As St. Irenaeus wisely said in the quotation at the head of this chapter, it is hazardous "to be making surmises" of a specific nature as to the identity of the Antichrist to come.

The Orthodox Tradition

Nero was but an "antichrist" with a small "a"—a prefiguration of the Antichrist to come. Nero cruelly persecuted the Church, burning Rome and laying the blame on the Christians. The historian Tacitus (A.D. 55–117), a contemporary of Nero's reign, records:

First, Nero had self-acknowledged Christians arrested. Then, on their information, large numbers of others were condemned—not so much for incendiarism as for their anti-social tendencies. Their deaths were made farcical. Dressed in wild animals' skins, they were torn to pieces by dogs, or crucified, or made into torches to be ignited after dark as substitutes for daylight. Nero provided his Gardens for the spectacle, and exhibited displays in the Circus, at which he mingled with the crowd—or stood in a chariot, dressed as a charioteer. Despite their guilt as Christians, and the

---

29 Ralph Martin & Peter Davids, eds., *Dictionary of the Later New Testament and its Development* (Downers Grove, IL: InterVarsity Press, 1997), s.vv. "Revelation, Book of."

ruthless punishment it deserved, the victims were pitied. For it was felt that they were being sacrificed to one man's brutality rather than to the national interest.[30]

It was during this period that Saints Peter and Paul were martyred. Overall, it would be hard to find a better example of what it means to be an "antichrist" than Nero. The very name must have conveyed the same sense of odiousness to Christians of John's day that the name Hitler conveys to us today. Nero's name therefore became a synonym for antichrist. In fact, to this day, one of the two Armenian words for "antichrist" is *Nerhn*, an apparent transliteration of the Greek *Neron*.[31] It was natural that when John wanted to write about the coming Antichrist, he would draw upon the Church's experience with Nero. Nonetheless, Nero is only a type of the Antichrist that is to come. As John himself wrote, "many antichrists have come," but the final "Antichrist is coming" (1 John 2:18).

Orthodox tradition evidences much speculation as to what to expect with regard to the coming reign of Antichrist. The *Didache*, a Syrian church manual written at the beginning of the second century, warns:

> But be frequently gathered together seeking the things which are profitable for your souls, for the whole time of your faith shall not profit you except you be found perfect at the last time; for in the last days the false prophets and the corrupters shall be multiplied, and the sheep shall be turned into wolves, and love shall change into hate; for as lawlessness increases they shall hate one another and persecute and betray, and then shall appear the deceiver of the world as a Son of God, and shall do signs and wonders and the earth shall be given over into his hands and he shall commit iniquities which have never been since the world began. Then shall the Creation of Mankind come to the fiery trial and many shall be offended and be lost, but they who endure in their faith shall be saved by the cure itself.[32]

The Antichrist, according to the *Didache*, comes as the culmination of all false prophets and lawlessness, and Christians must prepare by frequently gathering together to seek what is profitable for the soul. If the Christian is found "not perfect" at the last hour, then "the whole time of your faith shall not profit you," undoubtedly because he will be swept away in the

---

30 Tacitus, *Annals*, 15:44.

31 The more common word in Armenian, though, is *Haghachristos*, which literally translates "antichrist."

32 *Didache*, 16:2–5. The meaning of the last sentence seems to indicate a belief that each judgment of God contains within itself the possibility of repentance and salvation. In passing, it should also be observed that this passage implicitly contradicts a pretribulational rapture of the Church. The assumption is that the Church will go through the time of Tribulation and must be prepared to encounter the Antichrist, who will appear "as a Son of God."

spiritual deceptions of the Tribulation period. A sobering thought.

St. Irenaeus of Lyons, at the end of the second century, evidences a more developed concept of the coming Antichrist in the fifth book of his *Against Heresies*. He believes that Rome is the fourth empire of Daniel's prophecy and the last empire to arise on the earth (see Dan. 2:31–45). The Roman Empire will splinter into ten kingdoms, and then the Antichrist will arise to usher in the great apostasy (see Rev. 12:3; 13:1; 17:3–16). His reign will signal the completion of six thousand years of human history, and then Christ will overthrow the Antichrist at the Second Coming. Interestingly, Irenaeus draws upon New Testament passages for his description of the Antichrist rather than Daniel's characterization of the blasphemous despot.

Irenaeus believes the Antichrist will be Jewish, of the tribe of Dan in particular. He bases this primarily upon Jeremiah 8:16 according to the Septuagint rendering: "We shall hear the voice of his swift horses from Dan; the whole earth shall be moved by the voice of the neighing of his galloping horses: he shall also come and devour the earth, and the fulness thereof, the city also, and they that dwell therein." Irenaeus interprets "from Dan" in a genealogical rather than a geographical sense. The Antichrist will be a descendant of Dan, and this is why his name is missing from the tribes listed in Revelation 7:5–8, the Twelve Tribes from whence come the 144,000.

Judges 18 tells how the Danites adopted idolatry—a long and odious tradition with Dan also mentioned by the Prophet Amos (8:14)—and set up a pagan shrine that would in time become one of the national sanctuaries of the northern kingdom of Israel (see 1 Kin. 12:29). Thus Dan became a byword for apostasy among Jewish religious leaders, and the idea that the Antichrist would be a Danite later became a standard belief among the Church Fathers. According to Irenaeus, the Antichrist is an apostate Jew from Dan who sits enthroned in the Temple in Jerusalem and who is worshiped as God.

The most influential treatise on the Antichrist produced by the early Church was written about the year 200 by Hippolytus of Rome, simply called *On the Antichrist*. Johannes Quasten, internationally famous patrologist and professor of ancient Church history and Christian archaeology at the Catholic University of America, states that Hippolytus' *On the Antichrist* represents "the most comprehensive discussion of the problem of antichrist in patristic literature." [33] For the most part, though, Hippolytus simply expands upon Irenaeus' ideas. However, unlike Irenaeus, he draws heavily from the Book of Daniel for his description of the Antichrist.

Hippolytus, following Irenaeus, believes that Daniel predicted Rome

---

33 Johannes Quasten, *Patrology*, Vol. 2 (Westminster, MD: Christian Classics, 1986), 171.

would be the last world empire and that it would break down into ten king-doms. He notes Daniel 7:8, "I was considering the horns, and there was an-other horn, a little one, coming up among them, before whom three of the first horns were plucked out by the roots," and sees in this a future Roman emperor as the Antichrist. Hippolytus fancifully concludes from this verse:

> And under this was signified none other than Antichrist, who is also him-self to raise the kingdom of the Jews. He says that three horns are plucked up by the root by him, viz., the three kings of Egypt, and Libya, and Ethio-pia, whom he cuts off in the array of battle.[34]

Hippolytus later adds that once Egypt, Libya, and Ethiopia have been subjected to his rule, the Antichrist will begin to exalt his own divinity and proclaim himself the ultimate master of the world. He will then lead an expe-dition against the cities of Tyre and Bertus, supposedly in fulfillment of Isaiah 23:4, 5. Hippolytus sometimes would get carried away in this fashion with his end-times speculation. In his *Commentary on Daniel*, he even predicted the end of the world for A.D. 500!

With Irenaeus, Hippolytus also believed the Antichrist would be from the tribe of Dan and would in every way show himself to be the Son of God. Because the Savior raised up the Temple of His Body, the Antichrist will raise up a Temple of stone in Jerusalem and there proclaim himself God. As to the identity of 666, Hippolytus observes that "many names indeed we find, the letters of which are the equivalent of this number."[35] If he must choose, though, he prefers the name Latinus.

The Antichrist will reign seven years, and in the midst of this seven-year period Enoch and Elijah will be the two witnesses sent by God to proclaim repentance to the world. During the final three-and-a-half-year period of his reign, the Antichrist persecutes the Church until the Coming of the Lord, at which time the Lord destroys him. The resurrection also occurs at this point, and, incidentally, Hippolytus cites 1 Thessalonians 4:15–17—the famous "rapture" proof text—in support of this. (Obviously, therefore, he didn't be-lieve this verse referred to a rapture before the Tribulation.)

Victorinus of Petau, who died as a martyr in the persecution of Diocletian around A.D. 304, has left an interesting commentary on Revelation. His comments on Revelation 17 (which describes the great harlot and the beast) reveal that there was still, at the beginning of the fourth century, a close association in the minds of believers between the beast of Revelation and Roman emperors of the first century.

---

34 Hippolytus, *On the Antichrist*, 25.
35 Hippolytus, *On the Antichrist*, 50.

Commenting on Revelation 17:9 ("The seven heads are seven mountains on which the woman sits"), Victorinus indicates the woman refers to Rome. The next verse, Revelation 17:10, speaks of seven kings: "Five of which have fallen, one is, and the other has not yet come. And when he comes, he must continue a short time." On this verse, Victorinus explains, "The time must be understood in which the written Apocalypse was published." Revelation was published during the reign of Emperor Domitian, Victorinus observes. Domitian, therefore, is the one that "is" (Rev. 17:10). The five that have fallen preceded Domitian: Titus, Vespasian, Otho, Vitellius, and Galba. The "other [that] has not yet come" and who will rule "a short time" refers to Nerva, who reigned less than two years.

Victorinus then cites Revelation 17:11, which says, "The beast that was, and is not, is himself the eighth, and is of the seven, and is going to perdition." This he believes refers to Nero, who is "of the seven," since "before those kings Nero reigned." When Revelation says the beast "is the eighth," the Apostle John means that "when this beast shall come, reckon it the eighth place, since in that is the completion." Victorinus thus sees in the number eight a symbol of completion.

Victorinus goes on to contemplate the meaning of the last part of verse 11, "and is going to perdition." After the ten kings (ten "horns") mentioned by Daniel receive power, the beast will move from the east and head toward Rome with his armies. Three kings will be killed by the Antichrist, and the other seven become his vassals.

Victorinus then turns to Revelation 17:16: "And the ten horns which you saw on the beast, these will hate the harlot, make her desolate and naked, eat her flesh and burn her with fire." He comments on this verse:

> Now that one of the heads was, as it were, slain to death, and that the stroke of his death was directed, he speaks of Nero. For it is plain that when the cavalry sent by the senate was pursuing him, he himself cut his throat. Him therefore, when raised up, God will send as a worthy king, but worthy in such a way as the Jews merited. And since he is to have another name, He [God] shall appoint another name, that so the Jews may receive him as if he were the Christ.[36]

What is fascinating in Victorinus' commentary on Revelation 17 is how the image of the beast is interwoven with the image of Nero. In the above commentary on verse 16, he explicitly characterizes the Antichrist as a resurrected Nero.

---

36 Victorinus of Petau, *Commentary on the Apocalypse*, 17:16. See Alexander Roberts & James Donaldson, eds., The Ante-Nicene Fathers, Vol. 7 (Peabody, MA: Hendrickson, 1886), 358.

St. Cyril of Jerusalem, in his *Catechetical Lectures* (A.D. 350), also gives an intriguing description of what he thinks the coming Antichrist will be like. Much of what he says develops ideas set forth by Hippolytus:

> And now, in this same way, since the true Christ is to come a second time, the adversary [the devil] makes use of the expectations of the simple, and especially of those of the circumcision [i.e., the Jews]; and he brings in a certain man who is a magician, and who is quite expert in sorceries and enchantments of beguiling craftiness. This one shall seize for himself the power of the Roman Empire, and he shall falsely style himself Christ. By this name Christ he shall deceive the Jews, who are expecting the Anointed [i.e., the Messiah]; and he shall seduce the Gentiles by his magical illusions.[37]

The Antichrist thus usurps the throne of the Roman Empire. After becoming emperor, he will then claim to be Christ and deceive the Jews, who are looking for a Messiah. Cyril continues:

> This afore-mentioned Antichrist is to come when the times of the Roman Empire shall have been fulfilled and the end of the world is drawing near. There shall rise up together ten kings of the Romans, reigning in different parts, perhaps, but all reigning at the same time. After these there shall be an eleventh, the Antichrist, who by the evil craft of his magic shall seize upon the Roman power. Of the kings who reigned before him, three shall he humble, and the remaining seven he shall have as subjects under him. At first he shall feign mildness,—as if he were a learned and discreet person,—and sobriety and loving-kindness.[38]

Like Hippolytus and Irenaeus, Cyril believes that history will end with the Roman Empire, which will be partitioned into ten regions ruled by ten kings. The Antichrist will conquer these ten rulers and take over the empire, consolidating his rule by behaving mildly at first. His true nature, though, soon becomes apparent:

> Having beguiled the Jews by lying signs and wonders of his magical deceit, until they believe he is the expected Christ, he shall afterwards be characterized by all manner of wicked deeds of inhumanity and lawlessness, as if to outdo all the unjust and impious men who have gone before him. He shall display against all men, and especially against us Christians, a spirit that is murderous and most cruel, merciless and wily. For three years and six months only shall he be the perpetrator of such things; and then he shall be destroyed by the glorious Second Coming from heaven of the only-begotten Son of God, our Lord and Savior Jesus, the true Christ, who shall destroy him with the breath of His mouth, and shall deliver him over to the fire of Gehenna.[39]

---

37 Cyril of Jerusalem, *Catechetical Lectures*, 15:11.
38 Cyril of Jerusalem, *Catechetical Lectures*, 15:12.
39 Ibid.

The Antichrist, says Cyril, personifies—and outdoes—all previous wicked men of history. In particular, he will be the ultimate persecutor of the Christians. To convince the world that he is actually Christ, he will perform signs and miracles through the power of Satan. This will last three and a half years, then Christ will return and destroy the Antichrist. In his description of the Antichrist, Cyril looks to Daniel's depiction of the blasphemous and persecuting despot.

Sifting Wheat from Chaff

Having surveyed the tradition of the Antichrist, what conclusions can we draw? First, we should view skeptically any attempt to draw a detailed career description for the Antichrist by a subjective interpretation of isolated scripture texts. The Books of Daniel and Revelation say nothing specific, for instance, about a future monetary system run by supercomputers, or of microchips being inserted into hands and foreheads; these sorts of misinterpretations result from confusing the newspaper with the Bible.

Christians have always found the apocalyptic parts of the Bible, like Daniel and Revelation, difficult to understand; we must therefore approach these books with a degree of fear and trembling. It is a serious injustice to wrench passages from Holy Writ and arbitrarily read into them modern technological or political developments. By doing this, we are not reading prophecy "literally," but actually obscuring the scriptural message.

In the best of the ancient commentaries on the Book of Daniel, the Prophet's descriptions were interpreted typologically, taking into full account the historical background of the book. Verses like Daniel 8:8–12, which describe the little horn of a male goat, the Fathers would often interpret as describing the Antichrist. Yet the Fathers also understood that Daniel 8:21 explicitly states that the "male goat" is the Greek kingdom; thus, the little horn is a Greek despot (Antiochus IV Epiphanes). What the Fathers were doing was interpreting the despot in Daniel 8:8–12, Antiochus Epiphanes, as a "type" or prefiguration of the despot to come, the Antichrist. This is different from speculating on the particulars of Daniel's prophecy in order to piece together a detailed biography of the Antichrist, as today's prophecy hacks are so fond of doing.

Hippolytus, for example, saw multiple applications for the "abomination of desolation" spoken of in Daniel. Its primary fulfillment is in Antiochus IV Epiphanes, though its ultimate fulfillment lies in the Antichrist to come at the end of the world:

> Daniel speaks [in Daniel 12:11], therefore, of two abominations: the one of
> destruction, which Antiochus set up in its appointed time, and which bears

a relation to that of desolation, and the other universal, when Antichrist shall come. For, as Daniel says, he too shall be set up for the destruction of many.[40]

Aphrahat the Persian Sage, in his *Demonstrations* (written between A.D. 336 and 345), also applies many of these verses in Daniel to Antiochus Epiphanes:

> For Daniel said: "I was considering the ten horns that were upon the head of the beast. For the ten horns were ten kings" who arose at that time until Antiochus (cf. Dan. 7:8, 24). And he said: "A little horn arose from between those ten and three fell before it" (Dan. 7:8). For when Antiochus arose in the kingdom, he humbled three kings, and he exalted himself against the saints of the Most High and against Jerusalem. And he defiled the sanctuary. And he caused the sacrifice and the offerings to cease for a week and half a week, namely, for ten-and-a-half years. And he brought in fornicators into the house of the Lord, and he caused the observances of the Law to cease. And he slew righteous men and gave them to the birds of heaven and to the beasts of the earth.[41]

Aphrahat goes on to describe how Antiochus persecuted the Jews, citing Daniel 7:21 ("the horn made war with the saints"). He also applies Daniel 7:25 to Antiochus, saying that he "changed times and seasons and the laws, and they were given into his hand for a time, times, and half a time." Aphrahat doesn't contradict the interpretation that saw in these verses the Antichrist to come; he simply explains, based on his understanding of history, the actual historical context of these verses that other early Christian writers were applying typologically to the Antichrist.

So what conclusions can we draw concerning the Antichrist? First we should recall that the word Antichrist doesn't only mean "against Christ." The Greek prefix *anti* also means "in place of." Thus the Antichrist seeks to usurp the place of Christ in the hearts of men. He does this mainly by imitating the real Christ, thereby appropriating the glory, honor, and worship that by right are due to Christ alone. As Christ had a prophet (John the Forerunner) who pointed the people to Him, so the Antichrist will have a false prophet who will lead people to worship him (Rev. 13:11–17). As Christ died and rose again, so the Antichrist will seem to die and rise again (Rev. 13:3, 12, 14).

Many, like St. John of Damascus, have taught that the Antichrist will be

---

40 Hippolytus, *Commentary on Daniel*, 4:54. Included among the "Scholia on Daniel" for Hippolytus' exegetical works in The Ante-Nicene Fathers, Vol. 5, 191. Compare also the remark, "Daniel has spoken, therefore, of two abominations; the one of destruction, and the other of desolation. What is that of destruction, but that which Antiochus established there at the time? And what is that desolation, but that which shall be universal when Antichrist comes?" (p. 184).

41 Aphrahat, *Demonstrations*, "Of Wars," Demonstration 5:20.

the offspring of fornication—a sort of diabolical parody of the Virgin Birth. A very ancient Christian tradition asserts he will be a Jew from the tribe of Dan. The Antichrist will reign three and a half years, though a few Fathers of the Church say the reign will last seven years. His rule will at first be peaceful and he will give the appearance of sanctity, but before long he will reveal his true nature. He will probably rule from Jerusalem, likely rebuild the Temple that was destroyed in A.D. 70, and he will certainly declare himself to be God. The Antichrist to come will be all previous despots rolled into one.

Despite possible outward appearances, he will in reality be opposed to God, deriving his power from Satan. Orthodox tradition also suggests he will be a military genius and exercise his influence as a leader throughout the world. When he declares himself to be God, the Christians will refuse to worship him; and so he will persecute the Church. Those who do submit to the Antichrist can be said to have his "mark," though the exact nature of this mark is an open question. As we saw, the *charagma*, or "mark," could also be a document officially proclaiming one's apostasy. The mark signifies apostasy from the true Christian Faith. Ultimately, it is not the specific nature of the "mark" that is the issue; what damns the soul is apostatizing by submitting to the "beast."

Andrew of Caesarea in the fifth century, whose commentary on Revelation is highly regarded in the Eastern Church, wrote of the mark of the beast:

> He [the Antichrist] will strive to place upon all the outline of the ruinous name of the apostate and deceiver, "in their right hands," in order to cut off the doing of right and good deeds, and likewise "in their foreheads," in order to instruct the deceived to be bold in deception and darkness. But it will not be received by those sealed in their faces with the Divine Light (cf. Rev 7:3, 4). And the seal of the beast will be spread everywhere, in buying and selling, so that those who do not receive it will suffer a violent death from want of necessities.[42]

Surely the suffering caused by the Antichrist will be a test to all true believers in Christ; and the Antichrist's persecution of the saints will purify the Church and prepare her to enter the Kingdom that Christ will bring with Him when He returns. Despite the worst the Antichrist can do, he will not be able to overcome the Church of God. Cyprian of Carthage (A.D. 200–258) writes, "For even the Antichrist, when he shall begin to come, shall not enter into the Church because he threatens; neither shall we yield to his arms and violence because he declares that he will destroy us if we resist." [43]

---

42 Andrew of Caesarea, *Commentary on the Apocalypse*, 37. Cited by Taushev, *Apocalypse*, 194.

43 Cyprian of Carthage, *Epistle 54 to Cornelius*, 19.

Revelation describes as follows what will happen to the Antichrist at the Lord's return: "Then the beast was captured, and with him the false prophet who worked signs in his presence, by which he deceived those who received the mark of the beast and those who worshiped his image. These two were cast alive into the lake of fire burning with brimstone" (Rev. 19:20). The destruction of the Antichrist at the Lord's coming ushers in the Kingdom prepared for us from the foundation of the world (Matt. 25:34). It is this coming of the Lord in glory that is the subject of our next chapter.

Chapter Fourteen

"Our Lord Comes!"

Men of Galilee, why do you stand gazing up into heaven? This same Jesus, who was taken up into heaven, will so come in like manner as you saw Him go into heaven.
  —The Acts of the Apostles 1:11

Let grace come and let this world pass away. Hosannah to the God of David. If any man be holy, let him come! If any man be not, let him repent: Maran 'atha' [Aramaic: "Our Lord comes!"], Amen.
  —Eucharistic prayer from *The Didache* (A.D. 100–150)

THE BOOK'S FULL TITLE IS, *The Lord's Instruction to the Gentiles through the Twelve Apostles,* but it is normally referred to by the first word of its Greek title, *Didache,* the "Instruction." It was so renowned by the early Church that in many places it was considered Scripture, even being bound with the New Testament writings.

The *Didache* is a Syrian church manual, likely composed in Antioch shortly after A.D. 100, which was long thought to have disappeared altogether. It was considered one of the most important documents of the primitive Church aside from the New Testament itself, and scholars in the nineteenth century had tried to reconstruct its text from quotations of it in other sources. No one imagined that a copy of this precious work would ever be discovered.

Then, in 1873, a Greek manuscript containing the *Didache* was uncovered in the patriarchal library of Jerusalem at Constantinople. It had been copied by a certain notary named Leo in the year 1056. The Greek Orthodox Metropolitan of Nicomedia, Philotheos Bryennios, published the find in 1883. Today one can usually go to a bookstore and obtain a copy of the *Didache* in any collection of early Christian writings. The discovery of the *Didache* has greatly enriched our understanding of the primitive Church.

The *Didache* begins by explaining that there are two paths a person can walk, the way of life and the way of death. The book ends with a look at Christ's Second Coming:

> And then shall appear the signs of the truth. First the sign spread out in Heaven, then the sign of the sound of the trumpet, and thirdly the resurrection of the dead: but not of all the dead, but as it was said, "The Lord shall come and all his saints with him" (cf. Matt. 25:31). Then shall the world see the Lord coming on the clouds of Heaven.[1]

The *Didache* breaks off at this point with the Lord, accompanied by His saints, descending from Heaven to a suffering world. What exactly will happen when the Lord returns and what will it be like?

"Then shall the world see the Lord . . ."

When the New Testament speaks of Christ's Second Coming, it regularly uses one of three words to describe the event: *parousia*, *epiphaneia*, or *apokalupto*. The first word, *parousia*, denotes both the actual arrival and consequent presence of Christ in the world. The word was frequently used of official visits by high-ranking dignitaries, such as heads of state, and for divine visitations.

For example, James writes, "Therefore be patient, brethren, until the *parousia* of the Lord. . . . Establish your hearts, for the *parousia* of the Lord is at hand" (James 5:7, 8). Jesus says His coming will be quick: "For as lightning comes from the east and flashes to the west, so shall the *parousia* of the Son of Man be" (Matt. 24:27). John uses the word to denote Christ's presence after His coming: "And now, little children, abide in Him, that when He appears, we may have confidence and not be ashamed before Him at His *parousia*" (1 John 2:28).

As we mentioned in Chapter 9, "The Rapture versus Scripture," 1 Thessalonians 4:15–17, a major proof text for the rapture, indicates the "catching up" occurs at the *parousia* of the Lord, not seven years previously.[2] Second Thessalonians 2:1 also speaks of the Lord's *parousia* "and our gathering together to Him" as a single event, with no seven-year Tribulation period separating the two. (Some other verses that use the word *parousia* for Christ's Second Coming are Matt. 24:3, 37; 1 Cor. 15:23; 1 Thess. 3:13; 5:23; 2 Thess. 2:8; and 2 Pet. 3:4.)

---

1   *Didache*, 16:6–8.
2   "We who are alive, and remain until the *parousia* of the Lord . . ." (1 Thess. 4:15).

The noun *epiphaneia* is the Greek word from which we derive the English "epiphany." It literally means "a shining forth" or "appearing," and is used of Christ's First Advent in Bethlehem in 2 Timothy 1:10. It is used of His Second Coming in places like 1 Timothy 6:14 ("that you may keep this commandment . . . until our Lord Jesus Christ's *epiphaneia*"), 2 Timothy 4:1 ("the Lord Jesus Christ, who will judge the living and the dead at His *epiphaneia* and His kingdom"), and 2 Timothy 4:8 ("and not to me only, but also to all who have loved His *epiphaneia*"). Paul says Jesus will destroy the Antichrist with "the *epiphaneia* of His [the Lord's] coming" (2 Thess. 2:8). The word appears as a verb in Matthew 24:27 where Christ says His coming will be like lightning that "goes out from" the east and "shines as far as" the west. The word is also used in a verse traditionally understood by the prophecy pundits as referring to the rapture: "the blessed hope and glorious *epiphaneia* of our great God and Savior Jesus Christ" (Titus 2:13).

The verb *apokalupto* (noun *apokalupsis*) means "to uncover" or "reveal." The Book of Revelation is sometimes called by its Greek title, the Apocalypse. The word is used of Christ's Second Coming in Luke 17:30: "Even so will it be in the day when the Son of Man is revealed [*apokalupto*]." Paul tells the church at Corinth that they await "the *apokalupsis* of our Lord Jesus Christ" (1 Cor. 1:7). Peter counsels us to partake of Christ's sufferings and to endure persecutions gladly, for they will redound to our benefit when the Lord's glory is "revealed," *apokalupsis* (1 Pet. 4:13). Second Thessalonians 1:7 states that Christians will only have "rest" from tribulation "when the Lord is revealed [*apokalupsis*] from heaven with His mighty angels." Paul speaks of our works being "revealed [*apokalupto*] by fire" at Christ's coming (1 Cor. 3:13). That Day will be an *apokalupto* of our glory as well (Rom. 8:18). Peter also remarks on "the glory that shall be revealed [*apokalupto*]" at the Second Coming (1 Pet. 5:1).

The early Christians were conscious of the fact that the parables Christ told of His Second Coming tended to describe the event as taking place at night. In the parable of the five foolish virgins, the bridegroom returns at midnight (Matt. 25:1–13). Jesus said He might come during the various watches of the night (Mark 13:35). Peter states the Lord will come as "a thief in *the night*" (2 Pet. 3:10, emphasis added). Therefore a popular belief arose that the Second Coming would happen at night, giving birth to all-night prayer vigils. As there also existed a belief that Christ would come on the Lord's Day,[3] the Saturday night vigil took on a special prominence in the Church.

---

3   E.g., see Peter of Damascus' *A Treasury of Divine Knowledge, The Philokalia,* Vol. III, 192–193. Peter writes, "And on this day [Sunday] the general resurrection of the dead will also take place. . . . and it will also be the day of Christ's second coming."

This belief that Christ would return at night lasted a long time in the Church. Lactantius (A.D. 260–330) in his *The Divine Institutes* describes the heavens as being laid open at Christ's Second Coming "in the dead and darkness of the night . . . and there shall go before Him an unquenchable fire." [4] Preaching on Matthew 24:36–42 around the year 390 in Antioch, St. John Chrysostom remarked, "And to me He seems to declare that at night will be the advent. For this Luke too saith." [5] Luke 17:34 reads, "I tell you, *in that night* there will be two men [or more literally, "people"] in one bed; the one will be taken and the other will be left" (emphasis added).

A belief also arose that the Lord would come from the east. Jesus used the analogy of lightning coming from the east to describe His coming (Matt. 24:27). The east is where the sun rises from the earth, as if from a grave, and gives light to the world. In like manner, Jesus, the Sun of Righteousness (Mal. 4:2), rose from the grave and gave light to the world. The east was where Paradise was believed to have been planted, and it was also believed that Jesus had ascended into heaven toward the east. St. John of Damascus (675–749) writes:

> And when He was taken up, He ascended to the east and thus the Apostles worshiped Him and thus He shall come in the same way as they had seen Him going into heaven [cf. Acts 1:11], as the Lord Himself said: "As lightning cometh out of the east and appeareth even into the west: so shall also the coming of the Son of man be" [Matt. 24:27]. And so, while we are awaiting Him, we worship toward the east. This is, moreover, the unwritten tradition of the Apostles, for they have handed many things down to us unwritten.[6]

The practice of facing east during prayer appears very early in Church history. Origen in the early third century advocated facing east even during private prayer at home,[7] and St. Basil the Great (330–379) mentions the practice of facing east during the Liturgy as an unwritten apostolic tradition.[8] Blessed Augustine of the North African city of Hippo ended his homilies by enjoining the people to face east as the Eucharist was about to be celebrated, using the set formula, *Conversi ad Dominum* ("Turn to face the Lord"). In the Egyptian Church to this day, in all three Coptic liturgies—those of St. Cyril, St. Basil, and St. Gregory Nazianzen—the deacon cries out at the beginning of the eucharistic anaphora, "Look towards the east."

When church buildings began to be built, these were normally constructed

---

4   Lactantius, *The Divine Institutes*, 7:19.
5   John Chrysostom, *Matthew*, Homily 77:2.
6   John of Damascus, *On the Orthodox Faith*, Book 4:12.
7   Origen, *On Prayer*, 32.
8   Basil the Great, *On the Holy Spirit*, 66.

facing east. The *Apostolic Constitutions*, written in the late fourth century, describes the church building as a long ship "with its head to the east." The *Constitutions* goes on to describe the beginning of the eucharistic celebration: the people "all rise up with one consent, and looking toward the east, . . . pray to God eastward, who ascended up to the heaven of heavens to the east." [9] Eastern Orthodox churches are still normally constructed facing east. Since earliest times, Christians have prayed facing in the direction in which they believed their Lord had ascended into heaven—and from whence they believed their Lord would someday return.

Our Lord taught that His coming would be sudden, visible, and apparent to everyone (Matt. 24:26, 27; Mark 13:26; Rev. 1:7). The Lord's appearance will be unexpected, like a "thief in the night" (Matt. 24:39; Luke 12:40; 1 Thess. 5:2; Rev. 16:15). Assuming that the "last trump" references aren't apocalyptic symbolism, the Lord's return will not only be visible, it will be audible as well (1 Cor. 15:2; 1 Thess. 4:16). It will be preceded by "the sign of the Son of Man" appearing in heaven (Matt. 24:30). This sign has traditionally been understood by the Fathers of the Church to be the sign of the life-giving Cross. Christ's Second Coming is associated with a great earthquake (Rev. 16:18), and, when He appears, the Lord will be surrounded by an innumerable number of angels and saints (Matt. 16:27; 25:31; 1 Thess. 4:16, 17; Jude 14; Rev. 19:14). He will come in glory (Matt. 24:30) and consuming fire (Ps. 97:3; Is. 66:15, 16; Ezek. 38:22; 1 Cor. 3:13; 2 Thess. 1:7, 8; 2 Pet. 3:7, 12).

When Christ returns in glory, the general resurrection and judgment will take place. On that day, all the dead will be raised so that all of humanity will stand in judgment before Christ. According to the opinion of some Church Fathers since at least the early fourth century, Joel 3:2, 12 describes this judgment as taking place in the "Valley of Jehoshaphat" (which they associated with the Kedron valley between Jerusalem and the Mount of Olives).[10]

The Resurrection and Judgment
When discussing the resurrection of the dead with dispensationalists, what needs to be stressed most is that there is a single resurrection of both the just and the unjust. As a result of their two-phase understanding of Christ's return (rapture and Second Coming) and their earthly millennium, dispensationalists have come to believe there will be multiple resurrections of the dead: one at

---

9   *The Apostolic Constitutions*, Book 2:57.
10 The Valley of Jehoshaphat has been variously identified by biblical scholars, and it is possible the name is symbolic rather than a place designation. "Jehoshaphat" means "Yahweh has judged" in Hebrew.

the rapture spoken of in 1 Thessalonians 4:16, 17 for believers, one at Christ's coming at Armageddon for Old Testament saints and Tribulation martyrs (Rev. 20:5–10), and yet another for the unsaved after the millennium (Rev. 20:12, 13).

This, of course, goes directly against two thousand years of Christian teaching. Since citations from the writings of the early Fathers expressing the belief in a single, general resurrection could be produced endlessly, we'll content ourselves with the following from St. Justin Martyr. Writing in his *First Apology* (A.D. 150), Justin explains:

> The prophets have proclaimed His [Christ's] two comings. One, indeed, which has already taken place, was that of a dishonored and suffering man. The second will take place when, in accord with prophecy, He shall come from the heavens in glory with His angelic host, when He shall raise the bodies *of all men who ever lived.* Then He shall clothe the worthy in immortality; but the wicked, clothed in eternal sensibility, He will commit to the eternal fire, along with the demons.[11]

This citation from a very early Christian writer, and one well respected by the Church, expresses what has always been the belief of Christians. Since the millenarians frequently cite Justin Martyr as an authority for an earthly millennium, they ought to take seriously Justin's witness to the Christian belief in a single resurrection of all humanity.

Scripture doesn't speak of coming "resurrections" in the plural, but of a single resurrection. In Daniel, there is the prophecy: "And many of those who sleep in the dust of the earth shall awake, some to everlasting life, some to shame and everlasting contempt" (Dan. 12:2). There is here depicted a single resurrection of both the just and the unjust.

Isaiah 26:19 relates, "Your dead shall live [the dead of the land of Judah— see v. 1]; together with my dead body they shall arise. Awake and sing, you who dwell in dust; for your dew is like the dew of herbs, and the earth shall cast out the dead" (Is. 26:19). The phrase, "the earth shall cast out the dead," implies that not just some of the dead, but *all* of the dead of the earth, shall be raised in a single event.

When speaking to Jesus at her brother's grave, Martha said, "I know that he will rise again in the resurrection [singular] at the last day" (John 11:24). Jesus responded in the next verse, "I am the resurrection [singular] and the life" (v. 25).

Paul also preached "Jesus and the resurrection [singular]" (Acts 17:24), stating once before the governor Felix, "I have a hope in God . . . that there

---

11 Justin Martyr, *First Apology*, 52. Emphasis added.

will be a resurrection [singular] of the dead, both of the just and the unjust" (Acts 24:15). In his second letter to Timothy, Paul condemns those who say that the resurrection (singular) is already past (2 Tim. 2:18). We could go on, but the point should be clear. Scripture knows nothing of multiple resurrections; it speaks only of a single, general resurrection "of the just and the unjust."

Dispensationalists frequently point to scriptures that speak of only the just or the unjust being resurrected as evidence that the two are distinct resurrections separated by the millennium. For example, in John 5:29 Jesus speaks of those doing good as attaining the "resurrection of life" and those who have done evil the "resurrection of condemnation." However, Jesus is not enumerating in this verse different resurrections to occur at different times, but what different types of people can expect at the general resurrection: life or condemnation. The Lord Himself in the previous verse implied all are resurrected at the same time, at "the hour [that] is coming in which *all who are in the graves* will hear His voice" (John 5:28, emphasis added). Indeed, proof that the resurrection of the just and the unjust is one event can be found throughout the New Testament.

In Matthew 13, for example, Jesus speaks of the resurrection of the just and the unjust as being like the separation of wheat from tares at "the time of the harvest" (Matt. 13:30). This harvest of both the wheat and the tares, the just and the unjust, is at Christ's Second Coming: "the harvest is the end of the age" (Matt. 13:39). Jesus makes the same point with the parable of the dragnet: "So it will be at the end of the age. The angels will come forth, separate the wicked from among the just, and cast them into the furnace of fire" (Matt. 13:49, 50). Therefore, though Scripture sometimes speaks as though the just are raised first (as does the *Didache* cited above), Jesus taught that the resurrection of the just and the wicked is a single event taking place at the Second Coming.

There is a serious problem in denying that the Second Coming, the resurrection, and the judgment are simultaneous. Christ's Second Coming represents the divine crashing into the created world, when the infinite and abiding overwhelms the temporal and transitory. It is therefore misleading in the extreme to speak of "chronology" with regard to an event in which time itself passes away in the face of the eternal. Bishop Gerasimos of Abydos explains that all that takes place at the Second Coming takes place simultaneously, adding, "The Parousia, the resurrection, and the end are not separated in time but only in thought. There is no time here." [12]

---

12 Gerasimos of Abydos, *At the End of Time* (Brookline, MA: Holy Cross Orthodox Press, 1997), 14–15.

What will our resurrected bodies be like? The Fathers teach that they will be resplendent with the uncreated light of God, which they will reflect to the degree that they participated in the grace of the Holy Spirit in this life. For example, in *The Fifty Spiritual Homilies* attributed to St. Macarius of Egypt (300–390), we are told:

> Christ will descend from Heaven and raise up all generations of Adam that have fallen asleep from the beginning of time, as Holy Scripture proves. . . . Then shall [the saints'] bodies be surrounded with the divine glory because of their good works. They themselves will be filled with the glory of the Spirit which in this life they enjoyed in their souls. And thus, illumined by the divine light and caught up into Heaven "to meet the Lord in the air (as it is written), we shall be always with the Lord" (1 Thess 4:17), reigning with him forever and ever.[13]

Thus our bodies will be transformed to the degree to which they participate in the grace of the Holy Spirit in this life. The Fathers teach that, even as Christ was both God and man, so we shall become divine by grace while yet remaining created beings. While this may sound like a radical new teaching to some, it is firmly rooted in the Bible. Peter says that we are already "partakers of the divine nature" (2 Pet. 1:4). John tells us that "when He is revealed, we shall be like Him, for we shall see Him as He is" (1 John 3:2). Paul declares that the Lord will "transform our lowly body that it may be conformed to His glorious body" (Phil. 3:21), which of course is both human and divine. Jesus said we will be light even as He is light, and "then the righteous will shine forth as the sun in the kingdom of their Father" (Matt. 13:43).

Macarius describes this transformation as the result of our participating in the divine energies of God:

> Just as a needle that is put into a fire is changed in color, becoming like the fire, yet retaining its own nature as iron, so also in the resurrection all members [i.e., all our bodily parts] rise. . . . All things will become light. All are immersed in light and fire and are indeed changed, but are not, as certain people say, dissolved and transformed into fire so that nothing of their nature remains. For Peter is Peter, and Paul, Paul, and Philip is Philip. Each person in his own unique nature and personality remains, yet filled by the Spirit. . . . The former things now are made into light. So also humans are changed in the resurrection and their members are made holy and full of light.[14]

---

13 Pseudo-Macarius, *The Fifty Spiritual Homilies*, Homily 5:12. These homilies were ascribed to St. Macarius of Egypt only a few generations after his death, and were first published under his name by Johannes Picus in 1559. Today, though, nearly all scholars agree that the author was an unknown monk living in northeast Syria in the middle of the fourth century.

14 Pseudo-Macarius, *Spiritual Homilies*, Homily 15:10–11.

Macarius stresses that our resurrected bodies will be permeated by the deifying grace of the Holy Spirit, yet without obliterating our distinctiveness as human persons. Therefore, while our resurrected bodies will be fully human and will possess those individual qualities that render each of us unique, our bodies will also be of a spiritual nature, as St. Paul says in 1 Corinthians 15:44.

Our mortal human bodies will be spiritually transformed by the Holy Spirit to their original prefallen state, perfectly conforming to the divine image and likeness. St. Gregory of Sinai (1265–1346) explains:

> The body in its incorruptible state will be earthy, but it will be without humours or material density, indescribably transmuted from an unspiritual body into a spiritual body (cf. 1 Cor. 15:44), so that it will be in its godlike refinement and subtleness both earthy and heavenly. Its state when it is resurrected will be the same as that in which it was originally created—one in which it conforms to the image of the Son of Man (cf. Rom 8:29; Phil 3:21) through full participation in His divinity.[15]

Thus our resurrected bodies will be spiritual, incorruptible, and immaterial. Many Fathers say our bodies will be angelic (see Matt. 22:30; Luke 20:36).

When St. Gregory says that our resurrected bodies will be without "material density," it should be explained that Orthodoxy teaches that only God is truly immaterial and incorporeal. Our bodies will only be immaterial in comparison to our present earthly reality, not in comparison to God, who alone is truly immaterial and incorporeal. As St. John of Damascus (675–749) writes, "For all that is compared with God, who alone is incomparable, we find to be dense and material. For in reality only the Deity is immaterial and incorporeal." [16]

The fourteenth-century theologian, Nicholas Cabasilas, relates that the splendor of our resurrected bodies is an unveiling of the grace we receive in the Eucharist. This eucharistic grace begins to transform our bodies in this life, so that they will be irresistibly drawn to Christ at the Second Coming:

> On that day the righteous will shine with one brightness and glory. They will become bright by receiving that light, He [Christ] imparting it. For this bread, this Body, for which men in this life come to the table in order that they may bring it therefrom, is that which will then appear to all eyes upon the clouds (cf. Matt. 24:30) and in one instant of time will display its splendour to the east and to the west like lightning. . . . But when freedom appears they [our bodies] will rush to Christ with an irresistible motion in order that they may receive their proper place. Accordingly Paul, as he

---

15 Gregory of Sinai, *Texts on Commandments and Doctrines*, 46. *The Philokalia*, Vol. IV, 221.
16 John of Damascus, *Exposition of the Orthodox Faith*, Book 2:3.

shows that this rush cannot be restrained, calls it a "carrying up" [rapture], for he says, "we shall be carried off in the clouds to meet the Lord in the air" (1 Thess 4:14). The Saviour says that He will take them to Himself: "then two will be in the field; one is taken and the other left" (Matt. 24:20).[17]

A related problem with dispensationalism is that there are as many "last judgments" as there are resurrections. Dispensationalism postulates:

(1) a "believer's judgment" after the rapture, sometimes known as the "bema judgment" (based on 2 Cor. 5:10);
(2) a "judgment of the Jews" to take place in Jerusalem during the Tribulation (based on Matt. 24:20–31 and Zech. 14:1–11);[18]
(3) a "judgment of the nations" when Christ returns (Matt. 25:31, 32);
(4) another judgment at Christ's Second Coming, wherein Old Testament saints and the righteous who survive the Tribulation are rewarded by entering the millennial kingdom as mortals to serve Jesus while He reigns in Jerusalem; and
(5) a "Great White Throne judgment" of all the unregenerate after the millennium (Rev. 20:11, 12).

Neither Scripture nor Christian Tradition teaches a multiplicity of "judgments"; it is the dispensationalist teaching of a pretribulational rapture and an earthly millennium following Christ's Second Coming that makes a multiplicity of resurrections and judgments necessary.

To see how dispensationalists interpret biblical texts describing the judgment, consider John Walvoord's interpretation of Matthew 25:31–46, the so-called "judgment of the nations" passage. In this passage, Christ gathers "the nations" together at His return and separates them into "sheep" (the righteous) and "goats" (the unrighteous), the sheep entering the Kingdom and the goats going into everlasting punishment.

According to Walvoord in *Armageddon, Oil and the Middle East Crisis*, the sheep "are the ones who will have aided the Jews during their intense persecution. They will have visited them in prison, clothed them when naked, fed them when hungry, and hidden them from tormentors."[19] Conversely, the goats are those who exhibited a "selfish cruelty toward the Jews during

---

17 Nicholas Cabasilas, *The Life in Christ*, 4:19, 20. See the translation by Carmino deCatanzaro (Crestwood, NY: St. Vladimir's Seminary Press, 1974), pp. 146–147.

18 Dispensationalist author Clarence Larkin writes of this judgment, "The human agent the Lord will use will be the Antichrist, the awfulness of whose rule will be supplemented by the pouring out of the 'Vials of God's wrath' upon the earth." *Rightly Dividing the Word* (Glenside, PA: Rev. Clarence Larkin Est., n.d.), 153.

19 Walvoord, *Armageddon,* 198.

the Tribulation. These individuals, described as goats, will be cast into ever-lasting fire—signifying that they will be punished by being put to death. Just as unbelieving Jews will be judged, so too, unbelieving Gentiles will be judged." [20]

Walvoord explains in his book *Major Bible Prophecies* that his belief that Matthew 25:31–46 is a judgment of the Gentiles' treatment of Jews during the Tribulation is based upon the fact that Christ says in this passage, "Assuredly, I say to you, inasmuch as you did it to one of the least of these my brethren, you did it to Me" (Matt. 25:40; compare v. 45).[21] The "brethren" of Jesus are assumed by Walvoord to be the Jews.

Yet is this what Jesus meant by "brethren"? What does Jesus say elsewhere? "For whoever does the will of God is My brother," Jesus says in Mark 3:35 (see Matt. 12:50; Luke 8:21). Thus Jesus doesn't limit His definition of a "brother" to those having familial or racial blood ties; instead, He saw as His brethren all those who did the will of the Father.

Syrian Orthodox scholar and author Touma al-Khoury, commenting on dispensationalism's peculiar interpretation of the judgment in Matthew 25, also observes that the word "brethren" includes not only Jews, but the righteous of every nation.[22] He points to the use of the word "brethren" in Hebrews 2:10–13, where it describes the "many sons" among Jews and Gentiles being brought to salvation (v. 10), as evidence that this is how the Apostolic Church generally understood the word:

> For both He who sanctifies and *those who are being sanctified* [i.e., Christians] are all of one, for which reason He is not ashamed *to call them brethren*, saying: "I will declare Your name to *My brethren*; In the midst of the assembly I will sing praise to You [Ps. 22:22]" (Heb. 2:11, 12, emphasis added).

Such a use of the word "brethren" for fellow Christians is also found throughout the Acts of the Apostles. Recognizing what Jesus meant by the word "brethren" in Matthew 25:31–46, the Church has always understood those being persecuted and in need of compassion as Christians, those people made up of all races who do "the will of God" and are, as a result, the Lord's brethren.

Another misunderstanding of Matthew 25:31–46 involves who will participate in this judgment "when the Son of Man comes in His glory" (v. 31). Jesus tells us that "all the nations will be gathered before Him," and dispensationalists often argue that this is a judgment uniquely for "nations" and not for individuals. "All the nations," that is, *except* Israel—despite the fact that Jesus explicitly states that this judgment is for "*all* the nations."

Aside from being inconsistent, such an interpretation totally misses Jesus' point. When Jesus says that all nations will be gathered before Him, what He means is simply that *everyone* will stand before Him. "All the nations" means all people from all the nations on earth (nations are after all made up of individual persons).

Consider the use of the word "nation" as Jesus used it in the Great Commission: "Go therefore and make disciples of *all the nations*, baptizing them in the name of the Father and of the Son and of the Holy Spirit" (Matt. 28:19, emphasis added). How does one disciple and baptize a "nation"? All agree that Jesus meant we were to disciple and baptize all people in all nations. So why would anyone interpret "all nations" a few chapters earlier in Matthew 25 differently, as abstract sociological units instead of as the various peoples of the earth? Only a prior commitment to an artificial theological system could lead anyone to such a misunderstanding of the judgment in Matthew 25:31–46.

Scripture describes only one judgment that will follow a single resurrection when the Lord comes. We never find the expression the "days of judgment" in Scripture, but "the day of judgment" or "that Day." Jude, for example, speaks of "the judgment [singular] of the great day [singular]" (Jude 6). Paul in Romans 2:5–10 writes:

> You are treasuring up for yourself wrath in the day of wrath and revelation [Gr. *apokalupto*] of the righteous judgment of God, who "will render to each one according to his deeds" [Ps. 62:12]: eternal life to those who by patient continuance in doing good seek for glory, honor, and immortality; but to those who are self-seeking and do not obey the truth, but obey unrighteousness—indignation and wrath, tribulation and anguish, on every soul of man who does evil, of the Jew first and also the Greek; but glory, honor, and peace to everyone who works what is good, to the Jew first and also to the Greek. (Rom. 2:5–10)

Paul here describes a single judgment at the Second Coming (note the word *apokalupto*), wherein God renders to "every soul" according to his deeds, whether these be good or ill. Notice that the judgment includes *both* Jews and Greeks; in other words, it isn't just a judgment of Gentile nations based on how well they treated Jews. According to Paul, those who obey the truth go to eternal life. The others, the self-seeking who care not for the truth, go to wrath. Compare also what the Apostle writes to the Corinthians: "For we must *all* appear before the judgment seat of Christ, that each one may receive the things done in the body, whether good or bad" (2 Cor. 5:10, emphasis added).

Jesus said in Matthew 16:27 that "the Son of Man is going to come in his Father's glory with his angels, and then he will reward *each person* according to what he has done" (Matt. 16:27 NIV, emphasis added). "Each person" will stand before Christ to be judged at the Second Coming. Consequently, there will not be separate judgments for different groups of people, but a single judgment wherein each person receives his due "according to what he has done," whether it be good or ill. While there are other scriptures that we could look at, Matthew 16:27 is about as explicit as they get.[23]

As with the general resurrection, the teaching of a single, general judgment was clearly and consistently taught by the early Church. The following example is taken from Hippolytus' *Against the Greeks*, written sometime before A.D. 225. The work is now lost except for a long citation preserved in St. John of Damascus' *Sacra parallela*. Hippolytus is emphatic that everyone, the just and the unjust, will be judged together:

> And being present at His [Christ's] judicial decision, all, both men and angels and demons, shall utter one voice, saying, "Righteous is Thy judgment." Of which voice the justification will be seen in the awarding to each that which is just; since to those who have done well shall be assigned righteously eternal bliss, and to the lovers of iniquity shall be given eternal punishment. And the fire which is unquenchable and without end awaits these latter, and a certain fiery worm which dieth not, and which does not waste the body, but continues bursting forth from the body with unending pain. No sleep will give them rest; no night will soothe them; no death will deliver them from punishment; no voice of interceding friends will profit them. For neither are the righteous seen by them any longer, nor are they worthy of remembrance.[24]

Hippolytus' chilling description of the end of those who reject the grace of Christ is worthy of contemplation. Observe that Hippolytus says it is "lovers of iniquity" who shall be condemned, not "doers of iniquity." Of course, we have all been guilty of "doing iniquity," and if this were the sole standard for judgment we would all be lost. But a "lover of iniquity" isn't just someone who sins. Someone who is a "lover of iniquity" is someone who is wedded to his wickedness, who experiences no qualms for his iniquity, and is thus devoid of any inclination toward repentance. The eternal punishment that Hippolytus describes is for the truly unrepentant.

---

23 Those desiring further scriptural information on this subject should read *Amillennialism Today* by William Cox (Phillipsburg, NJ: Presbyterian and Reformed Publishing, 1966), 112–123.

24 Hippolytus, *Against the Greeks*, 3.

Repentance is the key to our fate in eternity. In a work ascribed to St. Theognostos of Alexandria, who flourished during the third century, we read that it is not merely our sins that condemn us at the fearful tribunal, but whether we repented of those sins during our lives:

> We will not be punished or condemned in the age to be because we have sinned, since we were given a mutable and unstable nature. But we will be punished if, after sinning, we did not repent and turn from our evil ways to the Lord; for we have been given the power to repent, as well as the time in which to do so.[25]

The fact that there will be a single, general judgment at the end of the age ought not to be an issue among God-fearing Christians. The only issue that Christians should be pondering is whether they are ready to stand before the awesome judgment seat of Christ. Have I repented thoroughly from the heart and turned my whole life toward Christ my God? We must constantly occupy ourselves with this question in the days allotted to us, not theorizing how many "judgments" there might be and where in the end-times flow chart they might occur.

During each Orthodox Liturgy, the priest or deacon calls out, "For a good defense before the dread judgment seat of Christ, let us pray to the Lord." And everyone responds, "Lord have mercy." As we consider the great Day in which we will all stand before Christ to render an account of our lives, let us pray that the Lord will have mercy on us and keep us by His grace.[26]

---

25 Theognostos of Alexandria, *On the Practice of the Virtues*, 47. *The Philokalia*, Vol. II, 369–370.

26 For those desiring to read something especially inspiring on the subject of the final judgment, St. Ephrem the Syrian's *Letter to Publius* cannot be recommended too highly. The work was virtually unknown in the Western world until 1901. In fact, the single surviving manuscript, dated to the twelfth century, was only edited and translated into English in 1976. One of only two letters that scholars acknowledge as having actually been composed by St. Ephrem (the only other is Ephrem's *Letter to Hypatius*), the *Letter to Publius* is a profound meditation on the judgment, rich in imagery and metaphor. An excellent English translation by Edward Mathews, Jr., can be found in *St. Ephrem the Syrian/Selected Prose Works*, The Fathers of the Church (Washington, D.C.: The Catholic University of America Press, 1994), Vol. 91, 338–355.

Chapter Fifteen

The New Heavens and Earth

Jesus answered, "My kingdom is not of this world."
—The Gospel According to St. John 18:36

Ideal society is a drama enacted exclusively in the imagination.
—George Santayana, *The Life of Reason* (1905–1906)

THERE HAVE ALWAYS BEEN imaginative persons who have dreamed of creating an earthly Utopia. In particular, the course of the twentieth century was greatly influenced by Karl Marx's vision of a utopian "dictatorship of the proletariat." Even outside of Marxist societies, utopian visions of greater or lesser ambition have thrived. The United States itself attempted to create the "Great Society" in the 1960s.

The utopian vision has at times even taken on Christian overtones. The late nineteenth century saw the creation of what was called "the social gospel." This was largely a vision of creating the ideal society based upon the principles of liberal Protestantism with its credo of the universal fatherhood of God and the universal brotherhood of man.[1] Conservative Protestants also had visions of Utopia; however, they disdained the "social gospel," believing that only Jesus Christ Himself could establish Utopia on earth. Their utopian vision consequently took the form of an earthly millennium established by Christ after His Second Coming.

The Millennium Is Now

We've already learned much about the millennium mentioned in the Book of Revelation, but now we need to look at the subject in a little more detail.

---

1 Adolf Harnack is credited with reducing Christianity to these two concepts in his book, *What is Christianity?*

To begin with, there are basically three approaches to the issue. There is the *premillennial* position that says Christ will return before establishing the millennium. There is also a position called *postmillennialism* that has recently made a comeback. Postmillennialism asserts there will be a golden period when Christianity will be absolutely ascendant, after which Christ will return. Then there is the Orthodox position, called *amillennialism*, which identifies the millennium mentioned in Revelation 20:2–10 with the Church age from the Resurrection of Christ to the Second Coming. The amillennial teaching therefore rejects an earthly millennial reign of Christ following the Second Coming ("amillennial" literally meaning "no millennium").

Evangelical scholar R. C. Sproul explains that the differences between these approaches to Revelation 20 amount to more than a mere disagreement over prefixes. How we understand the millennium in large part determines how we view the Christian Faith as a whole:

> These simple designations of *pre-*, *a-*, and *post-* help to establish the chronological relationship between the millennial kingdom and Christ's return. But in themselves they fail to capture the full measure of the alternate positions. What is in view is not simply *chronology*, but the *nature* of the kingdom of God. These positions also differ in their understanding of history, whether it be optimistic or pessimistic, and in their views of the church's strategy in fulfilling her mission.[2]

Premillennialism is based on a highly literal (mis)reading of Revelation 20. Basically, the symbols of Revelation are not really seen as symbols at all. To see how shallow such a reading becomes, look at Hal Lindsey's description of this supposed millennial kingdom:

> In fact, without getting too far ahead of myself, let me just tantalize you by saying that those of us who experience the Rapture will be living in a city hovering above the earthly city of Jerusalem and interacting with the Millennial Kingdom below. . . . We might visit relatives on earth. We might come down to have a midnight snack. We might even catch a movie, once in a while. But keep in mind the people down below will be living in their old human bodies—somewhat improved, but not a glorified resurrection body like yours.[3]

Lindsey has an astonishingly earthly and carnal conception of the existence of those who "shall be changed—in a moment, in the twinkling of an eye, at the last trumpet" (1 Cor. 15:51, 52). What is so "tantalizing" about leaving a hovering city to come to earth for a midnight snack or to "catch a movie"? Are things really so boring above that we'd want to return to earth

---

2   R. C. Sproul, *The Last Days According to Jesus* (Grand Rapids: Baker Books, 1998), 194–195. Emphasis in original.

3   Lindsey, *Apocalypse,* 258–259.

for recreation? Though Scripture states that at the Second Coming we will all be glorified and "shall always be with the Lord" (1 Thess. 4:17), Lindsey pictures eternal life as but a continuation of our present, everyday existence— an existence many today, in fact, would like to escape from (thus the popularity of movies). As for those with "somewhat improved" mortal bodies who are confined to the earthly millennial kingdom "down below," why should they be deprived of the benefits enjoyed by those who have a glorified resurrected body?

How alien all this is from the expectations of the early Christians! Athenagoras of Athens, for instance, wrote in A.D. 176,

> When we are removed from the present life we shall live another life, better than the present one, *and not earthly but heavenly*. Then we shall abide near God and with God, changeless and free from all suffering in the soul, not as flesh, even though we shall have flesh (cf. 1 Cor 15:44), but as a heavenly spirit.[4]

Unlike Lindsey, Athenagoras does not try to "tantalize" people with the future prospect of catching a late-night show in an earthly millennial kingdom. Like the vast majority of the early Christians, he was an amillennialist. The ancient Church taught that the millennium of Revelation 20 is a present reality as Christ reigns through His Church. In other words, the millennium is *now*, the Church age. According to the early Church, opposition to Christ's reign will continue to escalate until it climaxes with the rise of the Antichrist and the final persecution of the Church. The Lord's victory over the forces of evil will be consummated when He returns and completes His redemption, which will entail the overthrow of the Antichrist and his followers, the realization of the promised resurrection and judgment of all humanity, and the metamorphosis of creation into the eternal state.

This basic belief is reflected in the Nicene-Constantinopolitan Creed that Orthodox Christians recite in church every Sunday. We declare in the Creed that we believe in Christ, who "is enthroned at the right hand of the Father; who will come again with glory to judge the living and the dead; and of whose kingdom there shall be no end. . . . [we] look forward to the resurrection of the dead and the life of the age to come. Amen." Based on this, Orthodoxy proclaims a belief in (1) a physical Second Coming of Christ in glory, (2) a final resurrection and judgment of all humanity, and (3) an eternal age that will immediately follow.

As we saw in a previous chapter, the Fathers of the Ecumenical Council of Constantinople in 381 included the phrase, "and of whose kingdom there shall be no end," explicitly to reject millennial teachings. Therefore, when

---

4   Athenagoras of Athens, *A Supplication for the Christians*, 31. Emphasis added.

we pray, "Thy kingdom come," in the Lord's Prayer, we are not praying for a thousand-year kingdom; we are praying for a Kingdom of which "there shall be no end." According to the Creed, when Christ comes there will be a (single) resurrection followed by a (single) judgment, and then will begin the eternal Kingdom promised by Christ and preached by the Apostles.

A sort of summary of the Orthodox belief is found in 2 Peter 3:10: "But the day of the Lord will come as a thief in the night, in which the heavens will pass away with a great noise, and the elements will melt with fervent heat; both the earth and the works that are in it will be burned up." Thus Christ will come "as a thief in the night," followed by a new heaven and a new earth. What Peter does *not* say is that Christ will return, *followed by a millennium,* and then there will be a new heaven and a new earth. The Apostle Peter knew nothing of an earthly millennium.

How then do Orthodox Christians interpret the reference to a millennium in Revelation 20? Having studied the Book of Revelation for two thousand years, the Church holds that the millennium mentioned in Revelation must be seen as a symbol that can be understood correctly only within the context of all the other symbols in Revelation. The word "thousand" occurs thirty times in twenty different verses in the Book of Revelation, each time having a figurative rather than a literal meaning. For example, its very first appearance in the Book of Revelation describes the innumerable angelic beings that offer praise to God: "Then I looked, and I heard the voice of many angels around the throne, the living creatures, and the elders; and the number of them was ten thousand times ten thousand, and thousands of thousands" (Rev. 5:11 KJV).

The "thousand-year" millennium described in Revelation 20, therefore, should be interpreted symbolically rather than literally.

Revelation 20

Unfortunately, when the Orthodox say that Revelation 20 shouldn't be taken literally, many non-Orthodox take this to mean Revelation 20 shouldn't be taken *seriously*. This is not at all what the Orthodox Church is saying. The Orthodox take Revelation 20 quite seriously, just as they do the rest of Scripture. In fact, it might be said in all humility that an Orthodox reading of Revelation 20 takes the passage more seriously than a literal reading, since the Orthodox are seeking to dig underneath the surface wording of the text to arrive at its actual meaning.

What follows is a brief Orthodox commentary on Revelation 20, starting with verses 1–3:

Then I saw an angel coming down from heaven, having the key to the bottomless pit and a great chain in his hand. He laid hold of the dragon, that serpent of old, who is the Devil and Satan, and bound him for a thousand years; and he cast him into the bottomless pit, and shut him up, and set a seal on him, so that he should deceive the nations no more till the thousand years were finished. But after these things he must be released for a little while.

John's vision in Revelation 17—19 concluded with the beast and his armies defeated and cast into the lake of fire (Rev. 19:20). Revelation 20:1 begins with, "Then I saw . . . ," indicating the commencement of a new vision in the book. This new vision will recapitulate the victory of Christ over Satan, the beast, and his ungodly followers, described already in Revelation 17—19. Therefore, we do not interpret the millennium as following in chronological order the defeat of the beast at Christ's Second Coming in Revelation 19. (For a full explanation of this approach to Revelation that sees chapters 20—22 as a separate vision distinct from chapters 17—19, see the Appendix.)

In Revelation 20:1–3, we learn that Satan is bound by a chain in a bottomless pit for a thousand years so he cannot deceive the nations, and then he is released for a short time. This pit has a lid that can be both locked (Rev. 20:3) and unlocked with a key (see Rev. 9:1, 2). In Revelation 20:3, the lid is sealed after it is locked, the seal in ancient times being a special precaution against escape (e.g., Dan. 6:17; Matt. 27:66). Once placed upon the door of a prison cell, the seal was allowed to be broken only by a properly authorized person.

The first thing to bear in mind when reading Revelation 20 is that the Book of Revelation is full of symbols. The number 1,000 in chapter 20 is used symbolically, just as the chain and the bottomless pit in the passage are only symbols of Satan being bound. If one insists upon taking the thousand years literally in this passage, one is also obliged to believe Satan will literally be bound by a literal chain in a literal bottomless pit with a literal lid and a literal seal. It is absurd to interpret just one detail in this passage literally and all the rest symbolically! We must at least be consistent in our interpretation.

Here "a thousand years" means "a long time," not a literal thousand years. The same symbolic usage is found in Psalm 50:10, "For every beast of the forest is Mine, and the cattle on a thousand hills." The thousand hills are obviously not meant to be understood as a literal thousand hills. What is being said is that *all* the cattle (i.e., all things) on *all* the hills of the earth (i.e., throughout creation) are the Lord's. We use the number 1,000 the same way in English. Recall the expression, "If I've told you once, I've told you a *thousand* times . . ." What we literally mean is that we have told the person something "many times." The millennium in Revelation 20 is to be understood in a similar way: as a long period of time during which Satan's activity is restricted so he cannot "deceive the nations."

Revelation in many places reflects John's Jewish background. The use of a symbolic number to denote an indefinite period of time is consistent with the Jewish rabbinic tradition concerning the messianic age. Abraham Cohen writes in *Everyman's Talmud*, "Many Rabbis believed that the period of the Messiah was to be only a transitionary stage between this world and the World to Come, and opinions differed on the time of its duration." [5] These opinions ranged from forty years (the length of time Israel wandered in the wilderness) to a length of time equaling the age of the world when the Messiah came. Similarly, the symbolic "thousand" in Revelation reflects this basic uncertainty within Judaism of the length of time the messianic age would last.

Moreover, Cohen's description of the messianic age as "only a transitionary stage between this world and the World to Come" is a perfect description of the Church age. The history of Christianity is a story of transitional tension. During the Church age we look back upon Christ's first coming and await His Second Coming and the eternal age to come.[6]

If the millennium is the Church age, then according to Revelation 20:1–3, Satan must have been bound at the beginning of this age. Again, Abraham Cohen explains that, in the Talmud, the rabbis expressed "the view that the Messiah will only produce one result, viz. the freeing of Israel from his oppressors [meaning national oppressors like Rome]." [7] Jesus didn't free Israel from Roman tyranny, but He did set her free from oppressors far worse: He set Israel free from the oppression of the Law (Rom. 8:2; Gal. 4:24—5:1), of sin (John 8:32–36; Rom. 6:18, 22), and of death (Rom. 8:2; 2 Tim. 1:10). Orthodoxy asserts that Jesus conquered Satan himself and bound him so that the freedom contained in the gospel message could be spread unhindered.

This is a very difficult point for some people to accept, because they look around at our world and it certainly doesn't *look* as if Satan is bound. Premillennialists often quip, "If Satan is bound, he's got an awfully long chain!" Of course, much the same could be said regarding sin and death: Does it look as though sin and death have been conquered? Yet the Scriptures

---

5   Cohen, *Everyman's Talmud,* 356.

6   However, Cohen also says that "earlier generations of the Rabbis identified the messianic era with the World to Come." This would be in a "timeless sphere in which the righteous would lead a purely spiritual existence freed from the trammels of the flesh" (Cohen, *Talmud*, 364). Thus the messianic era would not be an earthly thousand-year period *before* the eternal state, as in dispensationalism, but would be identified with the eternal state itself.

7   Ibid.

clearly tell us this is so, and that this happened two thousand years ago at the Cross.

The first thing to observe is that Satan alone is not responsible for all the evil and suffering in the world. We contribute a little of it ourselves. Secondly, and most importantly, Revelation 20:3 states that Satan's binding is for a specific purpose: "so that he should deceive the nations no more till the thousand years were finished." Satan was bound in order to allow the Church to be established and spread its message freely. The fact that Satan is bound doesn't mean the world should be idyllic. In fact, Scripture states that Satan can still exert his influence (Acts 5:3; 1 Cor. 5:5; Eph. 6:11; 1 Pet. 5:8). Nevertheless, Satan has been "defanged" by Christ. His power is limited.

What evidence is there that Satan has been bound already? Jude tells us that "the angels who did not keep their proper domain, . . . He [God] has reserved in everlasting chains under darkness for the judgment of the great Day" (Jude 6). Even now there are fallen angels that God has bound in chains (as in Revelation 20:1–3) and imprisoned in a dark place, like the bottomless pit in Revelation 20. Is Satan, the most powerful of the fallen angels, now among them?

At Christ's First Advent, the Lord met Satan and defeated him, as was originally prophesied to Adam and Eve (see Gen. 3:15). Before Christ defeated him, Satan was the undisputed "ruler of this world." However, through His sacrifice on the Cross, Christ has overthrown the dominion of Satan: "Now the ruler of this world will be cast out. And I, if I am lifted up from the earth, will draw all peoples to Myself" (John 12:31, 32). The author of the fourth Gospel elsewhere states, "For this purpose the Son of God was manifested, that He might destroy the works of the devil" (1 John 3:8). To John, Satan has been overthrown through the Cross, his works destroyed.

Paul writes that through the Cross our Lord "disarmed principalities and powers, He made a public spectacle of them, triumphing over them in it [the Cross]" (Col. 2:15). We who were in captivity to Satan have been freed, and when our Lord ascended to sit enthroned at the right hand of the Father, "He led captivity captive" (Eph. 4:8). Hebrews tells us that through death Christ destroyed "him who had the power of death, that is, the devil" (Heb. 2:14).

In Luke's Gospel, Jesus says, "I saw Satan fall like lightning from heaven" (Luke 10:18). This is probably alluding to Isaiah 14:12–15 (and possibly Ezek. 28:17), though it is also reminiscent of Revelation 20:3, where Satan is "cast" into the bottomless pit. Jesus then says that we, who were once subject to Satan, now have authority over our old master: "Behold, I give you authority to trample on serpents and scorpions,[8] and over all the power of the

8 Like the serpent, the scorpion was associated with either chastisement or demons in the

enemy [i.e., Satan], and nothing shall by any means hurt you. Nevertheless do not rejoice in this, that the spirits are subject to you, but rather rejoice because your names are written in heaven" (Luke 10:19, 20). Because Satan has been cast down and bound, we now have authority over him through Christ (see Matt. 28:18).

With this background in mind, what Christ says in Matthew 12:28, 29 becomes conclusive: "But if I cast out demons by the Spirit of God, surely the Kingdom of God has come upon you. Or how can one enter a strong man's house and plunder his goods, unless he first binds the strong man? And then he will plunder his house." As in Revelation 20:1–3, we have mention of the Kingdom of God (in Revelation, a "millennium"), Satan (the "strong man"), and "binding" (the same Greek verb, *deo*, is used in both places).

What is Jesus saying in Matthew? He says the Kingdom has arrived, that Satan, the "strong man," has been bound, and that He is going to plunder Satan's house and make off with his goods. What is Satan's "house" that Christ breaks into? It is the world over which Satan had control, and the goods that Christ takes from him are we who are made in God's image. Notice that Christ says the strong man is bound first, and then the world is plundered of the enslaved human race. In other words, before the Lord wins human souls with the gospel, Satan must first be bound.

After the millennium, at the end of the Church age, Satan will be released again "for a little while" (Rev. 20:3). We saw in a previous chapter that during the Tribulation the Antichrist will be energized by Satan, and that the "dragon" will have a free hand at this time. Satan will be loosed during the Tribulation, but this is only "for a little while," after which the King of kings will return and claim the world as His own.

In Revelation 20:4–6 we read:

> And I saw thrones, and they sat on them, and judgment was committed to them. Then I saw the souls of those who had been beheaded for their witness to Jesus and for the word of God, who had not worshiped the beast or his image, and had not received his mark on their foreheads or on their hands. And they lived and reigned with Christ for a thousand years. But the rest of the dead did not live again until the thousand years were finished. This is the first resurrection. Blessed and holy is he who has part in the first resurrection. Over such the second death has no power, but they shall be priests of God and of Christ, and shall reign with Him a thousand years.

It is important to grasp that in Revelation 20 the millennium is not earthly, as the prophecy pundits teach, but heavenly. In Revelation 20:4, the millennial reign is depicted with thrones set up for the saints in heaven. Among those

---

ancient world (e.g., 1 Kin. 12:11, 14; 2 Chr. 10:11, 14; Rev. 9:3, 5, 10 NIV).

sitting on the thrones who rule "with Christ" in heaven are the martyrs: "And I saw the souls of those who had been beheaded for their witness to Jesus." Throughout Revelation, the throne of Christ and those of His saints are always in heaven (see Rev. 1:4; 3:21; 4:2). In Revelation 12:5, for example, we read that Christ was "caught up to God and to His throne."

Rather than being earthly, therefore, the millennium is heavenly and spiritual. As Archbishop Averky Taushev observes:

> St. John says, "I saw the souls of them that were beheaded." From this it is clear that these saints who participate in the thousand-year reign of Christ are reigning with Christ and performing judgment not on earth but in heaven, for it speaks here concerning their souls which are not united with their bodies. From this it is evident that the saints take part in the governing of the Church of Christ on earth.[9]

During the Tribulation, as Satan is released to do his will, there will be many martyrs for "Jesus and for the word of God." They will neither worship the Antichrist nor accept his mark (see Chapter 13 on the Antichrist). Whether they be from the early Church, from the Turkish persecution, from the communist persecution, or the new martyrs created during the Tribulation, the martyrs live and reign in heaven with Christ "for a thousand years," that is, during the Church age. Christ is reigning now at the right hand of the Father, and the martyrs at their death go to reign with the Lord at the Father's right hand until the Lord returns in glory. They will return with Him at the Second Coming, at which time the resurrection takes place. It should also be pointed out that nowhere in this passage is Christ said to rule as an earthly king from Jerusalem.

The reference to the "first resurrection" should be interpreted cautiously, for no resurrection is actually described. All that is said is that the saints "lived and reigned with Christ for a thousand years." Moreover, John doesn't mention a "second resurrection." In Revelation 20:12, all the dead are depicted at the judgment without any indication of how they were raised. What are we to make of this "first resurrection"?

As we've already learned, the New Testament speaks of only a single resurrection. However, the New Testament in several places does speak of our spiritual regeneration as a sort of "resurrection" (e.g., Luke 15:24; John 5:24; 11:25, 26; 11:15; Gal. 2:19; Eph. 2:1–6; et. al.). Paul explicitly describes baptism as a spiritual resurrection in Romans 6:4–11. This is a "resurrection" before the general resurrection, an anticipation of what is to come. The Fathers early on interpreted the "first resurrection" as baptism, and this seems to be the best understanding of this difficult passage in Revelation.

---

9   Taushev, *Apocalypse*, 254.

Like the "first resurrection," the "second death" that is mentioned in verse 6 also seems to indicate a spiritual reality. The second death in verse 14 is defined as being cast into the lake of fire to suffer eternal torment. It isn't earthly death as we commonly know it, but a spiritual state. As Bishop Gerasimos of Abydos sums it up: "Thus we have a physical death [the first death] and a spiritual death [the second death], and we also have a spiritual resurrection [the first resurrection] and a physical resurrection, which is the general resurrection." [10]

Revelation 20:7–10 gives us a picture of what the Tribulation will be like:

> Now when the thousand years have expired, Satan will be released from his prison and will go out to deceive the nations which are in the four corners of the earth, Gog and Magog, to gather them together to battle, whose number is as the sand of the sea. They went up on the breadth of the earth and surrounded the camp of the saints and the beloved city. And fire came down from God out of heaven and devoured them. The devil, who deceived them, was cast into the lake of fire and brimstone where the beast and the false prophet are. And they will be tormented day and night forever and ever.

Satan is freed and the Tribulation begins. He proceeds to gather the nations of the earth to join him in his final rebellion against God. We saw in a previous chapter that Gog and Magog are symbolic of all the nations that are hostile to God's people. They are attacking "the camp of the saints and the beloved city." The "beloved city" is undoubtedly the heavenly Jerusalem, the Church that is the "camp of the saints." In the following chapter of Revelation, the Church is again pictured as the New Jerusalem (see Rev. 21:2, 9–27). Here in Revelation 20:7–10 John is saying that at the end of this age Satan and the world will mount an all-out attack on the Church, which is "the camp of the saints and the beloved city." [11] Note that there is no mention in the text of nuclear, chemical, or biological weapons. This is primarily spiritual warfare, and the stakes are much higher than in military warfare: the eternal destiny of human souls.

Satan's desperate attempt, though, will fail miserably: God will send fire from heaven and destroy Satan and his minions. The image of fire descending from heaven in judgment occurs in several places in the Bible. In 2 Kings 1, we read that King Ahaziah, a devotee of Baal-Zebub, the god of

---

10 Gerasimos of Abydos, *At the End of Time,* 30.

11 Earthly Jerusalem is probably not being spoken of here, because John speaks very negatively of it elsewhere in Revelation. For John, earthly Jerusalem was not "the beloved city," but "the great city which spiritually is called Sodom and Egypt, where also our Lord was crucified" (Rev. 11:8).

Ekron, sent a captain and fifty men to arrest the Prophet Elijah. Elijah told the captain, "If I am a man of God, then let fire come down from heaven and consume you and your fifty men" (2 Kin. 1:10). After he said this, fire descended from heaven and the contingent of soldiers was reduced to ashes. Again the king sent a captain with fifty men, and again Elijah called fire down upon them (v. 12). After the second time, the king and his military learned a new respect for Elijah and his God.

Though the enemies of God send armies against those who bear the name of Christ, yet God will preserve them through prayer. In the darkest hours of Satan's final rampage, God's protecting hand will be there. As we learned in the last chapter, Christ will come again with fire; and as the general judgment mentioned in Revelation 20:11–15 immediately follows the destruction of Gog and Magog by fire from heaven, the Orthodox believe the battle of Gog and Magog occurs during the Tribulation before the Second Coming.

After Satan and the nations are defeated, Satan is thrown into the lake of fire. Then, in Revelation 20:11–15, John details the judgment before the great, white throne:

> Then I saw a great, white throne and him who sat on it, from whose face the earth and the heaven fled away. And there was found no place for them. And I saw the dead, small and great, standing before God, and books were opened. And another book was opened, which is the Book of Life. And the dead were judged according to their works, by the things which were written in the books. The sea gave up the dead who were in it, and Death and Hades delivered up the dead who were in them. And they were judged each one according to his works. Then Death and Hades were cast into the lake of fire. This is the second death. And anyone not found written in the Book of Life was cast into the lake of fire.

The throne and the books are also found in Daniel's vision of the Ancient of Days (Dan. 7:9, 10). It is Christ who sits on the throne and renders judgment upon mankind (Acts 10:42; 2 Cor. 5:10). At the sight of this scene, heaven and earth flee in anticipation of the new heavens and new earth that are about to come into existence for the new humanity the Lord has created (see Ps. 114).

Before this throne all the dead, from all classes and from every part of the world, are brought to stand judgment. Death and Hades are emptied of everyone; no one is left out. The sea is mentioned in Revelation 20:13 because, in the ancient world, those who died without burial, like those lost at sea, were thought to be forever forgotten in the world of the dead. Therefore to be left unburied was considered a terrible fate (see 1 Kin. 13:21, 22; 14:11; Jer. 8:1–3). John assures us that God will not overlook the unburied on the Judgment Day; they too shall stand before Christ and receive their reward, whether good or ill. If their names are in the Book of Life, then they will receive the reward of the righteous. John tells us, "And they were judged, each one according to his works" (Rev. 20:13). This recalls what Jesus said in Matthew 16:27, that when the Son of Man comes in His glory, "each person" will be rewarded "according to his works." Every single individual will stand before Christ at this judgment.

Following the judgment, Death and Hades are destroyed. After the Apostle Paul described the general resurrection and judgment in his first letter to the Corinthians, he stated that "the last enemy to be destroyed is death" (1 Cor. 15:26). In Revelation 20:14, John describes the same thing: "Then Death and Hades were cast into the lake of fire. This is the second death." Death and Hades are relics of Satan's rule over the world, and these join him in the lake of fire. After this the new heavens and earth are described in Revelation 21 and 22.

In interpreting Revelation 20, note that we didn't attempt to fit the chapter into a chronological scheme wherein the entire Book of Revelation is understood as a continuous timeline of the future. In such a chronological approach, the Tribulation occurs in chapters 4—18, the Second Coming happens in chapter 19, Christ's earthly millennium in chapter 20, and a new heaven and earth in chapters 21 and 22. Orthodox theologian Fr. Seraphim Rose once remarked on this chronological approach, "The chiliastic [i.e., millennial] interpretation of the Apocalypse proceeds also from another basic mistake of most Protestant interpreters: to take the text of the book in strict *chronological* order instead of seeing it as it is: a series of visions quite distinct in nature from each other." [12]

In fact, a careful reading of the Book of Revelation reveals that its events are not listed in any strict chronological order. For example, we have the opening of the seven seals, which includes the general destruction wrought by the four horsemen of the apocalypse and the death of a quarter of the earth's population (Rev. 6:1–8), widespread martyrdoms of the saints (Rev. 6:9–11), and cosmic disturbances (Rev. 6:12–17), *before* God commands the angels to withhold the judgments until the servants of God are protected (Rev. 7:3). It seems that not even the seven seals themselves are in a strictly chronological order.

In the approach adopted here, we have viewed Revelation as a series of mystic visions, each telling of Christ's ultimate victory over evil in a different way. Thus, for example, the vision of the seven seals parallels and recapitulates the vision of the seven trumpets. Or again, the opening of a

---

12 Fr. Seraphim Rose, "Translator's Introduction," Taushev, *Apocalypse*, 32. Emphasis in original.

bottomless pit by a descending "star" (an angel)[13] in Revelation 9:1–3, releasing a demonic plague of "locusts" (see Ex. 10:4–19), parallels and recapitulates the same event in Revelation 20:7–9.

This method of reading Revelation as a series of visions was favored by many early commentators. It is not that we interpret Revelation this way simply to avoid millenarianism; rather, we read it this way because this is how Revelation is written. Victorinus of Petau during the third century had millenarian tendencies, and even he understood Revelation as a series of visions rather than as a chronological account:

> We must not regard the order of what is said, because frequently the Holy Spirit, when He has traversed even to the end of the last times, returns again to the same times, and fills up what He had before failed to say. Nor must we look for order in the Apocalypse; but we must follow the meaning of those things which are prophesied.[14]

If a coming earthly millennium is not a biblical teaching, then why do so many people think they see it throughout the prophecies of the Old and New Testaments? In the opinion of this author, millenarianism is the result of an ignorance of Orthodox hermeneutics; more specifically, it is an inability to interpret the Old Testament in general—and apocalyptic literature in particular—in the light of the gospel of Christ. For instance: Dispensationalists seize upon passages like Zechariah 14:16–19, which describes the nations from all four corners of the earth coming to celebrate the Feast of Tabernacles in Jerusalem during the messianic age, and envision Gentiles performing a pilgrimage to Jerusalem. As dispensationalists can find no historical precedent for such a thing during the Church age, they figure this must happen sometime after Christ returns—thus the need for an earthly millennium.

The Orthodox understanding of such a passage is far different. The Feast of Tabernacles was originally a seven-day harvest festival (Deut. 16:13–17), and is probably the oldest feast in Judaism (see Judg. 21:19; 1 Sam. 1:3). The Law was publicly read and on the seventh day sacrifices were offered, meaning the Covenant was renewed with the people (see Neh. 8:13–18). Christians have traditionally interpreted this passage in Zechariah as meaning that God would in the messianic age include, or "harvest," all the Gentiles of the earth in a renewed covenant. In this New Covenant, the Word of the Lord would be proclaimed to the nations and the God of Israel would be acknowledged Lord throughout the earth—which is precisely what happened

---

13 Stars often symbolize angels in the Bible (see Job 38:7), as well as in apocryphal writings like 1 Enoch: "These are of the number of the stars of heaven which have transgressed the commandment of the Lord, and are bound here till ten thousand years, the time entailed by their sins, are consummated" (1 Enoch 21:6).

14 Victorinus of Petau, *Commentary on the Apocalypse*, 7:2.

after Pentecost, when the Apostolic Church began including Gentiles from all corners of the world in the New Covenant.

In another Old Testament passage, Amos 9:11, 12, there is a similar prophecy concerning the rebuilding of "the tabernacle of David" (the Davidic kingdom) and the Gentiles seeking the Lord. The Apostle James interprets this as the Gentiles coming into the Church (Acts 15:16, 17), and the Orthodox Church has for two thousand years followed suit. Again, dispensationalists are at a loss as to how this Old Testament passage could possibly be interpreted as being fulfilled in the Church and thus manufacture a millennium for the purpose.

As a result of this inability to see such prophecies fulfilled in the gospel, due in part to a nonspiritual method of reading the Bible, an earthly millennium is artificially created whereby these prophecies can find a literal fulfillment. Thus the millennium becomes a dumping ground for all the "unfulfilled" prophecies that, according to the dispensationalist system, don't seem to fit into the New Testament purview.

Such, for example, is frequently the case with Ezekiel's vision of the ideal Temple in Ezekiel 40—48. When asked why Christ should build a Temple when He returns—especially in light of the fact that the New Testament is adamant that the Cross has superseded animal sacrifices—the answer inevitably comes back that the Old Testament states such will be the case—and that settles the matter![15] There is absolutely no thought as to why Christ should return in order to build a thousand-year Jewish theocracy based on the very Mosaic Law He had fulfilled at His First Advent.

Obviously, the mission of the Church must be to educate people on how to read the Old Testament from a Christian perspective. In the final analysis, this is the only way of preventing people from fabricating a millennium into which they can dump Scripture passages that they otherwise find inexplicable.

---

15 This ideal Temple described by Ezekiel is supposed to be erected during the reign of the Messiah. Since the Church saw itself as the messianic Kingdom, this messianic Temple was thought to be the Church itself (see 1 Pet. 2:5–8). Indeed, Jesus equated the Temple with His Body (see John 2:19–21). By its participation in Christ, the Church is also the Body of Christ and, by extension, the messianic Temple. In the context of building up the local church at Corinth, Paul asked, "Do you not know that you are the temple of God and that the Spirit of God dwells in you?" (1 Cor. 3:16). The "you" in this passage is plural, meaning that Paul saw the entire Church community as the Temple of God. Paul went even further by declaring that each individual Christian, since he has within himself the Holy Spirit, is a temple (1 Cor. 6:19; 2 Cor. 6:16). It is also interesting that at the inauguration of the Church at Pentecost there were 120 people who trumpeted the gospel with the gift of tongues (Acts 1:15), just as there were 120 priests with trumpets at the inauguration of Solomon's Temple in 2 Chr. 5:12–14.

A New Heaven and a New Earth

We now arrive at the ultimate goal of human existence: eternal life with God. To describe this eternal life with God adequately is not merely difficult, it is quite impossible. The Book of Revelation describes the final union of Christ with the Church in an allegorical fashion, using a variety of different symbols. One of these is the wedding feast of the Lamb (Rev. 19:7–9). This image of God as the Bridegroom and His chosen people as the Bride is common in the Bible (e.g., Is. 50; 54; Eph. 5:32; Rev. 21:9), and it is probably one of the best ways of glimpsing what lies beyond the Day of Judgment.

In the ancient Hebrew world, a couple was betrothed after the proposed marriage was publicly announced. This was a union far more formal than our "engagement," since a betrothed couple was considered legally man and wife (see 2 Cor. 11:2). After the betrothal, there was a long period before the actual marriage. During this interval, if it hadn't already been done, the groom paid the dowry to the father of the bride (see Gen. 34:12). The end of the betrothal period was celebrated with a procession. The bride adorned herself, as brides do today, and awaited the arrival of her husband with the procession. When he came, he was in his best clothes and accompanied by all his friends, who would be singing songs. The groom and his retinue then escorted the bride to his home (Matt. 9:15; 25:1–10). When everyone arrived at the home of the groom, there was a wedding feast lasting around seven days (see the wedding feast of Cana in John 2).

Now consider the parallels to our relationship with God: The wedding of God with His people was announced throughout the Old Testament period. When God took on flesh and dwelt among us (see John 1:14), the betrothal took place; God then became "one flesh" (Gen. 2:24) with humanity in the womb of the Virgin. The dowry given to the Father of the Bride was paid by the Bridegroom on Calvary. Now the betrothal period has arrived when the Church adorns herself with good works (see Rev. 19:8) and awaits the arrival of the Bridegroom at the Second Coming. When the Bridegroom comes, He will be accompanied by all His friends, the hosts of heaven (Matt. 25:31). He will then take His Bride to His home in heaven where the joyous wedding feast of the Lamb takes place. There will be no divorce in this marriage; it will last throughout eternity![16]

It is the last part of this marriage analogy that we are interested in now. What actually happens after the Church is escorted to the home of the Bridegroom? Christ taught that "heaven and earth will pass away" (Matt. 24:35), echoing the Psalmist: "Of old You laid the foundation of the earth, and the

---

16 The above comparison was taken from Hendriksen, *More Than Conquerors,* 179–181.

heavens are the work of Your hands. They will perish, but You will endure; yes, they will all grow old like a garment; like a cloak You will change them, and they will be changed" (Ps. 102:25, 26). The Scriptures teach that the heavens and the earth created "in the beginning," as Genesis puts it, will pass away. They "will be changed," and a new heaven and a new earth will come into existence, as recorded in the final two chapters of the Book of Revelation.

Isaiah says, "For behold, I create new heavens and a new earth; and the former shall not be remembered or come to mind" (Is. 65:17). The old creation will not be obliterated, however, but transfigured even as we are being transfigured. Paul says that "if anyone is in Christ, he is a new [Gr. *kainos*] creation; old things have passed away; behold, all things have become new" (2 Cor. 5:17; compare Gal. 6:15; Eph. 4:24). The word *kainos* is the same one used in Revelation 21:1 of the "new" heavens and the "new" earth. *Kainos* means "new" in the sense of having a different character—as opposed to the Greek word *neos,* which means "new" in the sense of a replacement. Thus the heavens and earth, as well as ourselves, are renewed—not replaced, as when we get a new car to replace our old one. God loves His creation, and doesn't plan on replacing it with a newer model.

By stating that we are now new creations in 2 Corinthians 5:17, Paul in no way implies that we were destroyed and then totally recreated. Rather, we were spiritually transfigured, totally changed while yet remaining the same person for whom Christ died on the Cross. So will it be for the whole of the old creation. As St. Gregory Palamas (1296–1359) wrote, "The world will not lapse entirely into non-being but, like our bodies and in a manner analogous to what will happen to us, it will be changed by the power of the Holy Spirit, being dissolved and transformed into something more divine." [17]

God didn't create the universe only to destroy it. It is important for Orthodox Christians to understand that the Fifth Ecumenical Council (A.D. 553), in condemning the errors of the Origenists, solemnly and specifically condemned a false teaching that asserted the final destruction of matter.[18] The creation has been redeemed in Christ as well, and it will also "be delivered from the bondage of corruption into the glorious liberty of the children of God" (Rom. 8:21).

---

17 Gregory Palamas, *Topics of Natural and Theological Science and on the Moral and Ascetic Life,* 2. *The Philokalia,* Vol. IV, 346–347.
18 The Fifteen Anathemas Against Origen condemns, in anathema 11, "anyone [who] shall say that the future judgment signifies the destruction of the body and that the end of the story will be an immaterial *psusis* [an unknown Greek word which may have been invented by the Origenists], and that thereafter there will no longer be any matter, but only spirit [Gr. *nous*]: let him be anathema."

The Apostle Peter describes the transfiguration of creation like this:

But the heavens and the earth which are now preserved by the same word, are reserved for fire until the day of judgment and perdition [i.e. destruction] of ungodly men. . . . But the day of the Lord will come as a thief in the night, in which the heavens will pass away with a great noise, and the elements will melt with fervent heat; both the earth and the works that are in it will be burned up. Therefore, since all these things will be dissolved, what manner of persons ought you to be in holy conduct and godliness, looking for and hastening the coming of the day of God, because of which the heavens will be dissolved, being on fire, and the elements will melt with fervent heat? Nevertheless we, according to His promise, look for new heavens and a new earth in which righteousness dwells. (2 Pet. 3:7–13)

The alleged experts on prophecy frequently distort even this aspect of our hope in Christ, seeing the "passing away" of the old creation "by fire" as a total annihilation. They don't seem to appreciate the fact that Scripture often speaks of fire as a cleansing agent, able to renew something to a state of purity (e.g., 1 Cor. 3:11–15; Rev. 3:18; etc.). In fact, many of them even go so far as to characterize the "great noise," the heat, and the "dissolving" of the old creation in terms of the destruction of the old creation by an atomic explosion. In other words, God is going to blow away the universe in a nuclear blast!

Such an idea is simply contrary to the message of the Bible. Peter, in the same passage that describes the heavens being "dissolved," also speaks of when the world "perished" in the Flood (2 Pet. 3:5, 6); yet clearly God did not obliterate the earth at the Flood, but renewed it. Instead of interpreting Scripture in the light of Albert Einstein and the new physics, we need to learn to interpret it according to the Church Fathers and the Ecumenical Councils—that is, according to the historic Christian Faith.

In the late second century, Irenaeus of Lyons explicitly stated that the essence of this world will not be annihilated, since it is the creation of God, who "saw everything that He had made, and indeed it was very good" (Gen. 1:31). Rather, it is the present form of the fallen creation that will be changed:

For neither is the substance nor the essence of the Creation annihilated (for faithful and true is He who has established it), but "the fashion of the world passeth away" (1 Cor 7:31); that is, those things among which transgression has occurred, since Man has grown old in them. And therefore this [present] fashion has been formed temporary, God foreknowing all things; . . . But when this [present] fashion [of things] passes away, and Man has been renewed, and flourishes in an incorruptible state, so as to preclude the possibility of becoming old, [then] there shall be the new heaven and the new earth, in which the new Man shall remain [continually], always holding fresh converse with God.[19]

Consider also how the following Church Father, Ephrem the Syrian, wrote about the new heavens and new earth in his *Hymns on Paradise*, composed during his early period (*ca.* A.D. 306–337). To the refrain of, "Blessed is He who, in His Paradise, gives joy to our gloom," Ephrem poetically describes the renewed creation:

> In the world there is struggle,
>   in Eden, a crown of glory.
> At our resurrection
>   both earth and heaven will God renew,
> liberating all creatures,
>   granting them paschal [Easter] joy along with us.
> Upon our mother Earth, along with us,
>   did He lay disgrace
> when He placed on her, with the sinner, the curse;
>   so, together with the just, will He bless her too;
> this nursing mother, along with her children,
>   shall He who is Good renew.[20]

Around A.D. 350, Cyril of Jerusalem, commenting on Matthew 24:29 (where the Lord describes how the sun, the moon, and the stars would fall from the sky), wrote:

> Let us not sorrow, as if we alone died; the stars also shall die; but perhaps rise again. And the Lord rolls up the heavens, not that He may destroy them, but that He may raise them up again more beautiful.[21]

Similarly, Cyril of Alexandria, Patriarch from A.D. 412 to 444, explained this transformation of creation as follows:

> Christ, therefore, will come not secretly nor obscurely, but as God and Lord, in glory such as becometh Deity; and will transform all things for the better. For He will renew creation, and refashion the nature of man to that which it was at the beginning.[22]

St. John of Damascus (675–749), in his classic *Exposition of the Orthodox Faith,* specifically repudiated any notion that creation would be destroyed: "Nevertheless, the heavens will not be utterly destroyed. For they will wax old and be wound round as a covering, and will be changed, and there will be a new heaven and a new earth." [23] Similarly, in the early eleventh century,

---

19 Irenaeus, *Heresies*, 5:36:1.
20 Ephrem the Syrian, *Hymns on Paradise*, 9:1.
21 Cyril of Jerusalem, *Catechetical Lectures*, 15:3.
22 Cyril of Alexandria, *Commentary on the Gospel of St. Luke*, Homily 139.
23 John of Damascus, *Exposition of the Orthodox Faith*, Book 2:6.

St. Symeon the New Theologian, in his *Ethical Discourses,* described what
he understood the ancient tradition to be concerning the transformation of
the creation. After citing 2 Peter 3:10, he asks:

> How, then, are all things to be dissolved? In just the way that a copper
> vessel, when it has grown old and become quite spoiled and useless on
> account of rust, is taken by the craftsman and put in the fire to be re-forged
> by him and formed again as new. In the same way, creation, too, after hav-
> ing grown old and been spoiled by our sins, is dissolved in fire by the
> Maker of all, and then forged anew and transmuted, and becomes incom-
> parably brighter and newer than the world which we see now.[24]

St. Symeon asserts that, like man himself, creation too will become spiritual and incorruptible (see 1 Cor. 15:43, 44; Rom. 8:19–22). He repeatedly
states that "creation will not return to what it was created in the beginning,"
that is, "not become what it was before, material and perceptible, but be
transformed in re-birth into an immaterial, spiritual dwelling place, beyond
any perception of the senses." [25] As creation fell with man, so shall it be
renewed with him to bask in "the glory and splendor of the unapproachable
and infinite light" of the Trinity:

> All creation, too, once made new, will become spiritual, and together with
> paradise will be transformed into an immaterial, unchanging, eternal, and
> intelligible dwelling place. .... All things are beyond speech, transcend
> thought, save only that they are spiritual and divine, joined to the intelli-
> gible world, and comprise another, intellectual paradise and heavenly Jerusa-
> lem, made like and united to the angelic world, the inviolable inheritance
> of the sons of God.[26]

St. Symeon's description of the Kingdom as "immaterial," "unchang-
ing," and "eternal" raises some intriguing questions. In particular, if God is
changeless, the "same yesterday, today, and forever" (Heb. 13:8), and if Christ
will hand over the kingdom to the Father so that "God may be all in all"
(1 Cor. 15:28), does this imply our eternal destiny will be a sort of static
existence?

St. Maximus the Confessor (580–662) once pondered this profound question, comparing the instability of nature to the immutability of Providence
(i.e., God) and what their ultimate union might mean in the age to come:

> The world is a finite place and possesses but limited stability. Time is cir-
> cumscribed movement. It follows that the movement of living things is

---

24 Symeon the New Theologian, *First Ethical Discourse,* 4. Taken from a translation of
Symeon's *Ethical Discourses* entitled, *On the Mystical Life,* Vol. 1: The Church and the
Last Things. Alexander Golitzin, trans. (Crestwood, NY: St. Vladimir's Seminary, 1995), p. 36.

25 Symeon the New Theologian, *First Ethical Discourse,* 5. *On the Mystical Life,* 38–39.

26 Ibid., 41.

subject to change. When nature passes beyond place and time, actively and inwardly . . . it is united directly with providence, and finds in providence a principle which is by nature simple, stable, without limitation and thus completely without movement. . . . When nature has come to exist in God through the essential unity of Him in whom it was created, it will possess an ever-moving stability and a stable and changeless form of movement generated eternally round that which is one, unique and always the same.[27]

Since the created can never be fully like the uncreated, this means that we can never fully be "changeless" like God. St. Maximus therefore concludes that creation will continue to "move," that is, continue to grow and change, but it will be a movement "in God," so it will be "an ever-moving stability."

The dynamic quality of our lives in the age to come is described by the Fathers as a constant growth in holiness, an infinite ascent from grace to grace. St. Gregory of Nyssa in the fourth century described this as an unlimited movement toward the good motivated by unbounded love:

There is no limit to the operation of love, since the beautiful has no limit, so that love might cease with the limit of the beautiful. The beautiful is limited only by its opposite. But whatever by its nature cannot admit anything worse will proceed towards the limitless and unbounded good.[28]

St. Gregory of Sinai (1265–1346) writes that "in the life to come the angels and saints ever increase in gifts of grace and never abate their longing for further blessings. No lapse or veering from virtue to vice takes place in that life." [29] Therefore, if we harbor any childish notions of idly loitering on white clouds and strumming harps for all eternity, we must discard them immediately. Nor are we to think of the Kingdom as merely a static contemplation of God. Heaven will be dynamic and yet stable, for we will be ever moving in grace toward divinity.

It is at this point that the marriage metaphor of our eternal union examined earlier becomes especially poignant: at the consummation of this age, the Church is to become "one flesh" (see Gen. 2:24) with the Bridegroom's deified flesh.[30] The Bible in several places describes in beautiful terms the love that ought to exist between a husband and a wife. After characterizing

---

27 Maximus the Confessor, *Various Texts on Theology, the Divine Economy, and Virtue and Vice*, 5:47, 48. *The Philokalia*, Vol. II, 272.

28 Gregory of Nyssa, *On the Soul and the Resurrection*, Catharine Roth, trans. (Crestwood, NY: St. Vladimir's Seminary, 1993), 81.

29 Gregory of Sinai, *On Commandments and Doctrines: One Hundred and Thirty-Seven Texts*, 54. *The Philokalia*, Vol. IV, 222.

30 This idea of our becoming "one flesh" with Christ's deified flesh in the age to come is anticipated each time we partake of Holy Communion, when we partake of the Body and Blood of Christ. Thus in communion we experience a foretaste of the marital union that will occur at the Second Coming.

the relationship of Christ to the Church as being like a marital relationship, Paul writes: "Nevertheless let each one of you in particular so love his own wife as himself, and let the wife see that she respects her husband" (Eph. 5:33).

Imagine what great love is ours if Christ, the Church's divine Husband, loves us "as himself"! Yet we know that such a love is ours from the lips of the Savior Himself, when He prayed to His Father "that the love with which You loved Me may be in them, and I in them" (John 17:26). Even now we live in this divine love, but when the fullness of the Kingdom arrives we will experience it in all its fullness, a love unspeakable and unbreakable (Rom. 8:38, 39). The vow "till death do us part" in this marriage will be not only meaningless, but absurd—for there will be no death to cruelly convert love into grief.

The truth of the Kingdom that our Lord has in store for us is beyond mortal speech. The Apostle Paul was given a vision of heaven and "heard inexpressible words, which it is not lawful for a man to utter" (2 Cor. 12:4). One is reminded of a comment by St. Maximus the Confessor: "Perfect silence alone proclaims Him, and total and transcendent unknowing brings us into His presence." [31]

No doubt Paul spent much time pondering his vision of heaven. Perhaps this led Paul, while commenting on our salvation, to paraphrase Isaiah in the following manner: "Eye has not seen, nor ear heard, nor have entered into the heart of man the things which God has prepared for those who love Him" (1 Cor. 2:9; compare Is. 64:4).

Sometimes people fall into thinking of the corrupt world around us as "reality" and the Kingdom to come as "fantasy," as pie-in-the-sky-when-you-die. If anything, the reverse is true. In this world our perception of the full scope of reality is clouded and distorted. In many ways, we live out our lives in a fantasy. As Paul observed, "For now we see in a mirror, dimly, but then [when we finally reach spiritual maturity in heaven] face to face. Now I know in part, but then I shall know just as I also am known" (1 Cor. 13:12). When the Kingdom is fully manifested at the Lord's coming, we will be able to perceive reality much more clearly than we do now.

Since our spiritual perception is so limited and immature in the here and now, any description of the coming Kingdom of our Lord tends toward vain speculation. Like St. Paul, we must declare the Kingdom to be inexpressible. We can only say that the Kingdom—though even now within us (Luke 17:21)—is yet to come. Anything more is best expressed in silence.

---

31 Maximus the Confessor, *Various Texts on Theology, the Divine Economy, and Virtue and Vice*, 5:43. *The Philokalia*, Vol. II, 271.

Chapter Sixteen

Apocalypse Now! . . .
Or Maybe Next Year

Therefore be patient, brethren, until the coming of the Lord. See how the farmer waits for the precious fruit of the earth, waiting patiently for it until it receives the early and latter rain. You also be patient. Establish your hearts, for the coming of the Lord is at hand.
—James 5:7, 8

From my understanding of biblical prophecies, I'm convinced that the Lord is coming for His Church before the end of 1981. I could be wrong, but it's a deep conviction in my heart, and all my plans are predicated upon that belief.
—Chuck Smith, *Future Survival* (1978)

A S THE ABOVE QUOTATION SHOWS, Chuck Smith of Calvary Chapel in Costa Mesa, California, was convinced that the Lord would come to rapture the Church in 1981. And because he was head of one of the largest churches in America, his conviction was influential in the lives of the many who followed him. Smith arrived at his 1981 date as a result of Hal Lindsey's reasoning concerning the parable of the fig tree, the rebirth of Israel in 1948, the forty-year generation that would "by no means pass away," and so forth. If the Lord was to return around 1988, as Lindsey intimated, then the rapture should occur seven years before, in 1981.

Obviously, 1981 came and went with no rapture. To his credit, however, Chuck Smith learned from the experience. Though he still believes in the imminence of Christ's return—which is perfectly acceptable—and that these are the times of the end, Smith now admits he was rash to set a date for the Lord's return. Date setting, he now says, is wrong.[1]

---

1   Alnor, *Soothsayers,* 41.

Doomsday Delayed

Of course, Smith has not been alone in setting dates for Christ's return. Another unfortunate instance involved Edgar Whisenant, who in the 1980s published a 58-page book entitled *88 Reasons Why the Rapture Will Be in 1988*. This former NASA rocket engineer predicted the rapture for September 11, 12, or 13, 1988. "It was all supposed to happen in Little Rock [Arkansas] . . . just before the disaster of nuclear war." [2] The tenor of the book can be gauged from reason number 16: 1988 is the year based on the fact that Adam was created on a Friday in 3975 B.C. at the age of thirty. [3]

This book, which reportedly sold 4.5 million copies, prompted some to put their pets to sleep, sell all their earthly possessions, and camp out on hilltops waiting for Christ's return. They had placed all their hopes and dreams on a coming thousand-year reign of Christ on earth, the so-called millennium. After the predicted September, 1988, date came and went, Whisenant admitted his error—and then "corrected" his prophetic timetable, setting the new date for 1989. [4] Editions of *The Final Shout: Rapture Report 1989* have continued to be reprinted every year since 1989, with only the dates being changed.

Similarly, Harold Camping's best-seller *1994?*, which picked September, 1994, as doomsday, sold fifty thousand copies by early 1993. The *Bookstore Journal* revealed that *1994?* was the fourth bestselling book on prophecy during February, 1993. [5] Harold Camping, though, is not the only one oblivious to the truism that God does not give us prophecy to enable us to prophesy. More recently, the likes of Pat Robertson, James McKeever, Grant Jeffrey, Marvin Byers, Robert Van Kampen, and Jack Van Impe have all peered through their Bible telescopes and have pointed to the year 2000.

However, the ultimate date setter has to be Charles Taylor, who started his career in Bible prophecy as a teenager in 1932. In the past few decades, he has pointed to September 6, 1975 (the Jewish Feast of Trumpets), 1976, 1980, 1981, 1982, 1983, 1985, 1986, 1987, 1988, 1989 . . . well, the reader gets the picture.

A more recent doomsday fad was the "year of jubilee." The jubilee year is based on a law found in Leviticus 25:8–17, 29–31. Every fiftieth year in ancient Israel was supposed to be a special year wherein liberty was proclaimed to all Israelites in bondage to their countrymen. Also, ancestral land was supposed to be returned to those who had been forced to sell it due to

---

2   Chandler, *Doomsday*, 273.
3   Ibid.
4   Alnor, *Soothsayers*, 15.
5   Oropeza, *99 Reasons*, 12.

poverty. The jubilee year was a time when the land was allowed to remain fallow, and people were to eat simple food either already in storage or that grew naturally on the land.

Many prophecy buffs, particularly within the charismatic movement, picked up on this jubilee theme as 1998 approached. They pointed out that Israel became a nation in 1948, and that 1998 represented Israel's fiftieth year as a nation. The year 1998 was therefore Israel's jubilee year, a prophetically significant year of release, recovery, and restitution. God was therefore expected to rapture the Church in 1998, beginning the process of reclaiming the earth for the millennium. This jubilee message was trumpeted without end on television via the Trinity Broadcasting Network (TBN), the main disseminator of the charismatic message.

Of course, 1998 has come and gone, and the prognosticators of the end have already moved on to the next prophetically "significant" year: the year 2000. In particular, many are fixated upon the Y2K (Year 2000) problem, which posits a massive computer failure for New Year's Day of the year 2000. It is naturally too much to expect that the coincidence of the dawn of a new millennium and the possible technological crash of Western civilization would simply be ignored by the Armageddon crowd. As might be expected, many of them have happily infused the situation with a massive dose of apocalypticism, busily warning the world of its impending demise while they stockpile provisions, survival gear, and—weapons. The stockpiling of weapons has especially alarmed the FBI, which still vividly recalls the tragedy of the Branch Davidian doomsday cult in Waco, Texas. A special task force has been set up by the federal agency that is closely monitoring what it considers to be "high-risk" sects, meaning groups that it believes might be inclined to "help" the apocalypse along in anticipation of the Second Coming.

When Christ Will Return

Our Lord expressly ruled out speculating on the date for His return and the end of the age. He said, "But of that day and hour no one knows, not even the angels of heaven, but My Father only" (Matt. 24:36). The Lord is even more emphatic in Mark 13:32–37:

> But of that day and hour no one knows, not even the angels in heaven, nor the Son, but only the Father. Take heed, watch and pray; for you do not know when the time [Gr. *kairos*] is. It is like a man going to a far country, who left his house and gave authority to his servants, and to each his work, and commanded the doorkeeper to watch. Watch therefore, for you do not know when the master of the house is coming—in the evening, at midnight, at the crowing of the rooster, or in the morning—lest, coming suddenly, he find you sleeping. And what I say to you, I say to all: Watch!

In Mark 13:33, note that the "time" when the Lord returns cannot be known. The word "time" translates the Greek word *kairos*, which can encompass a long period, even centuries (see Rom. 8:18; 2 Cor. 6:2; 2 Tim. 4:3; 1 Pet. 1:10, 11). It could, depending upon the context, also be translated as "era." What Jesus is saying is that we cannot know the particular time period of His return. We cannot even know, for instance, the month or the year of Christ's Second Coming.

The above passage is remarkable in that Jesus says *even He* doesn't know when He will come again! Many Church Fathers, such as St. Athanasius[6] and St. Gregory the Theologian[7] in the fourth century, have interpreted this to mean that in His humanity Jesus was ignorant of the time of His own return, though in His divinity He was omniscient (all-knowing) and knew "that day and hour." This interpretation emphasizes that Christ didn't become just *partly* human, but took on the fullness of our humanity with all its limitations— including human ignorance.[8] St. John Chrysostom at the end of the fourth century makes the pertinent observation that "by saying 'neither the Son' [Jesus] forbids them [His disciples] not only to learn, but even to inquire [of the time of the Second Coming]." [9]

Luke reports Jesus as telling His disciples to "be ready, for the Son of Man is coming at an hour you do not expect" (Luke 12:40). Paul says in relation to Christ's "appearing" (Gr. *epiphaneia*) that He will be manifested "in His own time," implying it won't be a time of our choosing (1 Tim. 6:14, 15).

Ever since our Lord ascended into heaven, the Church has been awaiting His sudden reappearance. In a way, the Ascension and the Second Coming

---

6   Athanasius of Alexandria, *Four Discourses Against the Arians*, 3:46. See The Nicene and Post-Nicene Fathers, second series, Vol. 4 (Peabody, MA: Hendrickson, 1994), p. 419.

7   Gregory Nazianzen, *Theological Orations*, Oration 30 ("The Fourth Theological Oration, Which is the Second Concerning the Son"), 15. See ibid., Vol. 7, p. 315.

8   Another common interpretation of the Fathers was that Jesus actually knew the time of His return, but was deliberately withholding this from the disciples since the information would not have been good for them to know. Starting with Hilary of Poitiers (315–367), Jesus' profession of ignorance concerning the time of His return began to be interpreted as something of a figure of speech. According to Hilary, "nor the Son" in Mark 13:32 meant that it was neither the right time for the Lord to act nor the right time to reveal the imminence of the Parousia to the Apostles (*On the Trinity*, Book 9:58–67). Impressed by Hilary's intricate reasoning and biblical examples of ignorance ascribed both to God and to Christ (e.g., Gen. 18:20, 21; 22:12; Matt. 7:23; 25:12), Augustine of Hippo enthusiastically took up this interpretation (see Augustine's *On the Trinity*, 1:12:23; *Letter 180 to Oceanus*, 3; *On the Psalms*, 6:1).

9   John Chrysostom, *Matthew*, Homily 77:1. Chrysostom is commenting upon a phrase found in some versions of Matt. 24:36, "neither the Son." It is included in the best representatives of the Alexandrian and Western text types, and most scholars consider it original. It is contained in newer translations of the verse, like the RSV, NIV, and NASB.

Icon of the Ascension

are slightly blurred within Orthodoxy. In certain Orthodox icons of the Ascension, it is difficult to tell whether Christ is going up into heaven or is descending from heaven to earth with the entire Church on the ground waiting to receive Him. Indeed, Jesus is even depicted in this icon as He is in the icons of the Last Judgment.[10] Christ, having defeated Satan and ascended into heaven, now rules at the right hand of the Father— yet we are awaiting the full manifestation of this reality, which could happen at any moment. The icon of the Ascension reflects a certain ambiguity in the Church's existence: the Kingdom is in our midst (Luke 17:20, 21), yet we continue to wait for it (Luke 17:23, 24).

Though the scriptures just cited indicating the unknowability of the Second Advent seem straightforward and clear, the oracles of the end are not dissuaded. Like many who see little difference between the Bible and a crystal ball, Edgar Whisenant has asserted on the radio that, though we cannot know "the day or the hour" of His return, we can nevertheless know the week, the month, and the year!

By contrast, we must concur with biblical scholar D. A. Carson when he says that "it is ridiculous quibbling divorced from the context [of Matt. 24:36] to say that though the day and hour remain unknown, we ascertain the year and month."[11] It indeed seems pedantic to argue over such a ludicrous twist on Jesus' words. The idea the Lord wished to convey was a notion common to Judaism at the time our Lord taught His disciples (which, alas, ought to be more common within Christianity today), namely, that it is folly to try to calculate the coming of the Messiah. Examine the following citations from Tractate Sanhedrin (97) in the Talmud:

> Rabbi Shmu'el bar-Nachmani said in the name of Rabbi Yochanan, "May the bones of those who calculate the end [that is, the time of the Messiah's coming] be blasted away! As soon as the time [which they have determined] arrives and the Messiah has not come, they say, 'He will never

---

10 Leonid Ouspensky and Vladimir Lossky, *The Meaning of Icons*, trans. G. E. H. Palmer and E. Kadloubovsky (Crestwood, NY: St. Vladimir's Seminary Press, 1989), 197.

11 Carson, *Matthew*, 508.

come!' Rather, wait for him, as it is written, 'Though he tarry, wait for him' (Habakkuk 2:3)." [12]

This rabbinic citation contains an especially pertinent observation: As in the story of the boy who repeatedly cried "wolf," people will stop believing in Christ's Second Coming after so many false alarms. Those who continually predict the Second Coming may unwittingly be helping to fulfill 2 Peter 3:3, 4, which states that in the last days scoffers will come, asking, "Where is the promise of His coming? For since the fathers fell asleep, all things continue as they were from the beginning of creation."

Another citation from the Talmud reads:

> Whenever Rabbi Zera' came upon scholars trying [to calculate when the Messiah would arrive], he would say to them, "It has been taught that three things come when the mind is diverted: the Messiah, finding a lost article, and a scorpion. So don't postpone his coming by thinking about it!" [13]

Remember Jesus' parable of the wicked servant in Matthew 24:45–51? The evil servant believes the master is delaying His coming, and so the servant begins to abuse his fellow servants and act in a reprobate manner. Jesus' point is that the master, Jesus Himself, will come at a time when the evil servant is not expecting Him and punish that servant. Referring to Edgar Whisenant's prediction of Christ's return in September, 1988, B. J. Oropeza remarks on the parable of the evil servant, "If we interposed Whisenant's date into the parable, couldn't the servant continue beating his fellow servants and getting drunk all the way until September 1988 without having to worry about his master dropping in unexpectedly?" [14] The point is obviously that even picking the month and year is in defiance of what Jesus taught us.

Blessed Augustine of Hippo (354–430) has sage counsel for those tempted to calculate the Second Coming:

> It is in vain . . . that we try to reckon and put a limit to the number of years that remain for this world, since we hear from the mouth of the Truth that it is not for us to know this. And yet some have asserted that 400, 500, or as much as 1,000 years may be completed between the Lord's ascension and His final coming. But to show how each of them supports his opinion would take too long; and in any case it is unnecessary, for they make use of human conjectures, and quote no decisive evidence from the authority of canonical Scripture. [15]

---

12 Cited by David Stern, *Jewish New Testament Commentary* (Clarksville, MD: Jewish New Testament Publications, 1992), p. 76.

13 Ibid.

14 Oropeza, *99 Reasons,* 40.

15 Augustine of Hippo, *City of God*, Book 18, Chapter 53.

Augustine goes on to command those who engage in such calculations to give their fingers a rest from counting the number of years left to mankind. He then cites the last words our Lord uttered before ascending to the Father, that it is not for us "to know times or seasons which the Father has put in His own authority" (Acts 1:7).

Those who presume to have special "inside" information on the mystery of Christ's Second Coming bear a certain resemblance to the Gnostics of the early Church, who also believed they had a special knowledge of the unspeakable mysteries of God. What Irenaeus of Lyons said to the Gnostics in the second century may equally be said to those today who are convinced they know the time of the Lord's return:

> The Gnostics presumptuously assume acquaintance with the unspeakable mysteries of God. Remember that even the Lord, the very Son of God, allowed that the Father alone knows the very day and hour of judgment. . . . If then the Son was not ashamed to ascribe the knowledge of that day to the Father only, but declared what was true regarding the matter, neither let us be ashamed to reserve for God those enigmatic questions which come our way.[16]

The mystery of Christ's Second Coming is not to be figured out, but is to be reverently reserved for God alone. Ultimately, the attempt to unlock the mystery of Christ's return is an attempt to lower God to our level, to make God as predictable as anything else in the natural world. Such a "god" is no God at all, but an idol of our own imagining. The true and living God does not come on a schedule like a bus.

To speculate on the date of the Second Coming, even if it be only the year, is to seek to wrest a secret from God that Jesus explicitly states only the Father possesses. Therefore, speculating on the timing of our Lord's return is arrogance bordering on blasphemy. As Bible commentator William Barclay explains, "It is not any man's duty to speculate; it is his duty to prepare himself, and to watch."[17] Barclay's point is well taken. The aim of Jesus' discourses on the Second Coming was always to one end: not to give us clues to date His return, but to exhort us to be prepared.

The Signs of the Times

Are there then no signs by which we can know when the time is at least near? In fact, there are some. First, though, let's review the overall teaching of the Church on this matter.

---

16 Irenaeus, *Heresies*, 2:27:6.
17 William Barclay, *The Gospel of Matthew*, rev. ed., Vol. 2 (Philadelphia: The Westminster Press, 1975), 315.

When our Lord came at His First Advent, He defeated Satan in fulfill-ment of Old Testament prophecies (e.g., Gen. 3:15). Satan is now "bound" and his power limited so the gospel can be spread; people are free either to accept it or to reject it of their own free will. We are consequently living in the millennium and Christ is reigning at the right hand of the Father.[18] The millennium will end with Satan's release and the Tribulation.

Scripture indicates that the Church, the fulfillment of Israel, will suffer persecution and tribulation as long as it is in the world (John 15:20; 16:33; Acts 14:22; Rom. 5:3; 1 Thess. 3:3; Rev. 1:9; 2:10). This will get worse until it culminates in the Great Tribulation, when Satan will be released for a short while to empower the Antichrist (2 Thess. 2:9; Rev. 20:3). Our Lord, how-ever, will protect the Church throughout the coming hardship and persecu-tion (John 17:15; 1 Thess. 1:10; Rev. 20:9).

At the end of this Tribulation, our Lord will come suddenly and in a visible manner. There will be a resurrection of the righteous and a catching up of the saints still living. The Lord will then come bodily in great glory accompanied by His saints and the hosts of heaven. Upon His return, Christ will cast Satan, the Antichrist, and the false prophet into the lake of fire. Simultaneously, there will be the "resurrection of condemnation" followed by the general judgment, which will forever separate the righteous from the wicked. After the righteous have received their rewards and the wicked their condemnation, Death and Hades will be destroyed and a new heaven and a new earth will be brought forth. This will be a transfiguration of the old creation, cleansed by fire. Then the Kingdom promised by our Lord and de-picted in Revelation 21 and 22 will become fully manifest, and the Church will enter eternity.

In connection with this general teaching, there are certain signs that point to the imminent time of Christ's return. One is an extraordinary increase in evil. The Apostle Paul wrote in 2 Timothy 3:1–5:

> But know this, that in the last days perilous times will come: for men will be lovers of themselves, lovers of money, boasters, proud, blasphemers, disobedient to parents, unthankful, unholy, unloving, unforgiving, slander-ers, without self-control, brutal, despisers of good, traitors, headstrong, haughty, lovers of pleasure rather than lovers of God, having a form of godliness but denying its power. And from such people turn away! (2 Tim. 3:1–5)[19]

---

18 See Dan. 7:13; Mark 16:19; Acts 7:56; Rom. 8:34; Eph. 1:20; Col. 3:1; Heb. 1:3, 13; 8:1; 10:12; 12:2; 1 Pet. 3:22.

19 Some argue that Paul was not speaking of a future reality, but was describing the situation as it existed when he wrote. Thus in v. 5 Paul tells Timothy, "And from such people turn away!" St. John Chrysostom comments on v. 5: "'From such turn away, [Paul] says [to

This certainly describes our own times fairly well—but then it also describes much of the world in the midst of the Middle Ages. While we may in truth be witnessing the fulfillment of this scenario in our own days, we must be prudent when contemplating the prophecy. Are our own times really worse than former eras? Is the disintegration of the moral order truly universal, or is it localized to certain Western societies that have bought into the philosophy of secularism? Such an evaluation of our world must be circumspect and take into account all of human history.[20]

Related to the sign of increasing evil is the sign that apostasy will be general before the Second Coming. Jesus asked, "Nevertheless, when the Son of Man comes, will He really find faith on the earth?" (Luke 18:8). Actually, the Greek reads *tes pistin*, which could be translated "the Faith." [21] When the Lord comes, it will be at a time when the genuine Christian Faith will be hard to find.

Many Orthodox in fact do believe we are witnessing the final apostasy from the Faith. The late Fr. Seraphim Rose was convinced we are seeing the advent of this final apostasy. In his book *Orthodoxy and the Religion of the Future*, he gave an insightful evaluation of the religious currents in our society and how these are affecting the Church. Though written in the 1970s, his critique of the developing non-Christian religious "consciousness" of our modern Western world is as valid today as when it was first written.

As the end draws near, many false christs will arise performing impressive signs and wonders (Matt. 24:24; Mark 13:22), saying, "I am the Christ" (Matt. 24:5). The Lord warns us not to follow after those who claim that

---

Timothy]. But how is this, if men are to be so 'in the latter times'? There were probably then such, in some degree at least, though not to the same excess. But, in truth, through him he warns them all to turn away from such characters." *Homilies on 2 Timothy*, Homily 8 on 2 Timothy 3:5.

20 For a good book from an Orthodox perspective arguing that are we seeing the apostasy and lawlessness predicted by Paul for the end times, see Fr. Seraphim Rose, *Nihilism: The Root of the Revolution of the Modern Age* (Forestville, CA: Fr. Seraphim Rose Foundation, 1994). Fr. Seraphim argues that civilization is going through four stages of the nihilist dialectic: liberalism, realism, vitalism, and anarchy (the "nihilism of destruction"). Writing in the early '60s, Fr. Seraphim believed we are on the path to the lawlessness described in Scripture for the end of human history.

21 Modern translations, however, don't translate Luke 18:8 this way. I. Howard Marshall gives what is probably the standard thought on the phrase: "The use of *pistis* with the article is unusual. It could refer to acceptance of Jesus and his message, which could be a developed Christian usage . . . , but more probably it signifies faithfulness, expressed in unfailing prayer. The presence of the article is an Aramaism . . . The question as a whole presupposes a time of tribulation for the disciples in which they may be tempted to give up faith because their prayers are not answered . . ." *Commentary on Luke*, The New International Greek Testament Commentary (Grand Rapids: Eerdmans, 1978), 676.

Christ is already present (Matt. 24:23). False prophets will be ubiquitous and speak lies in the name of God, seeking to lead us astray (Matt. 24:11, 24; Mark 13:22; 2 Pet. 2:1). As a result of widespread apostasy and spiritual deception, false religions and "spirituality" will flourish while Christianity will be marginalized for its exclusive claims to the truth.

Paul also speaks of this apostasy: "Let no one deceive you by any means; for that Day will not come unless the falling away comes first and the man of sin is revealed, the son of perdition" (2 Thess. 2:3). Here the coming apostasy is directly linked to the appearance of the Antichrist.

In 2 Thessalonians 2:3 cited above, it is stated that the time before the Lord's return will see the rise of the Antichrist who will promote this apostasy from Christ. We saw in our chapter on the Antichrist that he will be a world leader who will be the sum of all previous persecuting despots, like Nero and Antiochus Epiphanes. He will proclaim himself God and demand worship, forcing true Christians underground.

During the reign of the Antichrist, the two witnesses described in Revelation 11:3–12 will appear, prophesying and performing miracles. They will confront the Antichrist with the truth, exposing his lies to all. These two witnesses will be martyred, resurrected, and assumed into heaven. Orthodox Tradition, as we learned in Chapter 12, has strongly identified these two witnesses as Enoch and Elijah, who were both taken into heaven without suffering death. Scripture is explicit about the coming of Elijah: Malachi prophesied, "Behold, I will send you Elijah the prophet before the coming of the great and dreadful day of the Lord" (Mal. 4:5). In Matthew 17:11, Jesus said to His disciples, "Indeed, Elijah is coming first and will restore all things." The Fathers of the Church consistently tell us that the second witness is to be Enoch.

These signs may be a bit too vague to satisfy the curiosity of many. They want to know *when* Christ will return! "What good are signs that don't tell us when He's coming?" many might wonder.

It would seem that the vagueness of the signs of the end has two purposes. The first is to instill a vigilance so that we are always prepared for the ever-present possibility of the coming of the Lord and the final judgment. By contemplating the possible nearness of the Lord's return, we are motivated to prepare for this inevitable encounter with Truth by turning toward the truth now.

The second likely reason for the lack of specificity of the signs is to lead us to a prayerful contemplation of the direction our world is heading. Father Michael Pomazansky writes, "However, the unknowability of the time of the Lord should not prevent Christians from reflecting deeply on the course of historical events and discerning in them the *signs* of the approach of the time of the 'last day.' " [22]

Such contemplation of the imminent Second Coming must be approached with a degree of caution, however. According to St. Gregory of Sinai, a great spiritual master of the fourteenth century, the general resurrection, the awesome Second Coming of Christ, eternal torment, and the Kingdom of heaven

> . . . are yet to come and still unmanifest, but are clearly contemplated and recognized by those who have attained complete purity of mind through grace. Let him who approaches this without the light of grace know that he only builds fantasies, and does not contemplate; since, ensnared by the spirit of dreams and fantasies, he is but a dreamer.[23]

This is an important observation. To contemplate such profound and mysterious things as the Second Coming and the Kingdom of heaven requires a spiritual discernment attained only through purity of mind. Only a person enlightened by the grace of the Holy Spirit can hope to explore the final consummation of all things in Christ without lapsing into vain speculation, dreams, and fantasies.

Only those who have purified their hearts through prayer and fasting receive the necessary illumination from God to understand—however dimly— the present flow of historical events. Yet even then God does not reveal the day or the hour of the Lord's return. We can only gratefully accept whatever grace we are given, and leave the rest to God.

---

22 Michael Pomazansky, *Orthodox Dogmatic Theology*, 2nd ed. (Platina, CA: St. Herman of Alaska Brotherhood, 1994), 336. Emphasis in original.

23 Gregory of Sinai, *Texts on Commandments and Dogmas*, 130. E. Kadloubovsky & G. E. H. Palmer, trans., *Writings from the Philokalia on Prayer of the Heart* (London: Faber and Faber, 1992), 70.

Chapter Seventeen

The Joyful Penitent

And now there is waiting for me the prize of victory awarded for a righteous life, the prize which the Lord, the righteous Judge, will give me on that Day—and not only to me, but to all those who wait with love for him to appear.
    —Second Timothy 4:8 (Today's English Version)

Abba Theodore [of Pherme] was asked, "If there was a sudden catastrophe, would you be frightened, abba?" The old man replied, "Even if the heavens and the earth were to collide, Theodore would not be frightened." He had prayed God to take away fear from him and it was because of this that he was questioned.
    —*The Sayings of the Desert Fathers* (fourth century)

IN THE INTRODUCTION, it was stated that the Second Coming of Christ is not a peripheral part of the Christian Faith; rather, it is the goal towards which all of salvation history leads. What role then ought the teaching of Christ's Second Coming to play in the Christian's life?

Let's begin by first stating what the teaching of the Second Coming should not introduce into our lives: *fear*. Though the Fathers call the fear of God "a life-giving medicine" that cleanses the soul of sin, fear of Christ's return and the end of the age is something far different. We must not think that God would allow any evil to befall His people. As Christians, we have placed all our trust in the God who became man in order to redeem us, trampling down our death by His death. In Him we have died, and now our lives are "hidden with Christ in God" (Col. 3:3).

Liberated by the knowledge that God cares for our welfare even more than we do, we are empowered to live a victorious life in Christ. The late

Bishop Gerasimos of Abydos, an Orthodox theologian who spent a lifetime in prayerful meditation upon the Bible, explains:

> A Christian life is required of us, not curiosity about years and times "which the Father has placed under his own authority" (Acts 1:7). We do not live our lives as Christians out of fear that the coming of Christ is near, nor because we hope to gain rewards. We are Christians because we believe in the love of God, and we live a life in Christ out of love, being always ready to receive Him with great anticipation.[1]

The key word here is *love*: a love for God that manifests itself in an authentic Christian life, ever moving away from sin and toward our Savior. Thus contemplation of Christ's return leads Orthodox Christians not to tremble at the horrors of the Tribulation, or to chart road maps of the future, or to set dates, but to repent.

The Lord's last recorded words in the Bible are, "Surely I am coming quickly" (Rev. 22:20). We don't know when the Lord is coming; we do know, however, that He is coming soon and that we must be prepared, having thoroughly repented of our rebellion against God. The Lord could come today. Or He could come a millennium from now. When is not the issue; our readiness is all that matters. If we are prepared, then the Apostle John's exclamation can be ours as well: "Amen. Even so, come, Lord Jesus!" (Rev. 22:20).

When Christ tells us to "watch therefore, for you do not know what hour your Lord is coming" (Matt. 24:42), He doesn't mean we are merely to "watch" world events in the news and try to match these with certain prophecies. The Fathers teach that Christ is commanding us to watch our hearts to guard against evils and passions that can creep in and darken our souls. In each of the three parables on Christ's Second Coming given in Matthew 25, the message is to be vigilant and prepared. The Apostle John delivers the same message even more directly: "And now, little children, abide in Him, that when He appears, we may have confidence and not be ashamed before Him at His coming" (1 John 2:28).

We should be ever mindful of the judgment to help us abide in Christ, to help us always live righteously so we will not "be ashamed before Him at His coming." Thus, in the Saturday Vespers commencing the eighth Sunday before Pascha (Easter), when the Orthodox Church reads the judgment account given in Matthew 25:31–46, the Church sings the following hymn:

> When Thou shalt come, O righteous Judge, to execute just judgement, seated on Thy throne of glory, a river of fire will draw all men amazed before Thy judgement-seat; the powers of heaven will stand beside Thee, and in fear mankind will be judged according to the deeds that each has done. Then

---

1   Gerasimos of Abydos, *At the End of Time*, 8–9.

> spare us, Christ, in Thy compassion, with faith we entreat Thee, and count
> us worthy of Thy blessings with those that are saved.[2]

Similarly, at the same Vespers service, we also sing,

> When we hear Him call the blessed of His Father into the Kingdom, but
> send the sinners to their punishment, who shall endure His fearful condem-
> nation? But, Saviour who alone lovest mankind, King of the ages, before
> the end comes turn me back through repentance and have mercy on me.[3]

We grow in the Christian life by constantly reflecting upon our Lord's
coming in judgment. Contemplating the imminent Second Coming and judgment inspires a greater fervor for prayer, fasting, and all-night vigils. Ilias the
Presbyter wrote in the early twelfth century, "Blessed is the soul that, because it expects its Lord daily, thinks nothing of the day's toil or of the night's,
since He is going to appear in the morning." [4] Evagrius of Pontus (345–400),
while living as a monk in Egypt, is once reported to have said that if you "do
not forget the eternal Judgment, then there will be no fault in your soul." [5]

Sometime between the seventh and ninth centuries, St. Theodoros the
Great Ascetic, a monk of the monastery of St. Sabas near Jerusalem (who
subsequently became bishop of Edessa in Syria), wrote eloquently on the
need to meditate constantly upon our heavenly rewards and upon the "end-
less joy" that awaits us when Christ returns. After describing these rewards,
he advised:

> Let these thoughts dwell with you, sleep with you, arise with you. See that
> you never forget them but, wherever you are, keep them in mind, so that
> evil thoughts may depart and you may be filled with divine solace. Unless
> a soul is strengthened with these thoughts it cannot achieve stillness. For a
> spring which has no water does not deserve its name.[6]

The more we contemplate Christ's glorious Second Advent, the more we
repent. The more we repent, the more the Holy Spirit reveals to us about the
age to come. St. Thalassios, a priest and abbot at a monastery in Libya in the
seventh century, writes:

> The blessings that lie in store for the inheritors of the promise are beyond
> eternity, before all ages, and transcend both intellect and thought. . . .

---

2   Kontakion for the Saturday Vespers commencing Meatfare Sunday. As in the Bible, the
    day begins in the Orthodox Church at sundown of the previous day. See Mother Mary &
    Kallistos Ware, trans., *The Lenten Triodion* (South Canaan, PA: St. Tikhon's Seminary
    Press, 1994), 150.

3   Ibid., 151.

4   Ilias the Presbyter, *Gnomic Anthology*, 4:102. *The Philokalia*, Vol. III, 60.

5   Ward, *Sayings*, 64.

6   Theodoros the Great Ascetic, *A Century of Spiritual Texts*, 59. *The Philokalia*, Vol. II, 25.

According to the degree to which the intellect is stripped of the passions, the Holy Spirit initiates the intellect into the mysteries of the age to be.[7]

Christ has trampled down the evil of the world, thoroughly defeating it through His Cross (Eph. 2:16; Col. 2:14). We but await the full manifestation, the *epiphaneia*, of this victory at His Coming. In the eucharistic *anaphora* of the Orthodox Liturgy, after repeating Jesus' command to His disciples to "do this in remembrance of Me," the priest prays silently:

> Having in remembrance, therefore, this saving commandment and all those things which have come to pass for us: the Cross, the grave, the Resurrection on the third day, the Ascension into heaven, the seating at the right hand, and the second and glorious Advent: [*out loud*] Thine own of Thine own we offer unto Thee, in behalf of all, and for all.

What is so striking about this prayer is that "the second and glorious Advent" is spoken of as a past event. The Second Coming is so certain a reality that we speak of it in the Liturgy as already accomplished! We are certain of the future coming of Christ because, when celebrating the eucharistic Liturgy, we transcend time itself and enter eternity, where past, present, and future coalesce into a single vision of the divine economy. It is from this perspective that we view the Lord's return as an accomplished fact. The imminent Second Coming is therefore just as sure a reality as those redeeming events that have already transpired, and we can consider our salvation as already consummated even though the full manifestation of that salvation is yet to come.

The Second Coming is not only something we are to experience during Sunday worship. Metropolitan Hierotheos of Nafpaktos explains that we not only look for the Kingdom in the future, but we are to live it every day as a present reality:

> We Orthodox are not waiting for the end of history and the end of time, but through living in Christ we are running to meet the end of history and thus already living the life expected after the Second Coming. St. Symeon the New Theologian says that he who has seen the uncreated light [of God] and united with God is not awaiting the Second Coming of the Lord but living it. So the eternal embraces us at every moment of time. Therefore past, present and future are essentially lived in one unbroken unity.[8]

---

7   Thalassios the Libyan, *On Love, Self-Control and Life in accordance with the Intellect*, Century 4:71, 75. *The Philokalia*, Vol. II, 329.

8   Metropolitan Hierotheos of Nafpaktos, *Orthodox Psychotherapy: The Science of the Fathers*, Esther Williams, trans. (Levadia, Greece: Birth of the Theotokos Monastery, 1994), 25.

This present experience of the age to come contributes to the joy, awe, and majesty so characteristic of Orthodox liturgical and spiritual life. Paradoxically, not only repentance, but joy is also a fruit of contemplating Christ's Second Coming. According to the proper interpretation of Scripture, it is not nuclear annihilation, but joy that is at the heart of the Lord's teaching on His eventual return. Jesus described His coming in terms of a wedding feast at which there is great rejoicing for those who have wedding garments (Matt. 22:2–14; 25:1–13; Luke 14:16–24), that is, for those who have prepared themselves through good works for His Coming (see Rev. 19:8). On that Day, He will say to His good and faithful servants, "Well done . . . Enter into *the joy* of your Lord" (Matt. 25:21, 23, emphasis added). Again, after clarifying the Christian teaching on Christ's glorious return, Paul told the Thessalonians, "Rejoice always" (1 Thess. 5:16).

A thousand years ago, St. Peter of Damascus wrote a wonderful discourse on Christian joy and explained how, joyfully looking forward to that Day, the Christian is constantly reminded of the Second Coming of his Lord in everyday occurrences. After repenting of his former life of sin,

> Slowly the man emerges from the tears of distress and from the passions, and enters fully into the state of spiritual joy. Through the things that bring him pleasure, he is made humble and grateful; through trials and temptations his hope in the world to come is consolidated; in both he rejoices, and naturally and spontaneously he loves God and all men as his benefactors. . . . In thunder and lightning we see the day of judgment; in the call of cocks we hear the trumpet that will sound on that day; in the rising of the morning star and the light of the dawn we perceive the appearance of the precious and life-giving Cross (cf. Matt. 24:30); in men's rising from sleep we see a sign of the resurrection of the dead, and in the rising of the sun a token of the second advent of Christ. Some, like the saints caught up in the clouds on the last day (cf. 1 Thess 4:17), we see go forth to greet Him with song, while others, like those who will then be judged, are indifferent and remain asleep. Some we see rejoicing throughout the day in the offering of praise, in contemplation and prayer, and in the other virtues, living in the light of spiritual knowledge, as will the righteous at the second coming; while others we see persisting in the passions and in the darkness of ignorance, as will sinners on that day. . . . May we all be found worthy to inherit that kingdom through His grace and love.[9]

Repentance and rejoicing must be, as it is in the New Testament, the central note of the Church's proclamation of the Second Coming. Yes, we may very well be living in the twilight of the present age; but rather than merely presenting the world a message of impending calamity, we must work harder to spread the Good News of Christ, proclaiming the joy that awaits

---

9   Peter of Damascus, *Twenty-Four Discourses*, 22. *The Philokalia*, Vol. III, 261–263.

those who are ready for His return. Instead of lingering over the expected agonies of the wicked who will be thrown into "outer darkness," we must exhort sinners to repent and join us in joyfully looking forward to the coming salvation.

As we look toward that Day, our one concern as the Church must be to remain faithful, finishing the race as strongly as we began it on the Day of Pentecost so long ago. Over the centuries, the Church has suffered much in the way of persecutions and martyrdoms, enduring unrelenting oppression and debasement in many parts of the world. The Church will yet suffer many things before Christ returns; nevertheless, we must not be ashamed, for we know in whom we have believed and are persuaded that He is able to keep what we commit to Him until that Day (see 2 Tim. 1:12).

In a spirit of both repentance and joy, the Church has for many centuries waited patiently and in faith, praying together each day in the prayer our Lord Himself taught us, "Thy kingdom come . . ." And as joyful penitents, we will continue to wait, to watch, and to pray, until that great Day our Lord told us about indeed comes, and the centuries give way to the ages of ages.

Appendix

The Book of Revelation

A S STATED PREVIOUSLY, the Book of Revelation is not read in the regular liturgical services of the Orthodox Church. The exception is the Saturday night Vigil, when all the New Testament Epistles—including the Book of Revelation—are appointed to be read between Vespers and Matins; however, this service is seldom celebrated anymore. Nevertheless, Orthodox Christians who read Revelation will at once recognize its images, for they have been incorporated wholesale into the Orthodox Liturgy. The incense (Rev. 8:3, 4) and the "thrice holy" (Rev. 4:8) ought to make any Orthodox reader feel right at home.

There is no "official" interpretation of the Book of Revelation in the Church, though certain commentaries, like the one by St. Andrew of Caesarea (written in the fifth century), have greatly influenced Orthodox thought on this inspired book. Rather, the Church has tended only to declare that there are certain doctrines that *are not* to be found in Revelation—in particular, a literal earthly millennium. This is obviously a rather negative stance that permits us considerable freedom to interpret the book in a variety of ways. Below I will suggest an approach to Revelation that allows the reader to interpret the book in an Orthodox manner. I want to stress, though, that it is only one possible approach to this complex book. There is no intention to be dogmatic.

Author and Date of Composition

Revelation itself claims to be written by someone named John (1:1, 4, 9; 21:2; 22:8). Is this John the same person as the Apostle John, who composed the fourth Gospel? The early Church largely believed this to be the case. In fact, the early witness to the apostolic authorship of the book is one of the best in the New Testament: St. Justin Martyr, St. Irenaeus of Lyons, Clement of Alexandria, Origen, Tertullian, and Hippolytus all accepted the apostolic provenance of Revelation. Also witnessing to the widespread acceptance of

Revelation, the Muratorian Canon, a second-century document written in Rome, lists the Revelation of John as among those books received and read in the churches.

The association of Revelation with the millennial fantasies of the Montanist heresy placed the book under a cloud of suspicion during the third century. Dionysius of Alexandria (*d.* 265), a pupil of Origen and one of the great minds of the third-century Church, openly questioned the apostolic origin of the book. Dionysius based his rejection upon the differences he found between the fourth Gospel and Revelation. He noted differences in the character of the writer (e.g., the author of Revelation mentions his name whereas the author of the fourth Gospel does not), differences in thought and style, and linguistic differences. Many contemporary scholars in fact agree with Dionysius that the Greek of Revelation is arguably the worst in the New Testament, breaching more rules of grammar than even a simple schoolboy would have dared to do. This is in sharp contrast to the fourth Gospel.[1]

Eusebius of Caesarea also questioned the apostolic authorship of Revelation, ascribing the book to another John also living in Ephesus. Many others began to agree with Eusebius. Thus it started to be reasoned that all those second-century Christians who thought Revelation was written by the Apostle John were in error, and so the alleged apostolic authorship of Revelation was simply chalked up to an extraordinary case of mistaken identity. St. Cyril of Jerusalem in his *Catechetical Lectures* (A.D. 350) excluded Revelation from the list of canonical books read in the churches.[2] Though Cyril frequently cited John's Gospel and epistles in his *Lectures*, he nowhere alludes to Revelation.

The council of Laodicea (A.D. 360) did not include Revelation among its list of canonical books (Canon 60); nor is it listed among the "venerable

---

1   Eusebius of Caesarea preserves the following from Dionysius of Alexandria: "And furthermore, on the ground of difference in diction, it is possible to prove a distinction between the Gospel and the Epistle on the one hand, and the Revelation on the other. For the former are written not only without actual error as regards the Greek language, but also with the greatest elegance, both in their expressions and in their reasonings, and in the whole structure of their style. They are very far indeed from betraying any barbarism or solecism, or any sort of vulgarism, in their diction. For, as might be presumed, the writer possessed the gift of both kinds of discourse, the Lord having bestowed both these capacities upon him, viz., that of knowledge and that of expression. That the author of the latter, however, saw a revelation, and received knowledge and prophecy, I do not deny. Only I perceive that his dialect and language are not of the exact Greek type, and that he employs barbarous idioms, and in some places also solecisms. These, however, we are under no necessity of seeking out at present. And I would not have any one suppose that I have said these things in the spirit of ridicule; for I have done so only with the purpose of setting right this matter of the dissimilarity subsisting between these writings" (Eusebius, *History*, 7:25:24–27).

2   Cyril of Jerusalem, *Catechetical Lectures*, 4:36.

and sacred books" set forth in Apostolic Canon 85 (fourth century). In the Syrian church, Revelation was excluded from the fifth-century Syriac translation of the Bible known as the Peshitta (though the later sixth-century Philoxenian Version included it).

Today, scholars who reject the Apostle's authorship of Revelation do so largely for the same reasons as Dionysius of Alexandria. However, while Dionysius' observations concerning the fourth Gospel and Revelation are valid as far as they go, they don't necessarily rule out the Apostle John as the author of both books.

The Apostle John is believed to have written the fourth Gospel in Ephesus between A.D. 85 and 94. John was by then an old man, and Orthodox tradition tells us that John had a scribe, a certain Saint Prochorus, to whom he dictated the Gospel. Tradition identifies this Prochorus as one of the seven deacons listed in Acts 6:5. This dictation to Prochorus is depicted in the Orthodox icon of the Apostle John.

Upon close examination, the work of a scribe seems particularly evident in the Gospel. For example, the one who witnessed the crucifixion is distinguished from the actual writer in John 19:35. The same distinction is again made in John 21:24 (". . . and we [Prochorus?] know that his [John's] testimony is true"). The frequent mention of "the Jews" (e.g. John 1:19; 2:18, 20; etc.) also suggests that the fourth Gospel was actually penned by a non-Jew; John, who was a Jew himself, would be less likely to refer to fellow Jews as "the Jews" (though he might have done so for the sake of his Gentile audience).

The use of a scribe would also explain why the Apostle John is identified in the Gospel as the "beloved disciple," instead of by his name. "Beloved" by whom? Jesus? Would John have actually been so openly egotistical as to identify himself as the disciple whom Jesus loved as against the other eleven? It would seem only a faithful disciple of John acting as a scribe would identify John as the uniquely beloved disciple. On the other hand, if the expression "beloved disciple" is understood as describing the disciple of Jesus especially beloved by the church for which the Gospel was written, this also points to its composition by a scribe.

Tradition asserts that the Apostle John wrote Revelation while he was exiled to the island of Patmos (see Rev. 1:9) during the reign of Emperor Domitian, between A.D. 91 and 96. St. Irenaeus of Lyons, in the second century, states the Apostle John wrote Revelation toward the end of Domitian's regime.[3] Clement of Alexandria (150–215) mentions in passing that the

---

3   Irenaeus, *Heresies*, Book 5:30:3. He writes: "For that [i.e., John's apocalyptic vision] was seen no very long time since, but almost in our day, towards the end of Domitian's reign."

Icon of St. John the
Theologian dictating
his gospel to St. Prochorus

Apostle John was exiled on Patmos and then returned to Ephesus on the death of the emperor.[4] Jerome (342–420) offers more detail on John's sojourn on the island. In his *Concerning Illustrious Men*, Jerome tells us that John was exiled to the island of Patmos fourteen years after Nero's death, that is, around A.D. 94, and was freed on the death of Emperor Domitian, around A.D. 96.[5]

Revelation was therefore likely written about A.D. 95 on the island of Patmos.[6] Patmos (modern Patino) was a barren, rocky prison colony thirty-five to forty miles off the western coast of Asia Minor.[7] The island is crescent-shaped with its points facing east, and is eight to ten miles long and five miles wide at its widest point. John would have been subjected to hard labor in the quarries, scourging from military overseers, constant chains and fetters, lack of proper food and clothing, and sleepless nights on the cold, open ground or in a prison cell. John's company would have been composed of simple criminals, provincials, and slaves. Obviously John would not have had the luxury of a scribe, so he would himself have committed to writing the visions he experienced. As John's original language was Aramaic rather than Greek, it is not

---

4   Clement of Alexandria, *Who Is the Rich Man That Shall Be Saved?*, 42. Clement mentions the Apostle John as the author of the Apocalypse in his *Stromata*, Book 6:13.

5   Jerome, *Concerning Illustrious Men*, 9. "In the fourteenth year then after Nero, Domitian having raised a second persecution, he [John] was banished to the island of Patmos, and he wrote the Apocalypse . . . But Domitian having been put to death and his acts, on account of his excessive cruelty, having been annulled by the senate, he [John] returned to Ephesus under Nerva . . ."

6   Kenneth Gentry, Jr., however, makes an interesting case for a pre-A.D. 70 date for Revelation in *Before Jerusalem Fell*.

7   Some commentators question whether Patmos was actually a penal colony, preferring to argue that John was merely banished to the island by Roman authorities, which was occasionally done to those who threatened public interest. Others suggest John went to Patmos voluntarily to preach the gospel, or went there for a sort of ascetic "retreat." The idea that John went to the tiny island of Patmos to preach the gospel seems unlikely in light of the fact that Patmos had at best a small population, and there were certainly other more populated areas in Asia Minor needing John's special apostolic ministry. Moreover, persecution for bearing witness to Christ is one of the overriding themes of Revelation (e.g., 6:9; 20:4), which leads us naturally to believe that when John tells us he was on Patmos "for the word of God and for the testimony [Gr. *martyrion*] of Jesus Christ" (Rev. 1:9), he was there as a result of active hostility to the gospel.

surprising that the crude Greek of Revelation reads at times more like a literal rendering of Aramaic into Greek.

One name alone is sufficient to explain the differences between the fourth Gospel and Revelation: Prochorus, the Apostle's scribe. However, in pointing out the differences, the remarkable similarities between the fourth Gospel and Revelation must not be overlooked (see John 3:36 with Rev. 22:17; John 10:18 with Rev. 2:27; John 20:12 with Rev. 3:4; John 1:1 with Rev. 19:13; John 1:29 with Rev. 5:6). These obviously suggest common authorship. Given the weight of the witness of the early Church in the Apostle's favor, it is therefore reasonable to conclude that the Apostle John is the likeliest author of Revelation.

Genre and Audience

Is the Book of Revelation prophetic or apocalyptic literature? Prophetic literature is normally characterized as focusing on the present with its assorted moral, social, economic, and political difficulties. In general, prophetic literature is a call to hear the voice of God in the present and turn towards Him. As far as "predicting the future" is concerned, this largely focuses upon (though is by no means restricted to) the impending judgment or blessing of God, depending upon the people's decision to continue in sin or to turn and repent. In short, a prophecy is a message from God to repent.

Whereas the prophetic tradition was rooted in the spoken word, the apocalyptic tradition was always a literary one. The apocalyptic genre was popular between 200 B.C. and A.D. 200. Apocalyptic literature didn't expect a societal reformation and didn't call for one. Rather, it focused upon the imminent coming of the Messiah, who would bring destruction upon the wicked and vindication for the people of God. Apocalyptic literature usually consisted of a vision mediated by a heavenly being, such as an angel. An apocalypse was written in a highly symbolic manner and usually claimed to be written by a great historic figure, like Abraham or Enoch; in the case of Christian apocalyptic writing, we have works claiming to be written by the Apostle Peter and the Virgin Mary that were widely read in the early Church.

Although the Book of Revelation is normally classified as apocalyptic literature for many of these reasons, it is perhaps more accurate to say that it has elements of both the prophetic and apocalyptic traditions. Revelation itself is called a prophecy by John (Rev. 1:3; 22:7, 10, 18, 19). As such it is the uttered "word of God" (1:2). As in prophecy, moral considerations are important in Revelation, as exemplified by the seven letters to the seven churches in Revelation 2 and 3. Revelation is also unlike other apocalypses in a number of other ways. Whereas apocalypses explicitly claim to be written by an ancient figure of great spiritual stature, Revelation simply claims to be written by someone named John, without actually stating that it is the *Apostle* John. Again, while apocalypses normally attempt to retrace history as though the events were prophesied beforehand, Revelation seems firmly rooted in the contemporary situation of the early Church.

Given that Revelation is so preoccupied with the situation of the first-century Church, it is therefore right to conclude that the primary audience to which John was writing was his own "parishioners" in the first-century Church rather than us at the beginning of the third millennium. This is worth repeating: John did not write an encrypted book that could be decoded only by the last generation before the end of history. Revelation was written primarily as God's response to the persecuted Christians of Asia Minor during the first century.

Does this therefore mean that Revelation has nothing to say to us today? Not at all. Consider the examples of the Gospel of Luke and Paul's epistles. Though the Gospel of Luke was written for a first-century Christian named Theophilus (Luke 1:3), and Paul wrote his epistles for first-century Christian communities and individuals, nevertheless these divinely inspired works are timeless. They are as relevant to Christians today as they were two thousand years ago. So it is with Revelation. Revelation was not written only for those seven churches in Asia Minor. Revelation speaks to us as well, especially when we suffer persecution for righteousness' sake. The opening of Revelation makes this clear: "Blessed is he who reads and those who hear the words of this prophecy, and keep those things which are written in it; for the time is near" (1:3).

Methods of Interpretation

By common consent, the Book of Revelation is the most difficult book of the Bible to interpret. This is in large part because of its highly symbolic nature. As a result, it has been interpreted variously in the history of the Church. Below is a brief description of some of the main approaches taken to Revelation.

Preterist. The word "preterist" comes from the Latin word for "past." Accordingly, this approach interprets Revelation entirely in terms of the first-century situation. In essence, Revelation is a cryptic Christian pamphlet intended to encourage Christians under persecution. This is the approach favored today by most biblical scholars. While it takes seriously the actual situation of the Church during the composition of Revelation, the preterist approach, when unmodified, can sometimes reduce Revelation to a historical curiosity. If Hal Lindsey interprets Revelation wholly through today's news-papers, the preterist interprets it entirely according to yesterday's.

Futurist. The great popular appeal of this method is that it makes Revelation immediately relevant to the current generation reading it, which inevitably sees itself as the final, "terminal" generation. Whereas the major flaw of the preterist position is that it sometimes renders Revelation directly relevant to only one generation of Christians, that of the first-century Church, the futur-ist approach also renders Revelation directly relevant to only one generation of Christians—the last one. Even worse, since we cannot know which gen-eration is the last, there is no control on what Revelation's symbols mean. Thus we've seen elsewhere in this book that the smoke covering the sky in Revelation 9:2 can be understood as the result of gunpowder by a nineteenth-century commentator and as the radioactive fallout of a thermonuclear explosion by a twentieth-century one. (How will it be interpreted by a twenty-first-century commentator?) Lacking any objective checks and balances, imagination tends to run loose in this approach; and the symbols ultimately mean nothing, precisely because they can mean anything.

Historicist. This approach was started by Joachim of Fiore and was popular with the Protestant Reformers, notably Luther and Calvin. As the name implies, this approach holds that Revelation is an outline of history that high-lights God's Providence from John's day to the Second Coming. As comfort-ing a message as this might be, this perspective on Revelation renders nearly the entire book unintelligible to John's original readers, who obviously wouldn't know the history supposedly being described. Interpreters using this approach have also tended to see in Revelation a focus on the events of Western Europe, as though God thought the events of Western Europe alone important enough to be revealed beforehand to the whole human race! More-over, historicists radically disagree among themselves as to precisely which events were predicted by Revelation, seriously undermining the credibility of this approach.

Idealist. This method of interpretation sees Revelation as containing few or no references to historical incidents, either in the past or in the future. Rather, Revelation is seen as being wholly concerned with conveying spiritual truths about good and evil that are relevant to all Christians at all times. The advan-tage of this method is obvious: it is the only approach that makes Revelation immediately relevant to each generation of Christians. On the other hand, few are willing to concede that John does not have in mind an actual histori-cal setting for his symbols. This much all but the idealists can agree upon!

Archbishop Averky of the Russian Church Outside of Russia once gave a good summary of these four approaches to Revelation:

> One may divide all these commentaries [on Revelation] into four groups. Some of them refer all the visions and symbols of the Apocalypse to the "last times"—the end of the world, the appearance of the Antichrist, and the Second Coming of Christ. Others give to the Apocalypse a purely historical significance, referring all the visions to the historical events of the first century—to the times of the persecutions raised against the Church by the pagan emperors. A third group strives to find the realization of apocalyptic prophecies in the historical events of recent times. In their opinion, for example, the Pope of Rome is Antichrist, and all the apocalyptic misfortunes are announced in particular for the Church of Rome, etc. A fourth group, finally, sees in the Apocalypse only an allegory, considering that the visions described in it have not so much prophetic as a moral meaning, and allegory is introduced only to increase the impression, with the aim of striking the imagination of readers. The most correct commentary, however, is one that unites all these approaches, keeping in mind that, as the ancient commentators and Fathers of the Church clearly taught, the content of the Apocalypse in its sum is indeed directed to *the last part of the history of the world*.[8]

More and more interpreters are coming to see that to fully understand Revelation requires that we use a combination of all four approaches. With the preterist, we must see that John had an actual Christian community in mind while he was writing, and any interpretation of Revelation must be firmly rooted in this reality. We must understand Revelation within its own historical context. With the futurist, we must see that John is trying to give his readers an eternal perspective, that all God's purposes will be realized at Christ's Second Coming. With both the historicist and the idealist, we must recognize that John is intending to convey spiritual truths and how these will work themselves out in the general course of human history. By combining, for example, the idealist interpretation (which seeks the spiritual meaning) with the futurist interpretation (which sees Revelation as applying to our own day), fine commentaries have been written that are also excellent commentaries on contemporary society judged in the light of the Apocalypse. In the final analysis, John is giving us not merely a detailed road map to history (either past, present, or future), but rather a peculiarly Christian historical *perspective* by which to judge human events.

Archimandrite Athanasios Mitilinaios explains that, while the Second Coming is the central theme of Revelation, the book actually encompasses all of the divine economy, not only its dramatic conclusion at the Second Coming:

---

8   Taushev, *Apocalypse,* 53–54. Emphasis in original.

Thus, if Genesis describes the Creation of the world and Man, and his fall, Revelation prophetically describes the course of the Church and Creation in time, the rebirth of Man, the recreation of the created, visible world and their eternal glory. In brief, Revelation contains the whole Mystery of the divine Economy, from the Incarnation of God the Word where the Woman-Theotokos with the male child, Jesus, is persecuted and her male child is snatched up into Heaven—that is, the Ascension of Jesus Christ [see Rev. 12]. Revelation refers to the establishment on earth of the Kingdom of God, that is, of the Church to Her historical presence and Her worldwide expansion. It refers to the result of the Church's battle with the ungodly powers, the final blows which will fall upon unrepented Mankind. Finally, it refers to the appearance of the Antichrist, his ultimate crushing, the Second Coming of Christ as Judge, the resurrection of the dead from ages past, the final judgement, the eternal punishment of the impious, the eternal glory of the faithful, the revelation of the New Jerusalem—the Kingdom of God—the renewal of the visible created world, and the eternal communion of the deified believers with Christ. The Second Coming of Christ always remains the central idea of the book.[9]

Of equal importance with noting historical allusions is noting that John makes extensive *scriptural* allusions. A conservative count tells us there are more than four hundred allusions to the Old Testament—especially to Isaiah, Daniel, Ezekiel, Psalms, Genesis, Exodus, Jeremiah, and Zechariah—and any interpretation that fails to take this fully into account simply fails. Revelation must be read in the context of the entire biblical message.

The Parallel Structure of Revelation

Archimandrite Athanasios Mitilinaios in his brief commentary on Revelation writes that there are basically two ways to approach the structure of the various visions in Revelation. The first he calls the theory of repetition or recapitulation, which sees the separate visions as all relating the same events. The second theory sees the book as basically chronological, a "periodic progress of the events symbolized by the particular visions." His conclusion is that "the best of the Orthodox commentators, old and new, accept the first theory [of repetition or recapitulation] without excluding the second one." [10] In other words, even though the visions of Revelation repeat themselves, there is still a rough chronological sequence detectable in each vision and in the book as a whole.

Most people reading Revelation for the first time inevitably approach it as they would a simple narrative: as a series of sequential events. A careful

---

9   Athanasios Mitilinaios, *The Book of the Revelation of St. John the Evangelist* (Wescosville, PA: St. Nikodemos the Hagiorite Publication Society, 1993), 4.

10   Mitilinaios, *Revelation*, 23.

study of the structure of Revelation, on the other hand, shows that a "chronological" reading is not likely the way the book was originally intended to be read. Having stated that there is no particular "Orthodox interpretation" of Revelation, I will now offer one that has its roots in the most ancient commentaries of Revelation still extant, as well as modern exponents like the late William Hendriksen.[11] This interpretation sees Revelation as having seven parallel sections, each laying out the course of salvation history from the time of our redemption to history's consummation at the Second Coming. As I hope to show, recognizing Revelation's natural structure goes a long way to making the book more intelligible.

As any superficial reading of Revelation quickly makes apparent, the number seven plays a significant role throughout the book. In the twenty-two chapters of Revelation, the word "seven" occurs fifty-five times. Compare this to nine times in the Gospel of Luke, which has twenty-four chapters, or to no occurrences of the word in the twenty-one chapters of the Gospel of John. (It should be noted, however, that the concept of seven is important in the structure of John's Gospel—e.g., Jesus performs seven signs.) Moreover, no matter which way one turns in Revelation, one bumps into combinations of seven. There are seven beatitudes spread out across the entire book: 1:3; 14:13; 16:15; 19:9; 20:6; 22:7, 14. One can even focus on a single verse, such as Revelation 5:12, in which we find seven attributes of the Lamb, Jesus Christ.

The number seven was commonly regarded as a holy number among ancient Middle Eastern people. In Hebrew, the word for "swear" and "oath," *shaba*,[12] is derived from the Hebrew word for seven, *sheba*. An oath in biblical times was a sacred commitment whereby the deity was invoked to attest to the truth of what was promised or declared. The number seven also carried with it the idea of completeness, fulfillment, and perfection. The act of creation was seen as "completed" on the seventh day, when God rested, and not on the sixth day when the actual work of creating was finished with the generation of Adam from the dust of the earth. In creating the world in seven days—as opposed to instantaneously—God also reveals that He did not intend merely to be the Great Manufacturer, but to enter into a solemn commitment with His Creation, that is, a covenant relationship. In creating in seven days, God entered into an oath with His creation.

The number seven subsequently played a central role in the Mosaic covenant with Israel. One thinks of the Sabbath rest on the seventh day

---

11 See Hendriksen, *More than Conquerors*.
12 Literally, "to seven" oneself, probably by repeating the oath seven times.

(Ex. 20:10), the sabbatic year (Lev. 25:2–6), and the year of jubilee celebrated every fiftieth year (the year following seven times seven years—Lev. 25:8). The Feasts of Unleavened Bread and of Tabernacles lasted for seven days each (Ex. 12:15, 19; Num. 29:12). The Day of Atonement was in the seventh month (Lev. 16:29). In Old Testament liturgical worship, a bullock's blood was sprinkled seven times (Lev. 4:6), a cleansed leper was sprinkled seven times with water (Lev. 14:7), and seven lambs under one year old were sacrificed as a burnt offering at the beginning of each month (Num. 28:11). Naaman needed to wash seven times in the Jordan to be "completely" clean (2 Kin. 5:10), and Samson's "perfect" strength was in his seven braids of hair (Judg. 16:19). The Psalmist offered perfect praise to God by praying seven times a day (Ps. 119:164).

Simply focusing on occurrences of "seven" in the Book of Revelation, a significant pattern emerges: the entire book can be divided into seven sections. Moreover, each section completely summarizes the whole of salvation history from Christ's first coming to His glorious Second Coming. Let's look at each of these sections.

Revelation 1—3. This is the section of the seven letters sent to seven churches, represented in the first chapter as seven golden lampstands. One naturally thinks of the seven-branched candlestick in the tabernacle of the Israelites (Ex. 25:32). As seven is the number of completeness, Christians very early on understood the seven churches as symbolically representing the whole Church. In 1:5, Jesus' First Advent is summarized: He is the firstborn among the dead and now rules the earth from heaven. In His First Advent, He "freed us from our sins by his blood" (1:5 NIV). In verse 6, the present reality of the Church is proclaimed: we are now kings and priests to God the Father. Then, in verse 7, Jesus' coming in glory in the clouds is confidently asserted. This in a nutshell is the whole history of mankind from the First to the Second Advents.

In chapter 2, John outlines the present situation of the Church in seven letters: persecution, temptation, false religion, laxness, and so forth. These are perennial problems that will always plague the Church. John ends this section with Jesus standing at the door and knocking, proclaiming, "Behold, I stand at the door and knock. If anyone hears My voice and opens the door, I will come in to him and dine with him, and he with Me" (3:20). The image of Christ entering our world and eating a meal will return with particular vividness with the "marriage supper of the Lamb" at the Second Coming described in Revelation 19. The first section, therefore, ends with Christ "at the door," hinting at the imminent Second Coming.

Revelation 4—7. In this next section of the book we again view the same events, but from a heavenly vantage point. The section begins with an allusion to the prophecy in Genesis 49:9, 10 and Christ's first coming (5:5). Christ appears as a slain sacrificial lamb who is the only one able to approach "the right hand of Him who sat on the throne" of heaven (5:6). Christ has ascended and is mediating for the Church, so golden bowls of prayers are offered to the Father who sits on the throne (5:8). Christ then opens seven seals and reveals what is to occur on the earth: persecution, poverty, the sword, hunger, and death. In the fifth seal, we hear the cry of the martyrs; and then the sixth seal is broken. This seal results in an earthquake, the sun becoming black and the moon becoming as blood. The stars fall from heaven and the sky rolls up like a scroll. Mountains and islands collapse. This language is virtually identical with Jesus' description of the Second Coming found in Matthew 24:29. In Revelation 6:15, 16 it is noted that not a single class of men will repent even as the wrath of God falls upon them: "For the great day of His wrath has come, and who is able to stand?" (6:17). Chapter 7 reveals that Christians will be sealed so as not to suffer the wrath of God. Their ultimate bliss is described in 7:15–17.

Revelation 8—11. The seventh seal opens onto the beginning of the next sequence, which starts back at the beginning. The prayers of the saints are again shown ascending before the throne of God as in Revelation 5:8 (8:4), and there is silence in heaven (8:1). God's silence precedes judgment (see Zeph. 1:7; Zech. 2:13; Hab. 2:20). Seven trumpets then sound, bringing forth seven judgments, similar to those that afflicted Egypt at the time of the Exodus. We also remember that God's judgment on the Canaanites began at Jericho when the Israelites marched around the city seven times blowing seven trumpets (Josh. 6). At the sound of the fifth trumpet in Revelation 9:1, a star (an angel) falls from heaven and opens the bottomless pit. The Tribulation begins with the release of Satan. This is confirmed in Revelation 9:11: he is the king of the bottomless pit and is known as the "Destroyer" (Heb. *Abaddon;* Gr. *Apollyon*). All hell has literally broken loose upon the earth; but the torment is primarily spiritual, not physical. The demons let loose from the pit are not allowed actually to kill anyone (9:5, 6). The sixth trumpet reveals war and a mankind that refuses to repent of its sins (9:20, 21), just as we saw in the last section.

After a giant angel straddling land and sea pronounces "that there should be delay no longer" (10:6), then occurs the resurrection of the Church as exemplified by the two witnesses (11:11). They are caught up to heaven in a cloud, always associated with the Second Coming (11:12; compare 1:7). As in the last section (see 6:12), there is an earthquake at the Second Coming (11:13). The seventh trumpet reveals that "the kingdoms of the world have become the kingdoms of our Lord" (11:15). The standard formula for Jesus found first in Revelation 1:4, "the Lord who is and who was and who is to come," is changed in Revelation 11:17 to, "the One who is and who was." [13] There is no longer, "and who is to come." The Lord has come! In the next verse we have the general judgment: "that they should be judged, and that You should reward Your servants . . . and should destroy those who destroy the earth" (11:18).

Revelation 12—14. This section sets forth the story of the Church from an even more mystical perspective with the vision of the woman, the child, and the dragon. The woman is the Church, both of the Old and the New Testaments. As the Old Testament Church, she gives birth to the Messiah in Revelation 12:5. Satan tries to destroy the Child even as she is bringing Him forth, recalling the slaughter of children by Herod the Great. This "male Child" rules all the nations with a rod of iron (see Ps. 2:9). He then ascends to heaven and is seated on His throne as the woman flees, protected from the devil by God (12:6). Satan is thrown out of heaven to the earth (12:7–12) and persecutes the woman (12:13–17), the Church whose offspring are those "who keep the commandments of God and have the testimony of Jesus Christ" (12:17). In his war on the Church, Satan brings forth the beast who comes out of the sea (13:1–10) and the beast who comes out of the land (13:11–18), the Antichrist and his false prophet. After another vision of the Church represented as the 144,000 saints (14:1–5; compare 7:1–8) who are anointed and protected by God, judgment is pronounced upon "Babylon" (14:6–13), the corrupt political and religious world system.

Then the end comes: the Son of Man appears in the clouds again, as in each previous section (14:14). He wears a golden crown and has a sickle in His hand, ready to harvest the earth, symbolizing the final judgment (see Matt. 13:24–30, 36–43). In Revelation 14:20, the blood from this judgment is said to be as deep as a horse's bridle for 1,600 *stadia* (that is, a river of blood 200 miles long). Thus the river of blood encompasses geographically the entire land of Palestine, which is about 184 miles long. The number 1,600 is intended to be symbolic. In the Book of Revelation, the number four represents the four points of the compass, which is to say the whole world. The number ten represents an unlimited amount. Thus 1,600 (4 x 4 x 10 x 10) *stadia* of blood represents emphatically the wrath of God upon the whole

---

13 The KJV and the NKJV have, "and who is to come." This phrase, however, is a much later accretion to the Greek text added to make the verse conform to Rev. 1:4, 8 and 4:8.

world. The image of blood being as deep as a horse's bridle was a common metaphor in Jewish apocalyptic writings. The apocalypse of *1 Enoch*, for example, describes the fate of the unrighteous thus: "And the horse shall walk up to the breast in the blood of sinners" (1 Enoch 100:3).

Revelation 15 and 16. With chapter 15 we again return to the beginning. Now we have seven bowls of judgment that closely parallel the seven trumpets seen earlier. The seven lampstands of chapters 1—3, the seven trumpets in chapters 8—11, and the seven bowls depicted here in chapters 15 and 16, all have in common their association with Temple worship. God's judgment is liturgical in nature, thus revealing His divinity and glory.

The section begins with "the song of Moses . . . and the song of the Lamb" (15:3), followed by seven judgments, again recalling Moses' plagues upon Egypt. Compare these seven bowls with the seven trumpets: The first trumpet and the first bowl are poured upon the earth (8:7; 16:2). The second trumpet and the second bowl are poured upon the sea (8:3; 16:3). The third trumpet and the third bowl affect rivers and springs (8:10; 16:4). The fourth trumpet and the fourth bowl affect the sun and the heavens (8:12; 16:8). The fifth trumpet releases the demonic world (9:1–12); the fifth bowl releases "darkness" (16:10). Both the sixth trumpet and the sixth bowl dry up the Euphrates and lead to war (9:13–21; 16:12–16). The Euphrates is associated with Assyria and Babylon, the godless world.

The sixth bowl, like the sixth trumpet, leads to the Second Coming: "Behold, I am coming as a thief" (16:15). The next verse reveals the response of the world to Christ's coming: "And they gathered them together to the place called in Hebrew, Armageddon" (16:16). The seventh bowl is poured out, significantly, in the air (16:17). Christ will return "in the air" and execute judgment. God on His throne thunders, "It is done," meaning time is finished and eternity is about to be ushered in. Again there is a great earthquake accompanied by thunder and lightning (16:18). Again we have islands and mountains disappearing (16:20). Again, it is revealed that men are unrepentant to the end (16:21).

Revelation 17—19. We return once more to the beginning of the story, but this time the focus is upon the destruction of Babylon. We saw in section four (chapters 12—14) how Satan uses the beast, false prophet, and Babylon to work his will on earth. In this section, we specifically see the downfall of all three at Christ's coming. In chapter 19, Christ comes riding victoriously back to earth on His white horse with the armies of heaven. The world "gathered together to make war against Him who sat on the horse and against His army" (19:19). Notice that this recalls the wording in the last section: "And they gathered them together to the place called in Hebrew, Armageddon" (16:16). This is the same battle being described in both places. This section ends with Babylon overthrown and the beast with his false prophet thrown into the lake of fire.

Revelation 20—22. Again we are back to the beginning, with Satan being cast out of heaven and bound in the bottomless pit at Christ's first coming (20:1). After a thousand years Satan is released for "a little while," the Great Tribulation. This recalls Revelation 9 where "a star" opened the bottomless pit and then demons were released for "five months" to afflict the earth (9:1–10). In Revelation 20:4–6, we have a vision of the saints before the throne of God, as in previous sections. Again there is a battle at Christ's coming comprising "the nations which are in the four corners of the earth, Gog and Magog, to gather them together to battle, whose number is as the sand of the sea" (20:8). This phrase, "to gather them together to battle," echoes the previous two descriptions of this final battle (see 19:19; 16:16).

Christ's Second Coming is depicted as fire coming down from God in heaven (20:9). Christ's return is associated with fire elsewhere in the New Testament as well (1 Cor. 3:13; 2 Thess. 1:7, 8; 2 Pet. 3:7, 12; compare Ps. 97:3; Is. 66:15, 16; Ezek. 38:22). In the last section, it was the beast and the false prophet that were thrown into the lake of fire (19:20). The phrase, "And the devil . . . was cast into the lake of fire and brimstone where the beast and the false prophet are" (20:10) does not indicate that the beast and the false prophet were thrown into the lake and only a thousand years later does Satan receive the same punishment. There is no sequence indicated between the events in chapter 19 and those in chapter 20. Rather, the phrase is intended to inform us that the beast, false prophet, and Satan (who is the power behind the other two), all suffer the same fate. Then follow the general judgment (20:11–15) and the restoration of the heavens and the earth (chs. 21; 22). Viewing chapters 20—22 as a separate unit obviously renders a premillennial interpretation of Revelation 20:1–10 impossible.

Now that we have summarized the entire Book of Revelation by examining its seven sections, there is still another aspect of Revelation that must be observed. The seven different sections aren't totally isolated from each other; rather, they build on one another. There is a unity to the whole.

It should be observed that the groupings of seven are frequently divided into two units of either three and four or four and three. For example, each of the seven letters in chapters 2 and 3 has, with some variation, seven sections in itself: (1) a salutation; (2) Christ's self-designation; (3) a commendation; (4) a condemnation; (5) a warning; (6) an exhortation; and (7) a promise.

While this isn't an invariable pattern (e.g., the letter to Smyrna doesn't have either a condemnation or a warning), all the letters have an exhortation to "hear what the Spirit says to the churches" and a promise. The pattern in the first three letters is for the promise to follow the exhortation. In the last four, the exhortation follows the promise. This is a rough three/four division among the seven letters.

In the seven seals of Revelation 6, we have four horses in the first four seals followed by the other three seals, a four/three division. Among the seven trumpets in chapter eight, the first four affect the physical world: the earth, the seas, the rivers, and the heavens. An angel then warns "of the three angels about to sound" (8:13). These last three trumpets are spiritual judgments. As the bowls in chapter 16 mirror the trumpets, we find the same four/three division there as well.

This pattern shows itself in the seven major sections of Revelation, thus forming a major division down the middle of the book. The first part of the book consists of the first three sections: (1) Christ's letters to the seven churches in chapters 1—3; (2) the scroll with the seven seals in chapters 4—7; and (3) the seven trumpets in chapters 8—11. These together, according to scholars like William Hendriksen, comprise part one of the book and focus upon the "real world" problems of the Church, the earthly side of life. This earthly, everyday perspective is most evident in the first section—the seven letters to the seven churches—where the practical problems of these churches are identified. But as we enter the next two sections, we begin to see more vividly the spiritual underside to the Church's struggles.

In the second half of Revelation, we are exposed to the full spiritual reality of the Church's struggle on earth. This half comprises the last four sections: (4) the Woman, the Man-Child, and the dragon (along with the dragon's helpers: the beast, the false prophet, and Babylon); (5) the seven bowls of God's wrath; (6) the fall of Babylon, the beast, and the false prophet; and (7) the fall of Satan himself followed by the renewing of the heavens and earth. In this way, the everyday struggles of the Church depicted in the seven letters are shown to be what they really are—the ongoing struggle between Christ (in His Church) and Satan (in the harlot, beast, and false prophet).

Yet not even these two major divisions are absolute. We have already observed the close parallel between the seven trumpets and the seven bowls of God's wrath that connect the two sections. One interesting difference between the bowls and the trumpets is that the seven trumpets of judgment are expressed in fractions (a third of the trees burned up, a third of the sea becomes blood, a third of the fish die, a third of the rivers become bitter, etc.), whereas the seven bowls depict complete devastation ("and every living creature in the sea died"). The judgment of the trumpets is partial; the bowls represent total judgment. The bowls fulfill the trumpets.

One of the important functions of trumpets in the ancient world was to sound a warning (see Ezek. 33:3). In the partial judgments of chapter 8 we have a warning to the world that God's full wrath is coming. Let no one say that God hasn't throughout history sounded warnings of the impending judgment. Still, as Revelation shows in many places, mankind refuses to repent of its wickedness (e.g., Rev. 6:15–17; 9:20; 16:21). Therefore we are not sorrowful when the full bowls of God's judgments finally strike the world in chapter 16. Consequently, even though the trumpets in chapter 8 and the bowls in chapter 16 belong to two different halves of the book, they bring Revelation together to present a single coherent picture: God warns, man ignores, judgment falls.

The Book of Revelation presents us with an ever-deepening vision of reality: from reality as it exists on the surface (as presented in the first few chapters) to the eternal perspective of heaven, progressing deeper and deeper until we finally behold the new heavens and the new earth in the last few chapters. The book is a spiraling, progressive revelation of the destiny of · man from God's perspective. In this way we gain a spiritual insight into the meaning of the Church's struggles in the currents of human history. Instead of a road map with defined historical/political events, we are given an understanding of the deeper forces at work shaping the affairs of man. In the end, this makes Revelation a far more valuable book than if it were merely a newspaper written before the fact.

The Message of Revelation

So then, what specific message can we take away after reading Revelation? In 1995, Ecumenical Patriarch Bartholomew of Constantinople led a floating symposium of Orthodox, Catholic, and Anglican theologians to the island of Patmos to observe the 1,900th anniversary of John's apocalyptic vision. The Ecumenical Patriarch stressed that John's seemingly violent prophecy must be read in harmony with the rest of the Bible. God's justice on the world must also be balanced with what John says in his Gospel, that "God so loved the world" that He sent His Son to save it (John 3:16). "But to us [Orthodox], God is like the sun, emanating life, grace, and honor," the Patriarch stated. "Those who cut themselves off from that light find themselves in a hell of their own making." In a statement issued by Bartholomew's office in Constantinople, he added, "The future seems to be as uncertain and insecure [today] as it did to the people of the Eastern Mediterranean almost two millennia ago as they read God's message relayed to them by St. John in the

Book of Revelation. Its significance has been reinterpreted by successive generations seeking truth and rational confidence in periods of crisis."

The value of Revelation is especially felt when our Faith and our Church seem to be ever more marginalized in our present, secularized society. If these are indeed the final days before Christ's Return, then we can expect to be increasingly more marginalized in an increasingly godless world. In days such as these, Revelation reassures us that Christ and His Church will overcome Satan and his demonic accomplices: the beast, the false prophet, and all those with the mark of the beast who are in communion with "Babylon."

The Book of Revelation gives us this "rational confidence" (to quote Patriarch Bartholomew) by *revealing* to us that things are not wholly as they seem (this is why it's called "Revelation"). As the late William Hendriksen has pointed out, though our prayers *seem* to bounce off the closed doors of heaven, though God's saints *seem* to be defeated, though evil *seems* to conquer everywhere we look, the reality is just the opposite. Our prayers are coming to the very throne of God (Rev. 6:10); we are reigning even now on the earth (Rev. 5:10) as well as in heaven (Rev. 20:4), and, in the end, forever in the new heavens and the new earth (Rev. 22:5); and we learn that ultimately it is evil itself that will be conquered and thrown into the lake of fire.

Obviously, if Christianity were truly defeated and our Faith vain there would be no point in the forces of darkness attacking us in the first place. Revelation strips away the illusion of defeat and *reveals* the truth: we have already won through Him who loved us. As John records elsewhere, our Savior said at His seemingly darkest hour, "Be of good cheer, for I have overcome the world" (John 16:33). Our Lord who was, and who is, and who is to come, has already overcome, is now overcoming, and will come again to fully overcome an unrepentant world. Thus Satan is full of "great wrath because he knows his time is short" (Rev. 12:12).

In one important sense the futurists are correct in characterizing Revelation as a peek at things to come. The book gives us strength to go on when all seems lost precisely because we have seen the end of all things, and we know that ultimately Christ is victorious. This is why William Hendriksen back in 1939 chose Revelation 17:14 as best expressing the theme of Revelation: "These will make war with the Lamb, and the Lamb will overcome them, for He is Lord of lords and King of kings; and those who are with Him are called chosen and faithful." The Lamb has chosen us; let us therefore remain faithful to the end.

About the Author

T. L. FRAZIER has written numerous articles and books explaining and defending historic Christian beliefs. He has recently written *Holy Relics* for Conciliar Press, and has coauthored *Understanding the Orthodox Liturgy* with Fr. Michel Najim for the Fellowship of St. John the Divine. He resides in Southern California with his wife and two daughters.